DIVERSITY
IN SPORT ORGANIZATIONS

GEORGE B. CUNNINGHAM

TEXAS A&M UNIVERSITY

Consulting Editor, Sport Management Series

Packianathan Chelladurai

Holcomb Hathaway, Publishers
Scottsdale, Arizona 85250

Library of Congress Cataloging-in-Publication Data

Cunningham, George B.
    Diversity in sport organizations / George B. Cunningham.
        p. cm.
    ISBN-13: 978-1-890871-77-2
    1. Sports administration—United States.   2. Sports—Management.   I. Title.
    GV713.C86 2007
    796.06'9—dc22

                                                                    2006036740

Holcomb Hathaway, Publishers, Inc.
6207 North Cattletrack Rd.
Scottsdale, Arizona 85250
480-991-7881
www.hh-pub.com

10 9 8 7 6 5 4 3 2 1

ISBN 978-1-890871-77-2

DEDICATION

For Melissa, Harper, and Maggie.

Contents

PART I   FOUNDATIONS OF DIVERSITY   1

Overview of Diversity   3

Theoretical Tenets of Diversity   27

Prejudice and Discrimination   57

PART II   **CATEGORICAL EFFECTS OF DIVERSITY**   79

Race Issues in Sport Organizations   81

5 Sex and Gender in Sport Organizations   119

Categorical Effects of Age, Disability, and Obesity   155

Beyond Visible Demographics
RELIGIOUS BELIEFS, SEXUAL ORIENTATION, AND SOCIAL CLASS   179

PART III   COMPOSITIONAL AND RELATIONAL DIVERSITY   217

8 Compositional Diversity   219

Relational Diversity   241

Legal Aspects of Diversity   263

11 Managing Diverse Organizations   291

12 Managing Diverse Groups   319

13 Diversity Training   345

Preface

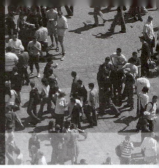

Diversity has been, and will continue to be, one of the most important issues managers encounter, and this is particularly true with sport and physical activity. The United States continues to become more diverse, both in terms of demographics and attitudes, and this diversity is evident in the organizational context, where dissimilarities among employees are now commonplace. These differences are important because they impact opportunities not only for employment but also for sport and physical activity participation. Following diversity-related legal requirements, or failing to do so, can have meaningful implications for an organization. The specific diversity management strategies used by an organization can influence employee attitudes, group processes, and the organization's overall effectiveness. Consequently, understanding the effects of diversity and the strategies to effectively manage those differences is of paramount importance. The purpose of this text, *Diversity in Sport Organizations,* is to provide students with such an understanding.

The book is divided into four parts. Part I provides an overview of diversity. Chapter 1 defines diversity and diversity management, and then analyzes why diversity warrants attention by students and managers. The focus of Chapter 2 is on the theoretical tenets of diversity. I discuss four approaches to the study of diversity, provide an overview of why theory is important to the study of diversity, and outline three primary theoretical approaches to the study of diversity—managerial, sociological, and social psychological—as well as the practical implications associated with each. Chapter 3 addresses prejudice and discrimination.

Part II is devoted to the categorical effects of diversity—the comparison of the experiences of members of one social group (e.g., lesbian sport participants) to those of another social group (e.g., heterosexual sport participants). Chapter 4 focuses on racial issues, while the concentration in Chapter 5 is on sex and gender. In Chapter 6, I discuss three physical aspects of diversity: age, disability, and obesity. Chapter 7 examines deep-level diversity characteristics that are often invisible—religion, sexual orientation, and social class.

Part III examines diversity from the group perspective. Chapter 8 is devoted to compositional diversity, or how a group's composition impacts subsequent processes and outcomes. For example, one might compare the cohesion of an all-male work group to another group composed equally of men and women. In Chapter 9, I focus on relational diversity, and how differing from others (whether in a group or dyad) impacts subsequent outcomes for the individual. For example, how does a middle-aged man respond to having a supervisor who is 25 years younger? The compositional and relational approaches to studying diversity move beyond simply comparing the experiences of individuals in different social units, as is done with the categorical approach.

Part IV focuses on effectively managing diversity in organizations. I outline diversity-related laws in Chapter 10 and discuss how those laws influence employment decisions and sport opportunities. In Chapters 11 and 12, I highlight several diversity management strategies that can be used to effectively manage dissimilar employees. The emphasis in the former chapter is on organization-wide strategies, while the focus in the latter is on smaller groups. Finally, Chapter 13 is devoted to diversity training. Here, I underscore the importance of this training and provide the steps to design, implement, and evaluate effective diversity training programs.

The book is intended for upper-level undergraduate and graduate students. Teachers, coaches, managers, marketers, and administrators also will benefit from the text's information. Because the sport industry is rather diverse, examples are drawn from a bevy of sources—professional sports, university athletics, fitness organizations, physical education, recreation and leisure settings, and nonprofit entities such as the YMCA.

Special Features

- **Diversity Challenge.** Each chapter opens with a Diversity Challenge, a real-life scenario introducing the chapter's topic. It is followed by a series of questions to prompt students to think about the issues raised.

- **Diversity in the Field.** Chapters also include Diversity in the Field boxes, which use real-life examples to help readers comprehend chapter concepts.

- **Professional Perspectives.** These recurring boxes reflect interviews of leading professionals with responsibilities in sport (e.g., professors, an elementary school principal, a university president, a president of a cruise line) and provide students with practical, informed opinions on the chapter content.

- **Alternative Perspectives.** Because so many topics and issues are subject to varying opinions, I have included Alternative Perspectives boxes to provide readers with additional sides of a discussion.

- **Questions for Discussion, Learning Activities, Supplementary Readings, and Web Resources.** Each chapter concludes with student activities and sources of additional information. Many of the Learning Activities are designed for students to explore in small groups. The Supplementary

Readings are annotated, and the Web Resources augment chapter material by providing links to professional associations, electronic methods of testing prejudicial attitudes, and resources for diversity training, among others.

■ **Ancillaries.** An Instructor's Manual and PowerPoint presentation are available for instructors who adopt this text for course use. The Instructor's Manual contains an overview of each chapter and questions that can be used for quizzes and exams.

I am excited about diversity and what it means for sport, sport organizations, and people associated with the sport industry. I hope I have reflected this enthusiasm in the text and that this enthusiasm is passed on to instructors and readers. I welcome your comments and look forward to any and all feedback. Please contact me in care of Holcomb Hathaway, Publishers; 6207 N. Cattletrack Rd., Ste. 5; Scottsdale, AZ 85250; sales@hh-pub.com.

Acknowledgments

would like to thank the wonderful colleagues and students with whom I have worked. In particular, I enjoyed the collaborative efforts I had with Dr. Michael Sagas, Dr. Janet Fink, and Dr. John Singer. A large debt of gratitude is owed to all of my students, especially Melanie Sartore and Jacqueline McDowell. Not only were they a joy to work with, but they also reviewed the book and provided very helpful and constructive feedback along the way. I am also grateful to my doctoral advisor, Packianathan Chelladurai, not only for his guidance in my professional preparation, but also for encouraging me to write this book.

I appreciate the very helpful comments and suggestions offered by the reviewers: Debra Blair, Temple University; Elaine Blinde, Southern Illinois University Carbondale; Glenna Bower, University of Southern Indiana; Willie Burden, Georgia Southern University; Alison Doherty, The University of Western Ontario; Christy Greenleaf, University of North Texas; Louis Harrison, Lousiana State University; Lori Head, Idaho State University; Fritz Polite, University of Tennessee; Brian Sather, Eastern Oregon University; John Singer, Texas A&M University; Ellen Staurowsky, Ithaca College; and Eli Wolff, Center for the Study of Sport in Society, Northeastern University. Their input was very helpful in the writing process.

I also thank Colette Kelly and others at Holcomb Hathaway, Publishers. I enjoyed working with them and will forever be indebted to them for the opportunity they gave me.

Finally, to those most important in my life: I thank my Lord and Savior, Jesus Christ, for his love, mercy, and grace. I am also thankful for my family: my wife, Melissa, and our two girls Harper and Maggie. They are my everything.

About the Author

George B. Cunningham (Ph.D., The Ohio State University) is an Assistant Professor of Sport Management in the Department of Health and Kinesiology at Texas A&M University. He also serves as the Director for the Laboratory for Diversity in Sport—a lab dedicated to producing and disseminating research related to all forms of diversity in the sport context. Author of over 80 articles and book chapters, Cunningham focuses his research in the areas of diversity, group processes, and employee attitudes. Within the diversity domain, he investigates the under-representation of various groups in leadership positions, the impact of dissimilarity on subsequent outcomes and behaviors, and strategies for ameliorating the potential negative effects of diversity. His research has been published in various journals, including those in the sport domain (e.g., *Journal of Sport Management*, *Journal of Sport and Exercise Psychology*, and *Sociology of Sport Journal*), the area of social psychology (e.g., *The Journal of Social Psychology*, *Journal of Applied Social Psychology*, *Sex Roles*, and *Group Dynamics*), and in various management journals (e.g., *Organizational Analysis*, *Journal of Business and Psychology*), among others. In 2005, Cunningham was named a Research Fellow of the North American Society for Sport Management.

Cunningham and his wife, Melissa, have two daughters, Harper and Maggie. His free time is spent with his family or playing (poorly, he says) soccer, basketball, and golf.

DIVERSITY

IN SPORT ORGANIZATIONS

Foundations of Diversity

Overview of Diversity

DIVERSITY CHALLENGE

LEARNING OBJECTIVES

Tennis, a sport played in various venues such as private clubs, schools, parks, and recreational facilities, provides its participants with the strenuous exercise needed to maintain a healthy lifestyle. Hispanics, however, are relatively unlikely to play tennis—they represent less than 10 percent of all participants. Participant numbers are even lower for members of other racial minority groups. Relative to Whites, Hispanics are more likely to play at recreational facilities (rather than private clubs), to begin playing tennis at a later age, and to have different motivations to participate. Because the discretionary income of Hispanics is generally lower than that of Whites, they also have fewer opportunities to participate in tennis. These differences are important because the Hispanic population is the fastest growing minority group in the United States and is the largest minority group in Texas, New Mexico, and California, states where minority group members represent the majority of the states' citizens. Recognizing this apparent contradiction, the Texas Section of the United States Tennis Association makes special efforts to target Hispanics and entice them to participate in tennis by using such strategies as increasing the availability of public courts, emphasizing the sport's health benefits, and advertising and promoting the sport in Spanish. Regardless of the strategy used, attracting Hispanics and members of other racial minority groups to tennis is essential for the sport's growth and survival.*

*Information adapted from Caldwell, A. A. (2005, August 11). Minorities become majority in Texas. *The Eagle*, pp. A7, A9; Fitzgerald, M. P., Fink, J. S., & Riemer, H. A. (2002). *USTA Texas Section marketing research report: Implications for growing tennis membership.* Austin, Texas: Authors.

After studying this chapter, you should be able to:

- Define diversity and diversity management.

- List and explain the different forms of diversity.

- Discuss the different factors that led to an increased interest in diversity.

DIVERSITY CHALLENGE **R E F L E C T I O N**

Imagine that you are the manager of the Texas Section of the USTA, then answer the following questions:

1. What strategies would you use to attract Hispanics and other minorities to tennis?
2. What are specific marketing or promotional activities that could be developed?
3. What changes are needed at an organizational level to attract minority participants?

Diversity is one of the most important topics for persons in the sport and physical activity context today. As the opening scenario illustrates, the United States' population is changing; therefore, organizations and the people who work in them must also change. Although the scenario focuses on current racial changes, other changes are also occurring, including those based on sex, age, beliefs, attitudes, and preferences. Due to these changes, managers must now implement alternative marketing and promotional activities to attract diverse participants and spectators, and structure their organizations so they are open to all people, irrespective of their demographic characteristics, preferences, or beliefs. Managers, athletic administrators, coaches, and others in the sport industry should be aware of the legal implications associated with having a diverse workforce and how various mandates and laws influence the human resource decisions they make. Because diversity is now a central issue for persons in sport organizations, it is critical that they understand the underlying dynamics and effects of diversity and implement strategies to maximize the benefits of having a diverse workforce.

This chapter provides an overview of diversity. The first section examines several definitions of diversity and diversity management, developing from them the definitions used throughout the text. This is followed by a discussion of the various forms of diversity and the ways in which people can differ. The third section identifies and analyzes the seven factors that contribute to the current interest in and importance of diversity. Finally, the last section provides a brief overview of the major diversity-related issues discussed in subsequent chapters.

Definitions

his section considers several definitions of diversity and diversity management in order to develop the working definitions used in the text.

Diversity

To begin developing a working definition of *diversity,* consider the following definitions used by others in this field:

> Diversity is "any mixture of items characterized by differences and similarities." (Thomas, 1996, p. 5)

> Diversity "refers to differences between individuals on any attribute that may lead to the perceptions that another person is different from self." (van Knippenberg, De Drue, & Homam, 2004, p. 1008)

> Diversity is the "distribution of personal attributes among interdependent members of a work unit." (Jackson, Joshi, & Erhardt, 2003, p. 802)

> Diversity refers to "differences among people that are likely to affect their acceptance, work performance, satisfaction, or progress in an organization." (Hayes-Thomas, 2004, p. 12)

> Diversity is "a mix of people in one social system who have distinctly different, socially relevant group affiliations." (Cox & Beale, 1997, p. 1)

> Diversity is "any characteristic used to differentiate one person from others." (Joplin & Daus, 1997, p. 32)

We can draw several points from these definitions. First, most of the definitions consider the group or dyad (i.e., two people working together, such as a supervisor and subordinate) as a requisite condition. People must be able to compare their attributes to the characteristics of others in the dyad or group. Without an ability to compare, people do not know if they are similar to or different from others. Thus, we can say that diversity is a dyadic or group-related topic.

Second, diversity is concerned with differences *and* similarities (Thomas, 1996); therefore, a truly diverse group has various characteristics. For example, some may view a group of five African Americans working in a sport marketing firm diverse because the group is comprised entirely of members of a racial minority. However, if the earlier definitions are applied, the group is actually homogeneous, not diverse, because each member is an African American. Another group in the same sport marketing firm has as its members two Hispanics, one White, one African American, and one Asian American. Clearly, with respect to race, this group has a broader array of attributes, as persons from four racial backgrounds are included. Relative to the group of five African Americans, the latter group is more diverse because it reflects more differences.

Third, note that van Knippenberg et al. (2004) asserted that differences between a person and other members of the group or dyad may lead to perceptions of being different. Others have noted that actual differences may lead to perceptions of being different (Riordan, 2000). This line of reasoning holds that it is the perceptions of being different, more so than the actual differences themselves, that impact subsequent outcomes. Refer again to the two groups in the sport marketing firm discussed previously. The members of the all African American group, because they are all racially similar to one another, are likely to *perceive* themselves as similar to one another as well. Because the Asian American in the second group is racially different from four other members, it is likely that this person *perceives* herself to be racially different from others in the group. Thus, actual differences result in perceptions of dissimilarity.

Finally, diversity is related to various work outcomes (Hayes-Thomas, 2004). These outcomes can occur at the individual level, such as the satisfaction a physical education student has with his teacher or the performance an employee realizes at work, and at the group level, including the conflict, cohesion, or creativeness of the group. Diversity also impacts organizational outcomes such as product innovation, personnel turnover, and organizational effectiveness. The benefits and possible shortcomings of diversity are discussed in greater detail later in this chapter and throughout the text.

Using the discussion and the previous definitions, diversity can be defined as *the presence of differences among members of a social unit that lead to perceptions of such differences and that impact work outcomes*. This definition highlights the (a) the presence of differences, (b) the dyadic or group nature of diversity, (c) the manner in which actual differences can influence perceptions of such heterogeneity, and (d) the impact diversity has on subsequent outcomes.

Diversity Management

In addition to defining diversity, it is also necessary to define *diversity management*. Consider first how other authors define diversity management:

> Diversity management is "an organizational practice which seeks to redress employees' negative responses to differences associated with age, gender, race, class, occupation, and religion, as well as physical ability and sexual orientation." (Lorbiecki, 2001, p. 345)

> Managing diversity is "creating a climate in which the potential advantages of diversity for organizational or group performance are maximized while the potential disadvantages are minimized." (Cox & Beale, 1997, p. 2)

> Diversity management "is the proactive management technique designed to utilize employee differences in order for an organization to glean a competitive advantage in the marketplace." (Fink & Pastore, 1999, p. 313)

> Diversity management is "the purposeful use of processes and strategies that make . . . differences among people into an asset rather than a liability for the organization." (Hayes-Thomas, 2004, p. 12)

Several conclusions about diversity management can be drawn from these definitions. First, diversity management is generally considered to be proactive and management-initiated (Fink & Pastore, 1999; Hayes-Thomas, 2004). This differs from reactive measures organizations may take to respond to federal or state initiatives such as affirmative action guidelines. Rather, diversity management is viewed as a purposeful, proactive strategy organizations use to realize a competitive advantage and organizational effectiveness.

Second, diversity management is aimed at improving the interactions among persons within a social unit who differ in some way (Lorbiecki, 2001). Although diversity has many benefits to the individual, group, and organization, dissimilarities among interacting people can also lead to friction, process losses, and other negative outcomes. The purpose of diversity management, therefore, is to minimize these potential pitfalls.

Finally, diversity management is a strategic action aimed at maximizing the benefits that diversity can bring to the social unit (Cox & Beale, 1997; Fink & Pastore, 1999; Hayes-Thomas, 2004). Just as organizations, departments, or teams set strategic objectives and initiatives to accomplish tasks and achieve goals, diversity management is a deliberate plan established to realize the benefits of diversity. Diversity can bring tangible benefits to an organization and serve as a source of competitive advantage (Robinson & Dechant, 1997); however, for these benefits to be realized, managers must be strategic in their policy and decision-making process. When managers fail to adopt an effective strategy or when they treat diversity as a "problem to be dealt with," the advantages diversity can bring to a social unit are not likely to materialize (Fink & Pastore, 1999). Thus, as Hayes-Thomas (2004) notes, effective diversity management entails making "differences among people into an asset rather than a liability for the organization" (p. 12).

Using the previous definitions and the discussion, diversity management may be defined as *a proactive, strategic action aimed at capitalizing on the benefits diversity can bring to an organization.* This definition highlights the strategic nature of diversity management and requires a proactive, rather than reactive, management plan that emphasizes the advantages of diversity while minimizing the potential downfalls.

Because people differ in so many ways, it is useful to classify the types of differences. The next section discusses the various forms of diversity.

Forms of Diversity

Much of the early work in diversity focused on demographic attributes, such as sex, race, or age. However, as our definition of diversity illustrates, examining only demographic differences takes an overly narrow approach to the study of diversity. Rather, diversity entails all the ways in which people can differ, including dissimilarities based on demographics, culture, language, physical ability, education, preference, attitudes, and beliefs.

Harrison, Price, and Bell (1998) identified two forms of diversity: surface-level and deep-level (see Exhibit 1.1).

Exhibit 1.1	Forms of diversity.

- **Surface-level diversity:** differences among individuals based on readily observable characteristics, such as age, sex, race, and physical ability.
- **Deep-level diversity:** differences among individuals based on psychological characteristics.
    - **Information diversity:** those differences based on knowledge and information, oftentimes resulting from variations in education, functional background, training, and organizational tenure.
    - **Value diversity:** those differences in values, attitudes, beliefs, and preferences.

Adapted from Harrison, D. A., Price, K. H., & Bell, M. P. (1998) and Jehn, K. A., Northcraft, G. B., & Neale, M. A. (1999).

Surface-Level Diversity

Surface-level diversity includes those dimensions that are readily observed—dissimilarities based on sex, race, age, and in some cases physical ability, socioeconomic status, and language. These variations are important because people make judgments as to how similar they are to others based on these characteristics. For example, when people enter a classroom, aerobics class, or workplace, they make almost instantaneous assessments of their similarity, or lack thereof, to others in the social unit with respect to demographic attributes. An African American coach who enters a room of White coaches almost instantly knows that he is racially different from the others. Surface-level diversity is also important because demographic attributes are permanent and potentially strong sources of member identity.

Similarly, cues about these differences are continually present in face-to-face interactions because of others' outward appearance. For example, members of face-to-face teams have a constant reminder of how other team members vary with respect to age, sex, race, and the like; as a result, the perceptions of difference are continually reinforced.

Deep-Level Diversity

The second form of diversity identified by Harrison et al. (1998) is termed *deep-level diversity*—dissimilarities among people based on psychological characteristics such as attitudes, beliefs, values, culture, or preferences. In general, deep-level differences only become apparent through the interaction with others. Consider once again the previous example of the African American coach in the room of Whites. If the African American coach engages in conversation with others in the room, he might learn that some have values, attitudes, and beliefs similar to his. Thus, even though the coaches may differ in surface-level characteristics, they may be quite similar with respect to deep-level characteristics. As this example illustrates, people can be different on one dimension, but similar on another.

Deep-level diversity can be divided into two categories as identified by Jehn, Northcraft, and Neale (1999): information diversity and value diversity.

Information diversity. Information diversity refers to differences based on knowledge or information that members bring to an organization or group. Members may vary in their functional background, level of education, amount of training, or tenure in the organization. For example, sport organization executive boards frequently comprise members from various business sectors in the community, including banking, coaching, and marketing. Thus, the board members bring a variety of experiences and sources of information to the board, thereby increasing the level of information diversity.

alternative
P E R S P E C T I V E S

Classifying Diversity. Chelladurai (2005) adopted an alternative approach to classifying the forms of diversity. His first form is based on appearance and visible features—age, sex, or race—and this form is synonymous with Harrison et al.'s notion of surface-level diversity. A second form is based on behavioral preferences; for example, food or dress preferences. Because these differences are readily observed, this is a form of surface-level diversity. Third, Chelladurai identified value and attitudinal differences. This form is more akin to the deep-level diversity that only comes to light after interacting with others. Finally, Chelladurai proposed that people could also vary based on their cognitive orientations and individual skills, also considered deep-level differences that can only be discerned through observing the individuals' task performance.

Value diversity. The second category of deep-level diversity is value diversity. A group has high value diversity when there are variations in members' attitudes toward work, personal preferences, or beliefs. These differences may be based on personality attributes such as conscientiousness, or personal traits such the value one attaches to sport and physical activity. Suppose some members of an athletic department put top priority on athlete education and moral citizenship, while others value individual and team performance. In this case, employees' attitudes toward athletics differ; thus, that athletic department is characterized by value diversity.

Interdependence of Surface- and Deep-Level Diversity

Thus far, I have discussed surface- and deep-level diversity as independent concepts. In reality, the two may be intertwined. In many cases, people's surface-level demographics might be representative of more deep-level characteristics. For example, a person, Jim, born in the 1930s is likely to have certain life experiences, expectations, preferences, and values that are quite different from a person, Jackson, born in the 1980s. Jim lived through World War II, the

Korean War, and the Vietnam War, worked in an era prior to the advent of computers and the Internet, and experienced a host of civil rights movements. These experiences, and others like them, shaped his values, beliefs, and attitudes.

Jackson, born in the 1980s, has not experienced as many wars, considers workplace technologies a fact of life, and only knows a workplace governed by equal employment opportunity laws. As with Jim, these factors shaped Jackson's values, beliefs, and attitudes. Thus, Jim and Jackson, who differ in the surface-level characteristic age, are likely to vary in their deep-level characteristics as well. Surface-level differences are likely related to deep-level dissimilarity (Cunningham, 2006; Thomas, Ravlin, & Wallace, 1996).

Understanding the Emphasis on Diversity

This next section considers why the topic of diversity is so important and receives such interest. The extant literature points to seven specific factors: changing demographics, changing attitudes toward work, changes in the nature of work, legal mandates, social pressures, the potentially negative effects of diversity, and the value-in-diversity hypothesis (see Exhibit 1.2). Each of these factors is discussed in greater detail.

Exhibit 1.2	Factors contributing to interest in and importance of diversity.

Changing demographics: increases in the median age, proportion of racial minorities, and women in the workforce.

Changing attitudes toward work: changes in the commitment and loyalty to employers and work–family conflict.

Changes in the nature of work: increases in the number of organizations that structure work around teams, the impact of globalization, and the frequency of mergers and acquisitions.

Legal mandates: federal and state laws that require equal employment opportunities for all persons, irrespective of demographic characteristics or background.

Social pressures: the notion that organizations have a moral and ethical obligation to have a diverse workplace.

Potential negative effects of diversity: diversity can potentially lead to negative outcomes such as low satisfaction, high conflict, and poor team performance.

Value-in-diversity hypothesis: diversity can positively influence desired individual, group, and organizational outcomes.

Changing Demographics

The most important factor spurring interest in diversity is the changing demographic makeup of the workforce. In the United States, significant changes in the racial, sex, and age composition of the country took place during the 20th century, and demographics are projected to continue changing. Shifts were also seen in socioeconomic status. Demographic changes in the population correspond to changes in the workforce, thus making diversity an organizational reality. These changes prompted managers and other professionals to take note of diversity and to devise strategies to manage such differences. I examine specific demographic shifts in further detail below.

According to the U. S. Census Bureau (www.census.gov), two of the most significant changes in the United States have been: (a) a sharp increase in the representation of racial minorities and (b) an increase in the population's median age. From 1980 to 2000, the Hispanic population in the United States doubled. Significant growth occurred for other racial groups as well. As seen in Exhibit 1.3, by the year 2000, Whites represented 69.4 percent of the U. S. population, followed by African Americans (12.7 percent), Hispanics (12.6 percent), Asian Americans (3.8 percent), and other races (2.5 percent). However,

Projected racial changes in the U. S. population. | *Exhibit 1.3*

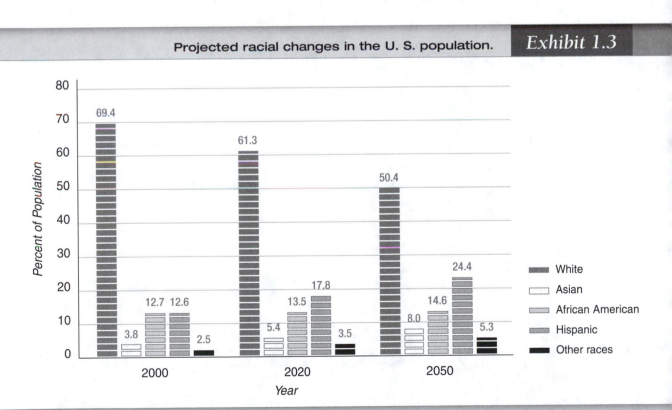

these figures are expected to change dramatically during the next 50 years. By the year 2050, Whites are expected to represent just 50.1 percent of the population, followed by Hispanics (24.4 percent), African Americans (14.6 percent), Asian Americans (8.0 percent), and other races (5.3 percent). These changes are expected to be reflected in the workforce, and as a result, employees of sport and physical activity organizations will grow more racially diverse. Consequently, people are likely to be working with, working for, or supervising someone who is racially different. Furthermore, potential customers will also become more racially diverse; therefore, managers will have to devise strategies aimed at attracting those customers to their goods and services.

Changes in the median age of the U.S. population have also been dramatic. According to the U. S. Census Bureau, at the beginning of the 20th century, the median age was 22.9 years. This figure increased over the 100-year span such that by the year 2000, over half of the U. S. population was over 35.3 years of age. Much of that change is a result of the large number of babies born in the 1940s and 1950s—the baby boom generation. As the baby boomers have grown older, so too has the overall population. The population of persons age 65 and older grew tenfold in the 20th century; furthermore, projections have the U. S. population continuing to grow older into the 21st century (see Exhibit 1.4). Not

Exhibit 1.4   Projected age changes in the U. S. population.

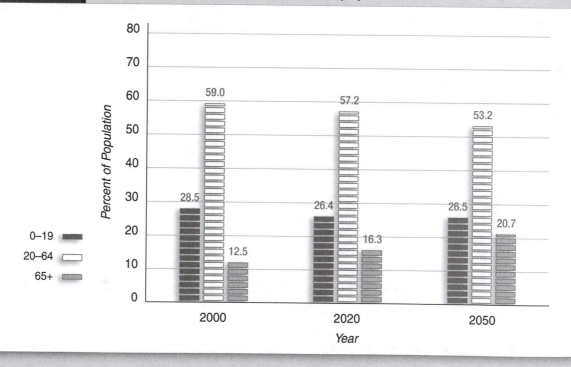

only is the nation growing older, but people are also working to a later age, resulting in a greater age diversity within all organizations, including those for sport and physical activity, and an older potential consumer base. Just as strategies are needed to attract persons from different racial groups to purchase an organization's goods and services, so too is there a need to devise plans to draw older customers to the organization.

Sex composition of the United States has also changed, though not as dramatically as the shifts in age and race. The U. S. Census Bureau reports that the U. S. population shifted from majority male at the beginning of the 20th century to majority female by the century's midpoint. At the end of the 20th century, women still outnumbered men (see Exhibit 1.5). Although women continue to enter the workforce in increasing numbers, they are still less likely to be members of the workforce than men. It should be noted, however, that the magnitude of the difference in the proportion of men and women in the workforce has decreased over time (see also Tsui & Gutek, 1999). As with the other forms of diversity, the increase in the proportion of working women means sex diversity in all types of organizations has increased as well.

Changes also have occurred with respect to socioeconomic status. Data from the U. S. Census Bureau indicate that in 1967, the mean income of the primary householder was $38,452, a figure that increased to $57,852 by 2002. In isola-

Sex changes in the U. S. population.   *Exhibit 1.5*

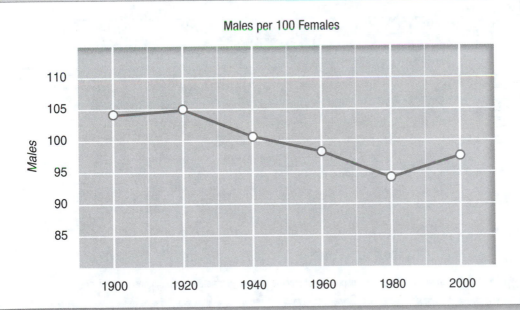

Males per 100 Females

U. S. Census Bureau data.

tion, these figures do not tell us much, as they simply indicate that people make more money over time, something that could be attributed to inflation. However, other data indicate that the share of aggregate income is increasingly unevenly dispersed. In 1967, the top 5 percent of all households possessed a 17.5 percent share of aggregate income. By 1980, the share had actually dropped to 15.8 percent. However, since that time, the share of aggregate income held by the top 5 percent increased, such that by 2002, the top 5 percent of all households possessed 21.7 percent of the aggregate income. The Gini Index, a measure that summarizes the dispersion of income over the entire income distribution, also increased during that time. This increase means that the income is increasingly being received by one group of people (see Exhibit 1.6). As this figure indicates, the socioeconomic status of the U. S. population changed over time, with the distribution of wealth growing increasingly inequitable.

Such changing demographics occurred in other areas of the world as well. Canada witnessed an increase in the proportion of native persons and other racial minorities during the last 20 years (Haq, 2004). New Zealand also witnessed increased racial diversity, primarily due to immigration from Asian countries (Haq, 2004). Further, the populations of a large number of European nations, as well as Japan and Australia, continue to increase in median age (Haq, 2004). Recent estimates suggest that women will account for 90 percent

Exhibit 1.6	Income changes in the U. S. population.

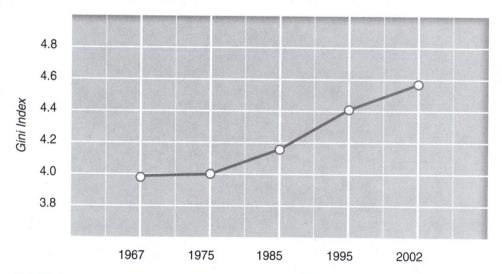

Note: The Gini Index measures the dispersion of income, with higher values representing greater inequality.

U. S. Census Bureau data.

of the increase in the British workforce in the next 10 years (Hewitt, 2002). These figures indicate that increasing diversity is occurring globally.

Changing Attitudes Toward Work

Just as the demographic composition of the workforce has changed, so too have employees' attitudes toward work (Korman, 1999; Thomas, 1996). Employees are no longer likely to spend their entire career with a single organization, moving up through the ranks as they progress in tenure and skills. Rather, employees are now likely to move from one organization to another several times in their career either by choice or as a result of changes outside of their control, such as downsizing, mergers, and so forth. The average person is likely to follow multiple career paths before retirement. As a result, employees may identify less with their organization and their job satisfaction may be affected. In general, employees' loyalties and commitments to their employers have lessened.

In addition to a more mobile workforce, a significant portion of the U. S. workforce now works part-time rather than full-time. This is meaningful because part-time workers have different attitudes about their work than do their full-time counterparts (Korman, 1999; Thorsteinson, 2003). For example, Thorsteinson reports that full-time employees strongly identify with their jobs and report higher pay satisfaction than do their part-time counterparts.

Finally, an increase in the number of women in the workforce, dual-career families, and single parents has resulted in greater emphasis on balancing work and family life (Thomas, 1996). The conflict between those two roles, termed *work–family conflict,* results in role conflicts and tensions in the workplace that have otherwise not been present.

New and evolving employee attitudes toward work increase the number of perspectives and variety of beliefs held in the workplace. Such changes result in greater deep-level diversity within organizations. Whereas demographic changes have increased the surface-level diversity in organizations, changes in attitudes and preferences have resulted in increased deep-level diversity.

Changes in the Nature of Work

The third reason diversity has become such a major issue for sport managers is due to changes in the nature of work. Many organizations are now structured around work teams (Marks, Mathieu, & Zaccaro, 2001). The level of interdependence among employees has increased, and consequently, people work more closely with their colleagues than they have in the past. When people work closely with one another, variations in talents, values, perspectives, and attitudes come to the forefront. Furthermore, differences, whether deep- or surface-level, between them are continually reinforced by the constant face-to-face interaction. These factors can influence the way work is experienced (Doherty & Chelladurai, 1999; Thomas, 1996).

Globalization has also influenced diversity within organizations. Many sport organizations, including pro sports, are recruiting employees and athletes from other countries (see Exhibit 1.7). There is also a growing proportion of foreign students enrolled in U. S. universities and participating in collegiate athletics (Ridinger & Pastore, 2000). It is incumbent upon managers, professors, and coaches to understand the cultures and backgrounds of the student-athletes in order to aid in their transition. Although many of these students return to their native countries upon graduation, others seek to remain and work in this country.

Sport organizations are striving to broaden the products and services offered to an international market. For instance, the National Football League (NFL) has affiliate teams placed in Europe as part of NFL Europe. The National Basketball Association (NBA) has teams in both Canada and the United States, and intends to expand to Europe (Whittell, 2002). Understanding different cultures and customs becomes paramount for the effective expansion into foreign markets.

Organizational diversity is also impacted by mergers and acquisitions. Mergers and acquisitions are commonplace in the business world, and the sport industry is no exception. For example, in 2003, NIKE purchased Converse for $200 million. Reebok spent roughly the same amount of money to buy The Hockey Company in April of 2004. And, in 2005, Adidas announced plans to purchase Reebok for $3.8 billion (Rovell, 2005). Such mergers have a bearing on diversity. When organiza-

Exhibit 1.7	MLB players from around the world.

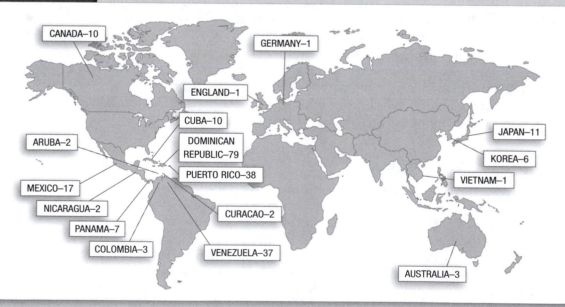

From http://mlb.mlb.com/NASApp/mlb/mlb/official_info/dbp/about_players.jsp

tions join together, so too do members of what were formerly different entities. Individuals with a great variety of backgrounds and experiences are expected to work effectively with one another. Information diversity increases in the workplace, which can be a positive change, but employee differences and differing organizational identities may make a true merging of talents difficult to accomplish (van Kippenberg, van Kippenberg, Monden, & de Lima, 2002). In general, mergers serve to increase deep-level diversity within organizations.

Legal Mandates

Legal mandates also spur interest in diversity. Diversity-related laws are discussed in greater detail in Chapter 10, so their significance is only briefly discussed here. No longer is it acceptable to discriminate based on race, national origin, sex, age, and so forth. Civil rights legislation passed in the 1960s and later in the 1990s made discriminatory practices illegal and mandated equal employment opportunities for all persons. These laws also required that the wages paid be based on work qualifications rather than personal demographics. As might be expected, these laws changed the way human resource decisions are made and generally serve to increase diversity within organizations.

Within the realm of sport, recreation, and physical education, Title IX represents the most significant legislation passed during the 20th century. This law requires that all persons, regardless of their sex, be afforded equal opportunities to participate in federally funded educational activities.

Social Pressures

Another factor thought to influence the interest in diversity is social pressures—there is a moral or ethical obligation for diversity within organizations. For example, Doherty and Chelladurai (1999) outlined how an organizational culture of diversity is likely the result of perceptions of a social responsibility to treat all employees fairly. Furthermore, DeSensi (1995) argued for an increase in the appreciation of and value placed on employee differences. For many

alternative
P E R S P E C T I V E S

Social Responsibility for Diversity. Although many argue that there is a social or ethical responsibility to have diversity, others suggest that such arguments are not realistic in an organizational context (Fink & Pastore, 1999; Robinson & Dechant, 1997). These authors submit that alternative, business-case arguments provide a more compelling reason for diversity, especially within for-profit organizations. Robinson and Dechant suggest that providing empirical data showing how diversity helps the business "bottom-line" provides a much more persuasive case for diversity than the social responsibility argument. Fink and Pastore, in their study of sport organizations, take a similar stance; they note that "while it would be wonderful for all of those in positions of power to realize the moral and social advantages of diversity, it may not be a realistic goal. Thus, for diversity initiatives to be truly embedded within the organization, those in power must be convinced of diversity's relationship to organizational effectiveness" (p. 314).

adopting this perspective, social responsibilities toward diversity should be the primary focus of diversity initiatives. Proponents of this perspective also may take umbrage with the term "managing diversity," as the term connotes "using" people to achieve organizational goals. This "using" of people stands in contrast to valuing and understanding employee differences in order to further benefit the employee and company (Prasad, Mills, Elmes, & Prasad, 1997). These social pressures have led to an increase in the diversity within organizations, especially with respect to surface-level differences.

Potential Negative Effects of Diversity

Although diversity does lead to positive outcomes, this is not always so. Thus, a sixth reason for the increased attention on diversity is the potential for negative effects of such heterogeneity. For some, diversity initiatives such as diversity management strategies, equal employment opportunity laws, and affirmative action mandates are seen as unfair, a form of reverse discrimination. Tsui and Gutek (1999) reported the negative feelings some employees felt toward diversity issues. As one employee noted, "minorities receive special attention. It is difficult to fire them because HR gets involved to minimize litigation. Managers do not want the hassle" (p. 2).

These negative attitudes are not just felt by Whites. Fitzgerald Hill, a former head football coach at San Jose State University and current president of Arkansas Baptist College, found that racial minority coaches often felt they were pigeon-holed into certain positions. As one research participant explained, Black coaches are only "hired to fill a quota, recruit the black athletes and become their mentor" (as cited in Brown, 2002). Thus, there is the perception among some African American coaches that, although they may have some access to certain positions, they are only hired to fulfill requirements or quotas set by organizations or legal mandates. Other research found that racial minorities have negative attitudes toward diversity initiatives when the plans are perceived as providing them an unwanted advantage (Highhouse et al., 1999).

People who are different from others in their social unit generally have negative experiences in that unit (see Williams & O'Reilly, 1998). This is true whether the differences are surface- or deep-level. A feeling of being different can negatively impact the attitudes people have toward the group or organization, as well as the group's ability to function. For example, consider Catherine, a female Asian American sport marketer who believes she is different from other employees with whom she works because of her race and the value she places on work and family. To the extent that these differences are meaningful to Catherine, she is unlikely to integrate well with her coworkers or have a positive experience in the workplace. On the other hand, if Bill, a White male in the same organization, feels that he is similar in demographics and values to others, then his experiences are likely to be positive. The same would also hold true for other demographics and deep-level differences, such as sexual orientation or religious beliefs.

As the examples illustrate, diversity can have a negative effect on organizational functioning. Because diversity is an organizational reality, managers have a responsibility to understand the potential for negative effects and to devise methods and processes to eliminate them.

Value-in-Diversity Hypothesis

The notion that diversity adds value to an organization represents the final factor that has led to an increase in the interest in diversity. To the extent that people can show that diversity brings real, tangible benefits to a group or organization, the value-in-diversity hypothesis (Cox, Lobel, & McLeod, 1991) is likely to result in the greatest acceptance of diversity by group or organization members.

Robinson and Dechant (1997) present several ways in which diversity might benefit an organization, the first of which is cost savings. Specifically, these authors contend that effectively managing a diverse workforce will result in lower turnover costs, a decrease in absenteeism, and a reduction in lawsuits. Indeed, business strategies, such as effective diversity management, that can reduce human resource costs and litigation fees are likely to be valued by any organization.

Second, Robinson and Dechant (1997) argue that effective diversity management plans will allow companies to successfully compete for talented human resources. They note, "winning the competition for talent means attracting, retaining, and promoting excellent employees from different demographic groups" (p. 24). Alternatively, if the available talent pool is limited to only persons from a certain demographic group (e.g.,

DIVERSITY *in the field*

Communication Barriers. Much of the research concerning the negative effects of diversity has focused on the organizational setting; however, these effects can be observed in all contexts. An example can be found among Little League baseball teams in Methuen, MA. In the summer of 2005, the Methuen team was playing Seekonk in Lakeville. Methuen was leading the contest 3–1 when the coach, Domingo Infante, gave instructions to his pitcher in Spanish. After the ensuing play, the umpire called timeout, briefly spoke to a Little League official, and then ruled that only English could be spoken during the game. At the time, there were no rules dictating the language to be spoken during the contest. A spokesperson for the League explained: "It appears the umpire was concerned that the coach or manager may have been using a language other than English . . . to communicate potentially 'illegal' instructions to his players." The Methuen coaches criticized the ruling, arguing that it demoralized the players, ultimately leading to a loss. A formal protest was denied, and the umpire did not face disciplinary action ("Ump's language," 2005).

The implication here is, of course, that those who are not speaking English must be trying to break the rules and gain an unfair advantage. Interestingly, it is acceptable in baseball to use signs and hand motions—a nonverbal form of communication that only team members can understand—to provide instructions. Even though the League rules do not ban other languages, teams who use languages other than English are penalized; thus, the players, coaches, and team are penalized for being different.

PROFESSIONAL
P E R S P E C T I V E S

The Importance of Diversity in Sport. Peter Roby served as the men's basketball head coach at Harvard University, then worked at Reebok International. He is currently the Director of the Center for Sport in Society, an entity that was created based on the idea that "sport can play an important role in helping to create social change." According to Roby, there are several reasons why diversity has become such a major issue in sport and physical activity. Primarily, he suggests that sport highlights differences among people, differences based on sex, age, race, religion, life experiences, and learning style. Roby explains that "there is a lot that people can benefit from as a result of being exposed to difference." In addition, "with regard to sport in particular, one of the values that we see in sport is how much it acts as a great common denominator—how it brings people from different backgrounds together under the common umbrella of sport." Sport serves as an educational tool—what people learn about diversity in the context of sport can be applied to their everyday life on a daily basis.

White, able-bodied, Protestant, heterosexual males), then a company is severely limiting the potential pool of human resources. Effective diversity management efforts not only attract diverse persons to the organization, but also help to retain them. Equal opportunities for training, development, and advancement for all persons, irrespective of their individual differences, bodes well for the employee retention process.

Organizational diversity can potentially drive business growth (Robinson & Dechant, 1997). One way business growth occurs is through improved marketplace understanding. For example, when NASCAR sought to increase the diversity of its spectators, it turned to former NBA great and successful entrepreneur Ervin "Magic" Johnson for help. NASCAR chief operating officer George Pyne noted, "Magic will help NASCAR achieve its goals to better educate new audiences and facilitate greater participation among the industry and communities of color" (as cited in "Magic," 2004). Other ways in which diversity spurs business growth include increased creativity and innovation, improved problem solving, enhanced leadership capabilities, and enhanced global technologies. The manner in which diversity influences these important outcomes is discussed in detail throughout this book.

The benefits, or valued outcomes, to an organization (e.g., cost savings, increased pool of talented human resources, competitive advantage) far outweigh any potential negative effects. Refer to the Professional Perspectives box for further discussion on why diversity is important within the context of sport and physical activity.

Putting It All Together

As the preceding discussions illustrate, diversity has become a central topic within organizations for sport and physical activity. Not only has the world around us become more heterogeneous, with respect to both demographic characteristics and attitudes, beliefs, and preferences, but the way work is accomplished has also changed. Legal and social pressures to diversify, as well as the evidence that diversity can both negatively and positively influence organizational outcomes, have all increased the interest in and attention paid to diversity.

The purpose of this text is to provide readers with an overview, understanding, and analysis of diversity in sport organizations. In Part I, I discuss the various ways we can look at diversity (Chapter 2). In doing so, I examine the theories used to guide this process. The focus of Chapter 3 is discrimination and prejudice. I provide definitions and key points, discuss the theoretical tenets behind those constructs, and outline the effects that discrimination and prejudice have on persons in the workplace.

Part II is devoted to the categorical effects of diversity. As discussed in Chapter 2, categorical diversity entails examining the experiences of people from one social group relative to the experiences of people in another group. In examining categorical effects of diversity, I focus on race and ethnicity (Chapter 4), sex and gender (Chapter 5), age, obesity, and disability (Chapter 6), and deep-level differences (Chapter 7).

Part III considers diversity in the dyad, group, and organization context. Chapter 8 examines the influence on subsequent outcomes of differences within groups, departments, and organizations. In Chapter 9, I discuss how differences in dyadic relationships, such as supervisor and subordinate, influence the outcomes of such relationships. For example, I consider how being different from others in the group impacts how well one might integrate into that group.

Part IV is devoted to strategies that can be used to create a diverse workplace and to capitalize on the positive effects of diversity. In this section, I first examine the legal aspects of employment diversity (Chapter 10), such as those dealing with equal employment opportunity, sexual harassment, persons with disabilities, and gender equity. Chapter 11 then provides an overview of various strategies that can be used to manage diversity at the department and organization levels. Chapter 12 examines diversity at the group level and how interactions and relationships among dissimilar people can be improved. Finally, in Chapter 13, I examine diversity training, the methods of conducting such training, and the influence of training on subsequent outcomes.

Chapter Summary

This chapter provided an opening glimpse of diversity in organizations. As seen in the Texas Section of the USTA Diversity Challenge, diversity is an important issue for all persons involved in sport and physical activity. In light of the ongoing changes in the workforce, coupled with other pressures for diversity, diversity will continue to be at the forefront for years to come. After reading the chapter, you should be able to do the following:

1. Define diversity and diversity management.

Diversity is the presence of differences among members of a social unit that lead to perceptions of such differences and that impact work outcomes. Diversity management is a proactive, strategic action aimed at capitalizing on the benefits diversity can bring to an organization.

2. List and explain the different forms of diversity.

Two forms of diversity were identified (Harrison et al., 1998): surface-level diversity, which is related to observable characteristics, and deep-level diversity, which is related to differences in psychological characteristics. Deep-level diversity is further broken down into information diversity, or those differences based on the knowledge and information members bring to the organization or group, and value diversity, which is related to differences in the values, attitudes, and preferences of group members (see Jehn et al., 1999).

3. Discuss the different factors that led to an increased interest in diversity.

The factors that have made diversity such an important topic include: (a) changing demographics in the workforce, (b) changing attitudes of organizational employees, (c) changes in the nature of work, (d) legal mandates, (e) social pressures, (f) the potential negative effects of diversity, and (g) the positive impact diversity can have on a group, department, or organization.

 ## Questions for Discussion

1. Why is it important to understand diversity and the influence of diversity in the sport and physical activity context?

2. Based on your experiences, how much emphasis is placed on diversity by managers and other personnel of sport organizations? Why is this so?

3. What are some potential pitfalls of diversity in the work context?

4. In what ways does diversity benefit people in sport organizations?

5. Some people raised concerns about the term "diversity management." What are some of those concerns, and what are the merits of each? Should these concerns change the management of diverse organizations?

6. Consider the various ways in which people differ. Are some forms of diversity more important than others? Would you expect some forms of diversity to have a stronger impact on attitudes and beliefs, or others to have a stronger impact on job performance? Why or why not?

7. Changing workforce demographics represents one of the major factors that has led to an increase in diversity. Suppose that a workgroup is demograph-

ically different (i.e., members from different races, sexes, ages, and so forth), but they all have the same attitudes, values, and beliefs. If the members all think and act in a similar fashion, is the group still considered diverse?

Learning Activities

1. Several demographic trends were noted in the chapter. Visit the U. S. Census Bureau website (www.census.gov) and gather data concerning other demographic and population trends. Also search for similar websites for other countries. How do the trends in the United States and in other countries differ? How are they the same?

2. Many people oppose diversity in the workplace or in educational settings. What are some of their arguments, and what are counterarguments you can use to alleviate these concerns? Divide into small groups, with each group adopting a particular position. Be prepared to present your position to the class.

Resources

SUPPLEMENTARY READINGS

Allison, M., & Schneider, I. (Eds.). (2000). *Diversity in the recreation profession: Organizational perspectives*. Bala Cynwyd, PA: Venture Publishing. (An edited text containing perspectives from professionals in the recreation field; discusses issues related to race, age, disability, sexual identity, social class, and gender.)

Stockdale, M. S., & Crosby, F. J. (Eds.). (2004). *The psychology and management of workplace diversity*. Malden, MA: Blackwell. (An edited text that contains essays from leading diversity scholars in the field; addresses issues related to the need for diversity, diversity management, and strategies for an inclusive workplace, among others.)

Takaki, R. (Ed.). (2002). *Debating diversity* (3rd ed.). New York: Oxford. (This edited text offers varying perspectives concerning race and ethnicity; also addresses topics such as Mexican immigration, affirmative action, and the diversity climate of America.)

WEB RESOURCES

- Center for the Study of Sport in Society (www.sportinsociety.org): organization devoted to the study of sport in society; focuses on issues concerning race and disability, among others.

- Diversity, Inc. (www.diversityinc.com): site devoted to diversity in the general organizational context.
- U. S. Census Bureau (www.census.gov): provides demographic data for the United States across a variety of contexts.

References

Brown, G. T. (2002). Diversity grid lock. *The NCAA News*. Retrieved February 15, 2003, from www.ncaa.org/news/2002/20021028/active/3922n01.html

Chelladurai, P. (2005). *Managing organizations for sport and physical activity: A systems perspective* (2nd ed.). Scottsdale, AZ: Holcomb Hathaway.

Cox, T., Jr., & Beale, R. L. (1997). *Developing competency to manage diversity: Readings, cases, & activities*. San Francisco: Berrett-Koehler.

Cox, T. H., Lobel, S. A., & McLeod, P. L. (1991). Effects of ethnic group cultural differences on cooperative and competitive behavior. *Academy of Management Journal, 34,* 827–847.

Cunningham, G. B. (2006). The influence of demographic dissimilarity on affective reactions to physical activity classes. *Journal of Sport and Exercise Psychology, 28,* 127–142.

DeSensi, J. T. (1995). Understanding multiculturalism and valuing diversity: A theoretical perspective. *Quest, 47,* 34–43.

Doherty, A. J., & Chelladurai, P. (1999). Managing cultural diversity in sport organizations: A theoretical perspective. *Journal of Sport Management, 13,* 280–297.

Fink, J. S., & Pastore, D. L. (1999). Diversity in sport? Utilizing the business literature to devise a comprehensive framework of diversity initiatives. *Quest, 51,* 310–327.

Haq, R. (2004). International perspectives on workplace diversity. In M. S. Stockdale & F. J. Crosby (Eds.), *The psychology and management of workplace diversity* (pp. 277–298). Malden, MA: Blackwell.

Harrison, D. A., Price, K. H., & Bell, M. P. (1998). Beyond relational demography: Time and the effects of surface- and deep-level diversity on work group cohesion. *Academy of Management Journal, 41,* 96–107.

Hayes-Thomas, R. (2004). Why now? The contemporary focus on managing diversity. In M. S. Stockdale & F. J. Crosby (Eds.), *The psychology and management of workplace diversity* (pp. 3–30). Malden, MA: Blackwell.

Hewitt, P. (2002, May 29). The way we work now: A shift in demographics and culture means Britain's labor market must become far more flexible. *The Guardian,* p. 19.

Highhouse, S., Stierwalt, S. L., Bachiochi, P. D., Elder, A. E., & Fisher, G. G. (1999). Effects of advertised human resource management practices on attraction of African American applicants. *Personnel Psychology, 52,* 425–442.

Jackson, S. E., Joshi, A., & Erhardt, N. L. (2003). Recent research on team and organizational diversity: SWOT analysis and implications. *Journal of Management, 29,* 801–830.

Jehn, K. A., Northcraft, G. B., & Neale, M. A. (1999). Why differences make a difference: A field study of diversity, conflict, and performance in workgroups. *Administrative Science Quarterly, 44,* 741–763.

Joplin, J. R. W., & Daus, C. S. (1997). Challenges of leading a diverse workforce. *Academy of Management Executive, 11*(3), 32–37.

Korman, A. K. (1999). Motivation, commitment, and the "new contracts" between employers and employees. In A. I. Kraut & A. K. Korman (Eds.), *Evolving practices in human resource manage-*

ment: Responses to a changing world (pp. 23–40). San Francisco: Jossey-Bass.

Lorbiecki, A. (2001). Changing views on diversity management: The rise of the learning perspective and the need to recognize social and political contradictions. *Management Learning, 32,* 345–361.

Magic Johnson to help NASCAR diversity efforts. (2004, May 20). SI.com. Retrieved September 2, 2005, from http://sportsillustrated.cnn.com/2004/racing/05/20/bc.rac.lgns.nascarmagicjohnson.r/index.html

Marks, M. A., Mathieu, J. E., & Zaccaro, S. J. (2001). A temporally based framework and taxonomy of team processes. *Academy of Management Review, 26,* 356–376.

Prasad, P., Mills, A. J., Elmes, M., & Prasad, A. (1997). *Managing the organizational meltingpot: Dilemmas of workforce diversity.* Thousand Oaks, CA: Sage.

Ridinger, L. L., & Pastore, D. L. (2000). A proposed framework to identify factors associated with international student-athlete adjustment to college. *International Journal of Sport Management, 1,* 4–24.

Riordan, C. M. (2000). Relational demography within groups: Past developments, contradictions, and new directions. In G. R. Ferris (Ed.), *Research in personnel and human resources management* (Vol. 19, pp. 131–173). Greenwich, CT: JAI Press.

Robinson, G., & Dechant, K. (1997). Building a business case for diversity. *Academy of Management Executive, 11*(3), 21–31.

Rovell, D. (2005, August 3). Reebok, Adidas have plenty issues to solve. *ESPN.* Retrieved September 1, 2005, from http://sports.espn.go.com/espn/columns/story?columnist=rovell_darren&id=2123332

Thomas, D. C., Ravlin, E. C., & Wallace, A. W. (1996). Effect of cultural diversity in work groups. In P. A. Bamberger, M. Erez, & S. B. Bacharach (Eds.), *Research in the sociology of organizations* (Vol. 14, pp. 1–33). London: JAI Press.

Thomas, R. R. (1996). *Redefining diversity.* New York: AMACOM.

Thorsteinson, T. J. (2003). Job attitudes of part-time vs. full-time workers: A meta-analytic review. *Journal of Occupational and Organizational Psychology, 76,* 151–177.

Tsui, A. S., & Gutek, B. A. (1999). *Demographic differences in organizations: Current research and future directions.* New York: Lexington Books.

Ump's language ban incites protest: Little Leaguers told to stop speaking Spanish on the field. (2005, July 29,). SI.com. Retrieved July 29, 2005, from http://sportsillustrated.cnn.com/2005/more/07/29/ll.spanish.ap/indiex.hrml?cnn=yes

van Knippenberg, D., De Drue, C. K. W., & Homan, A. C. (2004). Work group diversity and group performance: An integrative model and research agenda. *Journal of Applied Psychology, 89,* 1008–1022.

van Kippenberg, D., van Kippenberg, B., Monden, L., & de Lima, F. (2002). Organizational identification after a merger: A social identity perspective. *British Journal of Social Psychology, 41,* 233–252.

Whittell, I. (2002, March 12). NBA declares intention to expand to Europe. *The London Times,* 39.

Williams, K. Y., & O'Reilly, C. A. (1998). Demography and diversity in organizations: A review of 40 years of research. In B. M. Staw & L. L. Cummings (Eds.), *Research in organizational behavior* (Vol. 20, pp. 77–140). Greenwich, CT: JAI Press.

Theoretical Tenets of Diversity

DIVERSITY CHALLENGE

The YMCA is a nonprofit organization with an aim to "build strong kids, strong families, and strong communities." This goal is often achieved by way of sport, leisure, and recreational activities. As a nonprofit organization, its ultimate survival depends upon acquiring donated funds from community members and other organizations, a task often undertaken by the YMCA Executive Boards. The Executive Board of the YMCA in Calgary, Canada, consists of 17 (4 women, 13 men) members, most coming from various sectors of the business world. Some board members are dentists, others are in the energy sector, others work in local universities, and still others are from consulting and marketing agencies. Because the members' functional backgrounds differ, the Executive Board can be classified as cross-functional in nature. The board's cross-functional nature is important because this type of diversity influences group and organizational outcomes—outcomes that may benefit the organization or serve as an impediment. YMCAs with cross-functional boards are likely to generate a greater amount of donations than are YMCAs with homogeneous boards. Cross-functional groups can also create negative outcomes—lack of communication, lack of social integration, and other poor group processes. Thus, although cross-functional boards bring real benefits to the YMCA, there are negative effects as well.*

*Information gathered from www.ymcacalgary.org; Jassawalla, A. R., & Sashittal, H. C. (1999). Building collaborative cross-functional new product teams. *Academy of Management Executive, 13*(3), 50–63; and Siciliano, J. I. (1996). The relationship between board member diversity to organizational performance. *Journal of Business Ethics, 15,* 1313–1320.

LEARNING OBJECTIVES

After studying this chapter, you should be able to:

- Identify four approaches to the study of diversity.

- Understand what a theory is and why theory is important to understanding diversity.

- Discuss the different classes of theory used to understand diversity.

- Discuss how the different theories can be applied to diversity issues within organizations for sport and physical activity.

DIVERSITY CHALLENGE   **REFLECTION**

1. List some examples of cross-functional groups in other sport organizations.

2. Why do you think cross-functional groups generate more donations? What other benefits might they bring to their organizations?

3. What is it about cross-functional groups that results in negative outcomes?

4. List some other types of diverse groups that could help the YMCAs generate revenues.

As the YMCA board case illustrates, diversity is a complex issue. Although diversity brings many benefits to an organization, such as an increase in donations, it can also have negative effects, such as poor group dynamics. Not all types of diversity, however, have the same effects. Some types impact group and individual performance; others have a stronger impact on affective reactions and the attitudes people have toward one another and toward their work. The impact of diversity might also depend on the specific context.

How do we make sense of such complexity? Simply analyzing each case on an individual basis is daunting, inefficient, and counterproductive. This process does not allow for educated predictions about what might happen in the future concerning employee attitudes, group processes, or organizational outcomes. Therefore, there is a need to cognitively simplify the world around us; theory allows us to do this.

The purpose of this chapter is to provide the theoretical tenets associated with diversity. I begin by discussing four approaches to the study of diversity. This is followed by defining the term *theory* and explaining why theory is important in the study of diversity. Next, I discuss the three major categories of theories used to study and understand diversity, briefly outlining the specific theories within each category and the major tenets or propositions put forth by each. I also describe the application of each theory category to diverse organizations.

Four Approaches to the Study of Diversity

Of the many approaches to the study of diversity, one framework that has proven especially useful is that proposed by Tsui and Gutek (1999). According to these authors, there are three approaches to the study of diversity: categorical, compositional, and relational.

Although Tsui and Gutek used the term *demography* (e.g., compositional demography) because their focus is on demographic differences in organizations, the term *diversity* (e.g., compositional diversity) is used here because, as discussed in Chapter 1, differences can be based on any attribute—those that relate to demographics and those that do not. I have extended their work to include a fourth approach: diversity management strategy. An overview of the four approaches is provided in Exhibit 2.1, and an explanation of each follows.

Categorical Approach

When examining diversity using a categorical approach, the focus is on comparing the experiences and behaviors of members of one social unit (e.g., demographic group or work group) to those of another social unit; for example, comparing veteran NFL players to rookie players.

Approaches to the study of diversity.   *Exhibit 2.1*

Categorical:
- *Basic premise:* Compares the experiences and behaviors of members of one social category to those of another.
- *Example:* What is the level of job satisfaction of men compared to that of women?

Compositional:
- *Basic premise:* Examines the processes and outcomes of diverse social groups relative to those of homogeneous social groups.
- *Example:* What is the level of conflict present in cross-functional work groups relative to work groups with members from a single functional area?

Relational:
- *Basic premise:* Focuses on an individual's personal characteristics relative to the characteristics of the group.
- *Example:* How well do people socially integrate into a group when they are demographically different from the majority of the group members?

Diversity Management Strategy:
- *Basic premise:* Examines organizational strategies that can be used to capitalize on the benefits of diversity while reducing the negative effects.
- *Example:* What strategies do sport organizations use to attract and retain women and racial minorities?

DIVERSITY *in the field*

Native American Mascots. One shortcoming of the categorical approach to the study of diversity is the presumed homogeneity of the preferences and attitudes that members of a certain social group have—a presumption that is often unfounded. An example of an absence of such homogeneity relates to the issue of Native American mascots. In 2005, the National Collegiate Athletic Association (NCAA) ruled that teams using Native American mascots could not participate in postseason competitions or host tournaments because such mascots were deemed "hostile and abusive." This ruling meant that teams had to change their mascots or face exclusion from postseason competition. Many universities with Native American mascots appealed this ruling, including the Florida State Seminoles. The NCAA granted a waiver to Florida State because the Seminole Tribe of Florida endorsed the mascot's use. Max Osceola, the chief and general council president of the Seminole Tribe of Florida, considered it an "honor" to be associated with the university. However, not all Seminoles expressed similar beliefs, including members of the Seminole Nation of Oklahoma. General council member David Narcomey, in responding to the NCAA ruling, expressed the following: "I am deeply appalled, incredulously disappointed. . . . I am nauseated that the NCAA is allowing this 'minstrel show' to carry on this form of racism in the 20th century" (Wieberg, 2005). As this case illustrates, not all members of a particular social group, in this case Native Americans, have the same views concerning diversity-related issues.

Research

Research using a categorical approach might seek to answer such questions as:

- Do men and women coaches have the same career aspirations?

- Are there differences in the behaviors of new physical education teachers relative to those who have been teaching for a number of years?

- Do coaches whose religious and spiritual beliefs are important to them use leadership styles that vary from the styles used by those coaches whose religious and spiritual beliefs are a less central part of their lives?

According to research conducted using this approach, personal characteristics, also referred to as "simple demographics" by Tsui and O'Reilly (1989), provide important cues about how people will behave, the attitudes they will possess toward certain targets, and how they will be treated in the organizational context (Tsui & Gutek, 1999). Research shows that people's experiences can vary based on their sex, age, race, class, and education. Within the realm of sport and physical activity, various studies have found that:

- Men and women have different motivational goals for participating in sport and exercise (Kavussanu & Roberts, 1996).

- Social class influences recreation and leisure involvement, such that participation rates increase as one climbs higher in social class. This finding is valid for both North America (Crespo, Ainsworth, Keteyian, Heath, & Smit, 1999) and Europe (Collins & Kay, 2003).

- Persons with disabilities face significant barriers in their quest to participate in sport and leisure activities (French & Hainsworth, 2001).

- Racial minorities do not receive the same level of health care as do Whites in the United States (Schnittker & McLeod, 2005).

As these studies illustrate, both surface- and deep-level characteristics influence outcomes people experience. Fink, Pastore, and Riemer (2001) assert that people who are different from the majority (i.e., White, Protestant, heterosexual, able-bodied men) in the university athletics context face poor work experiences. Their assertion seems applicable to other realms of sport and physical activity as well. Specifically, persons who are demographically different from the majority not only face poorer work experiences, but they also have different attitudes toward sport participation and face obstacles to their efforts to participate in sport and leisure activities. As Tsui and Gutek (1999) note, the differential experiences are "due to the unique social–cultural perspectives or stereotypes" (p. 21) that are associated with a person's membership in a social category. In this way, membership in a particular social group is thought to be at the root of the varying experiences.

Potential Limitations

An underlying assumption of the categorical approach is that all (or most) members of a social category have similar experiences. It is further assumed, perhaps implicitly, that all members of a social group have similar values, attitudes, and preferences. If we compare, for instance, the recreational preferences of Native Americans relative to those of Whites, then we are making the assumption that Native Americans in our sample are relatively homogeneous in nature and can thus be grouped together. A similar assumption is made for the Whites in the sample as well. As a result of this presumed homogeneity, we can then make comparisons between all Native Americans and all Whites. Without making such assumptions, it is impossible to compare members of one group to another.

As you probably recognize, the assumption of homogeneity among members of a particular social group is oftentimes unfounded. Members of the Native American community may have quite divergent views of recreation and sport, preferences for leisure activities, and so forth. The categorical approach ignores these potential differences. The categorical approach also does not consider the influence of context. Sport and leisure activity preferences among Native Americans might vary from one situation to another; for example, a preference may depend on the racial makeup of the co-participants—other Native Americans versus persons from other racial groups. Research using the categorical approach has much to offer; however, there are potential concerns that limit its applicability.

Compositional Approach

The compositional approach to the study of diversity focuses on the social unit, such as a work group, athletic team, or physical education class (Pfeffer, 1983; Tsui & Gutek, 1999). This approach is used to study the processes and outcomes of a diverse social unit as compared to those of a homogeneous social unit.

Research

Research applying the compositional approach might attempt to answer such questions as the following:

- How do work groups with high tenure diversity (i.e., members have various organizational tenures) communicate relative to more homogeneous groups?
- How does the sex diversity within a group influence group performance?
- How does the value diversity of an athletic team impact the team's cohesion?

Such research examines the impact of group heterogeneity on subsequent group processes and performance. The key question is whether individuals within the group (or the group as a whole) are influenced by the dispersion of differences within the group.

Several studies demonstrated that diversity within the group does influence the functioning of that social unit. Consider the following:

- The mix of men and women within university athletic departments influences the communication patterns within those entities (Knoppers, Meyer, Ewing, & Forrest, 1993).
- Diversity in background and sex among YMCA Executive Boards influences the level of donations that organization receives (Siciliano, 1996).
- Increased racial diversity of university coaching staffs is associated with greater team performance (Cunningham & Sagas, 2004b).
- Tenure diversity on university coaching staffs is positively related with occupational turnover intentions and negatively related with occupational commitment (Cunningham & Sagas, 2004a).

As these examples demonstrate, the heterogeneity of a work group can have a meaningful impact on subsequent group outcomes. Tsui and Gutek (1999) assert that the distribution of differences within a group or organization is "crucial in understanding the experiences of employees and group processes such as communication, conflict, commitment, or performance" (p. 22). Diversity influences a group because of the meanings and values group members associate with individual differences.

Potential Limitations

Despite the efficacy of the compositional approach in understanding group dynamics and performance, the approach is not without its limitations (Tsui & Gutek, 1999). First, this approach ignores the characteristics of the individual. Because the group is the focus, the effects of individual characteristics within the group are not considered.

Second, the approach assumes that the characteristics of the group impact all group members the same. Of course, this may not be true. Recall the Calgary YMCA Executive Board discussed in the Diversity Challenge. One of the board's characteristics is sex diversity—it has 4 women and 13 men as members. Any study of this characteristic that applies the compositional approach must consider that it impacts all group members the same—it cannot contemplate that the characteristic may impact the men and women differently. This approach is limited in its ability to acknowledge the individual within the group context.

Relational Approach

The relational approach to the study of diversity focuses on the individual's characteristics in relation to those of the group (Tsui & Gutek, 1999). In doing so, the approach combines both the categorical *and* compositional approaches. The categorical approach is captured by considering the individual's characteristics; considering the entire group's characteristics uses the compositional approach. The fundamental premise of the relational approach is that the relationship between an individual's characteristics and those of the group will influence the behaviors, attitudes, and performance of that individual.

Research

Questions asked using the relational approach might include the following:

- What is the job satisfaction of a coach who is lesbian on a staff of all heterosexual coaches?
- How does being different from others in the class impact the motivation of a physical education student with physical disabilities?
- How does being racially different from others on a team influence subsequent performance?

Sport and physical activity research has examined questions such as these. In general, the studies indicate that being different from others in the group or organization negatively influences the experiences one has. Consider the following:

- University athletics personnel who differ from their athletic director in parental status or in race have varying perceptions of the diversity strategy employed by the department (Fink et al., 2001).
- Varsity athletes who are new to a team (i.e., differ in team tenure from other members) may face difficulty integrating into the team (Galipeau & Trudel, 2004).
- Girls participating on athletic teams communicate differently with their male coaches than they do with their female coaches (Officer & Rosenfeld, 1985).
- Spectators who perceive themselves to be different from their service provider at a professional tennis tournament express lower customer satisfaction (Cunningham & Sagas, 2006).

As these examples illustrate, the relational approach adds to our understanding of diversity. More important, the approach moves beyond the study of simple demographics by considering the interplay of one's membership in a social group and the proportion of group members who share that social category membership. For example, having a different religious faith from others in a work group may negatively influence one's work experiences, especially if that religious faith is a central part of the employee's identity. On the other hand, similarity to others in the group may positively influence the experiences one has at work. Thus, it is important to consider the comparative characteristics of others in the group.

Potential Limitations

As with the other approaches, the relational approach is not without its limitations. The main drawback is its focus solely on employee characteristics (both the individual's and the group's) without considering other contextual determinants. These determinants may be an organization's history, organizational climate, leadership behaviors, or the diversity strategy employed. Consider Jacqueline, an African American woman professor in a kinesiology department. We might expect that if most of her colleagues are White, her work experiences might be poorer than if most are African American. However, it is possible that the department's culture is one that values diversity and where diversity is seen as an asset (van Knippenberg & Haslam, 2003). If so, then Jacqueline's experiences will likely be positive because she knows that she contributes to the department's mission and goals. Simply analyzing Jacqueline's characteristics relative to her colleagues fails to recognize this dynamic.

Diversity Management Strategy Approach

As previously noted, Tsui and Gutek (1999) conceptualized three approaches to the study of diversity; however, a considerable portion of the diversity literature within the sport and physical activity domain focuses on the strategies used to realize the benefits of diversity in the workplace (Chelladurai, 2005; Cunningham, 2004; DeSensi, 1995; Doherty & Chelladurai, 1999; Fink & Pastore, 1999). Because diversity management strategies are discussed in detail in Chapters 11 and 12, only an overview is presented here.

Research

In general, the diversity management strategy approach seeks to answer such questions as:

- How do organizations capitalize on the benefits diversity can bring?
- What methods can managers and administrators use to reduce the potential negative effects of diversity?

■ What techniques can be implemented to improve the dynamics among diverse groups and teams?

Potential Limitations

This approach to the study of diversity has two potential limitations. First, most of the approaches focus on describing diversity in organizations instead of developing strategies that managers, educators, and coaches can use to better manage their workplaces. Obviously, developing strategies has more pragmatic value. Second, many of the current strategies have not been empirically tested. A key component of a strategy's validity is testability. If a strategy cannot be tested, then its ultimate utility is questionable. It should be noted here, however, that recent studies do demonstrate the effectiveness of various proposed strategies (see Cunningham & Chelladurai, 2004; Fink et al., 2001).

The Importance of Theory to the Study of Diversity

The preceding discussion provided a guide for classifying the various approaches to studying diversity; however, these classifications do not really explain (a) how diversity impacts subsequent group outcomes, (b) when being dissimilar from others is likely to result in low job satisfaction and when it is not, and (c) how organizational diversity potentially leads to greater effectiveness. To understand such issues, it is useful to discuss the various theories that have been adopted as a guide for understanding diversity's effects. First, it may be helpful to define theory and examine its uses in understanding organizational behavior, and specifically, diversity.

Definition

To develop a definition of *theory*, consider the following definitions used by others in the field:

> Theory is "a set of interrelated constructs (concepts), definitions, and propositions that present a systematic view of phenomena by specifying relations among variables, with the purpose of explaining and predicting phenomena." (Kerlinger & Lee, 2000, p. 11)

> Theory "is a statement of relations among concepts within a set of boundary assumptions and constraints. It is no more than a linguistic device used to organize a complex world." (Bacharach, 1989, p. 496)

> Theory is "any coherent description or explanation of observed or experienced phenomena." (Gioia & Pitre, 1990, p. 584)

We can draw several conclusions from these definitions. First, theory primarily consists of constructs and propositions (Bacharach, 1989; Kerlinger & Lee, 2000). For our purposes, it may be useful to consider a *construct* as a variable of interest, such as deep-level diversity or job satisfaction, and a *proposition* as the expected relationships among the constructs. For example, it may be proposed that people who are different from others in their work group have low job satisfaction.

Second, theory contains boundary conditions (Bacharach, 1989). Think of *boundary conditions* as assumptions about values, space, and time. Boundary conditions place "if–then" conditions or caveats on the expected relationships among the constructs set forth in the propositions. Using the previous deep-level diversity and job satisfaction constructs, we might expect that relationships are stronger among people who closely interact with one another relative to those group members who rarely work with one another (i.e., high task interdependence versus low task interdependence; see Doherty & Chelladurai, 1999). Thus, the negative relationship between deep-level dissimilarity and job satisfaction (i.e., the proposition that specifies the relationship between the constructs) may be dependent upon the level of task interdependence in the group (i.e., the boundary condition).

Third, and perhaps most important, theory organizes, explains, and predicts (Bacharach, 1989; Gioia & Pitre, 1990; Kerlinger & Lee, 2000). As Bacharach notes, "the primary goal of theory is to answer the questions of *how, when,* and *why,* unlike the goal of description, which is to answer the question of *what*" (p. 498, emphasis in original). Continuing with the previous example, we might explain that dissimilarity leads to low job satisfaction because dissimilar people are often considered to be in the out-group and receive less trust, liking, and so forth than do in-group members (see Riordan, 2000). These unpleasant work experiences may then translate into low satisfaction. Further, the relationship may be amplified for people who must work closely with others (high interdependence) because the differences are reinforced by the continued interaction (Doherty & Chelladurai, 1999). Explaining *why, how,* and *when* phenomena are likely to occur provides a richer understanding than simply describing *what.*

Practicality

Having defined theory, we next consider its usefulness in everyday life and in understanding diversity. As Lewin (1952) correctly noted, "there is nothing more practical than a good theory." Indeed, the ultimate effectiveness of a theory can be assessed by its usefulness and practicality (Bacharach, 1989). Coakley (2004) further suggests that "the best theories are those we understand so clearly that they help us make sense out of the social world" (p. 34). Good theories help us to make better sense of the world around us and, in doing so, cognitively simplify our social surroundings.

To further illustrate, consider Sue, who is dissatisfied with her job. Understanding *why* she feels the way she does, *how* that state of being arose, and *when* it occurred can help us resolve the situation. If we stop at the *what* of the situation (i.e., Sue is dissatisfied), we would not be able to remedy the situation or predict when it may occur again in the future. Because one of the goals of theory is to aid in prediction—by explaining why, how, and when—we are able to better understand *why* phenomena occur and make educated predictions about *how* and *when* they might occur in the future. Doing so allows us to take steps to reduce activities that might lead to negative outcomes, such as Sue's dissatisfaction, and capitalize on activities that might result in desired outcomes, such as commitment or high work performance from Sue. Further, we might be able to take steps to ensure that her dissatisfaction does not occur in the future. Thus, the practicality and utility of good theory is far-reaching.

PROFESSIONAL PERSPECTIVES

The Importance of Theory. Sally Shaw is a lecturer of Sport Management at the University of Otago in New Zealand. Shaw's research primarily focuses on gender and power relations in organizations for sport and physical activity. In commenting on her definition of theory, Shaw explained that "theory can be anything from a conversation in a pub to a highly developed, scientific set of ideas." To Shaw, understanding theory and its contributions is important because theory represents "a way of interpreting, or understanding, and of critiquing our social world and the ideas that go into that process." In short, theory is a "way to try to understand the world."

Theories Used to Understand Diversity

This next section examines several theories that are used to understand the effects of diversity. In general, the theories fall into one of three categories based on their focus: managerial, sociological, and social psychological. An overview of the three theory classes is provided in Exhibit 2.2. Not all proposed theories are included in this chapter; rather, I discuss those theories that have received the most attention in the diversity literature.

Managerial Theories

Managerial theories related to diversity have group and organizational functioning as a primary focus. These theories may focus on how diversity impacts group processes, such as conflict or cohesion, and group outcomes, such as creativity and decision-making comprehensiveness. They may also focus on the organization, and how diversity can influence the competitive advantage an organization is able to realize. Several theories fall under the managerial class, and are described below.

Exhibit 2.2	Theories of diversity.

Managerial:

- *Focus:* the impact of diversity on group/organizational processes and performance
- *Theories:* intervening process, information/decision-making, and resource-based

Sociological:

- *Focus:* issues such as structural determinants, power, and conflict, and how they influence diversity and persons who are different from the majority
- *Theories:* functionalism, conflict, critical, and interactionist

Social Psychological:

- *Focus:* how being different from (or similar to) others in a dyad or group influences subsequent affective reactions and behaviors
- *Theories:* social categorization framework and similarity-attraction paradigm

Intervening Process Theory

Pelled (1996) developed the intervening process theory to outline the manner in which various types of demographic diversity influence conflict within the group (i.e., the intervening processes) and subsequent outcomes. Pelled categorized demographic variables along two dimensions:

1. level of visibility, or the degree to which the form of diversity is easily recognized and observed by group members.
2. job relatedness, or the extent to which the form of diversity influences the skills and competencies related to cognitive tasks.

The form of diversity within each could either be high or low (e.g., high visibility or low job relatedness). Pelled then used these dimensions to classify the types of demographic variables:

- Low visibility–low job relatedness: no demographic characteristics
- High visibility–low job relatedness: age, sex, and race
- Low visibility–high job relatedness: organizational tenure, education, and functional background
- High visibility–high job relatedness: group tenure

Pelled (1996) also identified two forms of conflict: affective and substantive. *Affective conflict* represents those tensions raised as a result of emotional clashes among group members that are characterized by fear, distrust, and general negative affect. Such conflict is thought to give rise to negative outcomes such as member turnover. *Substantive conflict,* on the other hand, refers to differences in opinion among group members as to how to complete tasks, the importance of certain goals, and appropriate courses of action. This form of conflict is more productive, as it gives rise to divergent views and alternative ways of completing tasks. Therefore, substantive conflict is thought to be positively associated with group performance in cognitive tasks.

In integrating this information, *intervening process theory* holds that the different forms of diversity will impact group conflict. First, highly visible demographic diversity variables such as age, sex, and race are expected to positively influence affective conflict. This relationship is thought to arise from the strong emotions associated with being different from others based on race, age, or sex. Second, demographic variables associated with high job relatedness are believed to positively impact substantive conflict, sometimes referred to as task conflict. Variations in how long one has worked in a group or in an occupation, in education, and in functional background will likely result in a variety of conflicting perspectives related to how tasks should be completed, which goals a group should adopt, and so forth. Given these divergent perspectives, substantive conflict is likely to be present, increasing the breadth of decision making, the number of opinions, etc., thereby improving subsequent task performance. Diversity in highly visible demographic characteristics is thought to result in affective conflict, which is then expected to influence affective outcomes such as turnover. Diversity in highly job-related characteristics is believed to positively influence substantive conflict and result in more positive group processes and outcomes. A 1999 study by Pelled, Eisenhardt, and Xin demonstrated general empirical support for these propositions.

Information/Decision-Making Theory

Similar to the intervening process theory, the *information/decision-making* theory holds that diversity should impact the information and perspectives available in the group, thereby allowing for greater decision-making capabilities (see Gruenfeld, Mannix, Williams, & Neale, 1996; Williams & O'Reilly, 1998). These two theories are similar to the extent that diversity in demographics, education, functional background, and so forth is thought to increase the number of perspectives and ideas in the group. However, the information/decision-making theory departs significantly from intervening process theory where it concerns the manner in which diversity influences performance. Specifically, research has demonstrated that people are more likely to associate and converse with people who are similar to themselves (discussed in further detail in the social psychological theory section). This is important for diverse groups because individuals in such groups have access to information from similar others outside the group. The information obtained from persons outside the group is then brought back to the group and used to complete group tasks. Because diverse groups may have access to a greater variety of perspectives, the group's decision making will be enhanced, leading to better performance than the more homogeneous counterparts (see Ancona & Caldwell, 1992).

To illustrate, consider a cross-functional group tasked with developing a new clothing line for Titleist, a major manufacturer of golf products. The group consists of two members from research and development, two from marketing, and two from operations. These six persons have different ideas, perspectives, and beliefs about what product should be introduced. However, each pair from the three divisions also has access to persons from their functional background and the ideas and perspectives these people have to offer. Thus, Susan, a group member from research and development, may discuss the project with her colleagues from that area. They may have their own ideas about how the task should be completed and which products should be introduced. Susan then takes these ideas back to the original cross-functional group and presents them to her group members. If all of the cross-functional group members speak with members from their specific functional areas and bring ideas back to the group, then the number of ideas and perspectives available to the group increases dramatically. Clearly, this synergistic effect improves the number of alternatives from which the cross-functional group could choose, ultimately aiding their decision-making process and overall performance.

Resource-Based Theory

The final theory in the managerial class is the *resource-based* view (Barney, 1991). According to this theory, firms have various resources, including physical capital (e.g., technology, equipment, or physical structure), organizational capital (e.g., the firm's structure and planning mechanisms), and human capital (e.g., the personnel within the organization, and the training, experience, and capital they possess). To the extent that these resources are *valuable, rare,* and *difficult to imitate,* the firm realizes a competitive advantage. Some researchers argue that organizational diversity represents such a resource (Cunningham & Sagas, 2004b; Richard, 2000). Consider that:

- diverse groups have greater decision-making capabilities (see the earlier related discussion Gruenfeld et al., 1996; Pelled, 1996),
- diverse organizations are relatively rare, and
- it is difficult, if not impossible, to duplicate the effects of a diverse workforce without actually having a diverse workforce.

Research demonstrates support for the belief that diversity gives an organization a competitive advantage. For example, Cunningham and Sagas (2004b) found that racial diversity on coaching staffs was related to greater success for the athletic team. In a different context, Richard (2000) found that racial diversity in banks was related to greater financial performance when the bank followed a growth strategy. As these examples illustrate, diversity, because it is a rare and valued resource, brings benefits to groups and organizations.

Implications

The managerial theories have several implications for persons managing diverse groups or organizations. As all three theories illustrate, diversity increases the decision-making ability of groups. According to the intervening process and the information/decision-making theories, decision-making capabilities improve as a result of increases in the informational diversity of the social units. However, in drawing from Richard's (2000) work, it is also possible that racial diversity provides such benefits. The underlying assumption is that people who are dissimilar bring different sources of information, varying ideas, and an array of perspectives to the group. If creativity and breadth of decision making is desired, then group members should be persons from different educational, work, or perhaps racial backgrounds. This practice is oftentimes done with committees, task forces, and other short-term work groups that are responsible for creating policy, developing new product lines, and the like.

Second, although there are many benefits to diversity, there is also the possibility that increased diversity can bring negative outcomes such as affective conflict. As Pelled (1996) noted, highly visible sources of diversity are more likely to be associated with this detrimental form of conflict than are the less visible forms of diversity. Managers are then faced with a quandary, especially when it comes to racial diversity. This form of diversity can bring real benefits to a group or organization (Cunningham & Sagas, 2004b; Richard, 2000), but can also be associated with potentially high levels of affective conflict within that unit (Pelled, 1996). Furthermore, high levels of affective conflict may counteract the otherwise positive effects of substantive conflict (Pelled, 1996). Managers must effectively manage the levels of affective conflict within their social units. How to do so is discussed in Chapters 11 and 12.

Sociological Theories

Some researchers have adopted theories with a more sociological slant to study diversity. *Sociological* theories focus on issues such as power and conflict as they relate to diversity in society and organizations. These theories also tend to focus on more macro issues such as the impact of societal norms, institutional practices, and organizational policies on persons with diverse backgrounds. Eitzen and Sage (2003) outlined four theories that are used to study and understand diversity from a sociological perspective: functionalism, conflict, critical, and interactionist. Each theory is discussed next.

Functionalism Theory

According to Eitzen and Sage (2003), *functionalism* "attributes to societies the characteristics of cohesion, consensus, cooperation, reciprocity, stability, and persistence" (p. 9). Society is viewed as a system of parts working together in harmony because there is general congruence among the parts concerning the goals and values of society. As a part of society, sport is seen as something that brings people together, socializes youth who participate in it, and serves as a model for success and the achievement of excellence.

As an example, research by Brown et al. (2003) found that participation in sport helped to reduce racial tensions that otherwise might have been present. As the authors noted, "the use of integrated, organized team sports could be one way to help alleviate interracial tensions by urging individuals to shift the relative weight attached to being White or Black to the identity of teammate" (p. 177). In this way, sport is viewed as something that has the potential to unify people across racial boundaries.

Conflict Theory

Seen as an opposite of functionalism, *conflict* theory focuses on social processes that result in disharmony, social discord, and conflict (Eitzen & Sage, 2003). Political power and the distribution of wealth are also influential in conflict theory. Drawing heavily from the writings of Karl Marx, this theory holds that people tend toward competition, not cooperation, and this competition leads to disharmony among groups. Social structures and class differences play an important role in this theory, as those who are privileged (i.e., the upper class) are thought to use their status to maintain power and advantage within society, oftentimes at the expense of others (e.g., the lower class). This may be achieved explicitly, such as through a show of force, or more implicitly, such as through the media, schools, or other institutions.

People who adopt this approach to the study of diversity examine such issues as the underrepresentation of women and racial minorities in leadership positions or the resistance on the part of university athletic programs to follow gender equity laws (Eitzen & Sage, 2003). For example, Acosta and Carpenter (2006) have tracked the underrepresentation of women in coaching and leadership positions for over two decades. Their work is discussed in greater detail in Chapter 5.

Other research suggests that class influences the extent to which one can participate in or watch sport and leisure events (McGraw, 1998). A greater appreciation for this issue can be garnered by considering the average cost to attend professional sports in North America (see Exhibit 2.3). According to the Team Marketing Report's Fan Cost Index, the mean cost for a family of four to attend a professional sport event ranges from $112.53 (Major League Baseball [MLB]) to $261.34 (NFL). According to the U. S. Census Bureau, the median U. S. household income in 2003 was $43,300. By synthesizing these data, we see that attending all eight home games of an NFL team would account for roughly 4.8 percent of that household's income. Even more staggering, attending all 81 home games of an MLB team requires spending approximately 21 percent of the household income. These figures indicate that few households with an annual income of $43,300 can afford to spend from 4.8 to 21 percent

| | The cost of enjoying sport. | | | | | Exhibit 2.3 |

SPORT	TICKET	SODA	HOT DOG	PARKING	TOTAL	PERCENT OF INCOME
Major League Baseball	$79.28	$10.60	$12.16	$10.49	$112.53	21.05%
National Basketball Association	$181.12	$11.72	$12.80	$11.37	$217.01	20.50%
National Football League	$219.00	$12.92	$14.08	$15.34	$261.34	4.82%
National Hockey League	$174.28	$11.00	$12.04	$10.19	$207.51	19.65%

Team Marketing Report (www.teammarketing.com) and U. S. Census Bureau (www.census.gov) data. Prices for MLB, NBA, and NFL based on 2004 data. Because of the cancellation of the 2004 season, prices for the NHL are based on 2003 data. Prices of tickets, sodas, and hot dogs are based on four persons. Total price is based on attending a single game. Percent of income is based on attending all home games (MLB, 81; NBA, 41; NFL, 8; and NHL, 41) and using $43,300 as the median income.

of that income on sport events. Therefore, it can be argued that sport, and more specifically spectator sport, is structured in such a way that only individuals with incomes well above the median level can afford to purchase tickets and regularly attend major events.

Critical Theory

Critical theories are the third type of sociological theories used to study diversity in the sport and physical activity context (Eitzen & Sage, 2003). *Critical* theories seek to understand power and explain how power operates within social entities. These theories also emphasize human agency, or the choices people make concerning their actions and behaviors. Three theories are subsumed under this general heading: hegemony theory, feminist theory, and critical race theory.

Hegemony theory. *Hegemony* theory concentrates on the political, economic, and cultural patterns of power and dominance in a society. As Sage (1998) explains, "hegemony theory sensitizes us to the role dominant groups play in American government, economic system, mass media, education, and sport in maintaining and promoting their interests" (p. 10). This social dominance provides privilege to certain persons or groups at the expense of others, such as men over women, rich over poor, and Whites over racial minorities. Researchers applying this perspective examine how sport is related to race, gender, social class, and the production and control of resources (e.g., Whisenant, Pedersen, & Obenour, 2002).

Feminist theory. Most of the gender-related research in sport and physical activity has adopted a feminist approach. *Feminist* theory makes two basic assumptions. First, people's experiences, both within and outside the workplace, are gendered in nature. Gendered means that "the meaning, organization, and purpose of sports are grounded in the values and experiences of men and are defined to celebrate the attributes and skills associated with dominant forms of masculinity in society" (Coakley, 2004, pp. 51–52).

The second assumption is that because women have been oppressed and devalued in many contexts, there is a need to develop strategies to change those conditions (Coakley, 2004; Eitzen & Sage, 2003). By reversing the oppression of women, it is expected that women will become empowered and be able to transform their environments. Research examples in the sport realm include studies related to homophobia, the belittlement of women's accomplishments and activities, and the underrepresentation of women in leadership roles (e.g., Knoppers, 1992).

Critical race theory. Critical race theory represents the third critical theory oftentimes used to examine diversity issues in sport and leisure. As the name suggests, *critical race* theory places the issue of race at the forefront in studies of organizational, political, educational, and other social issues (Ladson-Billings & Tate, 1995; Tate, 1997). Tate (1997) outlines the theory's five key suppositions (see also Singer, 2005). According to these authors, critical race theory:

1. Argues that racism is endemic in the United States. Specifically, it is presumed that racism is a central part of U.S. society, embedded in the social institutions, laws, and culture.

2. Borrows from several different disciplines and "ways of knowing," including liberalism, feminism, and critical legal studies. Doing so allows for broader perspectives and a more gestalt analysis of the intersection of race and society.

3. Questions civil rights legislation and the effectiveness of such mandates, arguing that they are often undermined before they can be fully implemented. Furthermore, any progress that has been made in terms of equal employment opportunity legislation is seen as having been too slow.

4. Questions the notions of meritocracy, neutrality, color-blindness, and objectivity; these terms and ideas are viewed only as smoke screens for the self-interests of the powerful in society—the self-interests of Whites. As Singer (2005) notes, "Whites will tolerate or encourage racial advances for people of color only when they also promote White self-interest" (p. 468).

5. Supports context-specificity and relative truths, as opposed to a single truth being applicable in all situations across all contexts (see also Ladson-Billings & Tate, 1995). In this way, this theory emphasizes story telling as a "way of knowing" and a manner by which oppressed persons can have their voices heard.

Several studies in the sport management literature highlight the efficacy of using critical race theory. Singer (2002) incorporated focus groups and interviews to understand racism perceived by African American university football players. Using this technique, he was able to help the athletes develop strategies to overcome such barriers and to improve their overall experiences. Hylton (2005) used critical race theory to argue that sport and leisure managers should consider race, racism, and race equality when developing their policies and structures.

Interactionist Theory

Unlike the previous theories that focus predominantly on structural forces such as culture or social class, *interactionist* theory aims to understand how people give meaning to their lives. From this perspective, there is not a single reality of truth; rather, people define their own reality based on their interactions with others and through cultural influences. The process by which this reality is created is referred to as the social construction of reality (Eitzen & Sage, 2003). For example, the meanings we place on gender or race are socially constructed, and they may mean slightly different things to different people, depending on the experiences of each person. From a research perspective, the primary goal is to understand how people give meaning to their lives—something that is accomplished through observation and interviews; for example, asking about how sport socializes youth or what meanings gays and lesbians place on their role as athletes (see Anderson, 2005).

PROFESSIONAL PERSPECTIVES

Participatory Action Research. In addition to the theories highlighted in the text, others have proven helpful in the study of diversity. One such theory is called *participatory action research,* a subset of the larger sociological critical theories. Wendy Frisby, Chair of Women's Studies at the University of British Columbia, found this framework to be particularly useful in her research of women living below the poverty line. As Frisby explains, participatory action research is committed to the practical side of research. "It gets us thinking about how we can improve policies and practices" within the domain of sport and physical activity. Key to the theory is the word "participatory," as according to Frisby, "one way of building theory is to work with people who are the intended beneficiaries of our research." In the case of Frisby's studies, this means working with women who live below the poverty line to develop strategies aimed at improving the conditions of their lives, including increasing the level of physical activity. Because Frisby works with the women in a co-collaborator role, she can ask research questions that are relevant to the women's daily lives. The knowledge developed from this collaboration is much richer than otherwise would be possible because it is co-produced by Frisby and the women with whom she is working.

Implications

Sociological theories used to understand diversity have several implications for managers of sport and physical activity organizations. First and foremost is the recognition of the structural factors that influence people who are different from the majority. Because these societal determinants have a negative influence on such persons, it is necessary to critically analyze sport, sport organizations, and the people within them. To do so, we might ask questions such as (a) why are sport organizations structured the way they are and who benefits from this arrangement; or (b) how do power arrangements impact people within sport organizations? Sociological theory provides us with a means of answering these questions. Looking critically at these issues is an important step to remedying inequities within sport organizations.

Second, sociological theories put such issues as gender and race in the forefront. Whereas managerial theories explain the relationship between diversity and important organizational outcomes, sociological theories allow us to consider how personal demographics influence the manner in which people behave, the way organizations operate, and societal and cultural expectations. Sociological theories provide a different perspective from which we can understand diversity in sport organizations.

Social Psychological Theories

Whereas managerial theories focus on how diversity can bring value to the organization and sociological theories predominantly focus on structural issues related to diversity, *social psychological* theories focus on the individual in relation to others. Specifically, these theories focus on how being similar to or different from others in a social unit impacts subsequent affect and behaviors. Whereas sociological theories tend to focus on macro issues such as the impact of societal norms, institutional practices, and organizational policies on persons with diverse backgrounds, social psychological theories focus on the individual within social contexts. Sociological theories place an emphasis on society and culture, while social psychological theories emphasize the individual within these contexts. Two major frameworks are included in this general class of theories: the social categorization framework and the similarity-attraction paradigm, discussed next.

Social Categorization Framework

Most of the research adopting a compositional or relational perspective draws from the social categorization framework (see Riordan, 2000). Two theories contribute to this framework: *social identity* theory (Tajfel & Turner, 1979) and *self-categorization* theory (Turner, Hogg, Oakes, Reicher, & Wetherell, 1987). According to these two theories, people classify themselves and others into social groups. The classification can be based on a myriad of characteristics, including those based on surface-level attributes (e.g., age, sex), deep-level characteristics (e.g., liberal, conservative), or other memberships (Catholic, Protestant). Thus, people define themselves and others in terms of a social identity. People similar to the self are considered in-group members, while those who differ from the self are considered out-group members. In general, people hold more positive atti-tudes toward in-group members than they do toward their out-group counterparts. Therefore, there likely exists an intergroup bias, where differences exist in the affective reactions and helping behaviors given to in-group and out-group members. Within the group setting, this creates "us" and "them" dynamics. These social categorizations and related biases will be used in subse-quent interactions (Tsui & Gutek, 1999) such that attitudes formed toward out-group members in one situation are likely to be applied toward persons of the same social category in similar situations in the future. This is likely to take place because the categorization process leads to the formation of stereotypes about in-group and out-group members; thus, as Tsui and Gutek (1999) explain, "without categorization, stereotyping does not occur" (p. 48).

When discussing the categorization process, it is important to distinguish between social categorization and intergroup bias, as the two are not the same. *Social categorization* simply refers to the perceptual grouping of people into social units. *Intergroup bias,* on the other hand, refers to the more favorable attitudes, perceptions, and behaviors directed toward in-group members rela-tive to out-group members. Making such a distinction is important, because any negative effects of diversity observed from a social categorization are linked to intergroup biases and not the social categorization process, per se (van Knippenberg, De Dreu, & Homan, 2004).

These theoretical tenets are paramount to the discussion of diversity. As Tsui, Egan, and O'Reilly (1992) suggest, the formation of in-groups and out-groups is central to the tendency of people to prefer working in groups of persons similar to the self. In a similar way, Williams and O'Reilly (1998), after a review of over 40 years of diversity research, argued that the social catego-rization process was fundamental to the potentially negative effects of diversity in work groups and in organizations.

Let us consider two very different examples to illustrate the way that social categorization can influence how people interact with one another. The first example involves fans at a sporting event. As you enter the stands, you will see many fans around you. Some may be wearing gear with your team's logo and name, while others may be wearing hats and shirts representative of the opposing team. When you initially see all of the fans, you will immediately classify them as similar to or different from the self based on their apparel. People wearing your team's clothes might be considered in-group members (i.e., people similar to you), while those wearing the opposing team's apparel might be considered out-group members (i.e., people different from you). To the extent that being a fan of your team is an important part of who you are, you might prefer to sit close to other in-group members rather than out-group members. If you have ever sat in an opposing team's cheering section during an athletic contest, you can appreciate how different and perhaps uncomfortable that experience was.

The second example is set in the workplace. If you work in a group of seven persons and five of them are of a different race than you, then to the extent that race is a source of social categorization, you are surrounded by more out-group members than in-group members. Research shows that when this happens, it is possible that your experiences will be less positive than if you were surrounded by predominantly in-group members (Williams & O'Reilly, 1998). In both examples, the social categorization process is the impetus behind subsequent attitudes and behaviors. Exhibit 2.4 illustrates these trends.

Similarity-Attraction Paradigm

According to the similarity-attraction paradigm (Byrne, 1971), people who are similar to one another also demonstrate high interpersonal attraction and liking toward one another. The similarities might lead them to believe that they share common life experiences, have similar values and beliefs, and view their social worlds in a similar fashion. Thus, surface-level similarities are seen as resulting in the perceptions of more deep-level similarities as well (Chattopadhyay, 1999). People who find they share certain deep-level similarities might make assumptions as to congruence on other deep-level characteristics as well. As a result of this perceived similarity and increased liking, people are likely to have more positive affective and behavioral reactions

| Exhibit 2.4 | The effects of social categorization on fan and employee reactions. |

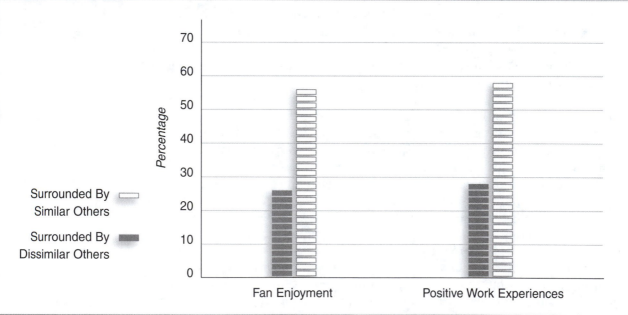

Data from Williams & O'Reilly, 1998.

when they are similar to their colleagues than when they differ.

Note that though the intervening mechanisms may differ, the end predictions that arise from the social categorization framework and the similarity-attraction paradigm are essentially the same (Tsui & Gutek, 1999). The social categorization framework holds that dissimilarity will lead to categorization, stereotyping, and ultimately poor work experiences. According to the similarity-attraction paradigm, dissimilarity results in a lack of perceived deep-level differences, a decrease in liking and communication, and ultimately, poor work experiences. Dissimilarity from others should result in poorer affective and behavioral reactions than being similar.

Implications

As previously noted, most diversity studies using the compositional and relational approaches adopt one of the social psychological theories. What is important for sport organization managers to understand is that being different, with respect to either surface- or deep-level characteristics, may be stressful or burdensome for the employee. As a result, communication among group members, helping behaviors, and positive affective reactions are likely to suffer. Of course, these outcomes are not necessarily consistent across all contexts; see the Diversity in the Field box.

DIVERSITY *in the field*

Overcoming Dissimilarity. One of the many ways that people can differ is their country of origin. Although differences among people from some countries may be trivial or unnoticed, such is not usually the case when discussing Israel and Pakistan. Indeed, these two countries, with different religious and political ideologies, are oftentimes at odds with one another concerning various issues. These differences made the relationship between Aisam-Ul-Haq Qureshi of Pakistan and Amir Hadad of Israel all the more noteworthy, as the two men paired to play tennis doubles at the 2002 Wimbledon. Not only did these players face potential difficulties playing with one another, but they were also subjected to pressures from their homelands. Qureshi was threatened with a ban if he continued to play with Hadad; however, the quest to excel on the court served as an overriding factor. As Qureshi noted, "If I believe that I can win at the Grand Slams and the big events with Amir then I'll stay and play with him." Hadad voiced similar sentiments, as he added, "I chose to play with him because of his talent, his skills as a tennis player, and I also like him as a person." Clearly, tennis served as a catalyst for the two players (Newbery, 2002).

Social psychological theories allow us to understand diversity beyond the organizational context. Specifically, these theories can be applied to employee–customer relationships, coach–player relationships, or any other dyadic or group relationship involving employees and persons outside the organization. For example, customer satisfaction can be dependent upon, at least in part, the (dis)similarity of the customer and the service provider (Cunningham & Sagas, 2006). Knowing this, managers can take steps to mitigate the potentially negative effects of employee–customer dissimilarity. Social psychological theories can have a meaningful influence on the way we understand diversity as well as the methods we take to manage differences in sport organizations.

Chapter Summary

This chapter focused on various theories and how they can be used to better understand diversity in sport organizations. As illustrated in the Diversity Challenge concerning the Calgary YMCA, diversity is a complex issue. The approach we use to study diversity influences the questions we ask, the focus of our examination, and the way we see the world in general. The same is true with the theory we choose to incorporate—it will influence the manner in which diversity is discussed and understood. After reading the chapter, you should be able to do the following:

1. Identify four approaches to the study of diversity.

Drawing primarily from Tsui and Gutek's (1999) work, four approaches to the study of diversity were identified: categorical, compositional, relational, and diversity management strategy.

2. Understand what a theory is and why theory is important to understanding diversity.

Using various early definitions (Bacharach, 1989; Gioia & Pitre, 1990; Kerlinger & Lee, 2000), the term *theory* was defined as a set of proportions concerning relationships among constructs, bound by assumptions of value, space, and time, with the purpose of organizing, explaining, and predicting social phenomena. Theory is important because of its practicality and its utility in helping managers understand their complex social surroundings.

3. Discuss the different classes of theory used to understand diversity.

Three classes of theory are used to study diversity: managerial, sociological, and social psychological. Managerial theories focus on the impact of diversity on organizational outcomes. Sociological theories focus on structural issues, power, and conflict, and how these factors influence diversity and persons who differ from the majority. Finally, social psychological theories focus on how being (dis)similar from others in social settings influences an individual's affect and behavior.

4. Discuss how the different theories can be applied to diversity issues within organizations for sport and physical activity.

The implications of each theory class for sport managers was discussed. The managerial theories illustrated the need to recognize how the various types of diversity influence outcomes (e.g., the influence of job-related aspects of diversity on substantive conflict). The sociological theories require managers to ask questions about how organizational factors, such as power structure, influence the experiences of persons different from the majority. Finally, social psychological theories suggest that managers should pay attention to the composition of work groups and employee–customer relationships, as surface- and deep-level differences within these relationships can lead to negative outcomes.

Questions for Discussion

1. Some students may express an aversion to a discussion of theory. Prior to studying this chapter, what were your attitudes toward theory? After reading the chapter, identify several benefits of studying theory.

2. Several definitions of theory were discussed in the chapter. What is a definition you can use that would allow you to describe what a theory is?

3. Four approaches to the study of diversity were identified. Which approach makes the most sense to you?

4. How do issues of power in organizations influence people who differ from the majority?

5. Social psychological theories suggest that being different from others in a dyad or group will negatively influence subsequent affective reactions and behaviors. How might a manager reduce these negative effects?

Learning Activities

1. Some people believe that students should not be taught theory, as it has limited applicability to workplace settings. Divide into groups and argue the pros and cons of understanding theory and theoretical principles as they apply to diversity in sport organizations.

2. Visit a local sport organization and ask the manager and employees how diversity impacts the workplace, group dynamics, and overall outcomes for the organization. Then, compare their responses with the theoretical tenets outlined in this chapter.

Resources

SUPPLEMENTARY READINGS

Cox, Jr., T. (1994). *Cultural diversity in organizations: Theory, research and practice.* San Francisco, CA: Berrett-Koehler. (Applies teaching, research, and consultation expertise to explore the dynamics behind diversity in the organizational context; useful for organizational development initiatives.)

Giulianotti, R. (2004). *Sport and modern social theorists*. Basingstoke, UK: Palgrave MacMillan. (Examines the contributions of major social theorists to our critical understanding of modern sport; includes contributions from Marx, Weber, Durkheim, Adorno, Gramsci, Habermas, Merton, C. Wright Mills, Goffman, Giddens, Elias, Bourdieu, and Foucault.)

Tsui, A. S., & Gutek, B. A. (1999). *Demographic differences in organizations*. New York: Lexington. (Provides an overview of different ways of studying diversity; outlines the social psychological theories used to study diversity; explores how demographic differences influence dyads, groups, and organizations.)

WEB RESOURCES

- Gender and Diversity in Organizations (http://division.aomonline.org/gdo/): a division of the Academy of Management; provides diversity resources related to research and teaching.

- Laboratory for Diversity in Sport (http://lds.tamu.edu): provides overview of research initiatives, as well as other diversity-related Internet sources.

- North American Society for the Sociology of Sport: (www.nasss.com): provides a resource center and directory of experts in several diversity-related areas.

References

Acosta, R. V., & Carpenter, L. J. (2006). *Women in intercollegiate sport: A longitudinal study—29-year update—1977–2006*. Unpublished manuscript, Brooklyn College, Brooklyn, NY.

Ancona, D. G., & Caldwell, D. F. (1992). Demography and design: Predictors of new product team performance. *Organization Science, 3,* 321–341.

Anderson, E. (2005). *In the game: Gay athletes and the cult of masculinity*. Albany: State University of New York Press.

Bacharach, S. B. (1989). Organizational theories: Some criteria for evaluation. *Academy of Management Review, 14,* 496–515.

Barney, J. (1991). Firm resources and sustained competitive advantage. *Journal of Management, 17,* 99–120.

Brown, T. N., Jackson, J. S., Brown, K. T., Sellers, R. M., Keiper, S., & Manuel, W. J. (2003). "There's no race on the playing field": Perceptions of racial discrimination among White and Black athletes. *Journal of Sport and Social Issues, 27,* 162–183.

Byrne, D. (1971). *The attraction paradigm*. New York: Academic Press.

Chattopadhyay, P. (1999). Beyond direct and symmetrical effects: The influence of demographic dissimilarity on organizational citizenship behavior. *Academy of Management Journal, 42,* 273–287.

Chelladurai, P. (2005). *Managing organizations for sport and physical activity: A systems perspective* (2nd ed.). Scottsdale, AZ: Holcomb Hathaway.

Coakley, J. (2004). *Sports in society: Issues and controversies* (8th ed.). New York: McGraw-Hill.

Collins, M., & Kay, T. (2003). *Sport and social exclusion*. New York: Routledge.

Crespo, C., Ainsworth, B., Keteyian, S., Heath, G., & Smit, E. (1999). Prevalence of physical inactivity and its relation to social class in U.S. adults: Results from the third national health and nutrition examination survey, 1988–1994. *Medicine and Science in Sport and Exercise, 31,* 1821–1827.

Cunningham, G. B. (2004). Strategies for transforming the possible negative effects of group diversity. *Quest, 56,* 421–438.

Cunningham, G. B., & Chelladurai, P. (2004). Affective reactions to cross-functional teams: The impact of size, relative performance, and common in-group identity. *Group Dynamics: Theory, Research, and Practice, 8,* 83–97.

Cunningham, G. B., & Sagas, M. (2004a). Group diversity, occupational commitment, and occupational turnover intentions among NCAA Division IA football coaching staffs. *Journal of Sport Management, 18,* 236–254.

Cunningham, G. B., & Sagas, M. (2004b). People make the difference: The influence of human capital and diversity on team performance. *European Sport Management Quarterly, 4,* 3–22.

Cunningham, G. B., & Sagas, M. (2006). The role of perceived demographic dissimilarity and interaction in customer service satisfaction. *Journal of Applied Social Psychology, 36,* 1654–1673.

DeSensi, J. T. (1995). Understanding multiculturalism and valuing diversity: A theoretical perspective. *Quest, 47,* 34–43.

Doherty, A. J., & Chelladurai, P. (1999). Managing cultural diversity in sport organizations: A theoretical perspective. *Journal of Sport Management, 13,* 280–297.

Eitzen D. S., & Sage, G. H. (2003). *Sociology of North American sport* (7th ed.). New York: McGraw-Hill.

Fink, J. S., & Pastore, D. L. (1999). Diversity in sport? Utilizing the business literature to devise a comprehensive framework of diversity initiatives. *Quest, 51,* 310–327.

Fink, J. S., Pastore, D. L., & Riemer, H. A. (2001). Do differences make a difference? Managing diversity in Division IA intercollegiate athletics. *Journal of Sport Management, 15,* 10–50.

French, D., & Hainsworth, J. (2001). "There aren't any buses and the swimming pool is always

cold!": Obstacles and opportunities in the provision of sport for disabled people. *Managing Leisure, 6,* 35–49.

Galipeau, J., & Trudel, P. (2004). The experiences of newcomers on a varsity sport team. *Applied Research in Coaching and Athletics Annual, 19,* 166–188.

Gioia, D. A., & Pitre, E. (1990). Multiparadigm perspectives on theory building. *Academy of Management Review, 15,* 584–602.

Gruenfeld, D. H., Mannix, E. A., Williams, K. Y., & Neale, M. A. (1996). Group composition and decision making: How member familiarity and information distribution affect process and performance. *Organizational Behavior and Human Decision Processes, 67,* 1–15.

Hylton, K. (2005). "Race," sport and leisure: Lessons from critical race theory. *Leisure Studies, 24,* 81–98.

Kavussanu, M., & Roberts, G. C. (1996). Motivation in physical activity contexts: The relationship of perceived motivational climate to intrinsic motivation and self-efficacy. *Journal of Sport & Exercise Psychology, 18,* 264–280.

Kerlinger, F. N., & Lee, H. B. (2000). *Foundations of behavioral research* (4th ed.). Fort Worth, TX: Harcourt College Publishers.

Knoppers, A. (1992). Explaining male dominance and sex segregation in coaching: Three approaches. *Quest, 44,* 210–227.

Knoppers, A., Meyer, B. B., Ewing, M., & Forrest, L. (1993). Gender ratio and social interaction among college coaches. *Sociology of Sport Journal, 10,* 256–269.

Ladson-Billings, G., & Tate, W. F., IV. (1995). Toward a critical race theory of education. *Teachers College Record, 97*(1), 47–68.

Lewin, K. (1952). *Field theory in social science: Selected theoretical papers by Kurt Lewin* (p. 169). London: Tavistock.

McGraw, D. (1998, July 13). Big League Troubles. *U.S. News and World Report, 125*(2), 40–46.

Newbery, P. (2002). Pakistani doubles star defiant. *BBC Sport Online.* Retrieved September 30,

2005, from: http://news.bbc.co.uk/sport1/hi/tennis/wimbledon/2079170.stm

Officer, S. A., & Rosenfeld, L. B. (1985). Self-disclosure to male and female coaches by female high school athletes. *Journal of Sport Psychology, 7,* 360–370.

Pelled, L. H. (1996). Demographic diversity, conflict, and work group outcomes: An intervening process theory. *Organization Science, 7,* 615–631.

Pelled, L. H., Eisenhardt, K. M., & Xin, K. R. (1999). Exploring the black box: An analysis of work group diversity, conflict, and performance. *Administrative Science Quarterly, 44,* 1–28.

Pfeffer, J. (1983). Organizational demography. In B. Staw & L. Cummings (Eds.), *Research in organizational behavior* (Vol. 5, pp. 299–357). Greenwich, CT: JAI Press.

Richard, O. (2000). Racial diversity, business strategy, and firm performance: A resource-based view. *Academy of Management Journal, 43,* 164–177.

Riordan, C. M. (2000). Relational demography within groups: Past developments, contradictions, and new directions. In G. R. Ferris (Ed.), *Research in personnel and human resources management* (Vol. 19, pp. 131–173). Greenwich, CT: JAI Press.

Sage, G. H. (1998). *Power and ideology in American sport: A critical perspective* (2nd ed.). Champaign, IL: Human Kinetics.

Schnittker, J., & McLeod, J. D. (2005). The social psychology of health disparities. *Annual Review of Sociology, 31,* 75–103.

Shaw, S., & Hoeber, L. (2003). "A strong man is direct and a direct woman is a bitch": Gendered discourses and their impact on employment roles in sport organizations. *Journal of Sport Management, 17,* 347–375.

Siciliano, J. I. (1996). The relationship between board member diversity to organizational performance. *Journal of Business Ethics, 15,* 1313–1320.

Singer, J. N. (2002). *"Let us make man": The development of Black males in a big-time college sports program.* Unpublished doctoral dissertation. The Ohio State University, Columbus, OH.

Singer, J. N. (2005). Addressing epistemological racism in sport management research. *Journal of Sport Management, 19,* 464–479.

Tajfel, H., & Turner, J. C. (1979). An integrative theory of intergroup conflict. In W. G. Austin & S. Worchel (Eds.), *The social psychology of intergroup relations* (pp. 33–47). Monterey, CA: Brooks/Cole.

Tate, W. F. (1997). Critical race theory and education: History, theory, and implications. In M. Apple (Ed.), *Review in research education 2* (pp. 191–243). Washington, DC: American Educational Research Association.

Tsui, A. S., Egan, T. D., & O'Reilly, C. A., III (1992). Being different: Relational demography and organizational attachment. *Administrative Science Quarterly, 37,* 549–579.

Tsui, A. S., & Gutek, B. A. (1999). *Demographic differences in organizations: Current research and future directions.* New York: Lexington Books.

Tsui, A. S., & O'Reilly, C. A., III (1989). Beyond simple demographic effects: The importance of relational demography in superior–subordinate dyads. *Academy of Management Journal, 32,* 402–423.

Turner, J., Hogg, M. A., Oakes, P. J., Reicher, S. D., & Wetherell, M. S. (1987). *Rediscovering the social group: A self-categorization theory.* Oxford, UK: B. Blackwell.

van Knippenberg, D., De Dreu, C. K. W., & Homan, A. C. (2004). Work group diversity and group performance: An integrative model and research agenda. *Journal of Applied Psychology, 89,* 1008–1022.

van Knippenberg, D., & Haslam, S. A. (2003). Realizing the diversity dividend: Exploring the subtle interplay between identity, ideology, and reality. In S. A. Haslam, D. van Knippenberg, M. J. Platow, & N. Ellemers (Eds.), *Social identity at work: Developing theory for organizational practice* (pp. 61–77). New York: Psychology Press.

Whisenant, W. A., Pedersen, P. M., & Obenour, B. L. (2002). Success and gender: Determining the rate of advancement for intercollegiate athletic directors. *Sex Roles, 47,* 485–491.

Wieberg, S. (2005, August 24). NCAA lets FSU keep "Seminoles." *USA Today*. Retrieved December 30, 2005, from www.keepmedia.com/pubs/USATODAY/2005/08/24/977842?extID=10032&oliID=213

Williams, K. Y., & O'Reilly, C. A., III (1998). Demography and diversity in organizations: A review of 40 years of research. In B. M. Staw and L. L. Cummings (Eds.), *Research in organizational behavior* (Vol. 20, pp. 77–140). Greenwich, CT: JAI Press.

Prejudice and Discrimination

DIVERSITY CHALLENGE

The University of Alabama football program has a long, distinguished history. Crimson Tide teams have won 8 national championships, participated in 52 bowl games, and had 91 All-American athletes compete on the squads. Given this long, rich history of football excellence, coaching at the University of Alabama is considered one of the most prestigious jobs in all of college football, with several of the game's most famous coaches, such as Paul "Bear" Bryant, having served at the helm.

In 2003, Mike Price was dismissed as the Crimson Tide head football coach after various indiscretions. Sylvester Croom was one of the many coaches considered for the position. Croom, an African American, was a native of Tuscaloosa, Alabama (the university's home), was a former All-American for the Crimson Tide, had served as an assistant coach for Bryant, and coached in the NFL for 17 years, many of the years as a coordinator. With these qualifications, many considered Croom's chances of receiving the position as very favorable. Such, however, was not the case. Rather, the university chose to hire Mike Shula, a White coach who, though having 12 years' experience as an NFL assistant coach, never served as a coordinator for offense or defense.

Fortunately for Croom, he was named the head football coach at Mississippi State the following year, thereby becoming the *first* African American head coach in the Southeastern Conference. However, that Croom later received a head coaching position represents the *exception,* not the norm. Indeed, this is just one example of a racial minority facing a discriminatory workplace and being denied access to a position (whether as assistant

LEARNING OBJECTIVES

After studying this chapter, you should be able to:

- Define and discuss the major tenets of prejudice.

- Understand the differences between traditional and aversive racism.

- Define discrimination and identify its two forms.

- Discuss the prevalence of discrimination in the sport context.

- Understand why discrimination occurs.

- Discuss the effect of discrimination on subsequent work outcomes.

or head coach) based on his demographic characteristics. In fact, at the beginning of the 2005 season, of the 117 NCAA Division I-A football teams, only three (2.56 percent) were guided by an African American head coach: UCLA (Karl Dorrell), Mississippi State (Croom), and the University of Washington (Tyrone Willingham).*

DIVERSITY CHALLENGE   R E F L E C T I O N

1. How much of a problem is discrimination in university athletics?

2. In what sectors of sport and physical activity does discrimination take place?

3. From your perspective, what group of people is most likely to face discrimination in the sport context?

4. What are some strategies that can be used to overcome discrimination in sport?

*Information adapted from Brown, G. T. (2002). Diversity grid lock. *The NCAA News*. Retrieved February 15, 2003, from www.ncaa.org/news/2002/20021028/active/3922n01.html; RollTide.com: The official site of University of Alabama athletics. Retrieved September 16, 2004, from www.rolltide.com/Football; Wade, D. (2004, August 21). Sylvester Croom a gift from the Tide. *Fox Sports*. Retrieved September 16, 2004, from http://feeds.foxsports.com/story/2669318.

As Sylvester Croom's situation seems to illustrate, even 40 years after major civil rights legislation was passed (e.g., the Civil Rights Act of 1964), discrimination may still play an important role in the personnel decisions, opportunity structure, and treatment of university football coaches. Such practices, however, are not limited to the football domain; many instances of discrimination have been documented in other areas of university athletics, in high school sports, and in other sectors of the sport industry. Furthermore, discrimination is not limited to persons from underrepresented racial groups; rather, anyone who is different from the typical majority in the sport industry—that is, White, Protestant, able-bodied, heterosexual males—may face inequitable treatment (Fink, Pastore, & Riemer, 2001). There is considerable evidence that facing such discrimination can have a negative impact on an individual's work experiences, career progress, and even life satisfaction (see Button, 2001). The purpose of this chapter, therefore, is to explore the issues of differential treatment in the sport industry.

Prejudice

his section provides an overview of prejudice and discusses both explicit and implicit prejudicial attitudes. In doing so, the theoretical tenets and outcomes associated with these constructs are presented.

Definition

To understand prejudice, it is first necessary to define the term. Consider the following definitions developed by others working in this field:

> Prejudice is "an unfavorable attitude toward another group, involving both negative feelings and beliefs." (Gaertner & Dovidio, 2000, p. 15)

> Prejudice is "an antipathy based on faulty and inflexible generalization. It may be felt or expressed. It may be directed toward a group as a whole, or toward an individual because he is a member of that group." (Allport, 1954, p. 9)

> Prejudice represents "negative attitudes toward a socially defined group and any person perceived to be a member of that group." (Ashmore, 1970, p. 253)

Several conclusions may be drawn from these definitions. First, prejudice is concerned with negative attitudes toward a group of people or persons within that group (Allport, 1954; Ashmore, 1970; Gaertner & Dovidio, 2000). Second, the negative attitudes are expressed toward a particular group or any person who is *perceived* to be in that group (Ashmore, 1970). Even if one is not a member of a certain group (i.e., is not gay), if that person is perceived to be a member, then negative attitudes will be directed toward him. Third, the negative attitudes are usually based on faulty information and rigid generalizations (Allport, 1954). Finally, these negative attitudes can be felt internally or outwardly expressed, such as by verbally expressing one's beliefs (Allport, 1954; Gaertner & Dovidio, 2000).

From a social psychological perspective, prejudice arises from intergroup bias (Gaertner & Dovidio, 2000). Consistent with the social categorization framework discussed in Chapter 2 (Tajfel & Turner, 1979; Turner, Hogg, Oakes, Reicher, & Wetherell, 1987), persons are thought to have differing evaluations of in-group and out-group members. In this way, in-group members (persons similar to the self) are viewed in a more positive light than are their out-group counterparts (persons who differ from the self).

Traditional and Aversive Racism

To explore the issue of prejudice further, it is necessary to understand the different forms or expressions of prejudice. To explain and illustrate the forms of prejudice, the discussion in this section will focus on racial prejudice, or racism, expressed toward African Americans. Later, I will describe how the discussion

DIVERSITY
in the field

Racism in Soccer. Racism is present in all parts of the sport world, and soccer (football) is no exception. Norway's John Carew and Daniel Braathen, for example, faced considerable racist abuse by Slovenian fans as Norway battled Slovenia in a World Cup qualifying match in September of 2005 ("Carew," 2005). Unfortunately for these two players, there is little they can do while playing on the field; however, team and stadium officials can take steps to curb such abuse. Benjamin Davis-Todd, who hurled racist insults toward a Peterborough United player during a match in 2005, was banned from Lincoln City games for three years ("Match," 2005). In addition to the fines and court costs he was ordered to pay, Davis-Todd was prohibited from visiting any town or city where Lincoln City or the English national team was playing while the ban was in place. Apparently, the court action had an effect on Davis-Todd. After the court case concluded, he noted, "I'm very sorry for what I did. I'm embarrassed not only for myself but for my family as well. I've been going to watch Lincoln City my whole life, so I'm absolutely gutted that I can't go to matches anymore." Perhaps penalties such as these will curb the abusive insults racial minorities hear while participating in soccer.

applies to other groups. This is done for the simplicity and ease of presenting a single illustration throughout.

Traditional (Explicit) Racism

Traditional, or explicit, prejudicial attitudes are those negative attitudes toward persons different from the self that people consciously and deliberately maintain (Dovidio, Kawakami, & Beach, 2001). This form of prejudice is normally deemed socially unacceptable. Within the context of race, traditional or overt racism might include (a) attributing negative characteristics, such as laziness, to African Americans; (b) directing negative attitudes toward the group, such as antagonism; and (c) promoting mandates that limit opportunities of African Americans, such as those related to housing or employment (Gaertner & Dovidio, 2000). For example, members of the Ku Klux Klan are generally expected to hold such attitudes and are classified as *traditional* or overt racists.

An example in the sport field involved Derek Jeter who experienced overt racism during the 2005 baseball season. In April of that year, he received hate mail calling him a "traitor to his race" because he was dating White women. The person who wrote the letter warned him "to stop or he'll be shot or set on fire." Abraham Foxman, the national director of the Anti-Defamation League, reacted to the story by commenting that "celebrity status does not immunize anyone from the poisonous arrows of hate" ("Report," 2005). See the Diversity in the Field box for other examples of traditional racism in the sport context.

Aversive (Implicit) Racism

Unlike explicit prejudicial attitudes, aversive, or implicit, attitudes operate in an unconscious fashion and are not necessarily the result of negative attitudes toward dissimilar others (see Devine, Plant, & Blair, 2001). Within the context of race, the absence of overt negative attitudes toward racial minorities is often equated with a lack of racial prejudice. Although much of the research devoted to studying prejudice and racism adopts this premise, Gaertner and Dovidio (2000) challenge this assumption. These authors suspected that some people, known as aversive racists, may not hold negative attitudes toward racial minorities, but may still discriminate in subtle ways. The specific mechanisms as to how this occurs are presented next.

Foundation. As Gaertner and Dovidio (2000) explain, aversive racism is a "form of prejudice that characterizes the racial attitudes of many Whites with egalitarian values, who regard themselves as nonprejudiced, but who discriminate in subtle, rationalized ways" (p. 17). *Aversive racism* is a form of ambivalence in which one's desire to treat all people justly and fairly conflicts with negative racial beliefs and attitudes of which the person may be otherwise unaware. These negative attitudes and feelings may result from a history of racism in a specific context or the categorization of persons into in-groups and out-groups. Whereas traditional racists are more likely to be political conservatives, aversive racists are more likely to be liberal and hold egalitarian values.

The social categorization process is a key component of aversive racism, but not in the same way that it is with traditional racism. Traditional racists categorize racial minorities into out-groups and have negative attitudes toward persons in that group; aversive racists also categorize racial minorities into out-groups, but the positive attitudes they have toward minorities are not as strong as the positive attitudes they have toward other White in-group members (Gaertner & Dovidio, 2000). Although aversive racists have positive attitudes toward racial minorities, a bias still exists because the positive attitudes toward other Whites are stronger than the positive attitudes toward minorities. This dynamic is illustrated in Exhibit 3.1.

| Traditional and aversive racism attitudes. | *Exhibit 3.1* |

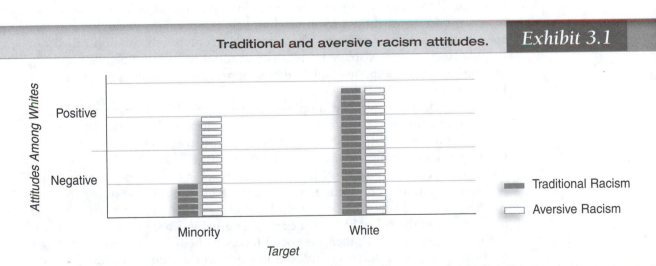

There are likely to be behavioral consequences of aversive racism because this intergroup bias does exist. Because aversive racists do not believe they are racists and they hold egalitarian values, they are unlikely to blatantly discriminate. They are also not likely to treat minorities and Whites differently when such differential treatment can be attributed to race. Rather, the differential treatment typically occurs when factors other than race can be used to justify such actions. As Gaertner and Dovidio (2000) explain, "in the absence of normative standards or when unfavorable treatment could be attributable to factors other than race, aversive racists could treat Blacks and Whites differently, yet not experience awareness that they are racially biased" (p. 18).

Illustration. Gaertner and Dovidio (2000) use the following example to illustrate their point. Suppose you invite people to your home for a holiday dinner. If you only invite family members, this does not connote ill-will toward those people who are not invited. Such an action is normal, socially acceptable, and only informs us of your positive attitudes toward your family members. On the other hand, suppose you also invite a select group of friends or withhold invitations from some family members. In these two instances, the attitudinal implications are clear: in the former example, we might expect that you have especially positive attitudes toward the select friends you invited, whereas in the latter example, we might expect that you have negative feelings toward the family members who did not receive an invitation.

A similar pattern of behavioral processes occurs when considering aversive racism. For example, when social forces to help someone are weak (i.e., not inhibiting), not helping someone who is racially different tells us very little about one person's attitudes toward another. After all, help is not necessarily expected, so the failure to help does not mean that there are negative attitudes involved. Rather, providing assistance in that situation suggests especially positive attitudes toward the person needing help. Conversely, when social forces suggest that action is necessary (i.e., strongly promote intervention), then not helping suggests the existence of negative attitudes toward the person requiring assistance. Several experimental studies support this rationale (see Gaertner & Dovidio, 2000, for a review).

Let us consider another example—one specific to the organizational setting. A group of sport marketers is working on a project, and one member, Len, is falling behind on the task. If Len puts forth considerable effort, but still has a hard time completing the task, social forces suggest that helping Len is the appropriate course of action. After all, Len is working on the project; he's simply having trouble completing it. Thus, whether Len is White or African American, he is likely to receive help from other team members regardless of their race. On the other hand, if Len is falling behind because he is procrastinating or "goofing off," then the social forces to help Len are minimal. Len's problem is his own doing because he has not worked diligently on the task. Drawing from the aversive racism literature, we might expect Len to receive help from Whites if he is White, but not to receive help from Whites if he is African American. Indeed, Frey and Gaertner (1986) found that when a person was considered to be undeserving of help (as with Len when he was procrastinating), Whites were helped more often than African Americans (93 percent of the time versus 30 percent). As this simple example shows, aversive racism can have a meaningful impact on work behaviors among colleagues.

Attitudes Toward Other Out-Group Members

Although the previous discussion used race as its focus, that should not imply that other out-group members do not experience prejudice. We can draw from the literature discussed earlier to formulate predictions about the nature of overt and implicit attitudes toward other persons, with the focus on such characteristics as sex, age, and sexual orientation.

As with the issue of race, overt forms of prejudice directed toward other out-group members are generally deemed socially unacceptable. For example, making blatantly derogatory remarks about women, the elderly, or persons with disabilities is likely to arouse a backlash directed toward the person making the remark. The same is generally true for overt behaviors directed toward these persons as well. It is interesting to note, however, that current research shows that negative attitudes toward gays and lesbians may be less likely to meet social criticism (e.g., Gill, Morrow, Collins, Lucey, & Schultz, 2006). Thus, not all forms of overt prejudice are treated the same or generate the same reactions.

Implicit behaviors and attitudes toward persons based on their sex, age, religious beliefs, and so forth are likely to follow the same pattern as with race. That is, helping behavior directed toward out-group members is likely to occur when the social pressures to intervene are high, while helping behavior is unlikely to take place when social norms dictating participation are low (for an extensive overview of these issues, see Dovidio et al., 2001).

Outcomes Associated with Overt and Implicit Prejudicial Attitudes

The existing literature shows that the traditional form of prejudice is associated with negative attitudes toward the out-group, while the aversive form of prejudice is associated with more positive attitudes toward the in-group (see Gaertner & Dovidio, 2000). Given this background, we might ask if the outcomes that result from the two forms of prejudice vary. The answer is mixed. With extreme instances of prejudice, yes, the outcomes are likely to differ. For example, the racial slurs hurled at Jackie Robinson or the death threats sent to Hank Aaron (both African American Hall of Fame baseball players) were likely made only by overt racists, not by people with egalitarian values who did not consider themselves as prejudiced (i.e., aversive racists).

However, with more subtle forms of prejudice, the demarcation in outcomes resulting from explicit and implicit prejudicial attitudes becomes blurred. As previously discussed, aversive racists provide help to others, at least in some situations, based on in-group or out-group membership (e.g., Frey & Gaertner, 1986). Although the reason *why* help was not given may vary (i.e., negative out-group attitudes versus pro in-group attitudes), the outcome—the African American not receiving help—is the same for both the traditional and aversive racist.

Various phenomena in the sport industry point to the incidence of prejudice beyond that demonstrated by overt racists. For example, that male coaches are more likely to hire other men than they are to hire women (Lovett & Lowry, 1994; Stangl & Kane, 1991) could be attributed to potentially negative attitudes men harbor toward women coaches (see Acosta & Carpenter, 1985, 1988). From another perspective, it is possible that male administrators have positive attitudes toward women coaches, but their positive attitudes toward male coaches are stronger than those felt toward women. In this case, the prejudice is implicit in nature. Drawing from the existing literature (e.g., Gaertner & Dovidio, 2000), we might expect that when social forces to hire a woman are weak (i.e., the applicants all have similar qualifications), the male athletic director may be more likely to hire the male coach. On the other hand, when social forces to hire the woman are strong (i.e., the woman applicant is clearly more qualified), the male administrator will select the woman. Of course, perceptions of qualifications may be tempered by the gendered nature of the selection process (e.g., Knoppers, 1992). Nevertheless, it does show the same outcome—the woman not receiving the coaching position—may be due to different underlying motivations and mechanisms than people have traditionally assumed.

Discrimination

This section begins by defining discrimination, including the two forms—access and treatment—the construct can take. The discussion then turns to theoretical explanation of why discrimination exists. This section concludes with the identification of discrimination outcomes.

Definitions

Gordon Allport (1954) defined *discrimination* as a behavior that "comes about only when we deny to individuals or groups of people equality of treatment which they may wish" (p. 51). Though related, prejudice and discrimination are conceptually distinct. According to Abercrombie, Hill, and Turner (2000), "prejudice, often the object of psychological study, is contrasted with *discrimination,* which refers to the outcome of social processes which disadvantage social groups" (p. 276).

Forms of discrimination.	**Exhibit 3.2**

Access discrimination:

- *Definition:* denies one access to an organization, job, or profession based on membership in a social category
- *Theoretical perspective:* social categorization framework
- *Example:* an African American who is more qualified than the other applicants is denied a managerial position

Treatment discrimination:

- *Definition:* members of a specific social category have less positive work experiences and receive fewer opportunities and rewards than they legitimately deserve based on job-related criteria
- *Theoretical perspectives:* critical theories, social categorization framework
- *Example:* an African American who performs better than her colleagues receives the lowest performance evaluation

Greenhaus, Parasuraman, and Wormley (1990) identified two types of discrimination: access and treatment (see Exhibit 3.2). *Access discrimination* prevents members of a particular social category from obtaining a job or entering a profession. This form of discrimination takes place while people are looking for a job, or when they are moving from one job to another.

Treatment discrimination occurs once people are employed. As Greenhaus et al. explain, this form of discrimination "occurs when subgroup members receive fewer rewards, resources, or opportunities on the job than they legitimately deserve on the basis of job-related criteria" (pp. 64–65). As this definition illustrates, the differences in treatment are the result of membership in a specific social category (e.g., being a woman), rather than poor performance at work. As previously noted, Fink et al. (2001) found that employees who are different from the majority in the sport context are likely to face difficult work experiences. Research in this area generally supports their thesis.

Access Discrimination

Several studies have demonstrated the existence of access discrimination in the sport and recreation context. Both Stangl and Kane (1991) and Lovett and Lowry (1994) found that women coaches faced discrimination in the hiring process, such that men (the persons who make the majority of the personnel decisions in this context) were more likely to hire other men than they were to hire women. In a similar *alternative*

P E R S P E C T I V E S

Discrimination Based on Language. Oftentimes, discussions of discrimination are related to differential access and treatment based on membership in a social group. For example, lesbian coaches might face more discrimination than their heterosexual counterparts. However, discrimination can also stretch beyond the way people look, their personal beliefs, or their sexual preferences. Others might face discrimination because of their language. Language discrimination is denying people access to particular opportunities or treating people differently in the workplace solely because of their native tongue or a specific characteristic of their speech. For example, requiring that only English be spoken in the workplace is likely to be considered language discrimination. Various U.S. Supreme Court decisions, dating back as early as 1926, have established the illegality of such actions. Furthermore, plaintiffs have successfully sued under Title VII of the Civil Rights Act of 1964. It is important to remember that discrimination is not only based on physical characteristics, beliefs, or preferences, but also on the language people use.

American Civil Liberties Union (www.aclunc.org/language/lang-report.html).

vein, Cunningham and Sagas (2005) found that African Americans faced access discrimination in the men's basketball context. These authors also found that the prevalence of discrimination was accentuated on staffs with a White head coach relative to those with an African American head coach (see also Hamilton, 1997, for similar effects in professional basketball). Longley (2000) found that French Canadians were underrepresented, both as players and as front-office personnel, on English Canadian NHL teams, relative to their U. S. counterparts. Other research has demonstrated that persons with disabilities (Hums, Moorman, & Wolff, 2003) and persons from a lower socioeconomic class are often denied access to sport and recreational opportunities. Finally, although research in other areas is lacking, it is reasonable to assume that other persons, such as religious minorities, may also face similar discriminatory practices.

Treatment Discrimination

Research suggests that treatment discrimination is widespread in the sport context. The research conducted among coaches illustrates this point. With respect to sex, various studies have shown that women, relative to men, face limited opportunities for advancement, both in their careers and within their organizations (e.g., Knoppers, Meyer, Ewing, & Forrest, 1991; Whisenant, 2003). Men are more likely than women to reap the rewards of extra training, education, and social contacts in the industry (Cunningham & Sagas, 2002; Sagas & Cunningham, 2004). Furthermore, women often encounter more negative work experiences than do men (e.g., Inglis, Danylchuk, & Pastore, 2000). Given this differential treatment, it should not be surprising that women in the sport industry often have different career goals and outcomes than do men. For example, research has shown that women coaches, relative to men, are likely to leave the profession at an earlier age (Cunningham & Sagas, 2003) and possess fewer career advancement aspirations (e.g., Cunningham & Sagas, 2002; Sagas, Cunningham, & Ashley, 2000).

Treatment discrimination is not just limited to women, however. With respect to race, research has shown that athletes of color face unique experiences on university campuses (Bruening, Armstrong, & Pastore, 2005). Among coaches, racial minorities are likely to perceive fewer advancement opportunities (Cunningham & Sagas, 2004) and to receive fewer promotions (Sagas & Cunningham, 2005). In addition, various studies have indicated that gays and lesbians face negative attitudes from others in the sport industry (Gill et al., 2006) and encounter treatment discrimination in the workplace (Krane & Barber, 2005). The general pattern of these studies supports the contention of Fink et al. (2001) that persons who are different from the majority often face discriminatory practices within the sport context.

Theoretical Explanations for Discrimination

With this background, the discussion turns to explanations of why discrimination exists. As was done previously, we examine theoretical perspectives related to access and treatment discrimination separately.

Theories Related to Access Discrimination

Although several theories could be used to understand access discrimination, a social psychological theory (see Chapter 2) works the best. Access discrimination is concerned with persons who differ from the majority

DIVERSITY *in the field*

Limited Access to Participation. Many times, access discrimination is discussed in terms of the limited opportunities persons from certain groups have to obtain particular jobs or work in a certain profession. However, people can also face access discrimination when it comes to participation in sports. Because athletes such as Jackie Robinson broke the "color barrier" over 50 years ago, many may assume that denying people access to participation opportunities based on their demographic characteristics is a thing of the past. However, this is not the case. For example, in the country club context, Augusta National, which hosts the Masters golf tournament, still denied membership to women as of 2005 (Daddario & Wigley, 2006). In a similar way, Shoal Creek did not admit persons of color as club members until its discriminatory admissions practices came under fire when the club hosted the 1990 PGA Championship. Such discriminatory practices are not limited to country clubs or to the exclusion of women and persons of color. Fernwood Women's Health Club is an organization designed as women-only fitness clubs. Other organizations, such as Fitness Etcetera for Women, have similar policies. As these examples illustrate, access discrimination occurs not only in an organizational context, but also in country clubs and fitness organizations.

being denied access to certain positions, organizations, or occupations (Greenhaus et al., 1990). When considering this lack of access, it is useful to identify who are keeping these people from obtaining such positions. Who are the decision makers and persons in charge of personnel decisions? As previously noted, within the sport context, these persons most often include men who are White, Protestant, able-bodied, and heterosexual (Fink et al., 2001). We can then use this information to make predictions about personnel decisions. Drawing from both the social categorization framework (Tajfel & Turner, 1979; Turner et al., 1987) and

alternative
P E R S P E C T I V E S

Questioning Different Work Experiences. Much of the literature in sport and leisure suggests that women have poorer work experiences than their male counterparts, thereby suggesting that they encounter treatment discrimination. There are some studies, however, that do not support this trend. Specifically, within the context of women's university athletics, several studies have shown that women coaches perceive more opportunity for advancement than do the men. For example, Sagas et al. (2000) asked assistant coaches of women's teams who had applied for head coaching positions why they did not receive the positions. Men were much more likely to indicate that discriminatory hiring practices prevented them from obtaining the position. That is, in the minds of these assistant coaches, administrators sought a woman for the position, not a man. Similar sentiments have been expressed by coaches in the field. In 2005, Michael Cox filed a discrimination lawsuit against Boston University, claiming that he did not receive a coaching position for the women's ice hockey team because he was a man (Levenson, 2005). Thus, although there is considerable evidence to suggest that women face treatment discrimination in sport and leisure, it is also possible that men, in some instances, also face differential treatment based on their sex.

similarity-attraction paradigm (Byrne, 1971), it might be expected that decision makers will select people who are similar to themselves. In this case, the people similar to the self are other White men who are able-bodied, heterosexual, and Protestant. This demographic profile mirrors that of most of the personnel in sport organizations today.

If we assume that people will hire others who are like them, then that also is true for persons who are not in the majority. Women who are in power, for example, will be more likely to hire other women. Using other demographic or deep-level characteristics to replace "women" in the previous example produces the same results. Current research supports this contention: Among NCAA Division I athletic departments, the proportion of women serving as head coaches of women's teams increases from 44.5 percent to 49.4 percent when the athletic director (the person charged with hiring decisions) is a woman (Acosta & Carpenter, 2004). Similar findings result when race is considered: Among NCAA Division I basketball teams, the proportion of African American assistant coaches increases from 30 percent to 45 percent when the head coach is an African American (Cunningham & Sagas, 2005).

These studies illustrate that all people, irrespective of their demographic characteristics, are likely to hire similar others. One way to reduce or eliminate access discrimination, therefore, is to change the sport organizations' power structure. If more women, racial minorities, or others who are different from the traditional majority are placed in decision-making roles, then the proportion of those persons in all levels of sport organizations is likely to increase.

Theories Related to Treatment Discrimination

Several theories have been adopted to explain the incidence of treatment discrimination; however, critical theories (see Chapter 2) remain the most often used. Feminist theory focuses on the gendered nature of organizations. In the context of many sport organizations, this means the organizational structures, the jobs within these organizations, and the activities within these entities are all defined in such a way that hegemonic masculinity is enhanced (Knoppers, 1992). Applying the feminist theory, sport organizations are places where men and the activities in which men participate are valued and celebrated, thereby privileging men and dominant forms of masculinity. As a result, women in these organizations face poorer work experiences than their male counterparts, and the activities in which they engage may be less valued.

Critical race theory also is used to explain discrimination in sport. Recall that one of the central tenets of this theory is that racism is endemic in society (Singer, 2005; Tate, 1997). Researchers who adopt this theory argue that racism is a central part of U. S. society, enmeshed in the society's institutions, legal system, and culture. This position supports the argument that the discrimination experienced by racial minorities is due, at least in part, to the racist institutions and systems present in American society.

Although most research adopts a sociological approach to studying treatment discrimination, recent research suggests that a social psychological approach can also be embraced (e.g., Cunningham, 2004; Sartore, 2006). Such an approach is especially useful when considering the presence of discrimination in work dyads, such as supervisor–subordinate pairs. It is assumed that managers (or coaches) categorize their subordinates into in-groups and out-groups based, at least in part, on the surface- or deep-level similarity to the self. In-group members, relative to their out-group counterparts, are then afforded greater trust, respect, and positive affect. In an organizational setting, such positive attitudes toward in-group members may also mean more challenging and meaningful work assignments, greater access to information, and more positive work experiences in general. Because most managers in sport organizations are White, able-bodied, Protestant, heterosexual men (Fink et al., 2001), people with similar characteristics are likely to be considered in-group members and have pleasant work experiences, while people with different characteristics are more likely to experience work poorly.

Discrimination Outcomes

This section discusses how discrimination influences subsequent outcomes—both for those who experience the differential treatment and for those who do not. The effects of access and treatment discrimination are addressed separately, though it is acknowledged that the two can interact and influence one another.

Outcomes Related to Access Discrimination

Because access discrimination denies people, based on their personal characteristics, the opportunity to obtain a particular job, enter an organization, or pursue a career in a certain profession (Button, 2001; Greenhaus et al., 1990), one of the most obvious outcomes is the limitations placed on the jobs and careers one can pursue. The statistics in this chapter's Diversity Challenge indicate that 97.44 percent of all NCAA Division I-A head football coaches are White—there is a strong history of excluding people who do not fit this demographic characteristic. Members of some racial groups, such as Asian Americans, have never served as a head coach for a Division I-A football team. For current assistant coaches in the profession, the message is clear: unless you are White, the chances of obtaining a head coaching position are slim. Although the focus here is on race and coaching, the same is true for others who differ from the majority—women, persons with disabilities, and so forth.

PROFESSIONAL
P E R S P E C T I V E S

Discrimination in the Hiring Process. Becky Heidesch is the founder and CEO of Women's Sports Services (WSS), an organization specializing in job placement for women, minorities, and professional athletes. According to Heidesch, the sports industry, like many others, is one that has traditionally been dominated by White males. Recently, however, this field has "been making in-roads" when it comes to diversifying the workforce. This progress grew from an awareness that a diverse staff can help a firm identify with and relate to people from different backgrounds. Although a push for greater diversity is evident, there are still many instances of discrimination, particularly among women and minorities. Those are not the only persons facing such barriers, however. As Heidesch notes, "certainly we see age discrimination across the board." Such discrimination oftentimes arises from perceptions among sport organization decision makers that older employees might not fit into the organization's culture. Discrimination can also take place based on the applicant's attractiveness. Heidesch notes that attractiveness plays a meaningful role in certain positions, such as those related to public relations, marketing, and advertising. Physical appearance is particularly important any time a person represents the company in public.

Access discrimination influences those who encounter it directly; for example, the woman who is denied a managerial role because of her sex (see the Professional Perspectives box for other examples). However, a history of access discrimination in a particular profession or industry also influences people who have not yet entered the field—namely, students. There is a growing body of literature that suggests that when people anticipate substantial barriers in a profession, they are unlikely to choose that career path (see Bandura, 2000; Lent, Brown, & Hackett, 1994). For example, if a student is considering entering the sport management profession, but observes that people with characteristics similar to hers face considerable discrimination and are not afforded an opportunity to progress, then it is unlikely that she will pursue that career. Instead, she may choose a career path that is more convivial to persons similar to her, and presumably then, to her as well (for an example, see Cunningham, Bruening, Sartore, Sagas, & Fink, 2005). Thus, access discrimination not only influences people who experience it, but also persons who may consider that career path.

Outcomes Related to Treatment Discrimination

Button (2001) argues that treatment discrimination can impact both tangible and subtle outcomes. Tangible outcomes include the job assignments one receives, the opportunities for development and training, the number and size of the raises one receives, and the number of promotions one is given. Subtle outcomes, while perhaps more difficult to quantify or observe, are equally as important. Such outcomes include differences in integrating into the workgroup, the support received from supervisors, and the discretion to execute job activities.

One of the primary ways treatment discrimination occurs is through performance appraisals (Ilgen & Youtz, 1986; Stauffer & Buckley, 2005). Unfair ratings have important implications for the employee's development, as well as the raises and promotions received. Recognizing the potential for bias in performance appraisals, Sartore (2006) drew from organizational psychology, social psychology, human resource management, and sociology literature to develop a conceptual model explaining how treatment discrimination, as manifested through performance appraisals, can influence subsequent work-related outcomes. This model is described next (see also Exhibit 3.3).

Using the social categorization framework (Tajfel & Turner, 1979; Turner et al., 1987), Sartore (2006) argues that the categorization of persons into in-groups and out-groups will influence performance appraisals, such that the performance ratings of in-group members will be higher than those of out-group members. This effect has been demonstrated in various contexts over many years (see Stauffer & Buckley, 2005). Sartore then suggests that this performance appraisal bias will result in self-limiting behavior. Self-limiting behavior refers to the decrease in abilities and loss of motivation that occur over time as a result of negative performance feedback. One's ability is likely to diminish because poor

The effects of performance appraisal bias.   *Exhibit 3.3*

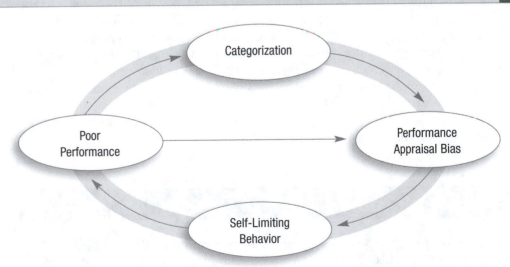

performance appraisals result in being assigned less meaningful work and being offered fewer training opportunities. Thus, opportunities to develop skills and abilities decrease. Motivation decreases because continually being exposed to negative performance feedback may impact one's confidence or the overall effort put forth to complete a task. We might expect that if people perceive that discrimination is the cause of the poor appraisal, they may become less motivated because they feel they cannot alter or control it.

As might be expected, when self-limiting behavior occurs, subsequent task performance becomes poor. When employees lose opportunities to develop their skills, lack confidence in their abilities, and demonstrate a lack of motivation, their performance is likely to diminish. Recognizing this relationship, Sartore (2006) proposes that self-limiting behavior is negatively related to task performance.

The subsequent poor performance has two expected outcomes: additional poor performance appraisals and stereotype confirmation. The former outcome is straightforward, as poor performance should result in a poor evaluation. With respect to the latter outcome, recall that out-group members were initially assigned poor performance evaluation scores not so much because of their actual job performance, but because they are different from the rater. These differences are related to negative attitudes toward the employee, or at the very least, less positive attitudes than are afforded in-group members. Thus, when out-group members perform poorly because of self-limiting behavior, this simply serves to reinforce initial stereotypes about that person.

Sartore (2006) further suggests that these relationships can be influenced by various factors, such as the amount of time the rater and ratee spend with one another, how closely the two parties work with one another, the extent to which the dissimilarities that lead to categorization are important to the rater, and the extent to which the rater and ratee consider themselves as belonging to a single, common in-group. Notwithstanding these potential caveats, Sartore correctly argues that rater–ratee differences can have a negative impact not only on immediate outcomes, such as the raise received, but also on more long-term outcomes as motivation, confidence, and performance. Furthermore, the categorization is not limited to demographic attributes, as research has shown that rater–ratee deep-level characteristic differences can also result in biased performance appraisals (Antonioni & Park, 2001).

Chapter Summary

The focus of this chapter was on discrimination and prejudice. As illustrated in the Diversity Challenge, these phenomena still play a major role in the context of sport and physical activity. Specifically, prejudice and discrimination influence the people who join an organization, the structure and policies an organization implements, the processes within the workplace, and various outcomes for the individual, group, and organization. After reading the chapter, you should be able to:

1. Define and discuss the major tenets of prejudice.

Four key points concerning prejudice were addressed. First, prejudice is concerned with negative attitudes toward persons from a specific social category. Second, the attitudes are expressed toward the group as a whole or to persons who are perceived to be members of that group. Third, the negative attitudes are oftentimes based on faulty information and rigid generalizations. Finally, prejudicial attitudes can be felt internally or outwardly expressed (e.g., by verbally expressing one's beliefs).

2. Understand the differences between traditional and aversive racism.

Traditional, or explicit, attitudes are those negative attitudes that people consciously and deliberately maintain. Aversive, or implicit, attitudes are held by persons who do not think they are prejudiced and hold egalitarian values. These persons only demonstrate prejudicial responses when social forces allow them to; that is, when such actions cannot be attributed to prejudice.

3. Define discrimination and identify its two forms.

Drawing from Allport (1954), discrimination was defined as a behavior that "comes about only when we deny to individuals or groups of people equality of treatment which they may wish" (p. 51). Greenhaus et al. (1990) further differentiated between two forms of discrimination: access and treatment.

4. Discuss the prevalence of discrimination in the sport context.

Research and anecdotal evidence both suggest that discrimination is widespread in the sport industry. With respect to access discrimination, people are denied access to certain positions within sport organizations or to participation opportunities in sport and recreation based on their personal demographics. With respect to treatment discrimination, research shows that people who differ from the typical majority are less likely to be rewarded for their career investment and success and generally have less positive work experiences.

5. Understand why discrimination occurs.

Several theoretical perspectives may explain discriminatory behavior. The social categorization framework is useful to understand access discrimination: in-group members are thought to be favored for positions over their out-group counterparts. On the other hand, critical theories, such as feminist theory and critical race theory, have most often been used to explain treatment discrimination. Although most research adopts a sociological approach to examine the issue of treatment discrimination, other research uses the social categorization framework to examine the differential experiences of in-group and out-group members.

6. Discuss the effect of discrimination on subsequent work outcomes.

Several outcomes are associated with discrimination. First, when people are denied access to a particular job, organization, or profession based solely on personal characteristics, they are denied the opportunity to pursue the vocation of their choice. Treatment discrimination results in such negative outcomes as decreased training opportunities, poorer job assignments, a lack of work group integration, and low supervisor support.

Questions for Discussion

1. What are the major differences between traditional and aversive racism? What are examples of each?
2. Which form of prejudicial attitudes is most prevalent in sport today? Are some sectors of sport and physical activity more likely to see certain types of prejudice than others?
3. With federal, state, and local statutes mandating equal employment opportunities, is discrimination still a problem? Why or why not?
4. What are the major distinctions between access and treatment discrimination?
5. Which form of discrimination has the more harmful effects? Why?
6. Several theories are used to understand why discrimination occurs. Which of the theories allows for the best explanation and why?

Learning Activities

1. Visit the Project Implicit website (https://implicit.harvard.edu/implicit/) and test your aversive, or implicit, attitudes toward different targets (e.g., age, race, disability).
2. Search the Web for recent examples of discrimination and prejudice in the context of sport and physical activity. Based on your search results, which group or groups are most likely to face discrimination?

Resources

SUPPLEMENTARY READINGS

Brown, R., & Gaertner, S. (Eds.). (2001). *Blackwell handbook of social psychology: Intergroup processes.* Malden, MA: Blackwell. (Edited collection of essays related to intergroup processes; contains specific sections of prejudice and changing intergroup processes.)

Colella, A., & Dipboye, R. (Eds.). (2005). *Discrimination at work: The psychological and organizational bases.* Mahwah, NJ: Lawrence Erlbaum Associates. (Edited volume with a focus on explaining discrimination, understanding discrimination against particular groups, and discussing the practical implications for reducing such behaviors.)

Dovidio, J. F., Glick, P., & Budman, L. A. (Eds.). (2005). *On the nature of prejudice: Fifty years after Allport.* Malden, MA: Blackwell. (An edited collection of essays from the leading social psychologists in the field; focuses on the contributions of Allport's original work related to prejudice; provides updates to the theory and directions for future inquiry.)

WEB RESOURCES

- Human Rights and Equality Commission (www.hreoc.gov.au/index.html): Australian agency aimed at eliminating discrimination in various contexts, including sport.

- Institute for Diversity and Ethics in Sport (www.bus.ucf.edu/sport/cgi-bin/site/sitew.cgi?page=/ides/index.htx): provides reports concerning diversity and discrimination in the university athletics and professional sport settings.

- Project Implicit (https://implicit.harvard.edu/implicit/): provides an electronic demonstration of how to test for implicit attitudes.

References

Abercrombie, N., Hill, S., & Turner, B. S. (2000). *The Penguin dictionary of sociology* (4th ed.). New York: Penguin Books.

Acosta, R. V., & Carpenter, L. J. (1985). Status of women in athletics: Changes and causes. *Journal of Physical Education, Recreation, and Dance, 56*(8), 33–37.

Acosta, R. V., & Carpenter, L. J. (1988). *Perceived causes of declining representation of women leaders in intercollegiate sports—1988 update.* Unpublished manuscript, Brooklyn College, Brooklyn, NY.

Acosta, R. V., & Carpenter, L. J. (2004). *Women in intercollegiate sport: A longitudinal study—twenty-seven year update—1977–2004.* Unpublished manuscript, Brooklyn College, Brooklyn, NY.

Allport, G. W. (1954). *The nature of prejudice.* Cambridge, MA: Addison-Wesley.

Antonioni, D., & Park, H. (2001). The effects of personality similarity on peer ratings of contextual work behaviors. *Personnel Psychology, 54,* 331–360.

Ashmore, R. D. (1970). Prejudice: Causes and curses. In B. E. Collins (Ed.), *Social psychology: Social influence, attitude change, group processes and prejudice* (pp. 245–339). Reading, MA: Addison-Wesley.

Bandura, A. (2000). Exercise of human agency through collective self-efficacy. *Current Directions in Psychological Science, 9*(3), 75–78.

Bruening, J. E., Armstrong, K. L., & Pastore, D. L. (2005). Listening to voices: The experiences of

African American female student athletes. *Research Quarterly for Exercise and Sport, 76,* 82–100.

Button, S. B. (2001). Organizational efforts to affirm sexual diversity: A cross-level examination. *Journal of Applied Psychology, 86,* 17–28.

Byrne, D. (1971). *The attraction paradigm.* New York: Academic Press.

Carew and Braathen abused by Slovenian fans. (2005, September 7). Retrieved September 30, 2005, from www.farenet.org/news_article.asp?int-NewsID=461

Cunningham, G. B. (2004). Strategies for transforming the possible negative effects of group diversity. *Quest, 56,* 421–438.

Cunningham, G. B., Bruening, J., Sartore, M. L., Sagas, M., & Fink, J. S. (2005). The application of social cognitive career theory to sport and leisure career choices. *Journal of Career Development, 32,* 122–138.

Cunningham, G. B., & Sagas, M. (2002). The differential effects of human capital for male and female Division I basketball coaches. *Research Quarterly for Exercise and Sport, 73,* 489–495.

Cunningham, G. B., & Sagas, M. (2003). Occupational turnover intent among coaches of women's teams: The role of organizational work experiences. *Sex Roles, 49,* 185–190.

Cunningham, G. B., & Sagas, M. (2004). Racial differences in occupational turnover intent among NCAA Division IA assistant football coaches. *Sociology of Sport Journal, 21,* 84–92.

Cunningham, G. B., & Sagas, M. (2005). Access discrimination in intercollegiate athletics. *Journal of Sport and Social Issues, 29,* 148–163.

Daddario, G., & Wigley, B. J. (2006). Prejudice, patriarchy, and the PGA: Defensive discourse surrounding the Shoal Creek and Augusta National controversies. *Journal of Sport Management, 20,* 466–482.

Devine, P. G., Plant, E. A., & Blair, I. V. (2001). Classic and contemporary analyses of racial prejudice. In R. Brown & S. L. Gaertner (Eds.), *Blackwell handbook of social psychology: Intergroup processes* (pp. 198–217). Malden, MA: Blackwell.

Dovidio, J. F., Kawakami, K., & Beach, K. R. (2001). Implicit and explicit attitudes: Examination of the relationship between measures of intergroup bias. In R. Brown & S. L. Gaertner (Eds.), *Blackwell handbook of social psychology: Intergroup processes* (pp. 175–197). Malden, MA: Blackwell.

Fink, J. S., Pastore, D. L., & Riemer, H. A. (2001). Do differences make a difference? Managing diversity in Division IA intercollegiate athletics. *Journal of Sport Management, 15,* 10–50.

Frey, D., & Gaertner, S. L. (1986). Helping and the avoidance of inappropriate interracial behavior: A strategy which perpetuates a non-prejudiced self-image. *Journal of Personality and Social Psychology, 50,* 1083–1090.

Gaertner, S. L., & Dovidio, J. F. (2000). *Reducing intergroup bias: The common ingroup identity model.* Philadelphia, PA: Psychology Press.

Gill, D. L., Morrow, R. G., Collins, K. E., Lucey, A. B., & Schultz, A. M. (2006). Attitudes and sexual prejudice in sport and physical activity. *Journal of Sport Management, 20,* 554–564.

Greenhaus, J. H., Parasuraman, S., & Wormley, W. M. (1990). Effects of race on organizational experiences, job performance, evaluations, and career outcomes. *Academy of Management Journal, 33,* 64–86.

Hamilton, B. H. (1997). Racial discrimination and professional basketball salaries in the 1990s. *Applied Economics, 29,* 287–296.

Hums, M. A., Moorman, A. M., & Wolff, E. A. (2003). The inclusion of the Paralympics in the Olympic Amateur Sports Act: Legal and policy implications for integration of athletes with disabilities into the United States Olympic Committee. *Journal of Sport and Social Issues, 27,* 261–275.

Ilgen, D. R., & Youtz, M. A. (1986). Factors affecting the evaluation and development of minorities in organizations. In K. Rowland & G. Ferris (Eds.), *Research in personnel and human resource management: A research annual* (pp. 307–337). Greenwich, CT: JAI Press.

Inglis, S., Danylchuk, K. E., & Pastore, D. L. (2000). Multiple realities of women's work experiences in coaching and athletic management. *Women in Sport and Physical Activity Journal, 9*(2), 1–26.

Knoppers, A. (1992). Explaining male dominance and sex segregation in coaching: Three approaches. *Quest, 44,* 210–227.

Knoppers, A., Meyer, B. B., Ewing, M., & Forrest, L. (1991). Opportunity and work behavior in college coaching. *Journal of Sport and Social Issues, 15,* 1–20.

Krane, V., & Barber, H. (2005). Identity tensions in lesbian intercollegiate coaches. *Research Quarterly for Exercise and Sport, 76,* 67–81.

Lent, R. W., Brown, S. D., & Hackett, G. (1994). Toward a unifying social cognitive theory of career and academic interest, choice, and performance [Monograph]. *Journal of Vocational Behavior, 45,* 79–122.

Levenson, M. (2005, July 5). BC coach alleges gender bias at BU: Files complaint over hockey job. *The Boston Globe.* Retrieved September 2, 2005, from www.boston.com/sports/colleges/womens_hockey/articles/2005/07/05/bc_coach_alleges_gender_bias_at_bu/

Longley, N. (2000). The underrepresentation of French Canadians on English Canadian NHL teams: Evidence from 1943–1998. *Journal of Sports Economics, 1,* 236–256.

Lovett, D. J., & Lowry, C. D. (1994). "Good old boys" and "good old girls" clubs: Myth or reality? *Journal of Sport Management, 8,* 27–35.

Match ban for racist Imps fan. (2005, September 26). Retrieved September 30, 2005, from www.farenet.org/news_article.asp?intNewsID=480

Report: Letter calls Jeter a "traitor to his race." (2005, September 26). ESPN. Retrieved September 26, 2005, from http://sports.espn.go.com/mlb/news/story?id=2172598

Sagas, M., & Cunningham, G. B. (2005). Racial differences in the career success of assistant football coaches: The role of discrimination, human capital, and social capital. *Journal of Applied Social Psychology, 35,* 773–797.

Sagas, M., & Cunningham, G. B. (2004). Does having the "right stuff" matter? Gender differences in the determinants of career success among intercollegiate athletic administrators. *Sex Roles, 50,* 411–421.

Sagas, M., Cunningham, G. B., & Ashley, F. B. (2000). Examining the women's coaching deficit through the perspective of assistant coaches. *International Journal of Sport Management, 1,* 267–282.

Sartore, M. L. (2006). Categorization, performance appraisals, and self-limiting behavior: The impact on current and future performance. *Journal of Sport Management, 20,* 535–553.

Singer, J. N. (2005). Addressing epistemological racism in sport management research. *Journal of Sport Management, 19,* 464–479.

Stangl, J. M., & Kane, M. J. (1991). Structural variables that offer explanatory power for the underrepresentation of women coaches since Title IX: The case of homologous reproduction. *Sociology of Sport Journal, 8,* 47–60.

Stauffer, J. M., & Buckley, R. M. (2005). The existence and nature of racial bias in supervisory ratings. *Journal of Applied Psychology, 90,* 586–591.

Tajfel, H., & Turner, J. C. (1979). An integrative theory of intergroup conflict. In W. G. Austin & S. Worchel (Eds.), *The social psychology of intergroup relations* (pp. 33–47). Monterey, CA: Brooks/Cole.

Tate, W. F. (1997). Critical race theory and education: History, theory, and implications. In M. Apple (Ed.), *Review in research education 2* (pp. 191–243). Washington, DC: American Educational Research Association.

Turner, J., Hogg, M. A., Oakes, P. J., Reicher, S. D., & Wetherell, M. S. (1987). *Rediscovering the social group: A self-categorization theory.* Oxford, UK: B. Blackwell.

Whisenant, W. A. (2003). How women have fared as interscholastic athletic administrators since the passage of Title IX. *Sex Roles, 49,* 179–184.

Race Issues in Sport Organizations

LEARNING OBJECTIVES

During the 1980s, Dexter Manley played professional football for the NFL's Washington Redskins. He was selected for the Pro Bowl based on his accomplishments as a defensive end and won two Super Bowl rings while playing with the Redskins. Despite these achievements and receiving a college degree from Oklahoma State University, Manley was illiterate until age 30. Manley's situation was not an isolated incident. Another player, Kevin Ross, was functionally illiterate but played four seasons at Creighton University. He was admitted to the university even though he scored only 9 out of 36 on the ACT entrance exam. While attending the university, other students took his exams for him and the athletic department hired a secretary to complete his homework assignments.

Dexter Manley and Kevin Ross are but two examples of players, particularly racial minorities, being used for their athletic talents so a university may benefit. In both cases, the players were streamlined into "easy" classes and had their assignments completed for them. After their eligibility was exhausted, the benefits stopped. Even though the NCAA and the U.S. Department of Education passed new rules concerning the academic progress of student-athletes, the abuses continue today. In a 2001 report, the NCAA analyzed graduation rates for men's basketball players who entered school between 1990 and 1994, or the equivalent of five straight recruiting classes. The NCAA study showed that 36 of the 323 Division I schools did not graduate *a single* African American athlete during that time. That some of the athletic programs were run by African

After studying this chapter, you should be able to:

- Define race, ethnicity, and minority group and describe the differences among these concepts.

- Discuss the experiences of racial minorities in the employment context, including variations in occupational status, wages earned, and employment decisions.

- Discuss the underrepresentation of racial minorities in the sport industry and identify factors that contribute to the underrepresentation.

- Understand the influence of race on the experiences of sport and physical activity participants.

American head coaches, such as Nolan Richardson at the University of Arkansas, indicates that the problem is not limited to those programs run by White head coaches.*

DIVERSITY CHALLENGE **R E F L E C T I O N**

1. How frequently are cases similar to those of Dexter Manley or Kevin Ross seen today?

2. Is a university "exploiting" a student-athlete if the school provides a scholarship in exchange for the basketball services?

3. Why do you think graduation rates of African American athletes are lower than those of White athletes competing in similar sports?

4. Are you surprised that some of the programs that graduated none of their African American athletes were run by African American head coaches?

---

*Information adapted from Moore, K. (2004, July 1). Tackling illiteracy: Former Washington Redskin Pro Bowl defensive end Dexter Manley keynote speaker, *The Connection Newspapers,* retrieved November 21, 2005, from www.connectionnewspapers.com/article.asp?archive=true&article=34303&paper=62&cat=109; *Outside the lines: Unable to read* (2002, May 17), ESPN: Page 2, retrieved November 22, 2005, from http://sports.espn.go.com/page2/tvlistings/show103transcript.html; Richardson: "I'm supposed to make a difference" (2002, February 28), ESPN.com, retrieved November 22, 2005, from http://espn.go.com/nbc/s/2002/0228/1342915.html.

A s the Diversity Challenge illustrates, issues of race are still a very important part of sport and physical activity. From an employment standpoint, race can impact the type of job one fills, access to certain jobs, the rate of promotion, and the representation in certain positions. From an athletic standpoint, one's race can influence the sports in which one participates, the positions played, and the treatment received while participating. Even decades after federal legislation outlawing racial discrimination, race influences virtually every aspect of sport and physical activity in some form or fashion.

The purpose of this chapter is to examine the categorical effects of race in greater detail by focusing on the experiences of racial minorities relative to those of Whites. The decision to focus the discussion in this manner was made for two reasons. First, racial oppression has been a significant factor in U.S. history. Feagin (2006, p. 2) claims that with its slavery ties, the United States represents "the only major Western country that was explicitly founded on racial oppression." Second, and in a related way, critical race theorists argue that such oppression is still present today and seen in the country's laws, cultures, and major institutions (Ladson-Billings & Tate, 1995; Tate, 1997). These two factors suggest that the experiences of racial minorities, as persons who have traditionally been oppressed, should be different from those of Whites. Similar trends have been observed in other countries around the world. As such, it is instrumental to consider the experiences of racial minorities relative to those of Whites.

In the first section, I define race, ethnicity, and minority group. The influence of race on general employment trends, such as occupational segregation and wages earned, is discussed next, followed by an examination of the factors that influence the underrepresentation of racial minorities in coaching and leadership positions within the sport industry. The chapter concludes with an examination of race on athletic participation.

Defining Race, Ethnicity, and Minority Group

To begin, it is important to understand the definitions of three key terms: race, ethnicity, and minority group (see Thomas & Dyall, 1999). Though race and ethnicity are used interchangeably at times, there are definite distinctions between them. As Eitzen and Sage (2003) explain, "race is a social category regarded as distinct because the members supposedly share some genetically transmitted traits" (p. 285). As this definition of *race* implies, classifying people into different races is based on biological characteristics and the presumed genetic dissimilarity of members of one race compared to members of another. *Ethnicity,* on the other hand, refers to the cultural heritage of a particular group of people, and as such, moves away from attempting to classify people based on biological characteristics (Coakley, 2004; Eitzen & Sage, 2003). Ethnic groups share a common culture, such as a language or dialect, a specific custom, or a shared history (Eitzen & Sage, 2003). Members of a specific ethnic group (e.g., Italian Americans, Irish Americans) share a way of life and have a common commitment to a specific set of norms, ideals, and values that construct their way of life.

Some research questions the scientific merit of the concept of race, with some suggesting that such classifications lack validity (Abercrombie, Hill, & Turner, 2000; Littlefield, Lieberman, & Reynolds, 1982). In fact, there are many more similarities than differences among people who are supposed to be from different races. Nevertheless, there are many reasons why its use continues. First, though classifications based on race have little scientific merit from a biological standpoint, there are social meanings attached to the term. As Coakley (2004) explains, the concept of race is ultimately based on socially constructed meanings associated with biological characteristics. In this way, race is a cultural creation. Second, the meanings people attach to race have substantial implications for everyone. The way people are treated, the social systems that are created, and privileges afforded to members of certain social groups are oftentimes centered around race. This is consistent with critical race theory, which supposes that race issues are at the forefront of organizational, political, educational, and other social issues (Ladson-Billings & Tate, 1995; Tate, 1997). It is, therefore, important to consider race, the meanings people attach to race, and various race theories in our study of sport and physical activity. In doing so, however, it is imperative to remember that *"traditional racial categories are based on the social meanings given to those similarities and differences, not on biology"* (Coakley, 2004, p. 288, emphasis in original).

Finally, we must understand the use of the term "minority." A *minority group* is a collection of individuals who share common characteristics and face discrimination in society because of their membership in that group (Coakley, 2004). Within the context of sport and physical activity, all members of non-White racial groups, such as African Americans, Hispanics, and so forth, are considered racial minorities. As Coakley (2004) notes, a minority group is simply an "identifiable collection of people who suffer disadvantages at the hands of others who define them as inferior or unworthy and have the power to affect their lives negatively" (p. 285).

General Racial Trends

To better understand the influence of race in society and the workplace in general, recall from Chapter 1 that the proportions of racial minorities in the United States are increasing, and consequently, the proportion of Whites is decreasing. According to U. S. Census Bureau estimates, though Whites represented 69.4 percent of the population in the year 2000, by 2050, they will account for just 50.1 percent. This growth is particularly evident in several regions throughout the United States where minorities are the majority in some states (e.g., California, Hawaii, New Mexico, and Texas). Other nations, such as Canada and New Zealand, have recently witnessed a sizeable growth in the proportion of some racial minority groups as well.

Though racial minorities represent a substantial proportion of the population, their treatment oftentimes is poor. In the United States, consider the history of slavery, laws in the 18th and 19th centuries legalizing segregation, the occurrence of race riots such as those in Los Angeles in the 1990s, the continued discrimination in certain sectors of society such as housing, and the increased incidence of hate crimes. According to the U. S. Census Bureau, relative to Whites, Hispanics, African Americans, and Native Americans are less likely to graduate from high school or from college. With regard to health, research shows that, relative to Whites, African Americans live shorter lives, have almost twice the number of infant mortalities, have lower self-reports of their health, and have a higher incidence of various illnesses including hypertension, AIDS, diabetes, and certain forms of cancer (see Schnittker & McLeod, 2005, for a thorough review of the literature). Although socioeconomic status has some bearing on these findings, the research found that race also has independent effects (e.g., Williams, 1997). Though some variations exist, similar trends are present for Hispanics and Native Americans (cf., Schnittker & McLeod, 2005). Thus, consistent with Coakley's (2004) definition, racial minorities are likely to be disadvantaged in society in general.

Race in the Employment Context

The negative impact of race seen in society at large is also observed in the employment context. Prior research shows that race influences earnings, positions held, and employment decisions (see Exhibit 4.1). Each of these issues is discussed in turn.

Earnings

U. S. Census Bureau data provide considerable evidence of the earnings differences among various racial groups. As of 2002, African Americans and Hispanics were much more likely to live in poverty (24.1 and 21.8 percent, respectively) than were Asians (10.3 percent) or Whites (8.0 percent). Another indicator of earnings differences is the median household income and how such incomes vary based on the householder's race. Incomes were highest for Asian

---

The influence of race in the employment context.   *Exhibit 4.1*

Earnings:

- Median income levels are lower for some racial minorities, such as African Americans and Hispanics, than for Whites.

Positions held:

- Whites are more likely to be employed in management and professional positions, while African Americans and Hispanics are more likely to work in service positions.

Employment decisions:

- Relative to Whites, African Americans and Hispanics are likely to have poorer interview ratings, lower performance evaluations, and lower ratings for promotion potential.

householders ($51,908) and lowest for African American householders ($29,423). Whites ($45,367) and Hispanics ($33,676) fell in between those two median incomes. Not surprisingly, the same pattern emerges when we examine the median income across races (see Exhibit 4.2). Asians reported the highest median income ($52,285), followed by Whites ($46,900), Hispanics ($33,103), and African Americans ($29,177). These data also indicate that Whites are much more likely to earn at least $50,000 (47.4 percent) than Hispanics (31.6 percent) or African Americans (27.2 percent) (see Exhibit 4.3). These figures demonstrate the influence of race on monies earned, as in each case, Hispanics and African Americans earned less than their White counterparts.

Positions Held

According to Cokley, Dreher, and Stockdale (2004), *occupational segregation* is "the extent to which individuals of various racial/ethnic backgrounds are disproportionately represented in various occupational groupings" (p. 170). The U. S. Census Bureau developed a taxonomy of six occupational groups: (a) management and professional; (b) service; (c) sales and office; (d) farming, fish-

| Exhibit 4.2 | Median incomes by racial group, as of 2002. |

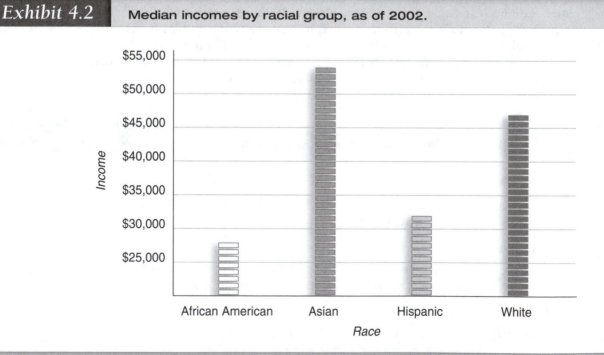

U. S. Census Bureau data.

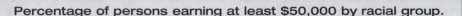

Percentage of persons earning at least $50,000 by racial group.   *Exhibit 4.3*

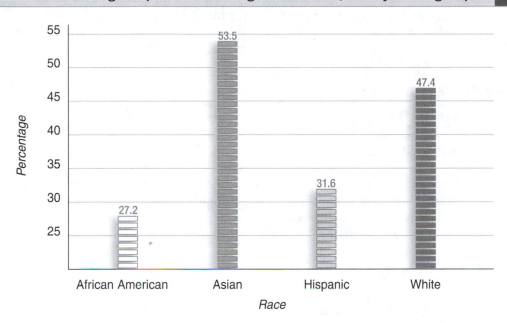

U. S. Census Bureau data.

ing, and forestry; (e) construction, extraction, and maintenance; and (f) production, transportation, and material moving. These six groups are further broken down into 509 occupation categories. For purposes of this discussion, we will only examine the influence of race on the proportion of people in the six major occupational categories.

Data from the 2000 Census indicate that there are differences in the positions people hold based on their race. For example, both African Americans and Hispanics are most likely to hold sales or office jobs (27.3 and 23.1 percent, respectively), while Whites are most likely to hold management, professional, and related positions (36.6 percent). Only 25.2 percent of African Americans and 18.1 percent of Hispanics reported having a management-type job. Furthermore, African Americans (22.0 percent) and Hispanics (21.8 percent) were more likely than Whites (12.8 percent) to hold service jobs.

Employment Decisions

In Chapter 3, I highlighted the two forms of discrimination and how such discrimination impacts various work outcomes, such as access to positions (access discrimination) and job performance ratings (treatment discrimination). Using this information, we can examine racial differences in three types of employment situations: job interview ratings, performance evaluations, and promotion potential ratings. In all cases, racial minorities receive lower scores than their White counterparts.

Interview Ratings

Huffcutt and Roth (1998) conducted a meta-analysis of 31 studies related to race and interview ratings. They found that, across all studies, African Americans and Hispanics were rated more poorly than Whites. The racial differences were even more pronounced when the interview was not structured and when the job was relatively simple in nature. These differences were nonexistent, however, when the job was complex. The authors reasoned that because highly complex jobs require extensive education, training, and expertise, the applicant pool was considered elite. Alternatively, it is possible that minorities who interviewed for these jobs were coveted by the organizations to which they applied.

Performance Evaluations

Stauffer and Buckley (2005) found that race influenced employee performance ratings. For White employees, ratings by African American supervisors were the same as those given by White supervisors; however, they found that for African American employees, White supervisors rated their performance significantly lower than did African American supervisors. Furthermore, the ratings White supervisors gave White employees were significantly higher than the ratings they assigned African Americans. Because of the importance of performance appraisals in the work context (e.g., Cunningham & Dixon, 2003), such bias severely limits the career success of African Americans.

Promotion Potential

Other research found evidence that race influences promotion potential ratings. Landau (1995) surveyed more than 1,200 employees of a Fortune 500 company, all of whom had either a moderate or high potential for advancement. After accounting for other variables that may influence the results (e.g., age, organizational tenure, position, salary, education, and satisfaction with support), she found that African Americans were rated as possessing significantly less promotion potential than their White counterparts. Similarly, Greenhaus, Parasuraman, and Wormley (1990) found that African Americans, relative to Whites, received lower ratings of promotion potential and were more likely to have reached their career plateau.

The Influence of Race on Employee Work Outcomes in Sport Organizations

As in the general employment context, research in the context of sport and physical activity demonstrates that racial minorities generally experience work negatively and are sometimes held to higher standards than Whites (Madden, 2004). There is also evidence of occupational segregation. The following section examines these trends. Because most, but by no means all, of the research in this area focuses on university athletics, the discussion here does as well. Where data are available, I also examine race and employee outcomes in other contexts. Exhibit 4.4 provides an overview of the primary areas addressed.

Representation of Racial Minorities

The representation of racial minorities is mixed and depends largely on the context (i.e., professional sport versus university athletics) and the employee's race. Lapchick's *2004 Racial and Gender Report Card* (2004) is a publication devoted to tracking the representation of women and minorities in various sport entities. Grades are assigned to the professional leagues and university athletics based on the proportion of persons of color in the league or university relative

---

The influence of race on work outcomes in sport organizations.   *Exhibit 4.4*

Representation of racial minorities:

- Racial minorities are overrepresented as players in some sports (e.g., basketball or football).

- Racial minorities are underrepresented, relative to the pool of potential applicants, in both coaching and administrative positions.

Occupational segregation:

- In many cases, racial minorities only have access to certain positions within sport organizations. For example, they may be overrepresented in some positions (e.g., academic advisor) and underrepresented in others (e.g., business manager).

Reasons for racial minority underrepresentation:

- Potential reasons for the underrepresentation of racial minorities in coaching and leadership positions include treatment discrimination, limited advancement opportunities, occupational turnover, and access discrimination.

to their representation in the general U. S. population. In his *2004 Report Card,* Lapchick assigned the following grades:

- National Basketball Association = A
- National Football League = B
- Major League Baseball = B+
- Major League Soccer = C+
- Women's National Basketball Association = A
- University Athletics = B–

In many cases, Lapchick notes differences within a specific context. For example, within university athletics, Lapchick wrote "opportunities for people of color in men's sports other than basketball remained poor." Given the abysmal hiring practices in other sports (e.g., football, see Chapter 3), Lapchick's conclusions in this area appear accurate.

Coaches

Lapchick's work is widely cited in both the popular press such as ESPN and in academic works, and his work has made a substantial contribution to the field. It is possible, however, that Lapchick's assessments are overly generous. Recall that grades in the *Report Card* are assigned based on the representation of persons of color in the league or university relative to the proportion of those persons in the general population. This rationale is based on affirmative action guidelines set by the federal government. However, from a practical standpoint, not all people in a population have an equal chance to enter a particular league or sport, especially as a coach. Rather, many researchers argue that former players represent the largest pool of potential coaches (e.g., Everhart & Chelladurai, 1998). Current research supports this contention, as most coaches once participated in university athletics (Cunningham & Sagas, 2002). Therefore, it is argued that the comparison should be to the proportion of racial minorities who played that sport (Cunningham & Sagas, 2005), not to the proportion of racial minorities in the general U.S. population. When this approach is adopted, a much different picture emerges related to coaches.

Using professional sports as an example (see Exhibit 4.5), in the NBA, persons of color represented 78 percent of all the players during the 2003–2004 season. This percentage has remained relatively stable over the years, as persons of color represented 79 percent of the players in the 1993–1994 season. Despite the large proportion of racial minorities as players, they represented just 37 percent of the head coaches and 29 percent of the assistant coaches. Of course, many factors contribute to the selection of head coach, of which only one may be previous playing experience. There are some head coaches, such as Laurence Franks of the New Jersey Nets, who did not play at the professional level.

However, such a large difference in the proportion of minority players relative to the proportion of minority coaches suggests that race may play a role in selecting head and assistant coaches.

The numbers are even more disproportionate when we examine other sports. In the NFL, racial minorities represented over 70 percent of the participants during the 2003 season, but just 9 percent of the head coaches and 33 percent of the assistant coaches (Lapchick, 2004). During the 2003–2004 academic year, racial minority athletes represented over 51 percent of Division I-A football players (Bray, 2005), yet constituted just 2.9 percent of the head coaches and 27.4 percent of the assistant coaches (DeHass, 2004). This trend is also seen in the high school ranks as evidenced in the Diversity in the Field box.

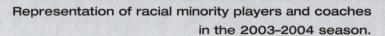

Representation of racial minority players and coaches in the 2003–2004 season.

Exhibit 4.5

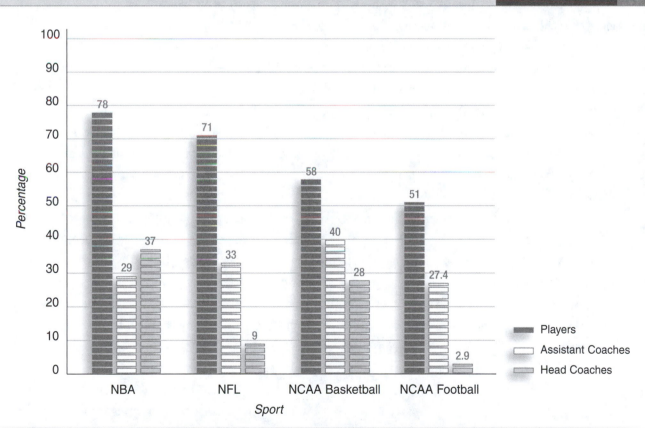

Adapted from Bray, 2005; DeHass, 2004; and Lapchick, 2004.

DIVERSITY *in the field*

Underrepresentation of African Americans as High School Coaches. The underrepresentation of African Americans as football head coaches is widely documented in the college and professional ranks. The problem also exists at the high school level, and sometimes to a greater degree than in other contexts. Matt Wixon of the *Dallas Morning News* documented this trend (Wixon, 2006). Specifically, Wixon found that although minorities might have access to positions in inner-city schools, they are oftentimes not afforded opportunities in suburban schools. In 2002, of the 66 Class 5A and 4A (the two largest classifications in Texas) football teams in the Dallas area, only 4 were led by an African American. The numbers grew even bleaker in 2006, as only 3 of 72 teams had an African American head coach.

Coaches and athletic directors in the area surveyed by Wixon pointed to several contributing factors. Mike Robinson, an African American head coach at Hillcrest, said that "It wasn't what you've done or what you know. It's who you know." Garland ISD athletic director Homer Johnson acknowledged this possibility when he suggested that some coaches don't get hired because the athletic directors do not know them that well.

Others suggested that African American coaches lack experience. Joe Barnett, the Irving ISD athletic director, suggested that "sometimes maybe they [African Americans] don't have the experience because they haven't been given the opportunity somewhere else. It's hard to get that experience if you don't get hired. It's a Catch-22."

Although the lack of experience may impede the progress of some coaches, there are other instances where very qualified assistant coaches were not afforded the chance to become a head coach. Dallas Carter coach Allen Wilson is one such example. Despite serving as an assistant coach on two state championship teams and having 19 years of experience, Wilson has repeatedly been denied a head coaching position.

The effects of continually being passed over for head coaching positions can have a harmful effect on African Americans. Kendall Miller, an African American who serves as the offensive coordinator at Lincoln High School, has applied for five positions over the past two years only to be passed over each time. He suggested that there is a "feeling of restriction" when it comes to the schools at which one can become a head coach. He explained that "after a while, it makes you think, 'Why go through with it?' because you've seen the track record. But at the same time, you have to make yourself go through with it because you don't want to allow the excuse, 'Well, they're not applying.'" Thus, despite the lack of opportunity, these African American high school coaches continue to press forward in their quest for head coaching opportunities.

Considered together, these figures represent a mixed picture with respect to coaching. On the one hand, basketball, both at the professional and university levels, appears to be relatively open to racial minorities. However, a closer examination of the proportions suggests that relative to the pool of potential coaches (i.e., the athletes), the proportions of racial minorities in coaching positions are lower than might be expected. These differences are further amplified when we consider other sports such as professional and university football. Overall then, it can be argued that minorities are underrepresented in coaching positions.

Administration

In the previous section, I suggested that past playing experience was often a requisite qualification for becoming a coach of a particular team. The same is not necessarily true for administrative positions. Understanding how to navigate the intricacies of a salary cap, knowing how to market a particular product, making personnel decisions, and so on require business acumen more than previous playing experience. Theo Epstein, who served as the general manager of the Boston Red Sox from 2002–2005, and Jon Daniels, who was hired as the Texas Rangers general manager in 2005, both exemplify this point—neither had professional playing experience. Therefore, all persons have as much of an opportunity to be an administrator of a sport organization as they do in any other organization. Because the opportunity is available to everyone, it is possible to use the proportion of racial minorities in the general U. S. population (31.6 percent) as a comparison marker when examining the proportion of minorities in administrative positions in sport organizations.

Even using this more conservative comparison point, the data still suggest that minorities are underrepresented in administrative positions. As shown by the following statistics, the majority of the senior administrators in all professional leagues and university athletics are White (DeHass, 2004; Lapchick, 2004):

- National Basketball Association: 84 percent
- National Football League: 84 percent
- Major League Baseball: 83 percent
- Major League Soccer: 90 percent
- Women's National Basketball Association: 81 percent
- National Collegiate Athletic Association: 89 percent

These figures illustrate that Whites are overrepresented as senior administrators within sport organizations (81–90 percent) relative to what is expected based on their proportion in the general U. S. population (69.1 percent). As with the coaching positions, racial minorities are underrepresented as senior administrators.

Occupational Segregation

Earlier in the chapter, I discussed occupational segregation in the general employment context, noting that racial minorities are more likely to hold certain jobs (e.g., service) than others (e.g., management). This segregation also occurs in the sport context. Using football as an example, racial minorities are likely to coach running backs and wide receivers (Anderson, 1993) and unlikely to serve as a coordinator of the defense or offense (DeHass, 2004). There is also some sentiment among minority football coaches that they are hired primarily to aid in the recruitment of minority athletes, not necessarily for their coaching expertise (Brown, 2002). Similar findings occur in the basketball context. Recent research shows that on basketball coaching staffs, Whites are significantly more likely to hold the first assistant position than African Americans; the second assistant position is more likely to be filled by an African American (Cunningham & Sagas, 2004a).

Similar trends exist among university athletics administrators. Data from the NCAA (DeHass, 2004) indicate that racial minorities are more likely to hold positions that involve contact with athletes, such as academic advisor (27.2 percent) or life skills coordinator (25.4 percent), than they are to hold positions dealing with budgetary or administrative duties. Only 13.1 percent of all business managers and 9.1 percent of all head athletic directors are racial minorities. Together, these data suggest that persons of color are likely to be "pigeonholed" into certain types of jobs, both in the coaching and administrative areas.

Reasons for Racial Minority Underrepresentation

This section examines the reasons for racial minority underrepresentation. The discussion here focuses on the underrepresentation in coaching positions, though many of the identified factors can be used to explain the underrepresentation in administrative positions.

In general, it is expected that treatment discrimination and limited advancement opportunities will combine to result in greater occupational turnover for minority coaches relative to White coaches. Note also that these two factors can negatively influence those athletes thinking of entering the profession. The high turnover rate among active coaches limits the potential applicant pool, leading to the underrepresentation of minority coaches. Other factors also contribute to the underrepresentation (e.g., access discrimination and donor/alumni expectations). Finally, these relationships are thought to be moderated by the context; that is, the sport coached. Each of these factors is discussed in greater detail next, and a summary is presented in Exhibit 4.6.

Treatment Discrimination

As discussed in Chapter 3, treatment discrimination "occurs when subgroup members receive fewer rewards, resources, or opportunities on the job than they legitimately deserve on the basis of job-related criteria" (Greenhaus et al.,

Reasons for the underrepresentation of racial minorities
in coaching positions.   *Exhibit 4.6*

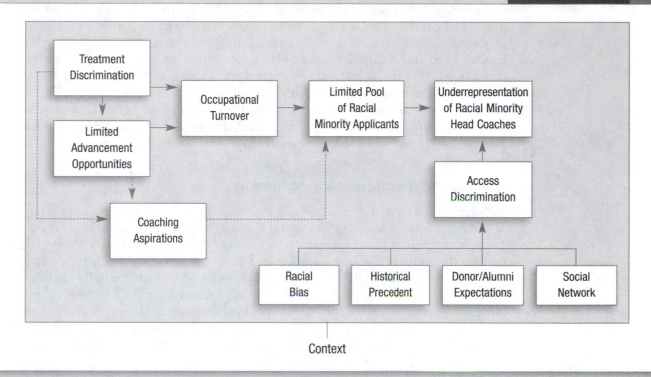

Reasons for the underrepresentation of racial minorities in coaching positions.

Exhibit 4.6

1990, pp. 64–65). There is considerable evidence pointing to the incidence of treatment discrimination among racial minority coaches. Some coaches face discrimination while coaching athletic contests. One athlete involved in a study recalled "one time, we were playing this one team and the (opposing) coach spit on him (our coach). One of our opponents we was playing, he spit on our coach and called him a nigger. Our coach stared at him, and just walked away. We were pretty shocked" (Lawrence, 2004, p. 106). Others report discrimination in their work as a coach. Brown (2002) reported that many minority coaches believed they were hired to fill a quota and were not treated the same as their White counterparts.

There is also empirical evidence to support these sentiments. Sagas and Cunningham (2005) surveyed 387 assistant coaches of NCAA Division I-A football teams. They assessed the coaches' human capital, social capital, and career success, as measured by career satisfaction, number of promotions, and proximity to the head coaching position. *Human capital* relates to one's investment in terms of education attained, previous playing experience, and tenure as a coach. *Social capital* is concerned with the contacts one has in the industry and the strength of such relationships. It is expected that the more people invest in their human and social capital, the better they will fare in their careers (Nordhaug, 1993; Seibert, Kraimer, & Liden, 2001). As expected, the human and social capital variables were, by and large, related to the various measures of career success. However, even after accounting for these investments, the coach's race still had independent effects on career success. Racial minority coaches enjoyed less career success than their White counterparts, even when considering the minority coaches' human and social capital investments. These results point to the treatment discrimination of racial minority coaches and support other sources documenting similar effects, both in university athletics (e.g., Brown, 2002) and in professional sport (Madden, 2004).

Limited Advancement Opportunities

Research suggests that persons of color face considerable challenges advancing in the profession. A study by Sagas and Cunningham (2005) showed that racial minorities received fewer promotions than their White counterparts. As noted earlier, the same is true for advancement from an assistant coach to a head coach. According to Hill (2004), there have been 381 head football coaching vacancies at the Division I-A level since 1982. Of those, only 19 were filled by African Americans, or roughly 4 percent. Furthermore, in the entire history of Division I-A football, African Americans were selected to lead a team only 21 times. These figures certainly paint the picture of limited opportunities for career advancement for coaches of color.

Occupational Turnover

Occupational turnover is another factor that contributes to the underrepresentation of racial minority coaches. When minority coaches leave at a faster rate than their White counterparts, or plan on leaving at an earlier age, this creates a limited pool of potential coaches from which to select head coaches. The available research in this area demonstrates racial differences in the occupational turnover of coaches. In one study, Cunningham, Sagas, and Ashley (2001) surveyed 152 assistant basketball coaches from Division I universities and asked them about their commitment to coaching and their intention to leave the profession. After controlling for personal characteristics (e.g., age, coaching tenure, and race of their head coach) and occupational commitment, race was still a significant predictor of occupational turnover intentions. Cunningham and Sagas (2004b) had similar results in their study of football assistant coaches. These results support the notion that race influences one's plans to leave coaching, such that racial minorities have greater turnover intentions than their White counterparts (for additional support, see Cunningham, Bruening, & Straub, 2006; Cunningham & Sagas, in press).

Access Discrimination

As noted in Chapter 3, access discrimination denies members of a particular social category an opportunity to obtain a particular job or enter a certain profession (Greenhaus et al., 1990). Access discrimination is prevalent in several areas of sport, and coaching is no exception (see Lapchick, 2004). As previously discussed, head coaching is oftentimes viewed as a position to which racial minorities have limited or no access. This may be because of historical precedent, social networks, racial bias on the part of those doing the hiring, or donor and alumni expectations. Each of these issues is discussed in turn.

Historical precedent. In light of the history of passing over racial minorities for coaching positions, hiring a person of color may be considered as something outside the norm. Even with today's social pressures to have a more diverse workplace (see Chapter 1), it may be easier for athletic directors and university presidents to hire White coaches than to hire a minority. This precedent may serve to limit the access of those who are not White to head coaching positions.

Social network. Social networks influence who is hired in several ways. It is incumbent upon the assistant coach to form social networks and contacts within the industry. Through the network, the coaches learn of job openings, identify who to contact, and meet people who will sponsor them for a coaching position; that is, they know people who will speak on their behalf once a position becomes available (see the Professional Perspectives box). Research shows that racial minority coaches have more racially diverse social networks than White coaches. This is significant because earlier research demonstrated that mixed-race social networks are generally weaker than those networks comprised of people of the same race as the coach (Ibarra, 1993; Kram, 1988). There is also less support and personal attraction among the network members when the network is mixed-race (Ibarra, 1993). Thus, minority coaches' networks are likely to provide fewer returns and benefits than the White coaches' networks.

PROFESSIONAL
PERSPECTIVES

Creating and Maintaining Networks. Gary Sailes is an applied sport sociologist who has considerable experience consulting with athletes and teams. His expertise and primary research interests are in the area of racial issues in university and professional sports. When asked what racial minorities could do to advance in the profession, Sailes indicated that networking was most important. "People hire people who they know. It's that simple. I don't care if you're Black, White, male, female, ethnic minority, or majority, people hire who they know. So you have to get yourself out there and meet the people who are doing the hiring," Sailes explained. Networking provides many advantages. It affords more visibility and provides greater access to information. In addition, Sailes believes that because networking allows people to know the applicant on a more personal level, any personal biases held by the decision maker may be overcome. As he notes, "This will go a long ways toward your advancement."

It is also important to examine the networks of those doing the hiring; namely, the athletic directors. Athletic directors have social networks that they rely on for information concerning potential applicants for a coaching vacancy, and these networks tend to be comprised of people demographically similar to the director (e.g., White, middle-aged men; Brooks & Althouse, 2000). As noted in an earlier chapter, people are more likely to hire someone racially similar to the self than someone who is racially different (Carington & Troske, 1998; Stoll, Raphael, & Holzer, 2004). This holds true for athletic directors when hiring coaches. Brooks and Althouse (2000) note, "coaches and athletic directors perpetuate their subculture by hiring their duplicates" (p. 97).

Racial bias. As noted in Chapter 3, racial bias can be either overt or subtle in nature. Overt racial bias, or traditional racism, is those negative attitudes toward persons different from the self that people consciously and deliberately maintain (Dovidio, Kawakami, & Beach, 2001). On the other hand, aversive racial biases operate in an unconscious fashion and are not necessarily the result of negative attitudes toward dissimilar others (Devine, Plant, & Blair, 2001). If organizational decision makers harbor biases, the opportunities for racial minorities to be selected as head coach are reduced.

Donor and alumni expectations. It is possible that the commercialization of university athletics and the need to generate monies from donors and alumni have hurt racial minorities' employment opportunities. Because athletic departments rely so heavily on donations, they staff with whom the donors can identify. This is especially the case for football, a sport that is oftentimes considered the "front porch" of an institution (Beyer & Hannah, 2000). As Michael Rosenberg of the *Detroit Free Press* (2004) notes:

> It is largely about money. It is about a face to show the alumni, especially the ones with big wallets. College coaches don't just coach; they are, in many ways, the public faces of their schools. And if the big donors don't like a coach because of his weight/accent/skin color, schools will stay away.

Lapchick (cited in Wong, 2002, p. 1) drew similar conclusions:

> I have had discussions with people in searches for coaches and athletic directors that the final decision was made to hire a White male because they were afraid their alumni, who also happen to be strong boosters of the football program, would not contribute nearly as much or as readily to an African American athletic director or football coach.

The preference for White coaches over coaches of color may be influenced by school boosters who have a need to identify with the head coach and do donate large sums of money to support the department's activities.

Relationships Among the Constructs

The discussion thus far focused on several constructs that are thought to impact the underrepresentation of racial minorities in head coaching positions. This section discusses the relationships among these constructs. As seen in Exhibit 4.6, treatment discrimination is expected to be positively related to turnover intentions and negatively related to career advancement opportunities. When people face discrimination at work, they are unlikely to have pleasant work experiences, have high job satisfaction, or be committed to their work (Button, 2001; Greenhaus et al., 1990). All of these factors likely contribute to people choosing to leave their line of work. In a similar way, people subjected to treatment discrimination are likely to have limited opportunities for promotion and advancement. This results from limited training and development opportunities, a lack of resources, poor work assignments, and general bias against them (Button, 2001; Greenhaus et al., 1990). Thus, treatment discrimination should impact both advancement opportunities and turnover behavior.

The higher turnover rate of racial minorities, relative to Whites, then creates a shortage of potential minority coaches to fill head coaching positions. Tsui and Gutek (1999) note that "small effects could accumulate and lead to non-trivial consequences. For example, a small tendency for the most different groups to leave can, over time, result in increasingly more homogeneous groups as one moves up the organizational hierarchy" (p. 40). There is evidence of this in Division I-A football, where racial minorities constitute approximately 28 percent of the assistant coaches, but less than 4 percent of the head coaches (DeHass, 2004). The limited pool of racial minority applicants, coupled with the incidence of access discrimination, directly relates to the underrepresentation of minority head coaches.

Note that Exhibit 4.6 has dashed lines from treatment discrimination and limited advancement opportunities to coaching aspirations. The lines are dashed because these two factors are thought to influence the aspirations not of current coaches, but of prospective coaches; that is, current athletes. Support for this prediction comes from a study (Cunningham, 2004) of NCAA football players, where African Americans were found to have less interest in becoming a head coach than White players. African Americans also reported fewer perceived opportunities to become a coach than did their White counterparts, and there was a relatively strong correlation between perceived opportunity and an interest in entering the coaching profession. Cunningham reasoned that because the African American players were aware of the discrimination and truncated career opportunities coaches of color face, they did not consider coaching a viable career alternative. Similar propositions are advanced here.

That racial minority athletes are less likely to enter the coaching profession than White athletes (Cunningham, 2004) creates a supply-side problem in terms of the pool of available coaches. If racial minorities are not likely to enter coaching and current minority coaches are likely to leave the profession at an earlier age than White coaches, then the pool of potential racial minority coaches from which to choose is limited.

The Sport Coached (as a Boundary Condition or Moderator)

In Chapter 2, we saw that theory contains boundary conditions, or *moderators*. Recall that boundary conditions are assumptions about values, space, and time. They place "if–then" conditions or caveats on the expected relationships among the constructs set forth in propositions (Bacharach, 1989). In our current discussion, the sport coached is thought to serve as a moderator. Persons of color do not face the same environment in all sports. Some contexts, such as basketball, are thought to be more convivial than others (e.g., football or hockey). Because of these potential differences, it is erroneous to assume that the previously discussed relationships will hold true for all racial minority coaches across all contexts.

Current research supports this rationale. Cunningham et al. (2006) conducted two studies—one qualitative in nature, the other quantitative—that examined the reasons for the underrepresentation of African Americans in head coaching positions. Across both studies, the researchers found dissimilarities between football coaches and basketball coaches. In general, racial minority football coaches, relative to basketball coaches of color, planned on leaving the profession at an earlier age, perceived less opportunity for career advancement, and perceived their race to serve as a barrier. Furthermore, in the basketball context, *White* coaches perceived opportunity for career advancement as a *greater* barrier than did African Americans. These results illustrate the need to consider contextual factors (such as the sport coached) and demonstrate that not all coaches experience work the same (see also Cunningham & Sagas, in press).

Race and Employee Outcomes in Other Contexts

Thus far, the focus was primarily on employees in the university athletics context. Though many of the overall trends are similar to those experienced by coaches and administrators, it is also useful to consider the effects of race on employees in other contexts, such as professors of color in higher education. Lavigne (2003) demonstrated that the proportion of racial minorities in faculty positions lags behind national population trends. In a similar way, Turner, Myers, and Creswell (1999) found that African Americans, Native Americans, and Latinos are underrepresented in faculty positions and that they receive poorer compensation than Asians or Whites. The same is true for faculty in kinesiology and physical education programs. Hodge and Stroot (1997) found that encountering racism is a fact of life among African American graduate students and faculty members in physical education programs. The racism is believed to manifest from the White undergraduate students, faculty members, and persons in the community. In a different study, Burden, Harrison, and Hodge (2005) interviewed nine African American physical education faculty members concerning the faculty members' experiences on primarily White campuses. In framing their study from a critical race theory perspective, these authors found that the faculty members experienced social isolation, were perceived as intellectually inferior, and were marginalized. These studies, and others like them, paint a consistent picture of racial minority faculty members facing considerable obstacles on university campuses.

Issues of race are also prevalent among people working in the recreation profession. Allison and Hibbler's (2004) qualitative study of recreational professionals illustrates this point. Professionals in their study argued that the racial makeup of the community in which the recreational agency operates should inform hiring decisions. As one professional noted, "I'm not saying that if you're in a barrio that's 95 percent Hispanic, that every single staff person should be Hispanic, but you should have a good representation of Hispanics on that staff" (p. 269). Similar sentiments were expressed concerning the language spoken (see the Professional Perspectives box). The professionals also noted that if there was a desire to design a program emphasizing diversity, it was left to the agency's racial minority members to design the program. Such programs were seldom seen as central or integral to the agency's functioning.

PROFESSIONAL PERSPECTIVES

Knowing the Language. Buffy Filippell is the President of Teamwork Online, LLC, an organization aimed at identifying and recruiting individuals for jobs in the sport industry. According to Filippell, sport organizations are making concerted efforts to diversify. As she explains, "There is a real push on behalf of the professional sports organizations that I'm familiar with to really try to reach out and capture as many diverse candidates and female candidates as possible." This push is much more intense than in years past. In addition to demographic diversity, sport organizations are increasingly looking to employ people who know a variety of languages. Filippell explains that for some sport organizations in the southwestern and western areas of the United States, such as Arizona and California, it is imperative that an employee be bilingual because much of the customer base is primarily Spanish-speaking. Thus, many forms of diversity are needed to ensure that sport organizations run effectively and efficiently.

The Influence of Race on Participants' Experiences

Just as it does for the sport and physical activity organizations' employees, race plays an influential role among participants. It influences the sports in which people participate, the positions they play on athletic teams, the stereotypes and attitudes toward athletes, athletes' treatment, and their career success. Each of these issues is discussed in turn (see Exhibit 4.7).

Sport and Leisure Participation

Historically, slavery, racism, and segregation limited the participation of racial minorities in sport. More recently, race influences sport participation primarily through two dynamics: socioeconomic status and cultural norms.

| Exhibit 4.7 | The influence of race on participants' experiences. |

Sport and leisure participation:

- Race influences the amount of participation and in which sport one participates. Other factors that contribute to sport and leisure participation include socioeconomic status and cultural norms.

Positions played on athletic teams:

- Racial minorities are overrepresented in some positions and underrepresented in others, a phenomenon known as stacking.

Stereotypes and attitudes:

- People develop stereotypes about sport participants related to their cognitive and "natural" athletic abilities.

Athlete treatment:

- Racial minority athletes are often treated differently than their White counterparts in such areas as academic advising, graduation rates, treatment by administrators and coaches, and opportunities for sport participation and in life after sports.

Socioeconomic Status

From a socioeconomic standpoint, the members of many racial minority groups are less affluent than Whites—a point discussed previously. Variations in household income levels often account for the differences in discretionary income—the more discretionary income one has, the more money can be spent on participating in sport, recreation, and leisure activities. This relationship explains, at least in part, why racial minorities are less likely to participate in some sport and leisure activities than their White counterparts (see Hibbler & Shinew, 2002).

Socioeconomic status influences not only the amount of sport and leisure participation, but also the types of activities in which one participates. Some sports, such as golf, require expensive equipment and high participation fees (e.g., green fees or club memberships). Therefore, only people with high levels of discretionary income participate in these sports on a regular basis. On the other hand, other activities, such as basketball or soccer, require fewer financial resources. Because access to a ball and a field or court is all that is necessary to take part in these activities, they are much more accessible to all segments of the population, irrespective of socioeconomic status. These equipment and cost variations, coupled with the racial differences in socioeconomic status, explain why Whites are overrepresented in some sports such as golf, while persons of color are overrepresented in others, such as basketball.

Cultural Norms

Cultural norms also influence sport participation. Eitzen and Sage (2003) report that two of the more popular sports among Hispanics are soccer and baseball. Both sports are popular in Latin American countries, and many of the sports' top stars (e.g., Alex Rodriguez, Carlos Delgado) have a Latin heritage. Furthermore, Univision, the largest Spanish-language television network in the United States, regularly broadcasts soccer contests. These factors spur the popularity of these sports among Hispanics, resulting in increased Hispanic participation, especially in relation to other sports.

Positions Played on Athletic Teams

Just as race influences the positions employees hold in organizations, it also impacts the positions athletes play on teams. This phenomenon, called *stacking,* occurs when "minority athletes are overrepresented in some playing positions and underrepresented in others" (Sack, Singh, & Thiel, 2005, pp. 300–301). Research demonstrates that stacking exists across a variety of contexts, including baseball (Gonzales, 1996), rugby (Hallinan, 1991), and hockey (Lavoie, 1989; see also the Alternative perspectives box). Understanding why stacking occurs, however, is less clear.

Two theories are traditionally used to explain the incidence of stacking: social closure theory and human capital theory. *Social closure* theory holds that organizational decision makers intentionally discriminate against women and persons of color, and as a result, the high-status, high-paying jobs are reserved for White men (Bonacich, 1972; Weeden, 2002). Applied to the sport context, this means that central, important positions (e.g., catcher in baseball) should be set aside for Whites, while more peripheral positions (e.g., right field in baseball) are occupied by racial minorities. Some authors also suggest that segregation occurs because of stereotypes about the players; for example, central positions are occupied by players with high

alternative PERSPECTIVES

Is It Really Stacking? Although many studies support the existence of stacking in various sport contexts, others question the premise behind stacking. Chelladurai (2005) argues that *geographically* central positions, such as the center or quarterback position in football, are not necessarily *functionally* central positions. Rather, it is primarily those who play wide receiver or running back who are charged with advancing the ball down field for a touchdown. The other team positions play only a supporting role. From this perspective, the wide receiver and running back positions are the team's key positions. As Chelladurai (2005) notes, "the assertion that there is discrimination against black players in football cannot be sustained by these data. In fact, it can be argued that it is whites who are precluded from the functionally central positions" (p. 409).

mental capabilities (e.g., Whites), while peripheral positions are occupied by those with "natural" athletic ability (e.g., minorities).

Human capital theory, on the other hand, holds that differences in position assignment should be a function of the variations in the skills and abilities one possesses (Nordhaug, 1993). In the sport context, human capital might include strength, speed, and size (Sack et al., 2005). Applying this theory, the position assignment for an athlete is based on the skills and abilities the athlete possesses, not the intentional discrimination by the decision maker.

Sack et al. (2005) tested these two theories in the MLB context. As expected, the authors found that 71 percent of the African Americans played in the outfield, relative to 25 percent of the White players and 36 percent of the Hispanic players. Furthermore, Whites were more likely than players of color to occupy the catcher position—a position central to the team's ability to function. After accounting for variations in speed and power, the effects of race on playing position still existed, albeit in a reduced fashion. These findings support the social closure theory by suggesting that baseball managers might be "assigning disproportionate numbers of African Americans to the outfield because of racial prejudice or for other reasons that have little to do with the skills the players bring to the league" (p. 313).

Stereotypes and Attitudes

Another way race influences the experiences of sport participants is through stereotypes and attitudes. The stereotypes primarily involve issues related to the athletes' cognitive and "natural" athletic abilities (Sailes, 2000). Stereotypes about athletes' academic prowess, or the lack thereof, have long been advanced (e.g., the "dumb jock"). Although all athletes may be, to some degree, the target of these stereotypes, African American athletes are especially vulnerable to such thinking. Some research suggests that White college students (a) perceive they perform better academically than African American athletes, (b) view African American athletes as academically unprepared to enter the university context, and (c) anticipate that African American athletes' academic performance will be poor (Sailes, 1993).

In addition to the negative opinions people have about the cognitive abilities of racial minority athletes, there are stereotypes concerning their athletic abilities (Sailes, 2000). For many athletes of color, athletic success is attributed to their "natural" abilities rather than their superior preparation, strategy, or motivation—an attribution that ultimately serves to diminish the athletes' accomplishments. These attitudes are also sometimes held by coaches, as is demonstrated in the Diversity in the Field box.

The stereotypes that negatively affect athletes of color also negatively impact White athletes. Coakley (2004) reports that many White athletes chose sports other than basketball and track because they believe that they cannot possibly compete with the more gifted racial minority athletes. As Coakley notes, the

White athletes' "whiteness, a taken-for-granted characteristic in the rest of their lives, had a major influence on their decisions about their athletic futures. In fact, they voluntarily limited their options because of their skin color" (p. 298).

In a similar way, Stone, Lynch, Sjomeling, and Darley (1999) found that racial stereotypes influenced actual athletic performance. The researchers asked students to participate in a golf activity and varied the information provided concerning the task. The results were striking. African Americans who were told that the task related to "sports intelligence" performed much more poorly than did those African Americans who did not receive such information. On the other hand, Whites performed poorly when they were told that the task involved an assessment of "natural athletic ability." These results suggest that athletic participants take cognitive stock of racial stereotypes and that such stereotypes influence their subsequent performance. Similar effects have been found with intellectual performance (Steele, 1997).

DIVERSITY *in the field*

Stereotypes About Athletic Performance. Stereotypes about the athletic performance of African Americans is nothing new, and they continue today. For example, in October of 2005, Fisher DeBerry, the head football coach at the Air Force Academy, attributed his team's loss to Texas Christian University (TCU) to the fact that TCU had more African Americans who "can run very, very well." He further noted that he planned to make a concerted effort to recruit more African Americans to his team, commenting, "it just seems to be that way, that Afro-American kids can run very, very well. That doesn't mean that Caucasian kids and other descents can't run, but it's very obvious to me they [African American kids] run extremely well."

Source: DeBerry, 2005.

Athlete Treatment

A fourth way that race influences sport participation is athlete treatment. The results of Singer's (2005) qualitative study with university athletes and data available from the NCAA identified several forms of differential treatment, including variations in academic advising, graduation rates, treatment by coaches and administrators, and available sport opportunities. Each of these issues is explained in the following sections.

Academic Advising

The Singer (2005) study demonstrated that African American athletes believed they were treated differently, from an academic standpoint, than White athletes. The athletes thought that Whites were allowed to freely choose their majors and academic career paths, while African Americans were funneled into particular courses, with only a limited number of majors available. As one athlete noted, "Sometimes, sometimes I feel like the academic counselors, they um, you know,

I don't know if they don't think that Black people are just as smart as the White people are, because you know, when it comes to the Black people, they want to, they just want to get us by, by giving us any old class" (p. 378).

Graduation Rates

Somewhat related to the academic advising differences are the graduation rates of minorities relative to White athletes. According to the NCAA, 60 percent of all athletes graduate within 6 years, a figure actually higher than the general student body (58 percent). A closer examination of the data reveals that athlete graduation rate variations are based on race, especially among men. Overall, 54 percent of all male athletes graduate in 6 years. White and Asian male athletes graduate at rates above that percentage, 58 percent and 57 percent, respectively. However, Native Americans (43 percent), African Americans (45 percent), and Hispanics (46 percent) all graduate at rates lower than their White and Asian counterparts (see Exhibit 4.8). Further, as noted previously, there are instances at many universities where the minority graduation rates in some sports, such as basketball, are at zero percent.

| *Exhibit 4.8* | **Graduation rates of male athletes based on race.** |

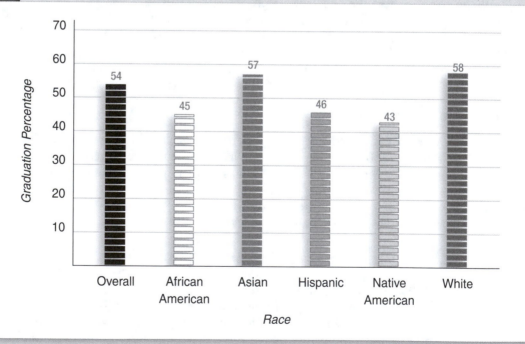

Data from NCAA, www.ncaa.org.

Treatment by Coaches and Administrators

Athletes of color also report being treated differently from White athletes by coaches and administrators. Singer (2005) reported that the African American athletes in his study believed that, in addition to the differential treatment related to academics, African American athletes, in general, were targeted more often for drug testing than White athletes. Other studies found that African Americans are more likely to feel exploited for their athletic talents (e.g., Sack, 1988). Moreso than their White counterparts, these perceptions led African American athletes to believe that they deserved workers' compensation, that they had the right to unionize, and that they should legitimately share in television revenues garnered by the university (Sack, 1988).

Sport Opportunities

Racial minority athletes believe that the available opportunities, both in their current sport participation and in their life after sport, are limited (Singer, 2005). Consistent with the discussion of stacking presented earlier, players in Singer's study believed that some positions, such as quarterback, were not available to African Americans. These same players believed that African Americans had to outperform their White counterparts to receive the same recognition; that is, they were held to higher standards. As Singer noted, participants in his study believed that "African American males must impress the White power brokers with their athletic prowess on the fields of play before they are even considered for opportunities to be in high management positions of leadership and authority" (p. 376). The same was not perceived to be the case for White athletes moving into such positions.

Race Issues Beyond University Athletics

The discussion thus far focused on the influence of race on coaches, administrators, and players in the university athletics setting. As might be expected, race significantly influences sport and physical activity in other contexts. These issues are examined below.

Compensation

Recall from previous discussions that discrimination can take various forms, including access to organizations, the number of promotions one receives, and the positions athletes play on teams. Another form of discrimination involves compensation differences, and research shows that racial minorities receive less compensation, relative to Whites, for their services, across a variety of contexts. For example, Hamilton (1997) examined the salaries of NBA players for the 1994–1995 season. No racial differences were present when looking at all players and all salary ranges. However, a more in-depth analysis revealed that, among the players receiving the highest salaries, Whites earned 18 percent more than their African American counterparts. Further analyses revealed that the general manager's race (i.e., the person who negotiates the salaries) *did not* influence compensation levels. Similar results have been observed across a variety of sports, as well as among professional sport team coaches (Pattnayak & Leonard, 1994).

Marketing and Sport Consumption

Research by Armstrong and Peretto Stratta (2005) illustrates that race plays a significant role in the area of marketing and sport consumption. These authors examined the preferences and behaviors of consumers who attended women's professional basketball games in two markets, one for a team in the Midwest and the other for a team in the South. Although there were many similarities between White and African American spectators, differences also existed. Promotional giveaways were more important in influencing African Americans to attend the events than in influencing Whites. The authors also found variations in the level of sport consumption. In the Midwest market, the team had a relatively even racial composition and had an all-White coaching staff. Whites and African Americans did not differ in the frequency of their game attendance for the Midwest team. However, the team located in the South was predominantly African American, including the team's star player, the head coach, and most of the front office personnel. In this market, African Americans attended games at a higher frequency than Whites. Further, the proportion of African American fans at these games (53 percent) was almost twice the proportion seen in the city's general population (26 percent). These findings support previous research in other areas—people of all races will consume products designed for the general public at equal rates; however, products geared primarily for an African American market will be consumed primarily by African Americans (Gouke, 1987). Race plays an influential role not only in who responds to promotional activities, but also in how the sport is perceived and the frequency of attendance.

Some companies and sport sponsors make efforts to target specific racial groups. For example, MasterCard used television, print, and electronic advertising to target the growing Hispanic population during its "Memorable Moments" campaign that was associated with the MLB (McKelvey, McDonald, & Cramer, 2005). Advertisements aired on Spanish-language television stations such as ESPN Desportes, while print ads ran in *MLB en Espanol* magazine. An advertisement also was posted on a special Spanish website, along with links that sent the consumers to mastercardespanol.com. These efforts were geared toward attracting Hispanic consumers to the MasterCard brand, using sport to achieve this end.

International Sport

As noted in Chapter 1, sport is a worldwide phenomenon, and many sport organizations can be considered multinational in nature. Those professional leagues that traditionally play games only in the United States are now venturing into other countries. The NBA, for example, considers China a viable alternative for expansion (Howard & Crompton, 2004). China is the largest country in the world (population 1.3 billion), has 7 percent annual economic growth, and high brand awareness among the youth of the NBA and its players. Therefore, the NBA believes there are many opportunities for product sales and television revenues within China.

Although intriguing business opportunities exist in China, as well as other countries, cultural and ethnic dissimilarities present potential hurdles. According to Ordish (2005), brand management and protecting intellectual property rights represent the primary concerns managers face when entering the sport marketing realm in China. For example, China maintains a "first-to-file" trademark registration system, meaning that companies should file papers early, as well as register the Chinese version of their trademark. Another consideration for sport marketers is negotiations with individual athletes. Because most Chinese athletes are supported by state-run sport organizations, the state retains the right to manage the athlete's commercial ventures. This was a hard lesson learned for Tian Lang, the 2000 and 2004 Olympic diving champion. Tian entered a sponsorship agreement with Emperor Entertainment Group without permission from the state. Afterward, Tian was expelled from the national diving team and placed on a provincial squad, bringing into doubt his participation in future Olympics. Further, the sponsor not only lost the sponsorship, but also the money it already paid Tian. As this situation illustrates, sport marketers must negotiate with the athlete, the team, and the state (Ordish, 2005).

Sport Experiences of Native Persons

The sport experiences of native persons (i.e., aboriginal peoples, indigenous peoples, First Nations) are oftentimes quite different from the experiences of persons of other races (Paraschak, 1997; Thomas & Dyall, 1999). Paraschak examined the sporting events of native persons in southern and in northern Canada and found variations among the events. Native persons in the northern part of Canada were largely isolated from Euro-Canadians, and consequently, were more in tune with their traditions and "native-derived lifestyle" (p. 16). Not surprisingly, sport events held in this region reflected this lifestyle, and the activities were structured according to their tribal values and traditions. This sport structure stood in contrast to the structure that existed for native persons in southern Canada. Native persons in this region had close interaction with Euro-Canadians, had largely adopted the Euro-Canadian way of life, and were considered "others" in that area. Because they could not maintain government support for their sport events, they were forced to develop a self-funded sport system—a system that largely reflected the ideals and policies of Euro-Canadians.

Robidoux's research (2004) on race relations in Southern Alberta, Canada, further exemplifies these points. Robidoux found that native persons frequently faced antagonistic environments while participating in sport, and Euro-Canadians sometimes viewed them in a negative light. Youth hockey participants in Robidoux's study told of being called a variety of racial slurs, such as "wagon burners" and "prairie niggers," by both the opposing players and those players' parents. On the other hand, Euro-Canadian hockey participants and their parents objected to the highly physical style of the native person teams and often advocated segregation. As one parent of a Euro-Canadian player noted, "Sportsmanship on the part of the Kaini team was nonexistent. . . . Perhaps these teams should make up their own league with their own 'rules' and be forced to travel long distances for competition" (p. 29). These studies illustrate the sometimes unique experiences of native persons while they participate in sport and the need for administrators and coaches to make sport accessible to *all* persons, irrespective of their race.

Entrance Into the Sport Industry

Race can also influence a person's desire and intention to enter the sport and leisure industry. Cunningham, Bruening, Sartore, Sagas, and Fink (2005), in their study of sport and leisure management students, found that discrimination played a key role in determining one's intention to enter the profession. Specifically, discrimination was negatively related to the students' belief that they could be successful in the field.

Hums, O'Bryant, and Tremble (2003) report similar findings. These authors asked sport management program directors about barriers racial minorities might encounter in their attempts to enter the sport industry. Responses included: (a) discrimination, (b) lack of opportunities in the field, and (c) the prevalence of the "old boys" network. Both of these studies suggest that race and racial prejudice can influence racial minorities' opportunities in the field.

Chapter Summary

This chapter focused on the categorical effects of race in sport and physical activity organizations. As illustrated in the Diversity Challenge, race has a substantial impact on the way people are treated while participating in sport and leisure activities. The same is also true for employees, as race influences the way people are treated, people's behaviors in relation to their work and to others, and the aspirations people possess. After reading the chapter, you should be able to:

1. **Define race, ethnicity, and minority group and describe the differences among these concepts.**

Though sometimes used interchangeably, the concepts of race and ethnicity have distinct meanings. Race refers to a social category used to differentiate people based on supposed genetic differences. Ethnicity, on the other hand, refers to the cultural heritage of a particular group of people, with an emphasis on the common culture certain groups of people share. Finally, a minority group is a collection of persons who share common characteristics and face discrimination in society because of their membership in that group.

2. **Discuss the experiences of racial minorities in the employment context, including variations in occupational status, wages earned, and employment decisions.**

In general, racial minorities are disadvantaged in society, such that the overall health and well-being of minorities is impacted. The influence of race is also evident in the general business context. Relative to Whites, persons of color earn less money, have less access to prestigious jobs, and have less favorable ratings across a variety of employment situations, including interview ratings, performance evaluations, and assessments of promotion potential.

3. **Discuss the underrepresentation of racial minorities in the sport industry and identify factors that contribute to the underrepresentation.**

Racial minorities are underrepresented in both coaching and administrative positions. Several factors explain the underrepresentation in these positions. Treatment discrimination limits the advancement opportunities and influences the occupational turnover of minority coaches. The higher turnover rate of coaches of color, relative to White coaches, results in a reduced pool of potential applicants, thereby limiting advancement opportunities. This limited pool, coupled with the access discrimination prominent in hiring decisions, is thought to result in the underrepresentation of racial minorities as head coaches. Finally, these relationships are expected to be moderated by the context or sport coached.

4. Understand the influence of race on the experiences of sport and physical activity participants.

Race affects sport participation primarily through two dynamics: socioeconomic status and cultural norms. The positions people play in sport are also influenced by their race, a phenomenon known as stacking. Both social closure theory and human capital theory have been used to understand the stacking process. There is evidence that participants of color are treated differently than are their White counterparts.

Questions for Discussion

1. What are the primary distinctions between race and ethnicity? Which term do you prefer and why?

2. Though the proportion of racial minorities in various countries is increasing, they continue to be disadvantaged in several areas. What are some of the reasons for this differential treatment?

3. Various factors were identified to help explain the underrepresentation of racial minorities in the coaching profession. Which of these factors is most important and why?

4. Discuss the various ways that race influences sport and leisure participation.

5. Two theories—social closure theory and human capital theory—help explain stacking. In your opinion, which theory provides the best explanation of why stacking occurs, and why?

6. Race influences the treatment of sport participants in several ways. Which of the factors identified in the chapter has the largest impact on sport participants? Why?

Learning Activities

1. What is the best benchmark (or comparison point) to use when discussing the representation of racial minorities in coaching positions? What are the pros and cons of the different benchmarks discussed in the chapter (e.g., the composition of the general population versus the composition of former athletes)? Divide into two groups, with each group adopting one perspective, and discuss.

2. Using the Web, identify mandates in different countries that address either racial equality in general or racial equality in the sport and physical activity context.

Resources

SUPPLEMENTARY READINGS

Brooks, D., & Althouse, R. (Eds.). (2000). *Racism in college athletics: The African American athlete's experience* (2nd ed.). Morgantown, WV: Fitness Information Technology. (Edited collection of essays concerning the intersection of race and university athletics; touches on issues such as stacking, opportunities, and the intersection of gender and race, among others.)

Feagin, J. R. (2006). *Systemic racism: A theory of oppression.* New York: Routledge. (Provides a historical overview of race and racism in the United States; focuses on the racial realities held by members of different racial groups.)

West, C. (1994). *Race matters.* New York: Vintage Books. (Analysis of race issues in the United States, including leadership, affirmative action, sexuality, and the legacy of Malcolm X, among others.)

WEB RESOURCES

- Black Athlete (www.blackathlete.net): site devoted to issues and controversies concerning African American athletes of all ages and skill levels.

- Black Coaches Association (www.bcasports.org): contains several resources, including the annual Hiring Report Card for college football teams.

- Commission for Racial Equality (www.cre.gov.uk/): British association aimed at achieving racial equality in several contexts, including sport and physical activity.

References

Abercrombie, N., Hill, S., & Turner, B. S. (2000). *The Penguin dictionary of sociology* (4th ed.). New York: Penguin Books.

Allison, M. T., & Hibbler, D. K. (2004). Organizational barriers to inclusion: Perspectives from the recreation profession. *Leisure Sciences, 26,* 261–280.

Anderson, D. (1993). Cultural diversity on campus: A look at intercollegiate football coaches. *Journal of Sport and Social Issues, 17,* 61–66.

Armstrong, K. L., & Peretto Stratta, T. M. (2005). Market analyses of race and sport consumption. *Sport Marketing Quarterly, 13,* 7–16.

Bacharach, S. B. (1989). Organizational theories: Some criteria for evaluation. *Academy of Management Review, 14,* 496–515.

Beyer, J. M., & Hannah, D. R. (2000). The cultural significance of athletics in U.S. higher education. *Journal of Sport Management, 14,* 105–132.

Bonacich, E. (1972). A theory of ethnic antagonism: The split labor market. *American Sociological Review, 37,* 547–559.

Bray, C. (2005). *1999–00—2003–04 NCAA student-athlete ethnicity report.* Indianapolis, IN: The National Collegiate Athletic Association.

Brooks, D., & Althouse, R. (2000). African American head coaches and administrators: Progress but . . . ? In D. Brooks & R. Althouse (Eds.), *Racism in college athletics: The African American athlete's experience* (2nd ed., pp. 85–117). Morgantown, WV: Fitness Information Technology.

Brown, G. T. (2002). Diversity grid lock. *The NCAA News.* Retrieved February 15, 2003, from www.ncaa.org/news/2002/20021028/active/3922n01.html

Burden, J. W., Jr., Harrison, L., Jr., & Hodge, S. R. (2005). Perceptions of African American faculty in kinesiology-based programs at predominantly White American institutions of higher education. *Research Quarterly for Exercise and Sport, 76,* 224–237.

Button, S. B. (2001). Organizational efforts to affirm sexual diversity: A cross-level examination. *Journal of Applied Psychology, 86,* 17–28.

Carington, W. J., & Troske, K. R. (1998). Interfirm segregation and the Black/White wage gap. *Journal of Labor Economics, 16*(2), 231–260.

Chelladurai, P. (2005). *Managing organizations for sport and physical activity: A systems perspective* (2nd ed.). Holcomb Hathaway: Scottsdale, AZ.

Coakley, J. (2004). *Sports in society: Issues and controversies* (8th ed.). New York: McGraw-Hill.

Cokley, K., Dreher, G. F., & Stockdale, M. S. (2004). Toward the inclusiveness and career success of African Americans in the workplace. In M. S. Stockdale & F. J. Crosby (Eds.), *The psychology and management of workplace diversity* (pp. 168–190). Malden, MA: Blackwell.

Cunningham, G. B. (2004). Already aware of the glass ceiling: Race-related effects of perceived opportunity on the career choices of college athletes. *Journal of African American Studies, 7*(1), 57–71.

Cunningham, G. B., Bruening, J. E., & Straub, T. (2006). Examining the underrepresentation of African Americans in NCAA Division I head-coaching positions. *Journal of Sport Management, 20,* 387–417.

Cunningham, G. B., Bruening, J. E., Sartore, M. L., Sagas, M., & Fink, J. S. (2005). The application of social cognitive career theory to sport and leisure career choices. *Journal of Career Development, 32,* 122–138.

Cunningham, G. B., & Dixon, M. A. (2003). New perspectives concerning performance appraisals of intercollegiate coaches. *Quest, 55,* 177–192.

Cunningham, G. B., & Sagas, M. (2002). The differential effects of human capital for male and female Division I basketball coaches. *Research Quarterly for Exercise and Sport, 73,* 489–495.

Cunningham, G. B., & Sagas, M. (2004a). Examining the main and interactive effects of deep- and surface-level diversity on job satisfaction and organizational turnover intentions. *Organizational Analysis, 12,* 319–332.

Cunningham, G. B., & Sagas, M. (2004b). Racial differences in occupational turnover intent among NCAA Division IA assistant football coaches. *Sociology of Sport Journal, 21,* 84–92.

Cunningham, G. B., & Sagas, M. (2005). Access discrimination in intercollegiate athletics. *Journal of Sport and Social Issues, 29,* 148–163.

Cunningham, G. B., & Sagas, M. (in press). The influence of race and sport coached on explaining treatment discrimination and work outcomes among university coaches. *International Journal of Sport Management.*

Cunningham, G. B., Sagas, M., & Ashley, F. B. (2001). Occupational commitment and intent to leave the coaching profession: Differences according to race. *International Review for the Sociology of Sport, 16,* 131–148.

DeBerry, F. (2005, Oct. 26). DeBerry cites lack of minority players for struggles. ESPN.com. Retrieved February 2, 2006, from http://sports. espn.go.com/ncf/news/story?id=2203926

DeHass, D. (2004). *2003–04 race and gender demographics of NCAA member institutions' athletic personnel.* Indianapolis, IN: The National Collegiate Athletic Association.

Devine, P. G., Plant, E. A., & Blair, I. V. (2001). Classic and contemporary analyses of racial prejudice. In R. Brown & S. L. Gaertner (Eds.), *Blackwell handbook of social psychology: Intergroup processes* (pp. 198–217). Malden, MA: Blackwell.

Dovidio, J. F., Kawakami, K., & Beach, K. R. (2001). Implicit and explicit attitudes: Examination of the relationship between measures of intergroup bias. In R. Brown & S. L. Gaertner (Eds.), *Blackwell handbook of social psychology: Intergroup processes* (pp. 175–197). Malden, MA: Blackwell.

Eitzen D. S., & Sage, G. H. (2003). *Sociology of North American sport* (7th ed.). New York: McGraw-Hill.

Everhart, B. C., & Chelladurai, P. (1998). Gender differences in preferences for coaching as an occupation: The role of self-efficacy, valence, and perceived barriers. *Research Quarterly for Exercise and Sport, 68,* 188–200.

Feagin, J. R. (2006). *Systemic racism: A theory of oppression.* New York: Routledge.

Gonzales, G. L. (1996). The stacking of Latinos in Major League Baseball: A forgotten minority? *Journal of Sport and Social Issues, 20,* 134–160.

Gouke, C. G. (1987). *Blacks and the American economy.* Needham Heights, MA: Ginn Press.

Greenhaus, J. H., Parasuraman, S., & Wormley, W. M. (1990). Effects of race on organizational experiences, job performance, evaluations, and career outcomes. *Academy of Management Journal, 33,* 64–86.

Hallinan, C. (1991). Aborigines and positional segregation in the Australian Rugby League. *International Review for the Sociology of Sport, 26,* 69–81.

Hamilton, B. H. (1997). Racial discrimination and professional basketball salaries in the 1990s. *Applied Economics, 29,* 287–296.

Hibbler, D. K., & Shinew, K. J. (2002). Interracial couples' experience of leisure: A social network approach. *Journal of Leisure Research, 34,* 135–156.

Hill, F. (2004). Shattering the glass ceiling: Blacks in coaching. *Black Issues in Higher Education, 21*(4), 36–37.

Hodge, S. R., & Stroot, S. A. (1997). Barriers and support structures perceived by African American and Caucasian physical educators during their career development. *Equity & Excellence in Education, 30*(3), 52–60.

Howard, D. R., & Crompton, J. L. (2004). *Financing sport* (2nd ed.). Morgantown, WV: Fitness Information Technology.

Huffcutt, A. I., & Roth, P. L. (1998). Racial group differences in employment interview evaluations. *Journal of Applied Psychology, 83,* 179–189.

Hums, M. A., O'Bryant, C. P., & Tremble, L. (2003). Strategies for increasing minorities and women in sport management and physical education teacher preparation programs: Common recruitment and retention themes. *Women in Sport and Physical Activity Journal, 5*(2), 89–97.

Ibarra, H. (1993). Personal networks of women and minorities in management: A conceptual framework. *Academy of Management Review, 18,* 56–87.

Kram, K. E. (1988). *Mentoring at work: Developmental relationships in organizational life.* New York: University Press of America.

Ladson-Billings, G., & Tate, W. F., IV. (1995). Toward a critical race theory of education. *Teachers College Record, 97*(1), 47–68.

Landau, J. (1995). The relationship of race and gender to managers' ratings of promotion potential. *Journal of Organizational Behavior, 16,* 391–400.

Lapchick, R. E. (2004). *2004 Racial and Gender Report Card.* Accessed November 9, 2005, from www.bus.ucf.edu/sport/public/downloads/2004_Racial_Gender_Report_Card.pdf

Lavigne, P. (2003, August 6). Measuring minority advances. *The Dallas Morning News,* pp. 12A, 13A.

Lavoie, M. (1989). Stacking, performance differentials, and salary discrimination in professional hockey. *Sociology of Sport Journal, 6,* 17–35.

Lawrence, S. M. (2004). African American athletes' experiences of race in sport. *International Review for the Sociology of Sport, 40,* 99–110.

Littlefield, A., Lieberman, L., & Reynolds, L. T. (1982). Redefining race: The potential demise of a concept in physical anthropology. *Current Anthropology, 23,* 641–655.

Madden, J. F. (2004). Differences in the success of NFL coaches by race, 1990–2002: Evidence of last hire, first fire. *Journal of Sports Economics, 5,* 6–19.

McKelvey, S., McDonald, M., & Cramer, R. (2005). MasterCard and Major League Baseball: Metrics for evaluating a most "memorable" promotion. *Sport Marketing Quarterly, 14,* 253–261.

Nordhaug, O. (1993). *Human capital in organizations.* New York: Oxford.

Ordish, R. (2005). Sports marketing in China: An IP perspective. *The China Business Review, 32*(6), 34–37.

Paraschak, V. (1997). Variations in race relations: Sporting events for native peoples in Canada. *Sociology of Sport Journal, 14,* 1–21.

Pattnayak, S. R., & Leonard, J. E. (1994). Explaining discrimination in the National Football League: A study of coaches' salaries. *Sociological Viewpoints, 10,* 35–44.

Robidoux, M. A. (2004). Narratives of race relations in Southern Alberta: An examination of conflicting sporting practices. *Sociology of Sport Journal, 21,* 287–301.

Rosenberg, M. (2004). Two few: Of 117 football coaches, two are black; it's called institutional racism. *Detroit Free Press.* Accessed November 14, 2005, from www.freep.com/cgi-bin/forms/printerfriendly.pl

Sack, A. L. (1988). Are "improper benefits" really improper? A study of college athletes' views concerning amateurism. *Journal of Sport and Social Issues, 12,* 1–16.

Sack, A. L., Singh, P., & Thiel, R. (2005). Occupational segregation on the playing field: The case of Major League Baseball. *Journal of Sport Management, 19,* 300–318.

Sagas, M., & Cunningham, G. B. (2005). Racial differences in the career success of assistant football coaches: The role of discrimination, human capital, and social capital. *Journal of Applied Social Psychology, 35,* 773–797.

Sailes, G. A. (1993). An investigation of campus typecasts: The myth of black athletic superiority and the dumb jock stereotype. *Sociology of Sport Journal, 10,* 88–97.

Sailes, G. A. (2000). The African American athlete: Social myths and stereotypes. In D. Brooks & R. Althouse (Eds.), *Racism in college athletics: The African American athlete's experience* (2nd ed., pp. 53–63). Morgantown, WV: Fitness Information Technology.

Schnittker, J., & McLeod, J. D. (2005). The social psychology of health disparities. *Annual Review of Sociology, 31,* 75–103.

Seibert, S. E., Kraimer, M. L., & Liden, R. C. (2001). A social capital theory of career success. *Academy of Management Journal, 44,* 219–237.

Singer, J. N. (2005). Understanding racism through the eyes of African American male student-athletes. *Race Ethnicity and Education, 8,* 365–386.

Stauffer, J. M., & Buckley, R. M. (2005). The existence and nature of racial bias in supervisory ratings. *Journal of Applied Psychology, 90,* 586–591.

Steele, C. M. (1997). A threat in the air: How stereotypes shape intellectual identity and performance. *American Psychologist, 52,* 613–629.

Stoll, M. A., Raphael, S., & Holzer, H. J. (2004). Black job applicants and the hiring officer's race. *Industrial and Labor Relations, 57,* 267–287.

Stone, J., Lynch, C. I., Sjomeling, M., & Darley, J. M. (1999). Stereotype threat effects on Black and White athletic performance. *Journal of Personality and Social Psychology, 77,* 1213–1227.

Tate, W. F. (1997). Critical race theory and education: History, theory, and implications. In M. Apple (Ed.), *Review in research education 2* (pp. 191–243). Washington, DC: American Educational Research Association.

Thomas, D. R., & Dyall, L. (1999). Culture, ethnicity, and sport management: A New Zealand perspective. *Sport Management Review, 2,* 115–132.

Tsui, A. S., & Gutek, B. A. (1999). *Demographic differences in organizations: Current research and future directions.* New York: Lexington Books.

Turner, C. S. V., Myers, S. L., Jr., & Creswell, J. W. (1999). Exploring underrepresentation: The case of faculty of color in the Midwest. *The Journal of Higher Education, 70,* 27–59.

Weeden, K. A. (2002). Why do some occupations pay more than others? Social closure and earnings inequality in the United States. *American Journal of Sociology, 108,* 55–101.

Williams, D. R. (1997). Race and health: Basic questions, emerging directions. *Annals of Epidemiology, 7,* 322–333.

Wixon, M. (2006, May 17). Black coaches see dearth of opportunity in suburbs: High schools diverse, but few land top football jobs. *Dallas Morning News.* Retrieved May 17, 2006, from www.dallasnews.com/cgi-bin/bi/gold_print.cgi

Wong, E. (2002). The mystery of the missing minority coaches. *New York Times Online.* Retrieved January 15, 2002, from www.patrick.af.mil/deomi/Library/EOReadFile/Affirmative%20Action/Spring02/The%20Mystery%20of%20the%20Missing%20Minority%20Coaches.pdf 151

118

Sex and Gender in Sport Organizations

CHAPTER 5

DIVERSITY CHALLENGE

Sport participation by women has increased dramatically over time, and this trend is particularly true when it comes to university athletics. The average number of women's teams sponsored by NCAA universities has increased from two to eight since 1972, and similar trends are present in other contexts. During the same time frame, however, many men's teams were cut, those teams usually falling in the "Olympic sports" category (e.g., swimming, gymnastics, and wrestling). For example, since 1972, 441 universities have stopped sponsoring varsity wrestling programs.

What accounts for these practices? The answer largely depends on who is asked. Some people, such as Donna Lopiano (considered one of the most powerful persons in sports today) of the Women's Sport Foundation, suggest that the "arms race" in "big-time" college sports is to blame. Lopiano notes that Division II and III universities—schools with the smallest budgets and fewest revenues—generally do not drop men's sports, as might be expected; rather, these sports are most often cut by Division I programs, which have the largest budgets and most lucrative revenue streams of all athletic departments. Title IX and the associated mandates requiring equal participation opportunities are usually pitted as the culprits when such cuts are made. Lopiano contends that monies *are* available to support those sports, but college presidents and athletic directors spend lavishly and foolishly. The following is a list of actual events that occurred at schools claiming not to have the budget to carry Olympic sports any longer:

- A university spent $300,000 on lights for a football practice field, but the lights were never used. The coach claimed they were needed for recruiting purposes.

- A football team spent the night in a hotel the night prior to a *home* game so the coaches could monitor the players' behaviors. In addition

LEARNING OBJECTIVES

After studying this chapter, you should be able to:

- Understand the meaning of sex and gender and the differences between the two concepts.

- Discuss the differing experiences men and women have in the workplace.

- Be familiar with the influence of sex and gender on sport participation.

- Discuss the intersection of race and sex.

- Understand the influence of sex and gender on the marketing of sport.

to the 50 rented rooms and meals, the team also rented a movie theatre for entertainment purposes.

■ After a football season in which the team won seven games, the head coach treated the entire coaching staff, including the coaches' wives, to a trip to the Bahamas.

Citing these and other examples, Lopiano contends that fiscal irresponsibility is to blame for the cuts to men's Olympic sports, not Title IX mandates. Her position is supported by Walter Byers, the former head of the NCAA.

Not all people, however, agree with Lopiano and Byers. For example, renowned columnist George F. Will referred to Title IX as a "train wreck" because of what is perceived to be discrimination against men and men's teams. Researchers have statistically demonstrated that men's access to athletics realized a net decrease after the implementation of Title IX, leading to the conclusion that "men have been disenfranchised—we contend, from a disregard of demand." Sport economists Howard and Crompton argue that Title IX caused inordinate spending increases by university athletic departments. The spending increases are viewed as problematic because "women's sports at most institutions currently contribute no more than 5% to 10% of the total revenues generated by average collegiate athletic programs." Thus, there continues to be two sides to the Title IX debate—a debate that has been hotly contested and undoubtedly will continue to be for years to come.*

DIVERSITY CHALLENGE   **R E F L E C T I O N**

1. What are some of the arguments for and against the position that cuts to men's sports can be attributed to fiscal irresponsibility by university athletic departments? Which side is more compelling? Why?

2. What are some of the arguments for and against the position that cuts to men's sports can be attributed to discrimination resulting from Title IX mandates? Which side is more compelling? Why?

---

*Byers, W. (1995). *Unsportsmanlike conduct: Exploiting college athletes*. Ann Arbor, MI: The University of Michigan Press; Howard, D. R., & Crompton, J. L. (2004). *Financing sport* (2nd ed.). Morgantown, WV: Fitness Information Technology; Lopiano, D. (2001, May). The real culprit in the cutting of men's Olympic sports. *Women's Sports Foundation*. Retrieved January 3, 2006, from www.womenssportsfoundation.org/cgi-bin/iowa/issues/opin/article.html?record=76; McBride, D. K., Worcester, L. L., & Tennyson, S. L. (1999). Women's athletics and the elimination of men's sports programs: A reevaluation. *Cato Journal, 19,* 323–330; Will, G. F. (2002, May 27). A train wreck called Title IX. *Newsweek, 139,* 82.

itle IX and the funding of athletic teams is just one of many topics concerning men and women in sport organizations that continues to be hotly debated. Research and anecdotal evidence related to sex and gender in the workplace is abundant, but the extent to which men and women differ in that environment is mixed. Some research suggests that men and women do not differ in work-related outcomes. Other studies, however, have found differences in the way men and women experience work, the wages earned, the occupational status, and the attitudes toward work and careers. Therefore, managers must be cognizant of the potential for one group of people (e.g., women) to experience work in a more negative fashion than another group (e.g., men).

This chapter examines the experiences of men and women in sport organizations. As in Chapter 4, these experiences are examined from a categorical perspective. In the first section, the concepts of sex, gender, and gender role identities are presented. This is followed by a discussion of the experiences of men and women in the workplace. Next, I highlight the experiences of sport participants, and whether such experiences differ between men and women. This discussion is followed by an examination of the intersection between race and sex, and finally, the influence of sex and gender in sport marketing efforts.

Sex and Gender

hough the terms are often used interchangeably, this text makes distinctions between sex and gender (see Exhibit 5.1). According to Powell and Graves (2003), *sex* is a biological classification of individuals based on their physiological properties and reproductive apparatus. Men and women have different sex organs and physical characteristics that distinguish them from a sci-

Defining sex and gender.	*Exhibit 5.1*

Though often used interchangeably, sex and gender are distinct terms.

- **Sex:** a biological classification of individuals based on their physiological properties and reproductive apparatus.

- **Gender:** the social roles expected of men and women, including expectations related to attitudes, behaviors, and interests perceived to be appropriate for or typical of men and women. (The gender roles people adopt are influenced by at least three factors: parents, schools, and the mass media.)

PROFESSIONAL
P E R S P E C T I V E S

Using Sexist Language. A topic associated with gender issues concerns the use of sexist language; for example, the use of false generics such as "mankind" and the use of "girl" to refer to an adult woman. Sexist language connotes the notion that masculine is the norm and perpetuates male privilege in society. Research of this topic in the sport realm has largely been spearheaded by Parks and Roberton (1998a, 1998b, 2000, 2002, 2004). Their research shows that males generally endorse the use of sexist language more so than women, and the difference is relatively large, with Cohen's *d* values ranging from .72 to 1.43. The authors examined qualitative responses (e.g., "a woman . . . will never be one hundred percent equal to a man. It is a concept that needs to be faced," and "if women want to be men, have them get a sex change") to determine why such a difference is present.

Other research by Parks and Roberton shows that attitudes toward women in general mediate the relationship between one's sex and the endorsement of sexist language. Using their findings, they concluded that sexist language may be important, from a symbolic standpoint, to people who either consciously or unconsciously believe that men are superior to women. The question, then, is how is the use of sexist language reduced or eliminated? Their research indicates that emphasizing the harmful effects the use of such language may have on others will make people more aware of the words they use, and they may make greater efforts to reduce the use and endorsement of sexist language.

entific standpoint. *Gender,* on the other hand, is related to the social roles expected of men and women. Discussions of gender focus on the roles, attitudes, behaviors, and interests perceived to be appropriate for or typical of members of one sex relative to members of another. Such discourse usually focuses on notions of femininity and masculinity, where masculinity is associated with aggressiveness and independence, while femininity is affiliated with warmth, dependence, and gentleness (Abercrombie, Hill, & Turner, 2000).

The distinction between sex and gender is further clarified by considering the following. Sex differences are related to how men and women actually differ. They also influence people's dispositions and their proclivities to behave in certain ways in the workplace (Powell & Graves, 2003). For example, studies show that women have greater verbal abilities than men (Halpern, 2000). This is a sex difference as it pertains to the performance of verbal tasks in the workplace. On the other hand, gender differences are related to how people perceive or anticipate that men and women differ, or should differ. These perceptions influence one's reactions to other people in the workplace and are manifested in stereotypes, prejudice, and discrimination as discussed in Chapter 3 (Powell & Graves, 2003). For instance, women may be expected to take greater responsibility for child-rearing duties. This expectation could result in greater stress associated with the work–family interface for women than it does for men (Dixon & Bruening, 2005). As these examples illustrate, there are distinct differences between the terms *sex* and *gender,* thereby necessitating care in their use.

Some may question whether making such a distinction really matters. For example, if one discusses "gender differences" in personality, height, or any other immutable characteristic, is this incorrect or inappropriate? Furthermore, do people really make these distinctions, or is this simply something with which academics concern themselves? Pryzgoda and Chrisler (2000) examined these very questions through a survey of 137 college students. They asked participants to write down what they thought of when seeing the word "gender." The majority of the respondents (66.8 percent) indicated that they thought of biological terms, such as "sex," "male/female," or "boy/girl." Participants were also asked to provide definitions of the term *gender*. The most common responses included "male/female" (34.8 percent) and "sex" (34.8 percent), while references to masculinity and femininity were included approximately 12 percent of the time. Though used somewhat interchangeably from a definition standpoint, participants did make distinctions when completing sentences. Most participants selected "sex" to complete sentences related to biological features (e.g., "The _____ of the cat is male," p. 567) and "gender" to complete socially cued sentences (e.g., "Masculine is an adjective that best describes a person's _____," p. 567). Two exceptions occurred with the following sentences: "The girl's gender is _____," and "The boy's gender is _____" (p. 567). With both sentences, participants were as likely (if not more so) to choose a biological descriptor (e.g., female) as the socially constructed descriptor (e.g., feminine). Pryzgoda and Chrisler concluded that people may use gender to describe both anatomical and behavioral characteristics, but will otherwise make distinctions between the terms. Overall, these results indicate that, in most situations, people do make a distinction between sex and gender.

Gender Identity

For many years, gender identity was considered a dichotomous construct, with masculinity and femininity believed to be opposites (Powell & Graves, 2003). If a person was considered to be highly masculine, then he or she would have to be low in femininity, and vice versa. These dissimilarities were thought to mirror sex differences, such that men were highly masculine and women were highly feminine. A male who demonstrated feminine qualities (e.g., dependence, gentleness) was considered abnormal, as was a female demonstrating masculine characteristics (e.g., aggressiveness, independence).

Bem (1974, 1977) provides an alternative view of gender identity (see also Spence & Helmreich, 1978). Rather than viewing masculinity and femininity as being at opposite ends of a single construct, she suggests that the two concepts are distinct—one could conceivably be high on both attributes, low on both, or somewhere in between. Using this reasoning, Bem developed the Bem Sex-Role Inventory, consisting of 20 items measuring masculinity, 20 items measuring femininity, and 20 items disguising the purpose of the instrument. To complete the questionnaire, respondents rate themselves in relation to traditional concepts of masculinity and femininity. Based on their responses, people could then be classified into one of four categories:

- *Masculine:* high masculinity, low femininity
- *Feminine:* low masculinity, high femininity
- *Androgynous:* high masculinity, high femininity
- *Undifferentiated:* low masculinity, low femininity

Bem's notion of androgyny, which comes from the Greek words *andr* (meaning man) and *gyne* (meaning woman), was unique to the gender identity literature. People with androgynous characteristics were thought to have more desirable outcomes, such as high self-esteem and greater confidence, than people in other categories.

The relationship between gender identity and various outcomes has been reported at length in the sport literature. The research indicates that athletes have higher masculine and lower feminine gender orientations than nonathletes (Lantz & Schroeder, 1999). Furthermore, those persons with a feminine gender orientation who participate in highly competitive sports have low levels of athletic competence and poor perceptions of their own self-worth (Bowker, Gadbois, & Cornock, 2003). This pattern is true for both males and females. These results are consistent with the notion that sport has traditionally been considered a masculine domain; as such, people with gender orientations that are not masculine may not engage in competitive sports for long durations. These people may have more pleasant and positive experiences in less competitive or more socially oriented sport settings (Bowker et al., 2003).

More recently, Woodhill and Samuels (2003) conducted a more in-depth analysis of gender roles. Although androgyny was initially thought of as an ideal gender role that balances the best attributes of both masculinity and femininity (Bem, 1975), these authors convincingly argue that gender roles can be both positive and negative. Consider the following: An elite level swim coach who has high levels of independence, ambition, compassion, and tolerance would fit desirable masculine (the first two characteristics) and feminine (the latter two characteristics) gender roles and be considered *positively* androgynous. Another swim coach has the following characteristics: high levels of both selfishness and submissiveness, characteristics that are negative attributes of masculinity and femininity, respectively. The latter swim coach is considered *negatively* androgynous. The same distinctions can be made for people who are feminine or masculine, only. The demarcation of gender roles in this manner is useful when examining various outcomes such as overall well-being. Woodhill and Samuels, for example, found that positively androgynous people scored higher on indicators of mental health and well-being than did persons who were negatively androgynous, negatively masculine, negatively feminine, or undifferentiated androgynous. Thus, the gender roles one adopts can have a meaningful impact on a variety of outcomes, including sport participation and overall well-being.

Origins of Gender Socialization

As previously noted, because ideas about gender and gender roles are influenced by societal forces, there are several factors that influence one's gender role identity: parents, schools, and the mass media (Powell & Graves, 2003). Each factor is discussed in turn.

Parents. Parents play an influential part in children's gender role identity development. Parents who believe that men and women should enjoy equal opportunities in the "adult world" are more likely to encourage their children to deviate from traditional gender stereotypes (Eccles, Jacobs, & Harold, 1990). The parents' working status also influences gender role identities, as working mothers are more likely to have daughters who embrace egalitarian views toward gender roles than are stay-at-home mothers. These effects are less substantial on the attitudes sons hold toward gender roles (Hoffman & Youngblood, 1999). Research shows that both parents, but especially fathers, are likely to encourage gender-stereotypical behavior for both boys and girls, promote activities requiring motor skills for boys, and discourage aggressive behavior among girls (Lytton & Romney, 1991). This is consistent with other studies that show the father plays a significant role in the development of attitudes toward sport participation for both girls and boys. Furthermore, the lack of a female parent who participates in sport (or did not participate in the past) potentially conveys to children that sport is an exclusively male domain (Shakib & Dunbar, 2004). Finally, parents are also likely to purchase different types of toys for their male and female children, further reinforcing gender stereotypes (Pomerleau, Boldue, Malcuit, & Cossette, 1990).

Schools. Schools also influence the development of gender roles. Powell and Graves (2003) outline how girls generally perform better academically than boys in school—a trend that exists in all academic areas, including math and science, across all ages, and through all levels of education. The grade differences are not necessarily the result of varying cognitive ability; rather, they are the result of the girls' superior work habits and study skills. Ironically though, boys receive more attention, both positive and negative, in the classroom than girls. They are called on more often, praised more, criticized more, and have more ideas that are both rejected and accepted. Though girls volunteer to answer questions more often than boys do, they are called on less frequently and are afforded less time to provide answers. Powell and Graves maintain that the cumulative effects of these practices lead to lower self-esteem among girls relative to boys, findings that have been substantiated in empirical studies (Kling, Hyde, Showers, & Buswell, 1999). The lower self-esteem among girls, relative to boys, negatively influences their choice of academic course work, the degrees they seek, and the career paths they pursue.

Mass media. The media, television, print, radio, Internet, have a significant influence on individuals and the culture in which they live, prompting some to suggest that they "have become one of the most powerful institutional forces for shaping values and attitudes in modern culture" (Kane, 1988, pp. 88–89). The media help to affect how we think, influence our attitudes toward various topics, and shape our perceptions of the roles men and women should play in society. The same is true in sport, as research on the coverage of sport teams and participants demonstrates inequitable and biased representation. The media generally portray sport as a masculine venture (Cramer, 1994; Tuggle, 1997). Women participating in traditionally "feminine" sports such as golf or swimming are featured more frequently than women competing in "masculine" sports such as rugby (Fink & Kensicki, 2002; Lumpkin & Williams, 1991). When women do receive media or press coverage, they are likely to be depicted as sex symbols and/or in supportive rather than participating roles (e.g., cheering the contestants; Cuneen & Sidwell, 1998; Fink & Kensicki, 2002; Tuggle, 1997). Other research indicates that women and women's teams receive considerably less coverage than men and men's teams. This pattern exists across a variety of mass media, including sport magazines (Fink & Kensicki, 2002; Kane, 1988), newspapers (Wann, Schrader, Allison, & McGeorge, 1998), television (Tuggle, 1997), the Internet (Sagas, Cunningham, Wigley, & Ashley, 2000), and publications from professional organizations, such as the *NCAA News* (Shifflett & Revelle, 1994).

DIVERSITY *in the field*

Hitting "Like a Girl." Gender stereotypes are just as much a part of the sports world as they are any other part of society, if not more so. Phrases such as "you throw like a girl" are sometimes espoused among male participants with the intention of belittling someone. A similar situation took place at a golf tournament in November, 2005. Fred Funk, Tiger Woods, Annika Sorenstam, and Fred Couples were all competing in a tournament together. Woods told Funk that he (Funk) would never hear the end of it if Sorenstam hit the ball farther than he did, even on one hole. However, that is just what happened on the third hole. Afterward, Funk wore a pink skirt over his pants for the remainder of the hole (Van Sickle, 2005). It didn't matter that Sorenstam had more career wins and earned more prize money than Funk. Because she was a woman and hit the ball farther, he attempted to deflect the focus from his shortcoming by wearing the skirt for the remainder of the hole. This is but one of many examples of the way gender roles influence sport and sport participants.

Gender in the Sport Context

As this review illustrates, gender plays a significant role for all people—male and female—in all walks of life, including sport and physical activity. Parents, schools, and the media all significantly influence the gender roles boys and girls adopt. These gender roles are then used to define behaviors and participation in other areas of life, including sport and leisure. For example, girls' and women's participation in some sports thought to be masculine in nature, such as football or rugby, is limited. On the other hand, their participation in sports that are thought to be feminine in nature, such as gymnastics, oftentimes outnumbers the participation by boys. Boys generally have greater participation in all sports than girls (Carpenter & Acosta, 2005). These trends illustrate the gender roles adopted in the sport domain, especially in relation to choices of sport participation.

Gender stereotypes are seen throughout other areas of sport, including the workplace (discussed later), commercials, events, and facilities. Commercials promoting the beginning of the 2005 NHL season illustrate this point. The commercials showed a bare-chested hockey player sitting on a bench, with the sounds of drums and sabers rattling in the background. He is approached by a woman clothed only in a bra and gauzy robe who proceeds to help clothe him in his shoulder pads and jersey. Although seen as nothing more than a way to grab the viewers' attention to some, others disagree, suggesting that the advertisement depicts the woman as a "sexual ornament" ("Deeply," 2005). Another example is found in the University of Iowa's visitor's locker room at Kinnick Stadium—it has pink walls, carpet, showers, and lockers. Football officials contend that pink was used because the color is believed to have a calming effect on the opposing teams. Others see it differently, suggesting that the use of pink is demeaning and perpetuates negative stereotypes about women. After raising these objections, one professor on the campus received death threats ("Color," 2005). As these examples demonstrate, gender stereotypes are seen in many aspects of sport and influence people's behaviors, attitudes, and beliefs.

Men and Women in the Workplace

We next turn our attention to men and women in the workplace, examining the differences and similarities between men and women in workforce participation, earnings, and representation in management and leadership positions. We also consider several potential reasons for the under-representation of women in top-level positions. Each topic is discussed below.

Participation in the Workforce

Variations exist in the proportion of men and women in the workplace, though the extent of the differences has narrowed over time (see Exhibit 5.2). According to the U. S. Census Bureau, 19 percent of women and 80 percent of men were members of the U. S. labor force in 1900. By 1950, the proportion of women in the labor force had risen to 31 percent, while the proportion of men remained constant at 80 percent. By the year 2000, the gap had narrowed even further, as 60 percent of women and 75 percent of men were members of the U. S. labor force. To examine these figures from a different perspective, in 1900, four out of five women *did not* work, while in 2000, three out of five women *were* members of the labor force. This general trend is mirrored in the sport and physical activity context (Eitzen & Sage, 2003).

| Exhibit 5.2 | Percentage of women in the labor force since 1900. |

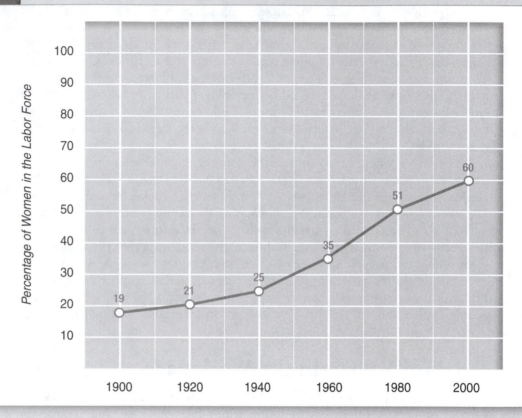

U.S. Census Bureau data.

Note that the proportion of women choosing to enter the workforce coincides with changing attitudes toward gender roles. In the early 20th century, "appropriate" gender roles called for women to raise their children and work in the home, focusing on domestic duties. Women who worked outside the home during this time were seen as challenging traditional gender roles. However, several legislative, political, and societal factors slowly helped to change these stereotypes. The ratification of the 19th Amendment (gave women the right to vote), World Wars I and II (resulted in women working in factories in the place of men away at war), the women's movements in the 1960s and 1970s, the Civil Rights Act of 1964 and Title IX (as discussed at length in Chapter 10) all influenced women's participation in the workforce and in sport. These changes challenged stereotypes, altered the perceptions about what a woman could do and who she should be, granted women rights not previously enjoyed in the workplace, and ultimately allowed women the right to choose to work away from home and participate in organized sport activities.

Earnings

Despite the increased representation of women in the workforce, men have traditionally received larger salaries than women—a trend that continues today. The U. S. Census Bureau reports that in 2004 the real median earnings of men over age 15 was $40,798, while the median earnings for women over age 15 was $31,223. This variation could be a function of the type of job the men and women hold. Exhibit 5.3 provides the median weekly earnings of full-time male and female workers across several occupations. The data indicate that men continually receive greater weekly earnings than women. Among persons in management occupations, men earn $1,215 a week, while women earn $871. Among educators, men earn $227 more a week than do women ($956 and $729, respectively). A similar trend is present for recreation and fitness workers, where men earn $585 a week and women earn $473. Comparable findings have been reported across a variety of countries, including Australia (Eastough & Miller, 2004) and Great Britain (Ward, 2001).

Salary discrepancies exist for men and women in sport organizations, but the picture is more complex. Consider the salaries of university basketball coaches. Among coaches of women's teams, women head coaches earn more than men (Humphreys, 2000); however, this statistic is only related to the

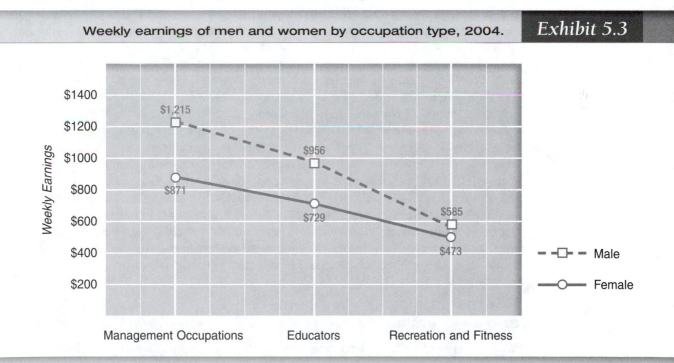

Weekly earnings of men and women by occupation type, 2004. *Exhibit 5.3*

U.S. Census Bureau data.

coaches of women's teams. Coaches of men's basketball teams earn almost double what coaches of women's teams earn. This is significant because in practice, the coaching positions for men's teams are reserved for men, but the same is not true for coaching positions of women's teams. Therefore, the womens' earning potential is substantially less than it is for men, and this same trend generally exists throughout university sports.

Consider the following example at the University of Texas, as outlined by Zimbalist (1999). Jody Conradt was hired as the head coach of the women's basketball team in 1976, and since that time, amassed a .771 winning percentage. The women's games regularly drew between 7,000 and 8,000 fans, among the top 10 in attendance in the nation. In the early 1990s, she was appointed athletic director for women's sports at the university while still fulfilling her head coaching duties. Her total compensation package for the 1998–1999 academic year was $237,235—substantially less than the compensation of Rick Barnes ($800,000), the head coach of the men's team with a .601 career winning percentage (.170 points lower than Conradt's). Note that Barnes did not fill two jobs, as did Conradt, yet he still received a compensation package worth more than three times Conradt's.

Some assert that because men's sports generate greater revenues, the coaches of those teams (men) should receive more compensation. Sport economist Andrew Zimbalist (1999) showed that this was not necessarily true because the coaches of men's teams earned greater salaries than what would be expected if the compensation was based on the financial return of their teams. Zimbalist suggests that differences in men's and women's salaries are a function of social factors (i.e., discrimination), not economic rationale.

It is interesting that these salary discrepancies between men and women do not necessarily result in outrage by women. Parks, Russell, Wood, Roberton, and Shewokis (1995) describe a phenomenon known as the "paradox of the contented working women," in which women receive lower pay than their male counterparts, yet are equally satisfied with their compensation, if not more satisfied. This is especially prevalent among women working in male-dominated professions. In the 1995 Parks et al. study of intercollegiate athletic administrators, the authors found that men earned $6,000 more, on average, than did the women. Despite this difference, the job satisfaction among men and women in their sample was the same. To explain their findings, Parks et al. suggest that "contemporary female administrators working in a male-dominated environment may incorrectly consider themselves to be 'pioneers' involved in 'men's work'" (p. 77), or just not be aware of the salary discrepancies.

Representation in Management and Leadership Positions

Women have historically been underrepresented in organizational management and leadership positions. As recently as 1972, women filled only 17 percent of all management positions. Times changed, however, and by 1995, women filled

42.7 percent of all management positions (Stroh, Langlands, & Simpson, 2004). These data suggest that women are making strides within organizational settings. A closer look at the data, however, reveals that women continue to be severely underrepresented in top management positions. A study by Catalyst (2000) found that only 12.5 percent of all corporate officers, 11.7 percent of all board directors, and two Fortune 500 chief executive officers were women. These data suggest that as we look up the corporate ladder, we find fewer and fewer women.

Similar trends are apparent in sport organizations. Women only represent 36 percent of the commissioners for the Australian Sports Commission (Australian Sports Commission, 2005) and less than a third of the council members in Sport England (Sport England, 2005). Within North America, women represent only 17 percent of the Executive Committee for the NCAA (National Collegiate Athletic Association, 2005), and only 38 percent of the directors of the Coaching Association of Canada (Coaching Association of Canada, 2005).

Women are also underrepresented as coaches. In 1972, women constituted over 90 percent of the coaches of NCAA women's teams. As a result of Title IX being enacted that same year, the coaching compensation and the prestige associated with coaching women's teams gradually increased. Consequently, being a coach of a women's team served as a viable alternative for men, and they steadily began to occupy a larger proportion of the coaching positions for women's teams (Acosta & Carpenter, 2006). By 1978, the percentage of women serving as the head coach of a women's team had dropped to 58.2 percent. In 2006, women represented less than half (42.4 percent) of the head coaches of women's teams—one of the lowest percentages ever recorded (Acosta & Carpenter, 2006; see Exhibit 5.4). There is evidence this trend may be continuing. Of the 270 new coaching jobs of women's teams to open between 2002 and 2004, men received approximately 53 percent (Acosta & Carpenter, 2004). Canada has also witnessed an influx of men coaching women's teams, to an even greater extent among NCAA teams (Danylchuk, & MacLean, 2001).

This underrepresentation of women in management and leadership positions is referred to as the "glass ceiling" (see Stroh et al., 2004). This concept describes the invisible, but certainly real, barrier that limits the upward progression of women in the organizational context. In addition to the glass ceiling, women also encounter "glass walls" (akin to occupational segregation discussed in Chapter 4). Glass walls prevent people from moving laterally within an organization or profession. For example, women are often employed in the administrative ranks of university athletic departments in positions called Senior Women Administrators. They are rarely seen in management positions in development or those that oversee men's sports even though men are routinely charged with overseeing women's sports (see DeHass, 2004). Rather, these positions, which have high prestige and may be considered a requisite stepping-stone to becoming a head athletic director, are generally reserved for men. These ideas are consistent with the notion of hegemonic masculinity, as discussed in Chapter 2.

Exhibit 5.4   Percentage of women coaching women's teams.

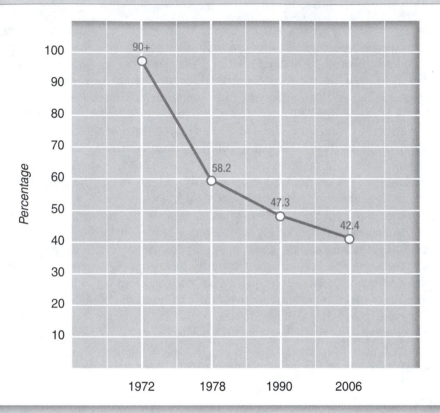

Data from Acosta & Carpenter, 2006.

Reasons for Underrepresentation

Understanding why women are underrepresented in management positions has been the subject of much research, both within and outside the sport context. Using this literature, we can identify three basic categories of factors that influence this phenomenon: stereotypes, structural forces, and personal characteristics. Each is discussed next (see Exhibit 5.5).

Stereotypes

Stereotypes influence the advancement of women in an organization in several ways. Specifically, they influence people's attitudes about whether women exhibit leadership characteristics and the job types considered appropriate for women.

Leadership. In her classic work, Schein (1973, 1975) compiled a list of 92 attributes believed to distinguish men and women, thus serving as the basis for

Factors that influence the underrepresentation of women in coaching positions.	*Exhibit 5.5*

Gender stereotypes:

- Leadership: Effective leaders are thought to possess masculine characteristics.

- Job type: Coaching is considered a profession best suited for men.

Structural forces:

- Discrimination: Athletic administrators favor men over women in the hiring process.

- Social networks: Women's social networks are not as strong as the "old boys club" with which men are associated.

- Nature of the coaching profession: The work–family conflict associated with coaching may have a stronger impact on women than it does on men.

Personal characteristics:

- Attitudes about being a head coach: Women have less positive attitudes about becoming a head coach than men.

- Intention to become a head coach: Women, when compared to men, have less desire to become a head coach.

- Occupational turnover: Women leave coaching at an earlier age than men do, thereby creating a shortage of qualified women coaches.

gender stereotypes. She asked a sample of middle managers to rate how those 92 characteristics fit women in general, men in general, and effective middle managers. As expected, she found that the characteristics believed to embody the successful middle manager were closely aligned with those thought to be representative of a man in general. This was true for both male and female respondent managers in her sample. Thus, to think of a successful manager was to think of a man, not a woman.

More recent research shows that people associate masculine characteristics with successful managers, and that people are more likely to use masculine, rather than feminine, pronouns when describing an ideal manager (Willemsen, 2002). A study by Shaw and Slack (2002) of sport national governing bodies in England supports these findings. They found that female leaders were usually described in terms of their elegance and style, with no mention of their leadership qualities being advanced. On the other hand, male leaders were noted for their vision and revolutionary style. Managers' behaviors are also cast in gender stereotypes. Shaw and Hoeber (2003) found that people within sport

alternative
P E R S P E C T I V E S

Women and Transformational Leadership. Thoughts about who makes an effective leader have traditionally favored men. This is due to the link between gender stereotypes and the perceived qualities of good leaders. Recent leadership theory questions assumption. Many researchers believe transformational leaders are the best type for an organization. *Transformational leaders* have charisma and provide inspirational motivation, intellectual stimulation, and individualized consideration. Because some of these attributes are thought to be consistent with feminine gender stereotypes, it is possible that women are more likely to be transformational leaders than men. Organizations led by transformational leaders are likely to have high levels of effectiveness and a committed workforce. Doherty (1997) found that coaches rated female administrators as demonstrating greater charisma and more individualized consideration. This finding suggests that, contrary to traditional stereotypes, women may be as suited as men to lead groups and organizations, if not more so.

organizations believe that "a strong man is direct and a direct woman is a bitch" (p. 347). See the Alternative Perspectives box for a further discussion of this issue.

As might be expected, these stereotypes can negatively influence women's career advancement. If organizational decision makers associate "being a manager" with "being a man," then women are at a distinct disadvantage in the hiring process. To the extent that primary decision makers hold such perceptions, stereotypes will limit the advancement of women.

Job type. Gender stereotypes concerning the type of jobs and activities considered appropriate for men and women also influence the proportion of women in leadership positions. The U. S. Census Bureau data document sex differences in occupational employment. For example, the top occupations employing men in 2004 included truck drivers, managers of retail sales workers, retail salespersons, and general laborers. On the other hand, the top occupations employing women in 2004 included secretaries, elementary and middle school teachers, registered nurses, cashiers, and retail salespersons. Note that only one occupation, retail salesperson, appears on both lists.

This pattern suggests that some job types are considered masculine in nature, and thus more suitable for men, while others are considered feminine and more appropriate for women. The gendering of jobs and activities also occurs within the sport and physical activity industry. Shaw and Slack (2002) found that men hesitated to fill some positions, such as regional development officer, in the sport organizations they studied because of the positions' legacy as "women's work" (p. 93). Similarly, Knoppers (1992) argues that coaching is associated with masculine qualities and as a place for men. This stereotype remains even though many of the activities associated with coaching, such as nurturing athletes, facilitating their play, and providing them with individualized consideration, are more feminine in nature than masculine. Because coaching is considered a job more suitable for men, women are disadvantaged in the profession.

Structural Forces

Structural forces refer to those forces in place, either in the coaching profession or the individual athletic departments, that serve to constrain the advancement of women. These forces include discrimination, social networks, and the nature of the coaching profession, as discussed below.

Discrimination. Much research points to discrimination, both access or treatment, as influencing the underrepresentation of women in coaching (Knoppers, 1992; Lovett & Lowry, 1994; Lowry & Lovett, 1997; Stangl & Kane, 1991). For examples in the leisure industry, see Aitchison, Jordan, and Brackenridge (1999). This discrimination takes several forms. Organizational decision makers could prefer men over women when filling coaching vacancies. In the athletics context, this means that athletic directors, most of whom are men, prefer other men to serve as coaches. This rationale is consistent with the social categorization framework and is supported by earlier studies. Acosta and Carpenter (2006) report that in Division I athletic departments run by a male, women represent 43.3 percent of the coaches of women's teams. This figure is less than the 48.5 percent of women coaching women's teams when the athletic director is female. When there are no women in an athletic department's administrative structure, women represent 38.5 percent of the coaches of women's teams.

Others adopt a different approach, suggesting that power is at the heart of the matter. Mary Jo Kane, director of the Tucker Center for Research on Girls and Women in Sport at the University of Minnesota, commented on the status of women coaching women's teams: "I think it can be summed up in one word: power. The stakes have gotten higher—there's money, scholarships, TV contracts. It's a new career for men, and men have taken it over" (as cited in Anderson, 2001, p. 88). Consistent with the previous discussion of gender stereotypes, Kane also suggests, "I think there is still some deep-seated cultural assumption that if you want to take your program big time, you want to get a *real* coach, so you should get a male coach" (as cited in Anderson, 2001, p. 88). Thus, gender stereotypes may lead organizational decision makers to consciously decide to hire men over women, thinking that men are more likely to have "what it takes" to be a successful coach.

Treatment discrimination also influences the underrepresentation of women in coaching positions. Because current women coaches are treated differently, there are variations in the career outcomes achieved by men and women. A study by Cunningham and Sagas (2002) lends credence to this position. These authors surveyed male and female assistant coaches of men's and women's university athletics teams and found that women had more valued human capital investments (e.g., playing experience, playing honors) than the men. In fact, 25 percent of all men in the sample never played university athletics, compared to just 3.3 percent of women without such experience. Nevertheless, men had longer coaching tenures and more desired attitudes toward coaching (e.g., head coaching intentions) than did the women. The authors reason that although women had greater human capital, they did not receive the return on such investments that the men did. Therefore, their attitudes toward the profession were not as positive as the men's attitudes. This reasoning is supported by various studies both in (Sagas & Cunningham, 2004) and out of the sport context (Kirchmeyer, 1998). To explain this pattern, Kirchmeyer notes, "low returns for female managers can be explained by perceptual distortions and cognitive biases among employers that lead to discriminatory practices" (p. 675). Thus, sex differences in the return on human capital investments negatively influence women's advancement in the coaching profession.

Social networks. The underrepresentation of women can also be attributed to dissimilarities in the social networks of male and female coaches. Social networks serve many important functions, including providing access to information, mentoring, and supporting upward mobility (Seibert, Kraimer, & Liden, 2001). People who are successful in forming social networks are likely to have greater career success than those who cannot form such alliances. Furthermore, people who have networks comprised of demographically similar others are likely to enjoy greater career success than those whose social networks are comprised of demographically different people (Seibert et al., 2001). This presents a quandary for women, especially in the sport context, as access to demographically similar social networks may be limited. That is, if coaching is considered a male domain and men are more likely to be coaches than are women, then men have a mathematically better chance of having other men in their social network than women do of having mostly women in their network. This is especially true when we consider those people in the network who are in high organizational positions, such as athletic director.

What impact does a social network have on female coaches? The answer is: a substantial one. Many point to the "good old boys" network prevalent in the sport context (for an example, see Lovett & Lowry, 1994) as a reason for the underrepresentation of women in coaching and leadership positions. Christine Grant, the women's athletic director at the University of Iowa, speaks to this issue: "I don't think there is a concerted effort to go and get qualified women. If you want well-qualified women candidates, you have to get on the phone and do your homework. Male athletic directors apparently aren't doing that. When they hire male coaches, they are on the phone with their buddies finding out what their recommendations are" (as cited in Anderson, 2001, p. 88). Thus, consistent with Grant's position, when it comes to coaching, or being considered for a coaching position, "who you know" might be just as important as "what you know."

Nature of the coaching profession. Coaching requires 12 to 15 hour workdays, extensive travel to games and events, and tireless hours spent watching game films, practicing, and recruiting quality players. The coaching profession's nature means that time spent performing other life activities such as those related to friends and family must be reduced, given half-heartedly, or put on hold for another time. As Dixon and Bruening (2005) note, women are more likely than men to experience stress resulting from conflicts between time spent at work and time spent with family, a phenomenon known as *work–family conflict*. As previously discussed, gender stereotypes call for the woman to spend more time than the man on family and domestic duties. Thus, women are more likely than men to have to choose between coaching and family or find a compromise between the two (but see also Greenhaus & Powell, 2006, for a discussion of work–family enrichment).

Women who do balance these roles either have support from friends and family or wait until later in life to begin a family. For Purdue swim coach Cathy Wright-Eger, the answer is a strong support network that includes parents, in-laws, sisters, and friends who all help with family issues while she is away coaching (Anderson, 2001). Pat Summitt, the women's basketball coach at the University of Tennessee, also notes the potential stress "for women who are trying to balance family and a coaching career, it is very difficult" (Anderson, 2001, p. 91). Summitt did not have her son until she was 38—after she was well-established in the coaching profession and could afford a full-time nanny. Of course, not all coaches are as successful as Summitt, have her financial security ($550,000 annual salary), or can afford a full-time nanny. Thus, discussions on how women can successfully manage their coaching life and their family life continue.

Personal Characteristics

Personal characteristics such as attitude toward being a head coach, intention to become a head coach, and the decision to leave the coaching profession influence women's underrepresentation. When discussing these factors, it is important to remember that personal characteristics are, by and large, shaped by gender stereotypes, societal expectations, and structural forces. Some factors, such as personality, are considered fairly stable over time and are at least partially due to genetics. Other characteristics (e.g., self-efficacy, outcome expectations, and head coaching intentions), however, are largely shaped by personal experiences; the influence of family, friends, and coworkers; and societal expectations and stereotypes. Thus, discussing the personal characteristics is not a "blame the victim" approach (Knoppers, 1987; Staurowsky, 1996); rather, not discussing such factors paints an incomplete picture of the phenomenon.

Attitudes about being a head coach. Research documents sex differences in attitudes toward being a head coach. For example, Sagas, Cunningham, and Ashley (2000) surveyed 112 assistant coaches (72 women, 40 men) of a variety of NCAA Division I athletic teams. They asked the coaches to indicate why they would not seek head coaching positions. The women in the sample listed the following as the most important factors: (a) they enjoy their current coaching situation and do not want to leave, (b) there is too much pressure to win as a head coach, (c) there is less stress associated with being an assistant coach, and (d) loyalty to their current team or head coach. Because the men in the sample had no aversion to being a head coach (a point discussed in the next section), they did not respond to these items. Other coaches express similar sentiments. Mickie DeMoss, a former head coach at the University of Florida and current associate coach at Tennessee, notes, "women establish relationships where they are, and there's a greater sense of loyalty with women than with men. If they get comfortable somewhere, that means more to women than to men" (as cited in Anderson, 2001, p. 90). The negative attitudes some women have toward being a head coach prevents them from seeking those positions.

Intention to become a head coach. An aspiration for career advancement is one of the most fundamental antecedents to progressing in one's career. Without such an aspiration, one is unlikely to make the human and social capital investments necessary to become a manager, to seek such positions, or to ultimately be promoted. Using this rationale, Cunningham and associates examined head coaching intentions among assistant coaches across a variety of contexts (Cunningham & Sagas, 2002; Cunningham, Doherty, & Gregg, 2005; Cunningham, Sagas, & Ashley, 2003; Sagas, Cunningham, & Ashley, 2000). The findings reliably show that women have less desire to become a head coach and are less likely to apply for such positions. Sagas, Cunningham, and Ashley found that 92.5 percent of men in their sample had a desire to become a head coach, compared to 68.1 percent of women. These findings were replicated in several studies, and hold for both American (Cunningham & Sagas, 2002; Cunningham et al., 2003) and Canadian (Cunningham et al., 2005) coaches. Consistent with these findings, Sagas, Cunningham, and Ashley (2000) also found men were more likely than women to have sought head coaching positions in the past (37.5 percent versus 15.2 percent).

That female assistant coaches have less desire to become a head coach than do men is one of the more salient factors influencing the underrepresentation of women in head coaching positions. If male assistant coaches are more likely to search for head coaching positions and express a greater desire to obtain such a position in the future, then the representation of women in head coaching positions is going to continue to lag behind that of men.

Occupational turnover. Differences in occupational turnover also influence the underrepresentation of women in head coaching positions. In a study by Sagas, Cunningham, and Ashley (2000), 68 percent of the women in the sample reported that they planned to leave the profession prior to age 45, a substantially higher percentage than men (15 percent) expressing similar plans.

Subsequent research supports this finding, both among assistant coaches (Cunningham & Sagas, 2002, 2003; Cunningham et al., 2003) and head coaches (Sagas & Ashley, 2001; Sagas & Batista, 2001). These findings are also consistent with research in other contexts, such as high school sports (Hart, Hasbrook, & Mathes, 1986). The problem associated with sex differences in occupational turnover is exacerbated when we consider that the vacancies are likely to be filled by men (Acosta & Carpenter, 2004; Hart et al., 1986).

Section Summary

Several factors contribute to the underrepresentation of women in coaching positions. Stereotypes about what women should do, who they should be, and what characteristics a successful coach should possess all work against women. When organizational decision makers, most of whom are male, seek to hire others who are demographically similar to themselves, the opportunity for women to be seriously considered is significantly reduced. Finally, not only are women less likely to seek head coaching positions, but they are also more likely to leave coaching at an earlier age than men, thereby creating a supply-side shortage of women coaches.

Sex, Gender, and Sport Participation

The discussion now turns to participation in sport and physical activity. Research shows few sex differences in physical activity levels among infants. However, as people grow older, differences emerge—in the toddler, youth, young adult, adult, and older populations, males are more physically active than females (Carron, Hausenblas, & Estabrooks, 2003).

There are several reasons for the sport participation differences between males and females. As previously noted in the discus-

PROFESSIONAL PERSPECTIVES

Women in Mexico. Although much of the research related to women in the sport industry takes place in the United States or Canada, it is also useful to consider women's work experiences in other countries such as Mexico. Gabriela Deyanira Martinez Garcia, who served as the women's athletic coordinator at Universidad Autonoma de Nuevo Leon from 2003 to 2005, explains that, in general, "women are not given the opportunity to hold decision-making positions in sports organizations either in universities, government, or any other organization." These limited opportunities are largely the result of men holding the power positions within sport organizations and selecting other men to fill vacancies. Garcia also notes that many men "consider that women have no right to be in leadership positions. The predominance of 'machismo' is the main factor why women are relegated and faced with limitations to do their work." (Note that machismo is a strong sense of masculine pride or an exaggerated masculinity considered to be present in many Latin cultures). She further notes that, although attitudes toward women are slowly changing, it will be a long time before women obtain decision-making positions based on their experiences and knowledge rather than the politics involved.

sion of gender stereotypes, parental influences, schools, and the mass media all connote sport and physical activity as more appropriate for males than for females. In the early 1970s, *Sports Illustrated* columnists Bil Gilbert and Nancy Williamson noted, "there may be worse (more socially serious) forms of prejudice in the United States, but there is no sharper example of discrimination today than that which operates against girls and women who take part in competitive sports, wish to take part, or might wish to if society did not scorn such endeavors" (as cited in Eitzen & Sage, 2003, p. 309). Given these stereotypes, it is easy to understand why girls and women chose not to participate in sport in the past.

However, over time, female involvement in sport increased substantially. Coakley (2004) points to five factors that influenced this increase:

1. Females have far more opportunities for sport participation today than ever before. Females have many sport and physical activity alternatives from which to choose.

2. Government mandates increased sport opportunities for girls and women. Most notably, Title IX requires equal opportunities for males and females participating in federally funded educational activities, including physical education courses and athletics. Title IX prohibits schools from offering sport opportunities and activities for one group (i.e., boys) and not the other (i.e., girls) in nearly all situations. Title IX is discussed in length in Chapter 10.

3. The global women's movement promotes that females are most complete as human beings when they develop their mental *and* physical abilities.

4. The health and fitness movement, which emphasizes the positive health benefits associated with sport participation, increased the awareness and appreciation of sport and physical activity, with an associated increase in those activities.

5. Increased media coverage of girls and women participating in sport prompted others to participate. Now, young girls have role models to show them that females not only can participate in sport, but can excel in it. These media images are powerful and inspiring, resulting in an increase in the interest in sport and physical activity among females.

The Intersection of Sex and Race

Thus far, the experiences of men and women were discussed in general terms. However, not all men and not all women have similar experiences in sport or sport organizations. Rather, other factors such as race may significantly influence one's experiences in the workplace. The effects of sex and race are likely not additive; rather, women of color are likely to have experiences that differ from those of men of color or White women. This section examines the intersection of sex and race among persons in the sport context (for further discussion of this issue, see Bruening, 2005).

Earnings

Sex and race interact to influence people's earnings. As previously indicated, men generally earn more than women, and Whites generally earn more than racial minorities. Examination of the data from the U. S. Census Bureau reveals other interesting patterns. For example, among men, African Americans and Hispanics earn 73.1 percent and 59.3 percent of what Whites earn, respectively. The variations are less pronounced among women, though the general pattern still remains. African American women earn 83.6 percent of what White women earn, while Hispanic women earn only 68.3 (see Exhibit 5.6).

An examination of sex differences within each race yields interesting findings as well. White women earn 72.9 percent of what White men earn. The magnitude of the earnings differences is less pronounced among African American men and women (83.3 percent) and Hispanic men and women (84.0 percent). Of course, White men earn the most among all people compared in this analysis, so that may contribute to these differences. Nevertheless, the figures reported here do illustrate how race and sex interact to influence earnings.

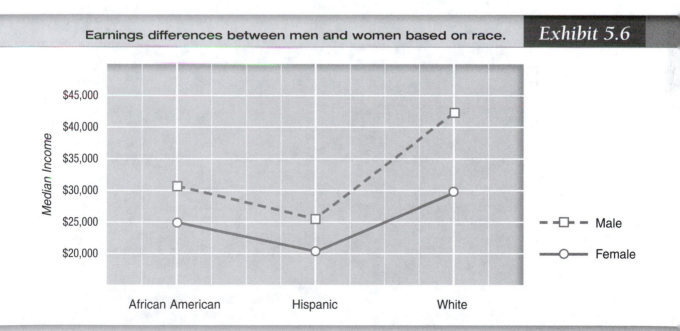

Earnings differences between men and women based on race.   *Exhibit 5.6*

U. S. Census Bureau data.

Representation in Management and Leadership Positions

As previously noted, women are generally underrepresented in management and leadership positions. The underrepresentation increases further when considering women of color (see Exhibit 5.7). For example, in the Australian Sports Commission, Sport England, the NCAA, and the Coaching Association of Canada, the proportion of White women far outnumbers that of minority women. On many of these boards, women of color are not represented at all. The same is true within university athletic departments. According to DeHass (2004), White women constitute 88.4 percent of the senior women administrators, compared to just 11.6 percent for women of color. These figures demonstrate that racial minor-

Exhibit 5.7   Racial differences in the representation of women in administrative positions within university athletics.

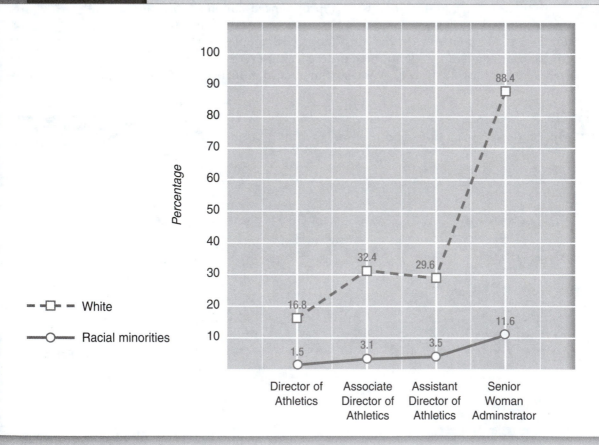

Data from DeHass, 2004.

ity women face particularly challenging obstacles in the workplace, both in their compensation and in their advancement up the organizational hierarchy.

Sport Participants

Women of color are more likely to have poor health (e.g., be overweight) and less likely to be physically active than White women (see Armstrong, 2001; Henderson & Ainsworth, 2001). Because physical activity improves one's health, several studies examined factors that influence participation in sport and recreational programs by racial minority women. Henderson and Ainsworth (2001), in their qualitative study of African American and Native American women, identified several factors that influenced physical activity levels. Job demands, family expectations and needs, economic constraints, and the lack of available facilities and opportunities were listed for women of both races as the major constraints to physical activity participation. Armstrong (2001) reports that the results of a nationwide research project consisting of mostly African American women indicate that lack of motivation, lack of time, lack of energy, and prohibitive costs are the top barriers to being physically active. Interestingly, younger women were more likely to cite these constraints than their older counterparts. In both studies, those women who participated in sport and recreational activities cited strong support networks. The support comes from friends, family, or other community members. Finally, in both studies, walking was reported as the most popular physical activity. As Henderson and Ainsworth note, walking was appealing because of its accessibility to all persons, the social and/or solitary dimensions of the activity, and the thinking that it is "not really exercise" (p. 28).

Using another perspective, the Women's Sports Foundation (Butler & Lopiano, 2003) commissioned a study to examine the influence of Title IX on men and women across races who participated in university athletics. The study was commissioned because anecdotal evidence suggested that women of color had not benefited from Title IX to the extent that White women had. The results indicate that this is not the case. Since 1971, the number of women of color participating in university athletics increased 995 percent, a figure much larger than the corresponding increase for White women (320 percent). Women of color also receive a percentage of the scholarship monies (19.5 percent) above what might be expected based on their proportion of all female athletes (14.8 percent). Finally, racial minority women athletes graduate at lower rates than White women athletes (55 percent versus 68 percent); however, this proportion is substantially higher than the proportion of minority women in the general student body (49 percent).

Based on this data, Butler and Lopiano arrived at several conclusions. First, claims that people of color are disadvantaged as a result of Title IX seem unfounded. Second, based on the representation of female athletes of color across all sports and their experiences while participating in those sports, sex and race discrimination are still present in the context of university athletics. Third, patterns of racial inequality are present in most women's sports, as clustering effects (i.e., the overrepresentation of athletes of color in some sports, but underrepresentation in others) are present in 20 of 25 (80 percent) of women's sports. Finally, there is no overt evidence of graduation rate or scholarship bias for athletes of color, as female athletes of color receive a greater proportion of scholarship dollars than would be expected based on their participation rates and also graduate at higher rates than their racially similar peers in the general student body. Overall then, Title IX can be seen as benefiting, not hurting, racial minority women who participate in university athletics.

The Marketing of Sport

The influence of sex and gender is evident in the marketing of sport and physical activity. Marketing efforts traditionally have been geared toward attracting the "average fan" to the event—that is, the efforts have been aimed at men (Fink, Trail, & Anderson, 2002). Today, women represent a growing segment of the fan base. Further, research shows that, relative to men, women are more likely to purchase team merchandise and remain loyal to the team in the future (Fink et al., 2002). Nevertheless, research suggests that men and women have different motivations for attending events and react differently to services provided at the event. Thus, it is important to understand these differences so more effective and efficient marketing efforts can be implemented.

Motives for Sport Consumption

Several studies examined different reasons men and women have for attending events. Swanson, Gwinner, Larson, and Janda (2003) argue that gender stereotypes guide motivations for sport consumption. They predicted that men, who are thought to be more aggressive and success oriented, might value those activities that are high in entertainment value, stimulate them, and provide a sense of self-worth when the team succeeds. On the other hand, women, with their presumed emphasis on feminine qualities such as communal concerns, might be more apt to seek activities that are family oriented. These predictions were largely supported, as men's attendance was primarily guided by the motivation to be emotionally aroused at the event (a concept known as eustress). Women, on the other hand, were primarily motivated to attend sport events for group affiliation reasons. Other researchers obtained similar results (Wann, 1995; Wann, Schrader, & Wilson, 1999).

Consuming Women's Sports

Other studies examined the reasons for attending women's sport events. Funk, Ridinger, and Moorman (2003) studied people who chose to attend women's professional basketball games. In addition to those motives identified in other sport contexts, the authors uncovered unique motivations for attending women's events, including players serving as role models, the need to support opportunities for women to compete in sports, and the perception of women's sports as a wholesome environment. The former two variables were especially influential in explaining the level of team support among the fans. As Funk et al. note, both of these factors could be leveraged by sport marketers to increase sport consumption among women, both young and old.

Customer Service

Team success is one of the most reliable indicators of fan loyalty; however, not all teams can be successful. As such, other factors such as customer service satisfaction become important in gaining consumer trust and loyalty. Trail, Anderson, and Fink (2002) found that women rated several service quality factors as more important than men did, including the cleanliness of the facilities, the quality of the restrooms, the audio experience, and the quality of the service personnel. These findings are consistent with research outside the sport context that shows that some service provider characteristics, such as the appropriateness of the attire, have a stronger influence on women's affective reactions than on men's (Shaoa, Baker, & Wagner, 2004). These results suggest that sex likely moderates the relationship between event factors other than performance and satisfaction with the event. Specifically, these factors may be more important to the formation of women's satisfaction with the event than men's satisfaction.

Promoting Sport

Finally, other studies examined gender issues in relation to promoting sport events. Fink, Cunningham, and Kensicki (2004) drew from the match-up hypothesis, which suggests that advertising endorsers are more effective when there is a match between them and the product. They examined the influence of athlete attractiveness and expertise in an advertisement promoting women's softball. Results from their experiment indicate that both attractiveness and expertise influence the fit of the endorser. Specifically, participants who believed the athlete was attractive and that she had a high level of expertise also believed that she was an appropriate endorser of the athletic event. Such fit perceptions are important because they influence both positive attitudes toward the event and the intention to purchase tickets for the event. That athlete expertise influences perceptions of endorser fit is expected, as highly skilled athletes, such as Serena Williams, are likely to be more effective endorsers of an athletic event than less skilled athletes. However, that attractiveness—an attribute that has nothing to do with how masterful a sport is played—also positively influences fit perceptions is consistent with gender stereotypes calling for women to maintain their femininity and beauty while participating in sports. Promoters of sport events remain mindful of this stereotype, as evidenced by the popularity of some attractive but not highly successful athletes as event promoters (e.g., Anna Kournikova).

Chapter Summary

This chapter focused on the experiences of men and women in the sport context. The Diversity Challenge demonstrated the substantial influence of sex and gender on who participates in sport, the allocation of resources, and attitudes toward sport. The same is also true in the workplace—work experiences, compensation, access to managerial and leadership positions, and attitudes toward their careers differ as between men and women. After reading the chapter, you should be able to:

1. **Understand the meaning of sex and gender and the differences between the two concepts.**

Sex refers to the biological characteristics, such as reproductive organs, that distinguish men and women. Gender, on the other hand, refers to the social roles expected of men and women, with an emphasis on the concepts of masculinity and femininity. Though the two terms are sometimes used interchangeably, especially when referring to biological differences (e.g., "his gender is male"), they have separate meanings and connotations.

2. **Discuss the differing experiences men and women have in the workplace.**

Across a variety of contexts, research shows that, relative to men, women are less likely to be members of the workforce, receive less compensation for their work, and are less likely to be in upper-echelon management positions. These trends are present in the sport and physical activity context as well. Considerable research examined why women are underrepresented in management and leadership positions, revealing three possible explanations: stereotypes, structural forces, and personal characteristics.

3. **Be familiar with the influence of sex and gender on sport participation.**

Women are generally less physically active than their male counterparts. This is due, in large part, to gender stereotypes emanating from various socialization agents (e.g., parents, school, media). More recently, women's participation in sport has increased, largely due to five factors: (a) increased opportunities, (b) governmental mandates, (c) the global women's movement, (d) the health and fitness movement, and (e) increased media coverage of women's sport.

4. **Discuss the intersection of race and sex.**

Research shows that women are generally disadvantaged when compared to men and that racial minorities are generally disadvantaged when compared to Whites. For women of color, these effects are magnified, such that their experiences, both in the general workplace and in sport, are considered to be poorer than people from other social groups. When compared to others, women of color receive the lowest salaries and are least likely to hold management positions. These effects are also seen among sport participants, as these women often face unique challenges when seeking physical activity participation opportunities.

5. Understand the influence of sex and gender on the marketing of sport.

Though sport marketing efforts traditionally have been geared toward a "male" prototype, there is a growing recognition that women and consumers of women's sports have unique motivations, wants, and desires when it comes to consuming sport. From a customer service perspective, the factors that women value in the service exchange oftentimes vary from those of men. Finally, research shows that gender stereotypes likely influence marketing and promotion efforts, as spokespersons for athletic events are generally better received when they are highly qualified *and* highly attractive.

Questions for Discussion

1. What are the primary gender stereotypes associated with men and women? Are those stereotypes still observed today?

2. What are the primary factors that influence the formation of gender stereotypes? Which is likely to have the strongest impact?

3. What is the influence of gender stereotypes on participation in sport and physical activity?

4. Why are sex differences in earnings still present today? Are they more likely to be seen in one context than in another?

5. Women are underrepresented in top management positions. What are some of the reasons for this phenomenon?

6. Several potential explanations for the underrepresentation of women in management and leadership positions were discussed in the chapter. Which is the most important in explaining this phenomenon?

7. Why does the participation of women in sport and physical activity lag behind that of men? What steps can sport managers take to reverse this trend?

8. This chapter suggested that women of color have experiences in sport and in the workplace that are unique to them. Why is this the case?

9. Are the experiences of all women of color likely to be the same? If not, why and what are examples of where this would not be the case?

Learning Activities

1. Suppose you are involved in searching for a coach for a women's team at your university. What emphasis would you put on the sex of the coach in the hiring process? What about the assistant coaches? Divide into two groups and discuss.

2. Using the Web, search for the presence of female administrators in national sport organizations such as United States Basketball.

Resources

SUPPLEMENTARY READINGS

Konrad, A. M. (2006). *Cases in gender and diversity in organizations.* Thousand Oaks, CA: Sage. (Provides real-life cases related to workplace discrimination, sexual harassment, work–life balance, organizational diversity programs, cross-cultural diversity, and entrepreneurship.)

Messner, M. (2002). *Taking the field: Women, men, and sports.* Minneapolis: University of Minnesota Press. (Argues that sport largely retains and continues its longtime conservative role in gender relations; considers the influences of the daily routines of sport participants, structural foundations in place, and the mass media.)

Powell, G. N., & Graves, L. M. (2003). *Women and men in management* (3rd ed.). Thousand Oaks, CA: Sage. (Comprehensive overview of the issues surrounding women in the workplace; examines historical aspects, sex and gender, and the influence of sex and gender on employment decisions, leadership, and career aspirations.)

WEB RESOURCES

- Black Women in Sport Foundation (www.blackwomeninsport.org/): examines intersection of race and sex for women participating in sport.

- National Association for Girls & Women in Sport (www.aahperd.org/nagws/template.cfm): division of the American Alliance for Health, Physical Education, Recreation, and Dance; good resource site.

- Women's Sports Foundation (www.womenssportsfoundation.org): provides a wide range of resources related to girls' and women's participation in sport.

References

Abercrombie, N., Hill, S., & Turner, B. S. (2000). *The Penguin dictionary of sociology* (4th ed.). New York: Penguin Books.

Acosta, R. V., & Carpenter, L. J. (2004). *Women in intercollegiate sport: A longitudinal study—twenty-seven year update—1977–2004.* Unpublished manuscript, Brooklyn College, Brooklyn, NY.

Acosta, R. V., & Carpenter, L. J. (2006). *Women in intercollegiate sport: A longitudinal study—twenty-nine year update—1977–2006.* Unpublished manuscript, Brooklyn College, Brooklyn, NY.

Aitchison, C., Jordan, F., & Brackenridge, C. (1999). Women in leisure management: A survey on gender equity. *Women in Management Review, 14*(4), 121–127.

Anderson, K. (2001, January/February). Where are all the women coaches? *Sports Illustrated for Women, 3*(1), 86–91.

Armstrong, K. L. (2001). Black women's participation in sport and fitness: Implications for sport marketing. *Sport Marketing Quarterly, 10,* 9–18.

Australian Sports Commission. (2005). *Board of the Australian Sports Commission.* Retrieved January 6, 2006, from www.ausport.gov.au

Bem, S. L. (1974). The measurement of psychological androgyny. *Journal of Consulting and Clinical Psychology, 42,* 155–162.

Bem, S. L. (1975). Sex role adaptability: One consequence of psychological androgyny. *Journal of Personality and Social Psychology, 31,* 634–643.

Bem, S. L. (1977). On the utility of alternative procedures for assessing psychological androgyny. *Journal of Consulting and Clinical Psychology, 45,* 196–205.

Bowker, A., Gadbois, S., & Cornock, B. (2003). Sports participation and self-esteem: Variations as a function of gender and gender role orientation. *Sex Roles, 49,* 47–58.

Bruening, J. E. (2005). Gender and racial analysis in sport: Are all the women White and all the Blacks men? *Quest, 57,* 330–349.

Butler, J. A., & Lopiano, D. A. (2003). *The Women's Sports Foundation report: Title IX and race in intercollegiate sport.* East Meadow, NY: Women's Sports Foundation.

Carpenter, L. J., & Acosta, R. V. (2005). *Title IX.* Champaign, IL: Human Kinetics.

Carron, A. V., Hausenblas, H. A., & Estabrooks, P. A. (2003). *The psychology of physical activity.* New York: McGraw-Hill.

Catalyst Institute. (2000). *Census of women corporate officers and top earners for the Fortune 500.* New York: Author.

Coaching Association of Canada. (2005). *Board of directors.* Retrieved January 6, 2006, from www.coach.ca/eng/

Coakley, J. (2004). *Sports in society: Issues and controversies* (8th ed.). New York: McGraw-Hill.

Color controversy at Iowa: Prof. threatened for criticizing pink locker room. (2005, September 28). SI.com. Retrieved September 28, 2005, from http://sportsillustrated.cnn.com/2005/football/ncaa/09/28/bc.fbc.bigtennotebook.ap/index.html

Cramer, J. A. (1994). Conversations with women journalists. In P. J. Creedon (Ed.), *Women, media, and sport: Challenging gender values* (pp. 159–180). Thousand Oaks, CA: Sage.

Cuneen, J., & Sidwell, M. J. (1998). Gender portrayals in *Sports Illustrated for Kids* advertisements: A content analysis of prominent and supporting models. *Journal of Sport Management, 12,* 39–50.

Cunningham, G. B., Sagas, M., & Ashley, F. B. (2003). Coaching self-efficacy, desire to head coach, and occupational turnover intent: Gender differences between NCAA assistant coaches of women's teams. *International Journal of Sport Psychology, 34,* 125–137.

Cunningham, G. B., & Sagas, M. (2002). The differential effects of human capital for male and female Division I basketball coaches. *Research Quarterly for Exercise and Sport, 73,* 489–495.

Cunningham, G. B., & Sagas, M. (2003). Occupational turnover intent among coaches of women's teams: The role of organizational work experiences. *Sex Roles, 49,* 185–190.

Cunningham, G. B., Doherty, A. J., & Gregg, M. J. (2005). *Using social cognitive career theory to understand head coaching intentions among assistant coaches.* Unpublished manuscript.

Danylchuk, K. E., & MacLean, J. (2001). Intercollegiate athletics in Canadian universities: Perspectives on the future. *Journal of Sport Management, 15,* 364–379.

Deeply offensive to me: Martha Burk protests new NHL advertising campaign. (2005, September). SI.com. Retrieved September 23, 2005, from http://sportsillustrated.cnn.com/2005/hockey/nhl/09/23/burk.ads.ap/index.html

DeHass, D. (2004). *2003–04 race and gender demographics of NCAA member institutions' athletics personnel.* Indianapolis, IN: National Collegiate Athletic Association.

Dixon, M. A., & Bruening, J. E. (2005). Perspectives on work–family conflict in sport: An integrated approach. *Sport Management Review, 8,* 227–253.

Doherty, A. J. (1997). The effect of leader characteristics on the perceived transformation/transactional leadership and impact on interuniversity athletic administrators. *Journal of Sport Management, 11,* 275–285.

Eastough, K., & Miller, P. W. (2004). The gender wage gap in paid- and self-employment in Australia. *Australian Economic Papers, 43,* 257–276.

Eccles, J. S., Jacobs, J. E., & Harold, R. E. (1990). Gender role stereotypes, expectancy efforts, and parents' socialization of gender differences. *Journal of Social Issues, 46,* 183–201.

Eitzen, D. S., & Sage, G. H. (2003). *Sociology of North American sport* (7th ed.). New York: McGraw-Hill.

Fink, J. S., Cunningham, G. B., & Kensicki, L. J. (2004). Utilizing athletes as endorsers to sell women's sport: Attractiveness versus expertise. *Journal of Sport Management, 18,* 350–367.

Fink, J. S., & Kensicki, L. J. (2002). An imperceptible difference: Visual and textual constructions of femininity in *Sports Illustrated* and *Sports Illustrated for Women. Mass Communication & Society, 5,* 317–339.

Fink, J. S., Trail, G. T., & Anderson, D. F. (2002). Environmental factors associated with spectator attendance and sport consumption behavior. Gender and team differences. *Sport Marketing Quarterly, 11,* 8–19.

Funk, D. C., Ridinger, L. L., & Moorman, A. M. (2003). Understanding consumer support: Extending the Sport Interest Inventory to examine individual differences among women's professional sport consumers. *Sport Management Review, 6,* 1–31.

Greenhaus, J. H., & Powell, G. N. (2006). When work and family are allies: A theory of work–family enrichment. *Academy of Management Review, 31,* 72–92.

Halpern, D. F. (2000). *Sex differences in cognitive abilities* (3rd ed.). Mahwah, NJ: Lawrence Erlbaum.

Hart, B. A., Hasbrook, C. A., & Mathes, S. A. (1986). An examination of the reduction in the number of female interscholastic coaches. *Research Quarterly for Exercise and Sport, 57,* 68–77.

Henderson, K. A., & Ainsworth, B. E. (2001). Researching leisure and physical activity with women of color: Issues and emerging questions. *Leisure Sciences, 23,* 21–34.

Hoffman, L. W., & Youngblood, L. M. (1999). *Mothers at work: Effects on children's well-being.* Cambridge, UK: Cambridge University Press.

Humphreys, B. R. (2000). Equal pay on the hardwood: The earnings gap between male and female NCAA Division I basketball coaches. *Journal of Sports Economics, 1,* 299–307.

Kane, M. J. (1988). Media coverage of the female athlete before, during, and after Title IX: *Sports Illustrated* revisited. *Journal of Sport Management, 2*, 87–99.

Kirchmeyer, C. (1998). Determinants of managerial career success: Evidence and explanation of male/female differences. *Journal of Management, 24*, 673–692.

Kling, K. C., Hyde, J. S., Showers, C. J., & Buswell, B. N. (1999). Gender differences in self-esteem: A meta-analysis. *Psychological Bulletin, 125*, 470–500.

Knoppers, A. (1987). Gender and the coaching profession. *Quest, 39*, 9–22.

Knoppers, A. (1992). Explaining male dominance and sex segregation in coaching: Three approaches. *Quest, 44*, 210–227.

Lantz, C. D., & Schroeder, P. J. (1999). Endorsement of masculine and feminine gender roles: Differences between participation in and identification with the athletic role. *Journal of Sport Behavior, 22*, 545–556.

Lovett, D. J., & Lowry, C. D. (1994). "Good old boys" and "good old girls" clubs: Myth or reality? *Journal of Sport Management, 8*, 27–35.

Lowry, C. D., & Lovett, D. J. (1997). Women coaches: Does when dictate why they leave? *Applied Research in Coaching and Athletics Annual, 1997*, 35–53.

Lumpkin, A., & Williams, L. D. (1991). An analysis of *Sports Illustrated* feature articles, 1954–1987. *Sociology of Sport Journal, 8*, 16–32.

Lytton, H., & Romney, D. M. (1991). Parents' differential socialization of boys and girls: A meta-analysis. *Psychological Bulletin, 109*, 267–296.

National Collegiate Athletic Association. (2005). *Division I board of directors.* Retrieved January 6, 2006, from www.ncaa.org

Parks, J. B., & Roberton, M. A. (1998a). Contemporary arguments against nonsexist language: Blaubergs (1980) revisited. *Sex Roles, 39*, 445–461.

Parks, J. B., & Roberton, M. A. (1998b). Influence of age, gender, and context on attitudes toward sexist/nonsexist language: Is sport a special case? *Sex Roles, 38*, 477–494.

Parks, J. B., & Roberton, M. A. (2000). Development and validation of an instrument to measure attitudes toward sexist/nonsexist language. *Sex Roles, 42*, 415–438.

Parks, J. B., & Roberton, M. A. (2002). The gender gap in student attitudes toward sexist/nonsexist language: Implications for sport management education. *Journal of Sport Management, 16*, 190–208.

Parks, J. B., & Roberton, M. A. (2004). Attitudes toward women mediate the gender effect on attitudes toward sexist language. *Psychology of Women Quarterly, 28*, 233–239.

Parks, J. B., Russell, R. L., Wood, P. H., Roberton, M. A., & Shewokis, P. A. (1995). The paradox of the contented working woman in intercollegiate athletics administration. *Research Quarterly for Exercise and Sport, 66*, 73–79.

Pomerleau, A., Boldue, D., Malcuit, G., & Cossette, L. (1990). Pink or blue: Environmental stereotypes in the first two years of life. *Sex Roles, 22*, 359–367.

Powell, G. N., & Graves, L. M. (2003). *Women and men in management* (3rd ed.). Thousand Oaks, CA: Sage.

Pryzgoda, J., & Chrisler, J. C. (2000). Definitions of gender and sex: The subtleties of meaning. *Sex Roles, 43*, 553–569.

Sagas, M., & Ashley, F. B. (2001). Gender differences in the intent to leave coaching: The role of personal, external, and work-related variables. *International Journal of Sport Management, 2*, 297–314.

Sagas, M., & Batista, P. J. (2001). The importance of Title IX compliance on the job satisfaction and occupational turnover intent of intercollegiate coaches. *Applied Research in Coaching and Athletics Annual, 16*, 15–43.

Sagas, M., & Cunningham, G. B. (2004). Does having the "right stuff" matter? Gender differences in the determinants of career success among intercollegiate athletic administrators. *Sex Roles, 50,* 411–421.

Sagas, M., Cunningham, G. B., & Ashley, F. B. (2000). Examining the women's coaching deficit through the perspective of assistant coaches. *International Journal of Sport Management, 1,* 267–282.

Sagas, M., Cunningham, G. B., Wigley, B. J., & Ashley, F. B. (2000). Internet coverage of university softball and baseball Web sites: The inequity continues. *Sociology of Sport Journal, 17,* 198–205.

Schein, V. E. (1973). The relationship between sex role stereotypes and requisite management characteristics. *Journal of Applied Psychology, 57,* 95–100.

Schein, V. E. (1975). Relationships between sex role stereotypes and requisite management characteristics among female managers. *Journal of Applied Psychology, 60,* 340–344.

Seibert, S. E., Kraimer, M. L., & Liden, R. C. (2001). A social capital theory of career success. *Academy of Management Journal, 44,* 219–237.

Shakib, S., & Dunbar, M. D. (2004). How high school athletes talk about maternal and paternal sporting experiences: Identifying modifiable social processes for gender equity physical activity interventions. *International Review for the Sociology of Sport, 39,* 275–299.

Shaoa, C. Y., Baker, J., & Wagner, J. A. (2004). The effects of appropriateness of service contact personnel dress on customer expectations of service quality and purchase intention. The moderating influences of involvement and gender. *Journal of Business Research, 57,* 1164–1176.

Shaw, S., & Hoeber, L. (2003). "A strong man is direct and a direct woman is a bitch": Gendered discourses and their influence on employment roles in sport organizations. *Journal of Sport Management, 17,* 347–375.

Shaw, S., & Slack, T. (2002). "It's been like that for donkey's years": The construction of gender relations and the cultures of sports organizations. *Culture, Sport, Society, 5,* 86–106.

Shifflett, B., & Revelle, R. (1994). Gender equity in sports and media coverage: A review of the NCAA News? *Journal of Sport and Social Issues, 18,* 144–150.

Spence, J. T., & Helmreich, R. L. (1978). *Masculinity and femininity: Their psychological dimensions, correlates, and antecedents.* Austin: The University of Texas Press.

Sport England. (2005). *Who's who in Sport England.* Retrieved January 6, 2006, from www.sport england.org

Stangl, J. M., & Kane, M. J. (1991). Structural variables that offer explanatory power for the underrepresentation of women coaches since Title IX: The case of homologous reproduction. *Sociology of Sport Journal, 8,* 47–60.

Staurowsky, E. J. (1996). Blaming the victim: Resistance in the battle over gender equity in intercollegiate athletics. *Journal of Sport and Social Issues, 20,* 194–210.

Stroh, L. K., Langlands, C. L., & Simpson, P. A. (2004). Shattering the glass ceiling in the new millennium. In M. S. Stockdale & F. J. Crosby (Eds.), *The psychology and management of workplace diversity* (pp. 147–167). Malden, MA: Blackwell.

Swanson, S. R., Gwinner, K., Larson, B. V., & Janda, S. (2003). Motivations of college student game attendance and word-of-mouth behavior: The impact of gender differences. *Sport Marketing Quarterly, 12,* 151–162.

Trail, G., Anderson, D., & Fink, J. S. (2002). Examination of gender differences in importance and satisfaction with venue factors at intercollegiate basketball games: Effects of future spectator attendance. *International Sports Journal, 6,* 1–14.

Tuggle, C. A. (1997). Differences in televised sports reporting of men's and women's athletics: ESPN SportsCenter and CNN Sports Tonight. *Journal of Broadcasting and Electronic Media, 41*(1), 14–24.

Van Sickle, G. (2005, November). *Funk-y bunch: Skirt-wearing underdog brings life to Skins Game.* SI.com. Retrieved January 5, 2006, from http://sportsillustrated.cnn.com/2005/writers/gary_van_sickle/11/27/skins.game/index.html

Wann, D. L. (1995). Preliminary validation of the sport fan motivation scale. *Journal of Sport and Social Issues, 19,* 377–397.

Wann, D. L., Schrader, M. P., & Wilson, A. (1999). Sport fan motivation: Questionnaire validation, comparisons by sport, and relationship to athletic motivation. *Journal of Sport Behavior, 22,* 114–140.

Wann, D. L., Schrader, M. P., Allison, J. A., & McGeorge, K. K. (1998). The inequitable newspaper coverage of men's and women's athletics at small, medium, and large universities. *Journal of Sport and Social Issues, 22,* 79–87.

Ward, M. (2001). The gender salary gap in British academia. *Applied Economics, 33,* 1669–1681.

Willemsen, T. M. (2002). Gender typing of the successful manager: A stereotype reconsidered. *Sex Roles, 11,* 385–391.

Woodhill, B. M., & Samuels, C. A. (2003). Positive and negative androgyny and their relationship with psychological health and well-being. *Sex Roles, 48,* 555–565.

Zimbalist, A. (1999). *Unpaid professionals.* Princeton, NJ: Princeton University Press.

Categorical Effects of Age, Disability, and Obesity

DIVERSITY CHALLENGE

The fitness industry is a multibillion dollar segment of the U. S. economy and makes substantial economic contributions in countries worldwide. For example, Gold's Gym, founded in Venice Beach, California, in 1965, now has over 600 gyms in 25 countries around the world. Bally Total Fitness has over 400 gyms located in such countries as the United States, Canada, South Korea, China, and the Bahamas. The focus of these organizations, and others like them, is to help people reach their fitness goals. For many people, these goals are losing weight or increasing their overall health and fitness levels. Therefore, these gyms are open to all types of customers, young and old, fit and unfit.

Although fitness organizations are open to a diverse membership, the same is not always true for their employees. There may be a bias in favor of hiring individuals who appear fit over those who do not appear fit, suggesting the existence of anti-fat attitudes. Jennifer Portnick's situation supports this contention. Standing 5'8" and weighing 240 pounds, Portnick participated in high-impact aerobics for 15 years. Given her stamina and demonstrated excellence in the activity, her instructor, Kristi Howard, encouraged her to seek an aerobics certification with Jazzercise. Howard noted, "She has everything it takes. Jennifer is very healthy. She is not pooped out and sucking for air in class."

However, Ann Rieke, district manager for Jazzercise, saw things differently and denied Portnick's request for certification. Rieke wrote that although she believed Portnick "will be a fabulous instructor someday," she did not currently have the "fit appearance" needed to be a Jazzercise

LEARNING OBJECTIVES

After studying this chapter, you should be able to:

- Define age, disability, and obesity.

- Understand the importance of studying the physical aspects of diversity.

- Discuss the categorical effects of age, disability, and obesity for sport organization employees and sport and leisure participants and consumers.

- Discuss whether the aged, disabled, and obese should be considered minorities.

instructor. She further suggested that Portnick, who is primarily a vegetarian, change her diet and try body sculpting. After receiving Portnick's protest, Maureen Brown, the director for programs and services for Jazzercise, agreed with Rieke's initial conclusion. She indicated to Portnick that "a Jazzercise applicant must have a higher muscle-to-fat ratio and look leaner than the public. People must believe Jazzercise will help them improve, not just maintain their level of fitness. Instructors must set the example and be the role models for Jazzercise enthusiasts."

After Brown's decision, Portnick obtained certification through the Aerobics and Fitness Association of America and currently teaches six high-energy, low-impact classes a week. She also filed a discrimination suit against Jazzercise, arguing that she did not receive certification because the company's decision was based on her physical characteristics, not on her qualifications as a potential aerobics instructor. The suit was dismissed when Jazzercise agreed to eliminate the fit appearance as a prerequisite for the company's instructors and franchisees.*

DIVERSITY CHALLENGE　R E F L E C T I O N

1. How much should a fitness instructor's appearance influence customers' perceptions of the instructor's capabilities and ability to train them?

2. Should a fitness organization such as Jazzercise be able to select their employees and trainers based, at least in part, on the applicant's physical characteristics? Why or why not?

3. If you believe fitness organizations should be able to hire only those people who appear physically fit, should this same standard apply to all organizations? Why or why not?

4. What are other situations where employee physical characteristics might be considered a prerequisite to holding a particular position?

---

*Information adapted from Fernandez, E. (2002, February). *Teacher says fat/fitness can mix: S.F. mediates complaint Jazzercise showed bias.* SFGate.com. Retrieved January 18, 2006, from www.sfgate.com/cgi-bin/article.cgi?file=/chronicle/archive/2002/02/24/MN187100.DTL; Portnick's Complaint (2002, May 20). *People, 57,* 139; www.ballyfitness.com; www.goldsgym.com.

The focus of Chapters 4 and 5 was on the categorical effects of race and sex. Much of the research devoted to diversity and the attention paid by the popular press focus on these two dimensions; however, as noted in Chapter 1, limiting the discussion of diversity to race and sex issues restricts our understanding of the way people differ and the effects of those differences. As Jennifer Portnick's situation illustrates, the categorical effects of diversity impact a number of areas, including weight.

The purpose of this chapter is to broaden the diversity discussion by considering the categorical effects of age, disability, and obesity. I begin by defining these physical aspects of diversity and then consider why issues of age, disability, and obesity are important to study and understand. This is followed by a discussion of the categorical effects of the physical aspects of diversity on sport organizations, their employees, and their consumers or customers. The final section examines how the categorical effects of age, disability, and obesity may vary from the other forms of diversity studied thus far.

The Physical Aspects of Diversity

Bell, McLaughlin, and Sequeira (2004) describe the physical aspects of diversity as *age*, *disability*, and *obesity*. As you might guess, this terminology is used because these diversity characteristics relate to aspects of the body. Although important to study and understand, defining these physical aspects is challenging.

To an 18-year-old employee, a colleague who is 35 may seem old. That same 35-year-old may consider herself young, especially in relation to others or when contemplating she has lived less than half her expected lifespan. Thus, in some respects, what qualifies as "old" is in the eye of the beholder. This is not true when considering the statutes addressing age. The Age Discrimination in Employment Act (discussed in detail in Chapter 10) sets 40 as the *age* when people become "protected" from various organizational practices. For example, it is illegal to hire and fire employees simply based on their age. From this perspective then, we can consider persons 40 or older as "older" employees.

Determining what constitutes a *disability* is often difficult. For some impairments, such as a complete lack of sight or the ability to hear, the existence of the disability is clear. For others, such as a partial hearing loss or the beginning stages of arthritis, there is more debate. The Americans with Disabilities Act (discussed in detail in Chapter 10) governs what constitutes a disability within the employment context. The mental and physical aspects of disability are varied. Generally, physical conditions include diabetes, cancer, and AIDS, and mental disabilities include retardation, dyslexia, and emotional illness.

Finally, definitions of *obesity* also vary. For some, an obese person is one with an excessive amount of body fat relative to lean muscle, while others consider a person obese when she is at least 20 percent above her recommended body weight (see Bell et al., 2004). The Centers for Disease Control (CDC) considers people to be overweight when they have a body mass index (BMI) over 25.0 and to be obese when the BMI is over 30.0. The mathematical formula for BMI is:

$$BMI = (weight\ in\ pounds\ /\ height\ in\ inches^2)\ x\ 703$$

A person who is 5'9" and weighs 210 pounds has a BMI of 31.01 [(210/4761) × 703], considered obese according to the CDC's definition.

Of course, the BMI does not account for those people who have considerable muscle mass and therefore weigh more. They may be considered obese when in fact they are not. This is perhaps best illustrated by separate reports released in 2005 indicating that a majority of NFL players and a number of NBA players are considered obese according to their BMI (Kava, 2005). For example, Jevon Kearse is a defensive end for the Philadelphia Eagles and has about 5 percent body fat, indicating that he is very lean. At 6'4" and 265 pounds, however, Kearse is considered obese according to his BMI [(265/5929) × 703 = 31.4]. Dr. Ruth Kava, Director of Nutrition at the American Council on Science and Health, explains that the BMI is used as an index for sedentary people. For professional athletes, or those with an active lifestyle, the index is less useful (Kava, 2005).

alternative

P E R S P E C T I V E S

Non-Physical Aspects of Diversity. Bell et al. (2004) describe the physical aspects of diversity as age, disability, and obesity. Note, however, that not all forms of disability are physical in nature, as some persons have mental or sensory impairments. Thus, while Bell et al.'s classification scheme is useful in many respects, it is limited in others.

The Importance of Studying the Physical Aspects of Diversity

 ell et al. (2004) identify three reasons to study the physical aspects of diversity: changing populations, permeable boundaries, and work-related outcomes (see Exhibit 6.1). Each reason is discussed next.

Changing Populations

Populations across the world are changing, making it necessary to more thoroughly understand the physical aspects of diversity. DePauw and Gavron (2005) report that persons with disabilities became more visible in the 21st century. They also report that at least 10 percent of the U. S. population has a disability of some kind. With respect to age, U. S. Census Bureau reports indi-

The importance of studying the physical aspects of diversity.	*Exhibit 6.1*

Changing populations:

- There is an increase worldwide in the prevalence and incidence of persons who are aged, disabled, or obese.

Permeable boundaries:

- Unlike other forms of diversity, people do move into certain physical diversity categories by becoming older, disabled, or obese.

Work-related outcomes:

- Persons 40 or older, or with a disability, or who are obese are likely to face discrimination in the work context.

cate that the mean age of U. S. citizens has increased over time. This increase is seen in other countries, as well. In Japan, for example, the aging rate is faster than in North American countries (Haq, 2004). This is largely due to the fact that Japan has the lowest mortality rate and highest life expectancy rate in the world. Finally, the incidence of obesity has increased substantially in the United States. According to the American Obesity Association (2005), 127 million American adults are overweight and nearly 70 million American adults are classified as obese or severely obese.

These population changes are important for several reasons. First, *all* people grow older. As they do, the likelihood of becoming disabled or obese also increases. As one's age increases, so too does the incidence of heart disease, hypertension, and diabetes. These and other health problems can lead to weight gain, obesity, or other physical disabilities (Bell et al., 2004). Second, from an employment standpoint, various federal and state statutes protect persons with disabilities and older employees from being targeted for layoffs or discriminated against in promotions, hiring, and training. In some states, similar laws protect those who are obese. Third, in some countries, such as Japan, organizations are allowed to hire retired workers at lower salaries, meaning that the proportion of people age 65 and older working in Japan is almost three times that found in the United States and Canada (Haq, 2004).

Permeable Boundaries

Some physical characteristics (e.g., sex, race) are permanent features. The same is not true for such characteristics as age, disability (in some cases), or obesity. Bell et al. (2004) refer to these three group characteristics as having permeable boundaries. People do age, becoming "older" members of the workforce. They can become injured or ill, such that they are considered a person with a disability. Finally, people can gain and lose weight, thereby moving in or out of the obesity category. Therefore, the potential to experience certain effects of being physically diverse can ebb and flow over one's lifetime.

An example of the permeable nature of physical diversity is that of Michael Teuber of Germany. Teuber was an avid able-bodied wind surfer and snowboarder. After an automobile accident, however, he had limited use of his legs—about 65 percent of their previous capacity. He began mountain biking for rehabilitation reasons and soon became an avid cyclist. This love of cycling led him to compete, and he has done quite well. In fact, Teuber is a Paralympic world champion, a European cycling champion, and has won other medals in various forms of cycling, including road racing, trail racing, and pursuit racing (DePauw & Gavron, 2005).

Note that while some disabilities are permeable, others are not, as some people are born with disabilities. In these instances, the disabilities are permanent and are socially constructed, much like race and gender.

Work-Related Outcomes

The importance of studying the physical aspects of diversity derives from their relationship with important work outcomes (Bell et al., 2004) at the individual, group, and organizational levels. At the individual level, people may face antagonistic work environments if they are classified by others as too old, too young, disabled, or obese. This differential treatment can carry over and affect other work areas, such as group dynamics. Finally, organizational outcomes are influenced by various mechanisms (e.g., employee turnover, lawsuits).

Categorical Effects of the Physical Aspects of Diversity

The previous sections discussed the physical aspects of diversity and highlighted their importance. In this section, I discuss the categorical effects of the physical aspects of diversity in the sport industry, focusing on employees, participants, and consumers.

Age

Discrimination against persons on the basis of their age is referred to as *ageism* (Bell et al., 2004). Most discussions of the categorical effects of age focus on older populations, however the term *older* is defined, but this limited focus does not address all of the categorical effects of age. Thus, my discussion focuses on the two ends of the age continuum: the old and the young.

Employees

There are several negative stereotypes about older employees and their contributions to the organization's success (Thomas, Mack, & Montagliani, 2004; see also Kimmel, 1988). Older employees may be viewed as not capable of producing high-quality work, not understanding the current marketplace, or not likely to remain in a position long enough to make a substantial impact. Furthermore, the medical costs and days missed due to illness may be higher for older employees than for their younger counterparts. These factors negatively impact the perceived "payback" the organization receives relative to the monies spent recruiting, hiring, and training these employees.

However, as Thomas et al. (2004) note, empirical studies do not support the stereotypes that older employees are less qualified or less productive than their younger counterparts. Several indices such as job performance, capacity to learn, and overall competence are either unrelated to age or have a very small association. Most older employees possess several qualities that younger employees do not, such as a wealth of knowledge and experience accumulated over their lifetime. Those who have been with an organization for a number of years have accumulated institutional knowledge—a knowledge base of organizational practices and policies that reflect why particular decisions and changes were made. Thus, older employees are the living history of their organization. This sense of history is important, because as philosopher George Santayana noted, "Those who do not remember their past are condemned to repeat their mistakes."

Just as older employees may face certain biases because of their age, so too might younger employees. The social norms and historical precedents in some organizations question the appropriateness of a manager who is "too young." Perry, Kulik, and Zhou (1999) report that tensions might arise when employees have a manager who is the same age as their children, if not younger. They

alternative
P E R S P E C T I V E S

Caring for the Elderly. Although most research related to the categorical effects of age focuses on the employee's age, some research shows that the age of an employee's dependents can also influence important outcomes. Kossek, Colquitt, and Noe (2001) examined the effects of caregiving for elderly dependents (e.g., parents, in-laws) on subsequent well-being and performance. The authors note that because many cultures call for the separation of children from their parents such that the children form a personal identity independent of their parents, when these children are then required to care for their elderly parents, it produces a potential stressor, and the clear separation of identity becomes muddled or lost completely. This situation can have a negative effect on the employee both at home and in the workplace. For example, Kossek et al. found that employees who cared for elderly dependents performed poorly at work and reported lower well-being, relative to those who did not. Furthermore, home and family care decisions were more likely to have a negative impact on the employee when the organizational climate (or atmosphere) discouraged the sharing of family concerns. These findings show that the age of employees' dependents can influence the manner in which work is experienced.

found that those employees who were older than their upper-level supervisor were likely to miss work more often than those who did not have such incongruence.

There are, however, positive effects associated with having a younger manager. Doherty (1997), in her study of sport organization managers, found that younger managers were more likely than older managers to adopt a transformational style of leadership. Recall from Chapter 5 that transformational leadership is associated with high organizational effectiveness and strong employee commitment. Theo Epstein, for example, was hired in 2002 as the Boston Red Sox's general manager at age 28. At the time, he was the youngest person ever to hold that MLB position. Two years later, the team won their first World Series in over 80 years. Although tensions may arise from an incongruence in the age norms associated with the "ideal" manager, young managers can effect many desired outcomes for the organization.

Participants

Carron, Hausenblas, and Estabrooks (2003) report that as people grow older, they tend to exercise less. In fact, there is a 50 percent decrease in physical activity levels between the ages of 6 and 16. This trend continues over time—people get little to no physical activity after age 50 (Ruuskanen & Puoppila, 1995). Carron et al. offer two explanations for this occurrence. First, advancing age is associated with a number of ailments such as cardiovascular disease and arthritis. These impairments likely make it more difficult for older persons to engage in mild or moderate forms of physical activity. Second, the lack of physical activity could be a generational effect. People born in the early part of the 20th century may possess different attitudes toward physical activity and exercise than those born in the latter part of the century. Later generations might be more aware of the physical and mental benefits of sport and exercise and thus be more willing to participate. If this reasoning is correct, then the physical activity levels of later generations should remain constant, or only decrease slightly, as these people grow older. Only time will tell if this reasoning is correct.

Consumers

Discussions of the influence of age on sport consumption often center around Generation Y consumers (Bennett, Henson, & Zhang, 2003; Stevens, Lathrop, & Bradish, 2005), people born between 1977 and 1994. These people are highly sought after by sport marketers because of the generation's size (78 million in the United States) and spending habits. This generation's spending potential is expected to reach $300 billion.

As a result, much research is devoted to examining their preferences, attitudes, and behaviors. Stevens et al. (2005) found that persons in this demographic favored purchasing sports apparel and athletic shoes, and that the same-sex parent played an influential role in the purchase decisions for the child. Additional research by Bennett et al. (2003) shows that Generation Y consumers are Internet savvy and are likely to watch at least two hours of television daily. In terms of sport preferences, Generation Y consumers prefer to watch football, soccer, and track and field. They also prefer action sports such as the X-Games over more traditional sport forms such as baseball, basketball, and hockey. They also are more likely to watch the X-Games or Gravity Games on television than the World Series or the World Cup (Bennett et al., 2003). These findings suggest that the popularity of extreme or action sports may continue to grow, especially when considering the size and spending potential of Generation Y sport consumers.

Disability

Historically, opportunities for persons with disabilities in the workplace and in the sport context were limited. This changed, however, as persons with disabilities became more accepted in society. DePauw and Gavron (2005) argue that the intersection of disability and sport is a movement whose time has come. Although advances have certainly been made in many areas, persons with disabilities still face uphill battles in many situations. The categorical effects of disability are discussed next. Review Exhibit 6.2 for information (Pittz, 2005) on the intersection of disability with race.

Intersection of disability with race.   *Exhibit 6.2*

When discussing disability, it is important to remember that the incidence of various illnesses and disabilities *are not* equally dispersed among racial groups; rather, racial minorities are more likely to face health challenges than Whites. Recent research revealed the following:

- Compared to Whites, African Americans are 10% more likely to get cancer and 30% more likely to die from cancer.

- 25% of Native American and Alaskan Native children and 20% of African American children suffer from asthma.

- Hispanics, African Americans, and Native Americans are three times more likely than Whites to receive late or no prenatal care. This corresponds with the high infant mortality rate among racial minorities relative to Whites.

- Hispanics, African Americans, and Native Americans are more likely to have diabetes and die from the illness than Whites.

- In some parts of the United States, Native Americans can expect to live only into their 50s, while the life expectancy for Whites is in the 70s.

Adapted from Pittz, 2005.

Employees

Research shows that more and more people with disabilities are entering the workforce (Bell et al., 2004). For example, in 1986, 46 percent of those people with disabilities who were able to work chose to do so. This figure increased to 56 percent by 2000. Nevertheless, *ableism,* or discrimination against people with disabilities, is prevalent in many workplaces. Cox (1994) reports that some organizations may be reluctant to hire persons with disabilities because of the perceived increases in medical costs and absenteeism and a lower productivity capacity relative to able-bodied persons. When persons with disabilities do obtain employment, they are likely to be placed in less prestigious positions and to be assigned less challenging work roles (Bell et al., 2004). These discriminatory practices are likely to be stronger or more salient for those people whose disabilities are perceived to be of their own doing (e.g., drug addiction, alcoholism) than people whose disabilities occurred through no fault of their own (e.g., accident, birth) (Schwarzer & Weiner, 1991).

Although ableism does exist, Thomas et al. (2004) note that some firms have found that persons with disabilities are a major asset; they often express greater loyalty to the organization, thereby decreasing the costs associated with turnover—recruitment and training of new employees. Pizza Hut, for example, found that employees with disabilities had half the turnover rate of other employees. Furthermore, despite stereotypes related to performance decrements, empirical research shows that the performance of persons with disabilities is on par with or above that of employees without disabilities. For example, DuPont found that persons with disabilities, when compared to other employees, achieved greater performance levels, were absent less often, and paid greater attention to safety issues (Thomas et al., 2004). These data suggest that persons with disabilities are more likely to be an asset, not a liability, to an organization.

Other studies examined organizations' responses to accommodation requests made by persons with disabilities. The Americans with Disabilities Act (ADA) requires organizations with at least 15 employees to make "reasonable accommodation" for a person with a disability, so long as the accommodation does not place undue hardship on the organization (discussed later in Chapter 10). Such an accommodation for a hard-of-hearing employee might be having her manager face her and speak loudly when addressing her. The ADA places the responsibility for requesting an accommodation on the employee. Several factors influence whether employees will request accommodations, as well as the employer's reactions to such requests. For example, Baldridge (2005) found that people with supportive supervisors and coworkers are unlikely to withhold their requests. On the other hand, without such support, requests may not be made. As one participant in his study noted, "I hardly ever make requests to my new supervisor because she is so hostile. In her mind, any accommodation is unreasonable" (p. 2). Florey and Harrison (2000) found that managers who received a request from people perceived to be responsible for their disability responded negatively. They also found that managers responded favorably to requests from persons whose previous performance had been high.

Participants

DePauw and Gavron (2005) define *disability sport* as "sport that has been designed for or is specifically practiced by athletes with disabilities" (p. 80). This definition includes sports designed specifically for persons with disabilities such as goal ball for blind athletes; sports that able-bodied persons practice that are altered or modified to include athletes with disabilities such as wheelchair basketball; and sports that require little or no modification, such as swimming. These authors addressed three issues related to persons with disabilities in the sport context: attitudes toward athletes with disabilities, barriers to inclusion, and accessibility (DePauw & Gavron, 2005). Each issue is discussed below. For related information, see the Professional Perspectives box. Also note that, although the discussion focuses on disability sport, some persons with disabilities are also involved in mainstream sport, such as NCAA able-bodied teams.

Attitudes toward athletes with disabilities. Historically, athletes with disabilities were marginalized or excluded because sport traditionally required some form of physical prowess not possessed by those with physical impairments. These attitudes were reinforced throughout time by various socializing agents—parents, friends, schools, and the media. Because of these attitudes, people generally viewed disability sport as second class or illegitimate. The negative attitudes associated with disability sport result in athletes with disabilities receiving less media coverage, fewer rewards, and fewer opportunities for participation (DePauw & Gavron, 2005).

Barriers to inclusion. These negative perceptions of disability sport and its athletes have resulted in several barriers to inclusion, including a lack of:

- organized sport programs devoted to disability sport,
- informal sport experiences early in one's childhood,
- access to training programs and qualified and highly trained coaches,
- access to sport facilities, and
- financial resources for specialized equipment.

Although various statutes reduced these barriers somewhat, they still exist and curb participation in disability sport (DePauw & Gavron, 2005).

Accessibility. The lack of accessibility comes in several forms. First, limited access to adapted equipment serves to make sport participation impossible for many disability sport athletes. Second, even though current statutes require facilities to be accessible to persons with disabilities, many are not. Third,

PROFESSIONAL
P E R S P E C T I V E S

Trends and Issues in Disability Sport. Eli Wolff is a two-time Olympic soccer athlete, a graduate of Brown University, and current director of the Disability Sport Program at the Center for the Study of Sport in Society. According to Wolff, one of the major issues in the area of disability sport today is the inclusion and integration of persons with disabilities within the fabric of mainstream sport. How do mainstream sport organizations at every level of sport actually embrace disability sport opportunities? The answer, according to Wolff, is that full integration and inclusion is still a ways away. Wolff also points to two primary barriers for persons with disabilities who wish to participate in sport: attitudes toward such participation and the construction of disability sport in the media. Wolff notes that there is a misconception about "what it means to be a person with a disability in sport." Too often, people pity disability sport athletes rather than recognizing their efforts as athletes. The same trend occurs in the media, as athletes with disabilities are often portrayed as sources of inspiration for others. This stands in contrast to focusing on the athletes' accomplishments and athletic prowess. Seeking to overcome such barriers, Wolff argues that an awareness of these issues needs to be raised. People in the media, athletes, coaches, and supporters all need to know that the status quo is not how disability sport "has to be."

there is limited information, relatively speaking, about which disability sport opportunities exist. Persons with disabilities often have to make concerted efforts to track down the information from physical educators, sport managers, or park and recreation specialists. Finally, because there is a lack of coaches to guide the athletes, many are self-coached. For the most part, athletes without disabilities do not face these challenges to their sport participation (DePauw & Gavron, 2005).

Consumers

Marketers, including those who focus their efforts in the sport context, largely ignore persons with disabilities in their market segmentation efforts. A casual perusal of the sport marketing literature shows efforts to segment fans and consumers based on age, sex, race, and other characteristics, hoping to understand the preferences, attitudes, and purchase intentions of people within each demographic category. Why greater efforts have not been made to better understand consumers with disabilities or to market directly to these persons is unclear. After all, at least 10 percent of the U. S. population has a disability (DePauw & Gavron, 2005), and the spending potential of these persons is substantial. Recognizing this void, Stephens and Bergman (1995) identified five guidelines for marketing to consumers with disabilities, with the intent of helping marketers conform to the spirit of the Americans with Disabilities Act and potentially improve the effectiveness of their marketing efforts. Exhibit 6.3 provides a summary of these guidelines.

Although sport marketers typically opt not to use persons with disabilities in their commercials, Toyota was a sponsor of the 2004 Paralympic Games. (The Paralympic Games are an event held in conjunction with the Olympics.) The purpose of a Toyota advertisement was to convey the message

Guidelines for marketing to consumers with disabilities.	*Exhibit 6.3*

- Remember that different disabilities result in different consumer needs.

- Use language that connotes respect.

- Depict persons with disabilities in a deferential and accurate way.

- Be cognizant of your own biases about the quality of others' lives.

- Train employees to show respect to persons with disabilities.

that although the athletes had disabilities, they were still elite in their field. To express this idea, the advertisement showed an athlete running, with the lower half of the screen blacked out so the athlete appeared able-bodied. The voice-over commentary indicated that the athlete was winning. The full screen was then revealed, showing that the athlete possessed some form of disability. *B&T Weekly*, an Australian publication devoted to advertising, marketing, and media, noted that the advertisement was well-received and had the "wow factor" often sought when developing advertisements ("Simple," 2005).

Obesity

As with the other physical aspects of diversity, the categorical effects of weight have not been researched at great length. Nevertheless, the available research and anecdotal evidence do suggest that obese persons have unique experiences as employees, sport participants, and consumers of sport products.

Employees

Weight discrimination, which is sometimes referred to as *sizeism,* exists when people who are overweight, or perceived to be so, have limited access to organizations or receive fewer rewards than they legitimately deserve based on their weight. Research suggests that such discrimination exists in the workplace, as persons who are overweight or obese, relative to employees of a normal weight, are hired less often, promoted less frequently, disciplined more harshly, and fired more often (see Roehling, 1999, for a review). For example, Melville and Cardinal (1997) examined superintendents' hiring preferences for physical education teachers. They found that, all else being equal, those job applicants who were 20 pounds overweight were less likely to be hired than their counterparts

DIVERSITY *in the field*

Weighing the Coaching Options. There are several requisite qualifications to being a head coach in the NFL, including success as an assistant coach or administrator, leadership qualities, and quality coaching contacts. In addition to these qualities, Charlie Weis believed that most owners sought a coach with a certain body type. Therefore, the overweight Weis opted for gastric bypass surgery, a risky procedure designed to reduce the size of the stomach to allow for weight loss. Unfortunately for Weis, the surgery almost killed him. In fact, a Catholic priest gave last rites two days after the surgery. Weis ultimately recovered and went on to help the New England Patriots win a Super Bowl as their offensive coordinator. He was named head coach of the Notre Dame Fighting Irish in 2005. That he went to such lengths to obtain a head coaching position demonstrates two points: (a) there is the very strong perception that overweight or obese people do not have access to head coaching positions, and (b) people will go to great lengths to realize their dream of becoming a head coach (Mortensen, 2002).

who were 10 pounds overweight. Similar findings were made in a study of high school principals and their hiring preferences of physical education teachers (Jenkins, Caputo, & Farley, 2005).

The incidence of weight discrimination in the employment process is influenced by several factors. Women who are overweight are viewed more negatively than overweight men, thereby suggesting that it is less appropriate for a woman to be overweight than it is for a man (Pingitore, Dugoni, Tindale, & Spring, 1994). Male raters are more likely than female raters to evaluate overweight women harshly (Jasper & Klassen, 1990). The type of job also impacts such ratings. Obese people are more likely to be hired for those jobs that do not require face-to-face interaction, such as inside telephone sales, than they are to be hired for a job that does require such interaction (Bellizzi & Hasty, 1998).

That overweight and obese persons are likely to be the object of negative work-related decisions may be influenced by several factors, including physical attractiveness, negative stereotypes, pressure from others, and direct organizational costs (Roehling, 1999). It is possible that obese persons are considered less attractive than their normal weight counterparts, and because attractive people usually have favorable work outcomes (Jawahar & Mattsson, 2005), the lower attractiveness ratings will negatively influence obese employees' work experiences. Obese people are also likely to be the object of negative attributions, such being perceived as lazy, unkempt, and irresponsible, that are not generally applied to normal weight job applicants or employees. Roehling (1999) notes that although an evaluator does not personally hold biases, there may be pressure from customers and/or coworkers to hire more fit-looking employees. Finally, some employers believe that hiring obese employees results in direct costs to the organization—higher insurance premiums, more frequent absences, and any necessary special accommodation requirements. Any of these factors is likely to negatively influence the potential for overweight and obese persons to secure employment or to be treated fairly in the workplace.

Participants

Carron et al. (2003) report that obese men and women are less likely to exercise and participate in other physical activities than their normal weight counterparts, a finding that might seem intuitive given the link between regular exercise and body weight. The same is not necessarily true for children, however, as past research yielded equivocal findings related to the activity levels of obese and lean children (Carron et al., 2003).

Overweight and obese persons may choose not to exercise because they are self-conscious about others seeing them participate, especially when the activities are difficult for them to complete (Carron et al., 2003). This seems understandable, especially if many of the other participants have lean or muscular body types. Some people experience social physique anxiety, which is felt when they believe others are evaluating their body type (Carron et al., 2003). Those who experience such anxiety are likely to exercise in private (e.g., in their home) or wear loose fitting clothes. Social physique anxiety also influences the choice of activities. For example, Crawford and Eklund (1994) found that women with social physique anxiety were likely to have a positive attitude toward aerobics classes that did not emphasize the women's physique.

Consumers

Although little research has been conducted on the effects of obesity in sport and exercise marketing, the matchup hypothesis would predict that overweight or obese persons are unlikely to be used in sport-related advertisements because there should be a match or fit between the endorser and the product being endorsed. Till and Busler (2000), for example, found that athletes were more effective in promoting energy bars than actors. In a similar way, Fink, Cunningham, and Kensicki (2004) found that highly qualified and attractive athletes were considered a good fit as endorsers of an upcoming athletic event. Given that sport and exercise are often associated with power, strength, and physical fitness, it stands to reason that those people who embody these characteristics will be used to promote sport and exercise to consumers. A casual observance of such advertisements seems to support this reasoning.

What is interesting, however, is that these marketing efforts may not actually reach the primary target audience or the people who need sport and exercise the most—those who are overweight or obese. Recall from Chapter 2 that the social categorization framework for understanding diversity holds that people will have positive attitudes toward and trust those people who are similar to them (in-group members). If that is true, then using thin models with well-defined muscles to attract people to a fitness club would likely be effective only for those people who embody those characteristics. For persons who are overweight or obese, such product endorsers may be viewed as out-group members; hence, the positive attitudes toward and the trust afforded to such endorsers are

alternative P E R S P E C T I V E S

Dove Body Lotion. Companies often use ultra-thin models to advertise skin care or beauty products to entice consumers to purchase the products. In 2004, Dove began a new ad campaign, called *Campaign for Real Beauty,* for their hand and body lotions. The women in the advertisements are of varying ages, races, heights, and body types. Some are pregnant, some are curvaceous, others are thin. By incorporating "real women with real bodies and real curves," Dove broadened the definition of beauty. Olphie Camacho, Unilever de Puerto Rico general manager, praised the ad campaign. "It's positive, it's powerful, it's empowering women," she noted. The impetus for the campaign resulted, in part, from research Dove conducted. Dove found that people viewed the models most often used in commercials for beauty products as setting "an unrealistic standard for beauty." This empirical research was supported by comments women had provided Dove for years. The new campaign using models with "real bodies" has been wildly successful across the United States, Europe, and Latin American (Albanese, 2005).

likely to be low. Building from this argument, for more effective ads, sport and fitness organizations should use models who represent all body types. Of course, drawing from the matchup hypothesis literature, the product endorsers should still demonstrate some level of physical fitness. See the Alternative Perspectives box for an example of such an advertising campaign.

Research by Shapiro and King of Rice University shows that the general treatment of obese consumers is substantially poorer than the treatment of those whose weight is normal (Reyes, 2005). They designed a study in which 10 young women donned "fat suits" to make them appear heavier than they really were. The women shopped at various stores in the Houston area and noted the responses they received from the salespersons. In general, salespeople spent little time with the overweight women and, in some cases, even wondered aloud why an overweight shopper would bother patronizing a particular store. The researchers also found that the treatment the women received was better if they were drinking a diet cola or discussing weight loss. Reflecting on their findings, Shapiro noted that "obesity instantly gets you second-class treatment . . . it was distressing—an eye-opening experience" (as cited in Reyes, 2005, p. 125).

Minority Group Status

The final section of this chapter considers whether the aged, obese, and disabled should be considered minorities. Although the term *minority* is generally reserved for discussions of race, sexual orientation, and religion, some suggest that persons with physical diversity characteristics can also be considered minorities (Bell et al., 2004).

Recall from Chapter 4 that a minority group is a collection of individuals who share common characteristics and face discrimination in society because of their membership in that group (Coakley, 2004). Bell et al. (2004) extend this definition slightly by suggesting that four factors should be used to determine whether a group has minority status:

1. visibility
2. differential power
3. differential treatment
4. group awareness

By way of illustration, consider how these factors apply to racial minorities. In general, one's race is highly visible. It is this *visibility* that allows for the social categorization process to occur, resulting in the formation of in-groups and out-groups. Racial minorities, when compared to Whites, also have *differential power* and face *differential treatment* by society and within the sport context. *Group awareness* is related to the salience of a group membership. When people are part of a group that routinely encounters differential treatment, they may identify with that group and use pronouns such as "we" and "us" (e.g., *we* face discrimination). Research shows that this "we-ness" exists among African Americans, generally speaking. Applying these factors, African Americans are considered racial minorities in the United States.

This example shows the efficacy of using the concepts visibility, differential power, differential treatment, and group awareness to determine whether a group can be considered a minority or non-dominant group. Do people with physical diversity characteristics fit this model? The evidence points to the affirmative.

Visibility

For the most part, the physical aspects of diversity are visible. People can generally assess one's age almost immediately after seeing the person. Although 35- and 40-year-old men may look similar, they both are likely to appear younger than a 70-year-old man. The same is true for weight, as most people can distinguish between someone who is very thin and someone who is overweight or obese. Although some factors, such as the rater's weight, may influence the assessment of another's weight, research suggests that most people agree in their ratings of who is obese (Bell et al., 2004). For persons with disabilities, some disabilities are highly visible (e.g., a person in a wheelchair), while others may go unnoticed (e.g., a person with AIDS or dyslexia).

Differential Power

As discussed in previous sections, persons who are aged, have disabilities, or are obese hold less power in organizations than do their counterparts without such characteristics. Physically diverse have less decision-making power, fill lower-status jobs, and do not earn as much as others (Bell et al., 2004).

alternative PERSPECTIVES

Group Awareness. Though research suggests that group awareness is limited among the aged, obese, and disabled, it is important to note some agencies and centers do strive to increase that awareness. For instance, a primary goal of The Disability Rights Education and Defense Fund is to advance the civil and human rights for people with disability through advocacy, training, and other initiatives (see www.dredf.org). Thus, from an alternative perspective, group awareness is present.

Differential Treatment

The incidence of ageism, ableism, and sizeism present in many organizations supports the conclusion that physically diverse persons are stigmatized. As Major and O'Brien (2005) note, people who are stigmatized "have (or are believed to have) an attribute that marks them as different and leads them to be devalued in the eyes of others" (p. 395). This stigmatization process becomes the basis for treating people differently, thereby excluding them. This process is largely reflective of the experiences the aged, obese, and disabled have within the sport and organizational context.

Group Awareness

Bell et al. (2004) assert that there is limited group awareness among the aged, obese, and disabled. For example, their survey of persons with disabilities showed that only 47 percent shared a common identity with other people with disabilities. The lack of identification could be due to the diversity of each disability group (e.g., wheelchair-bound, deaf, blind). Each disability presents unique challenges that persons with other disabilities may not encounter. The same is true for the obese and aged. Despite the seemingly lack of group awareness, physically diverse people are highly visible, have differential power, and face differential treatment, thereby supporting their inclusion as a minority, as suggested by Bell et al. (2004).

Chapter Summary

This chapter focused on the physical aspects of diversity—age, disability, and obesity. Although many consider that diversity is only related to race and sex, thereby prompting the term "womenandminorities" (Tsui & Gutek, 1999), as discussed in Chapter 1, diversity is a much broader concept. As the Diversity Challenge illustrated, people who are older than the typical sport organization employee, who have a disability, or who are obese (as was the case with Portnick) are treated differently. After reading this chapter, you should be able to:

1. **Define age, disability, and obesity.**

"Older" employees in the organizational context are those age 40 and over. People are considered to have a disability if they have a mental or physical impairment that limits one or more major life activities. The CDC considers people to be overweight when they have a BMI over 25.0 and to be obese when the BMI is over 30.0.

2. **Understand the importance of studying the physical aspects of diversity.**

The three reasons why the study of the physical aspects of diversity is important are (a) changing populations, (b) permeable boundaries, and (c) work-related outcomes.

3. **Discuss the categorical effects of age, disability, and obesity for sport organization employees and sport and leisure participants and consumers.**

Employees who are especially old or especially young are likely to face stereotypes about their performance and contributions to the firm. The same is true for those with disabilities or who are overweight. Research shows that sport participation rates decrease with age and the incidence of obesity. Disability sport has grown over the years, though accessibility issues, negative attitudes toward the sport, and other barriers limit the participation opportunities available to persons with disabilities. Age, disability, and obesity all influence marketing efforts to sport consumers.

4. **Discuss whether the aged, disabled, and obese should be considered minorities.**

Physically diverse people are visible, experience differential power, and are subjected to discrimination. However, there is limited group awareness, or in-group identification, among persons who are aged, disabled, or obese. Nevertheless, considering the prevalence of the other factors associated with minority group membership, physically diverse people can generally be considered minority group members.

Questions for Discussion

1. Three reasons for studying the physical aspects of diversity were discussed. Which of these reasons is the strongest? Why?

2. Identify some of the factors that may influence requests for accommodation by persons with disabilities in the workplace? What might be done to overcome some of the potential barriers?

3. Some suggest that obesity should be considered a form of disability, while others disagree. What is your opinion? Why?

4. The possibility of fitness organizations using endorsers whose bodies more closely resemble their overweight or obese clientele was discussed. What are the advantages and disadvantages of such a practice?

5. Do you consider physically diverse persons to be minority group members? Why or why not? Does your opinion vary based on the form of diversity?

Learning Activities

1. What are the advantages and disadvantages to a sport organization that considers an applicant's weight or appearance in the hiring process? Does the applicant's sex make a difference? Divide into two groups, with each group taking one side, and discuss.

2. Using the Web, identify sport organizations and sport events targeted toward athletes with disabilities. Based on your search, how would you characterize the available sport and physical activity opportunities for persons with disabilities?

Resources

SUPPLEMENTARY READINGS

Brownwell, K. D., Schwartz, M. B., Pugh, R. M., & Rudd, L. (2005). *Weight bias: Nature, consequences and remedies.* New York: Guilford Press. (Edited text from leading scholars in the field; explores the nature and causes of weight discrimination, as well as ways to combat the discrimination.)

DePauw, K. P., & Gavron, S. J. (2005). *Disability sport* (2nd ed.). Champaign, IL: Human Kinetics. (Provides a historical account of disability sport and athletes with disabilities; also addresses the current challenges and controversies surrounding disability and sport.)

Gregory, R. F. (2001). *Age discrimination in the American workplace: Old at a young age*. New Brunswick, NJ: Rutgers University Press. (Provides an overview of discriminatory practices aimed at older workers; also addresses ways that older employees can respond to such acts.)

WEB RESOURCES

- National Disability Sports Alliance (www.ndsaonline.org): organization that serves as the governing body for competitive sport for persons with disabilities.

- National Senior Games Association (www.nsga.com): contains information about the National Senior Games, competitive sport events for persons age 50 or older.

- The Obesity Society (www.naaso.org): national society dedicated to the scientific study of obesity and obesity-related issues, including discrimination.

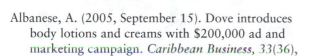

References

Albanese, A. (2005, September 15). Dove introduces body lotions and creams with $200,000 ad and marketing campaign. *Caribbean Business, 33*(36), 46.

American Obesity Association. (2005). *Obesity in the U.S.* Retrieved March 1, 2005, from www.obesity.org/subs/fastfacts/obesity_US.shtml

Baldridge, D. C. (2005). Withholding accommodation requests: The role of workgroup supportiveness and requester attributes. *Academy of Management Proceedings, 2005,* D1–D6.

Bell, M. P., McLaughlin, M. E., & Sequeira, J. M. (2004). Age, disability, and obesity: Similarities, differences, and common threads. In M. S. Stockdale & F. J. Crosby (Eds.), *The psychology and management of workplace diversity* (pp. 191–205). Malden, MA: Blackwell.

Bellizzi, J. A., & Hasty, R. W. (1998). Territory assignment decisions and supervising unethical selling behavior: The effects of obesity and gender as moderated by job-related factors. *Journal of*

Personal Selling & Sales Management, 18(2), 35–49.

Bennett, G., Henson, R. K., & Zhang, J. (2003). Generation Y's perceptions of the action sports industry segment. *Journal of Sport Management, 17,* 95–115.

Carron, A. V., Hausenblas, H. A., & Estabrooks, P. A. (2003). *The psychology of physical activity*. New York: McGraw-Hill.

Coakley, J. (2004). *Sports in society: Issues and controversies* (8th ed.). New York: McGraw-Hill.

Cox, T. H., Jr. (1994). *Cultural diversity in organizations: Theory, research, and practice*. San Francisco: Berrett-Koehler.

Crawford, S., & Eklund, R. C. (1994). Social physique anxiety, reasons for exercise, and attitudes toward exercise settings. *Journal of Sport and Exercise Psychology, 16,* 70–82.

DePauw, K. P., & Gavron, S. J. (2005). *Disability sport* (2nd ed.). Champaign, IL: Human Kinetics.

Doherty, A. J. (1997). The effect of leader characteristics on the perceived transformation/transactional leadership and impact on interuniversity athletic administrators. *Journal of Sport Management, 11,* 275–285.

Fink, J. S., Cunningham, G. B., & Kensicki, L. J. (2004). Using athletes as endorsers to sell women's sport: Attractiveness vs. Expertise. *Journal of Sport Management, 18,* 350–367.

Florey, A. T., & Harrison, D. A. (2000). Responses to informal accommodation requests from employees with disabilities: Multistudy evidence on willingness to comply. *Academy of Management Journal, 43,* 224–233.

Haq, R. (2004). International perspectives on workplace diversity. In M. S. Stockdale & F. J. Crosby (Eds.), *The psychology and management of workplace diversity* (pp. 277–298). Malden, MA: Blackwell.

Hogler, R. (2004). *Employment relations in the United States: Law, policy, and practice.* Thousand Oaks, CA: Sage.

Jasper, C. R., & Klassen, M. L. (1990). Perceptions of salespersons' appearance and evaluation of job performance. *Perceptual and Motor Skills, 71,* 563–566.

Jawahar, I. M., & Mattsson, J. (2005). Sexism and beautyism effects in selection as a function of self-monitoring level of decision maker. *Journal of Applied Psychology, 90,* 563–573.

Jenkins, A., Caputo, J. L., & Farley, R. S. (2005). Physical description and job attainment in physical education. *Physical Educator, 62*(2), 96–102.

Kava, R. (2005, March). Are our athletes fat? *CANSTATS Bulletins.* Retrieved January 20, 2006, from www.canstats.org/readdetail.asp?id=742

Kimmel, D. C. (1988). Ageism, psychology, and public policy. *American Psychologist, 43,* 175–178.

Kossek, E. E., Colquitt, J. A., & Noe, R. A. (2001). Caregiving decisions, well-being, and performance: The effects of place and provider as a function of dependent type and work–family climates. *Academy of Management Journal, 44,* 2944.

Major, B., & O'Brien, L. T. (2005). The social psychology of stigma. *Annual Review of Psychology, 56,* 393–421.

Melville, D. S., & Cardinal, B. J. (1997). Are overweight physical educators at a disadvantage in the labor market? A random survey of hiring personnel. *Physical Educator, 54*(4), 216–221.

Mortensen, C. (2002, July). *Seeking new image, Patriots' Weis almost loses life.* ESPN.com. Retrieved January 25, 2006, from http://espn.go.com/chrismortensen/s/2002/0724/1409547.html

Perry, E. L., Kulik, C. T., & Zhou, J. (1999). A closer look at the effects of subordinate–supervisor age differences. *Journal of Organizational Behavior, 20,* 341–357.

Pingitore, R., Dugoni, B. L., Tindale, R. S., & Spring, B. (1994). Bias against overweight job applicants in a simulated employment interview. *Journal of Applied Psychology, 79,* 909–917.

Pittz, W. (2005). *Closing the gap: Solutions to race-based health disparities.* Oakland, CA: Applied Research Center & Northwest Federation of Community Organizations.

Reyes, M. (2005). Who gets better service? *Glamour, 103*(8), 125.

Roehling, M. V. (1999). Weight-based discrimination in employment: Psychological and legal aspects. *Personnel Psychology, 52,* 969–1016.

Ruuskanen, J., & Puoppila, I. (1995). Physical activity and psychological well-being among people aged 65–84 years. *Age and Aging, 24,* 292–296.

Schwarzer, R., & Weiner, B. (1991). Stigma controllability and coping as predictors of emotions and social support. *Journal of Social and Personal Relationships, 31*(3), 111–136.

Simple and effective Paralympic campaign. (2005, January 14). *B&T Weekly, 54*(2502), 22.

Stephens, D. L., & Bergman, K. (1995). The Americans with Disabilities Act: A mandate for marketers. *Journal of Public Policy & Marketing, 14,* 164–168.

Stevens, J., Lathrop, A., & Bradish, C. (2005). Tracking Generation Y: A contemporary sport consumer profile. *Journal of Sport Management, 19,* 254–277.

Thomas, K. M., Mack, D. A., & Montagliani, A. (2004). The arguments against diversity: Are they valid? In M. S. Stockdale & F. J. Crosby (Eds.), *The psychology and management of workplace diversity* (pp. 31–51). Malden, MA: Blackwell.

Till, B. D., & Busler, M. (2000). The match-up hypothesis: Physical attractiveness, expertise, and the role of fit on brand attitude, purchase intent, and brand beliefs. *Journal of Advertising, 29,* 1–14.

Tsui, A. S., & Gutek, B. A. (1999). *Demographic differences in organizations: Current research and future directions.* New York: Lexington Books.

178

Beyond Visible Demographics

RELIGIOUS BELIEFS, SEXUAL ORIENTATION, AND SOCIAL CLASS

LEARNING OBJECTIVES

Anyone who is even vaguely familiar with NASCAR knows that the cars driven in the events are covered with company logos. These logos are representative of a variety of companies in various industries, including DuPont (on Jeff Gordon's #24 car), Goodwrench (on Kevin Harvich's #29 car), and Home Depot (on Tony Stewart's #20 car). In 2004, Bobby Labonte made headlines by promoting Mel Gibson's film *The Passion of the Christ,* a movie depicting the crucifixion of Jesus Christ, on his car's hood. According to Labonte, "It's a chance to get the word out. Someone who is curious about Jesus and has never been saved sees the races and says, 'Hmmm, I'd like to see what that's about.' . . . Maybe we can change their minds." That a driver chose to have close links to the Christian faith is nothing new to NASCAR, as its participants' strong ties to the Christian faith are long-standing. Church services often are held in the racetrack infield for the drivers, their crew, and race officials; prerace invocations are a regular occurrence; and there is a break in the racing schedule during Easter weekend. Other racers also include Christian material on their racing machines. Morgan Shepherd, for example, has a Jesus decal on his racing truck, and his racing team is called "Victory in Jesus."

Other sport leagues and their teams also have religious ties. The first line of the Little League pledge, which is recited by teams prior to each competition, is "I trust in God." The NBA's Portland Trailblazers had a "Family and Faith Night" at one of their 2004 contests against the Sacramento Kings. After the game, spectators stayed to listen to the Christian acappella group Rescue perform. The WNBA's Minnesota Lynx

After studying this chapter, you should be able to:

- Define religion and spirituality, and discuss the categorical effects of religious beliefs in sport organizations.

- Define sexual orientation and sexual prejudice, and outline the categorical effects of sexual orientation, both for the individual and for organizations.

- Define stratification, social class, and classism, and analyze the categorical effects of social class in sport organizations.

also offered a "Faith and Family Night," during which the Christian group Go Fish performed. As these examples illustrate, religious beliefs often are incorporated in sport and the entertainment associated with the events.*

DIVERSITY CHALLENGE   R E F L E C T I O N

1. Are you aware of any other sport teams that use religious themes to attract people to the event?

2. What are the advantages and disadvantages to sport organizations using such marketing techniques?

3. What are the advantages and disadvantages to those NASCAR drivers who have religious-themed logos or advertisements on their cars? What might be the impact on their fans? Or their potential or existing sponsors?

4. How else might employees' religious beliefs influence their attitudes and behaviors in the workplace?

---

*Information adapted from Newberry, P. (2004, February). *NASCAR mixing religion, racing.* Deseretnews.com. Retrieved February 4, 2006, from http://deseretnews.com/dn/print/1,1442,590042201,00.html; www.blazers.com; www.littleleague.org/about/pledge.asp; www.wnba.com/lynx/.

As the Diversity Challenge demonstrates, sport and religion are often intertwined. This relationship involves athletes (both amateur and professional), teams, and leagues. Is there a connection between religious and spiritual beliefs and individual, group, and organization work outcomes? What is unique about one's religious or spiritual beliefs, relative to some other diversity forms, is that the beliefs cannot be seen. Unless one chooses to wear certain religious clothing, displays religious symbols or messages, or publicly discusses his faith, others may not know of that person's religious or spiritual beliefs. This "invisibility" characteristic also applies to sexual orientation and in many cases, social class. Unless people choose to disclose their sexual orientation or social class, these characteristics typically remain unknown to others. This contrasts with the other diversity forms discussed thus far (e.g., race, sex, age, disability, and obesity), where people can identify others' membership in a social group simply by looking at them (e.g., "Juanita is a woman" or "Ted is obese").

The purpose of this chapter is to examine the categorical effects of three unseen or deep-level diversity characteristics—religious beliefs, sexual orientation, and social class. In the first section, I define religion and spirituality, considering the terms' differences and commonalities. This is followed by a discussion of the categorical effects of one's religious and spiritual beliefs—for athletes, coaches, and administrators. The second section addresses sexual orientation and the general attitudes people have toward gays, lesbians, and bisexuals, and examines the categorical effects of sexual orientation for athletes, coaches, and administrators. The final section focuses on social class, defining the terms *social class* and *social stratification,* examining class-related effects in the workplace, and investigating the interaction of sport participation and upward social mobility.

Religion

To understand the effects of religious beliefs in the workplace, it is first necessary to define basic terms. Durkheim (1965) defines *religion* as "a unified system of beliefs and practices relative to sacred things, that is to say, things set apart and forbidden—beliefs and practices which unite into one single moral community called a Church, all those who adhere to them" (p. 62). According to Durkheim, religion has several social functions. At the individual level, religion provides people with emotional support and an ultimate sense of meaning. Religion operates at an interpersonal level by creating a form of social bonding through the shared values and beliefs among people of a particular faith. At the institutional level, religion provides a form of social control by prescribing certain behaviors that are consistent with the values, norms, and beliefs of that faith and of society. Finally, religion provides a form of social integration, uniting people of a common faith. Religion brings together people of diverse backgrounds, reaffirms the basic customs and values of a society, and unites people in ways that transcend the individual self.

Some authors contrast religion with the concept of spirituality (e.g., Cacioppe, 2000; Mitroff & Denton, 1999). For them, *spirituality* is conceptualized as "the basic feeling of being connected with one's complete self, others, and the entire universe" (Mitroff & Denton, 1999, p. 83). Terms associated with spirituality include self-actualization, wholeness, meaning, purpose, life force, virtue, and interconnectedness, among others (Hicks, 2002). These authors who distinguish between the two concepts often view religion as being structured and organized, providing external controls, and as being divisive. On the other hand, spirituality is viewed as being broad and inclusive, providing inner peace, and being the ultimate end in itself (Mitroff & Denton, 1999). For example, one CEO in Mitroff and Denton's study explained, "not only do you not have to be religious in order to be spiritual, but it probably helps if you are not religious, especially if you want your spirituality to grow and be a basic part of your life" (p. 87).

Although these authors distinguish between spirituality and religion, Bailey (2001) asserts that "a meaningful conversation about spirituality sans religion is dubious" (p. 367). A similar position is advocated by others (Cash & Gray, 2000; Hicks, 2002) and is adopted for use in this chapter. Consider, for example, that many of the terms associated with spirituality such as passion, self-actualization, or virtue (Hicks, 2002) are also associated with many people's religious beliefs. Furthermore, Mitroff and Denton (1999) suggest that spirituality is:

- the basic belief that there is a supreme being that governs the universe,
- the notion that the higher power affects all things, and
- the ultimate source of meaning in one's life.

Christians, Jews, and Muslims would, for the most part, make similar statements about God and their religious beliefs. Given the similarities between and overlap of the two concepts, the subsequent discussion uses the terms religion and religious beliefs.

The Emphasis on Religion

Interest in the mix of religion and work has increased over the last 20 years, and this proliferation can be attributed to two primary factors. First, most of the world's population ascribes to a particular religious belief or faith. Kriger and Seng (2005) report that 82 percent of all persons follow one of the five major religions: Judaism, Christianity, Islam, Hinduism, and Buddhism. This number is significant because it is likely that those persons in leadership positions who ascribe to one of these belief systems have leadership and decision-making styles that are shaped, at least in part, by religious tenets.

The second factor is, as noted in Chapter 1, the major changes that have occurred in the workplace. Corporate scandals have eroded the trust employees have in upper management. Changing technologies and organizational restructuring have resulted in downsizing and variations in the nature of work. The loyalty previously expressed by organizations to employees is perceived as not as strong as it once was, making work life uncertain. Despite these negative changes, people are spending more time at work now than they ever have before. Time spent away from home in other activities such as attending social gatherings has decreased, while the hours spent at work have increased. This dynamic causes people to seek greater meaning in their lives, a quest that often leads to a greater integration of religious and work identities (Cash & Gray, 2000; Jurkiewicz & Giacalone, 2004). As they seek greater meaning, employees are likely to merge their religious beliefs, values, and identities into their work. The two identities are no longer separate, and religion is no longer viewed as something to be kept out of the workplace. For example, the Christian Faculty Network is found on many campuses and serves as a social network for university faculty and staff of the Christian faith.

Religion in the Workplace

Because religious beliefs can be important to people in their work life, it is useful to consider the categorical effects that integration evokes. Past research shows that religious beliefs can influence a variety of work-related outcomes, including strategic decisions, ethical behavior, leadership, and stress. Each is discussed in turn.

Strategic Decisions

The literature provides several examples of managers' religious beliefs influencing their strategic decisions. Malden Mills is a New England manufacturer of materials, most notably Polartec, used in winter clothing by such enterprises as Lands End and L.L. Bean. In 1995, the plant was ravaged by a fire, an incident that left many wondering whether the firm should move its operations overseas—a strategic decision that would have been economically advantageous. However, Aaron Feuerstein, the firm's owner and CEO, as well as a devout Jew, would hear nothing of it. He chose to rebuild the plant in the same community and, even more striking, continued to pay all of the workers for months, until the plant was again operational. When explaining his decisions, Feuerstein indicated that he felt a social responsibility to the workers—both blue- and white-collar—as well as the community, suggesting that leaving the community would have been "unconscionable." He further suggested that his religious beliefs and heritage played a significant role in his decision-making process (Shafran, 2002).

Though usually not as dramatic as the Malden Mills situation, religious beliefs impact decisions in the sport context. For example, Brigham Young University is an institution named after a former president of The Church of Jesus Christ of Latter-Day Saints. With its mission to assist individuals in their quest for perfection and eternal life, the university follows Mormon principles, which require that university athletic teams not participate in events on Sundays. This requirement certainly impacts the university's athletic scheduling practices and has influenced other entities as well. When the university's basketball teams play in the NCAA national tournament, they are always placed in those team brackets that play on Thursdays and Saturdays, as opposed to the alternative Friday and Sunday brackets.

Dunn and Stevenson (1998) found additional evidence of how religious beliefs influence strategic decisions in their study of a church hockey league. This hockey league was designed to promote the values and norms of evangelical Christians—a design reflected in many of the league rules. For example, body contact was prohibited—rare in the hockey context. Community prayers were said prior to the games, swearing was prohibited, as was beer in the locker rooms prior to and after the games. Finally, official team standings were not maintained—all teams made the playoffs. The league's cooperative nature, as evidenced by its rules, differs markedly from other recreational hockey leagues.

Ethical Behavior

It might be expected that people with strong religious beliefs, irrespective of the particular religion, will behave differently than those without strong beliefs, particularly with regard to their ethical behavior because certain forms of moral behavior (e.g., "love your neighbor as yourself") are common across the five major religions (Kriger & Seng, 2005). In some instances, this reasoning holds true. For example, people with strong religious beliefs are unlikely to use illicit or illegal substances (Khavari & Harmon, 1982). However, when it comes to business ethics, the picture is mixed, with some studies showing no relationship and others showing a strong relationship between religiosity and ethical behavior (see Weaver & Agle, 2002).

One potential way to understand these equivocal findings is to apply the social identity theory portion of the social categorization framework (see Chapter 2) to the issue (see Weaver & Agle, 2002). We know that people maintain various identities—student, man, golfer, Catholic, and the like. The salience of these identities is likely to change depending on the context. In some situations, being a fan of your favorite team is most important, and that identity shapes your attitudes and behaviors (e.g., giving a high-five to another fan at a game). For most people, however, being a fan is not the primary identity in all situations. At home, the role of being a husband or a father might be most salient, just as at church, being a Catholic might be most salient. Having a certain social identity be most salient in a particular context influences the attitudes, preferences, and behaviors someone exhibits in that context.

Social identity salience is particularly important to the discussion of religious preference and ethical behavior. If one's religious identity is salient across most social contexts, including work, then his attitudes, preferences, and behaviors are likely to be shaped by his religious beliefs. On the other hand, if a person's religious identity is primed on Sundays, but her work identity is primed at work, then it is less likely that her attitudes and behaviors at work will be guided by religious beliefs. "The more salient religion is for a person—that is, the larger role it plays in one's self-identity—the more difficult it will be for other factors to push aside or thwart the influence of religious expectations" (Weaver & Agle, 2002, p. 85).

Of course, there are several factors that could influence the expected positive relationship between religious identity and ethical behavior, including organizational commitment and the presence of others in the workplace who share the same religion (Weaver & Agle, 2002). If one is highly committed to the organization, this commitment will likely serve to counteract the salience of one's religious identity while at work. One cannot serve two masters; employees will either be committed and highly identified with their work or highly identified with their religion, but not both. Under such circumstances, the strong workplace commitment may negate (or at least reduce) the effects of one's religious beliefs on subsequent ethical behavior.

The presence in the workplace of others who share similar religious beliefs is likely to increase the salience of those beliefs. For example, if a Christian has many coworkers who also identify themselves Christians, the identity of being a Christian is likely to be reinforced at work. Furthermore, there is likely to be greater accountability for one's actions among the Christian coworkers. Because the religious salience is likely to be high in that work environment, the link between religious beliefs and ethical behavior will likely be positive.

Leadership

Several authors developed leadership theories based on religious and spiritual principles (Fry, 2003; Kriger & Seng, 2005; Whittington, Pitts, Kageler, & Goodwin, 2005). The theories demonstrate that people's leadership behaviors are largely contingent upon their spiritual and religious beliefs. For example, Whittington et al. (2005) developed a theory for what they termed "legacy leadership" that is based on the wisdom and behaviors of the Apostle Paul. Drawing from various biblical books written by Paul, as well as writings from more contemporary authors, Whittington et al. argue that the qualities of legacy leadership are unique and have long-lasting effects. Paul created "a self-perpetuating model of leadership" (p. 753) that impacted numerous people throughout the world, and leaders who follow this style are likely to have a similar impact on their organizations and employees. The characteristics of legacy leaders are listed in Exhibit 7.1.

Another leadership style with religious overtones is that of servant leadership (Greenleaf, 1977; Spears, 1998). Servant leaders recognize their moral

Characteristics of legacy leaders.	*Exhibit 7.1*

- Worthy of imitation
- Boldness in the face of opposition
- Authentic motives
- Assert influence without being authoritative
- Demonstrative and emotional
- Vulnerable and transparent
- Authentic
- Lead by actions
- Focus on others, not the self
- Life-changer (the primary outcome of legacy leaders)

Adapted from Whittington et al., 2005.

responsibility not only to the organization, but also to their subordinates, customers, and others with a stake in the organization. The moral compass servant leaders use is what separates them from other leaders. As Ehrhart (2004) notes, servant leaders "want their subordinates to improve for their own good, and view the development of the follower as an end in and of itself, not merely as a means to reach the leader's or organization's goals" (p. 69). These leaders "serve" their subordinates by helping them grow and mature, thereby realizing their full potential. This concern for others is likely to have positive effects. Ehrhart found that servant leadership was positively associated with followers' perceptions of fairness, as well as followers' citizenship behaviors such as helping and being conscientious. Thus, servant leadership is likely to positively influence several aspects of the organization.

Stress

One's religious beliefs can also produce stress in the workplace. This is particularly true in sport where the emphasis is on competition, superiority, and dominating others. These characteristics often contrast with the values of many religions, including cooperativeness, humility, and helping others. Bennett, Sagas, Fleming, and Von Roenn (2005) found evidence of this conflict in their case study of a university baseball coach. Specifically, they found that the coach experienced three contradictions between his religious beliefs and his role as a coach at a large university. First, he acknowledged a conflict between the emphasis on winning in sport and his spiritual beliefs. Second, as a coach who had won a national championship and currently led a major university team, his social status was exalted. The exaltation he received from others resulted in a certain degree of uneasiness. Finally, he struggled with his perception that his behavior on the field was incongruent with his spiritual beliefs. This conflict produced so much angst that he sometimes wept over his behaviors, noting that his "heart's desire" (p. 295) was to not behave in that manner.

Because these incongruities produced such stress for the coach, he developed three primary ways to resolve the contradictions. First, he used disassociation techniques—when he was away from work, he tried not to think about or discuss baseball. Second, he adopted the mind-set that he could walk away from coaching if that is what he felt "led" to do. Third, he relied heavily on his faith for comfort and reassurance (Bennett et al., 2005). Although this study focused on a single baseball coach, research shows that these contradictions also are felt by others who closely adhere to their religious beliefs (see Freshman, 1999).

Religion on the Field

Religious beliefs affect sport participants in two ways. First, religion influences who participates in sport and their reasons for doing so. Second, some athletes rely on their religious beliefs while participating.

Sport Participation

One's religious beliefs can influence the degree of sport participation and the reasons for that participation. Eitzen and Sage (2003) provide a historical account of the issue. According to them, primitive societies used sport and physical activity to defeat their foes, influence supernatural forces, or to increase crop and livestock fertility. The ancient Greeks also used sport in a religious context. In fact, the early Olympics was actually a religious performance aimed at pleasing Zeus. Although these cultures used sport in various religious capacities, early 17th-century Puritans viewed sport as antithetical to Christian ideals. Eitzen and Sage note that no Christian group opposed sport and sport participation more than the Puritans. This view was largely maintained by Christian churches in North America until the 20th century. Subsequently, however, changes in the United States—industrialization, urbanization, and an awareness of the health benefits of sport and physical activity—resulted in a more positive relationship between sport and religion. Eitzen and Sage (2003) note that "church leaders gradually began to reconcile play and religion in response to pressure from medical, educational, and political leaders for games and sport. These activities were believed to aid in the development of physical, mental, and indeed, more health" (p. 168). Consequently, churches now include sport in their social programs, and attendees are often actively involved in sport and physical activity (see also Hoffman, 1999).

Other religions also influence who participates in sport and their reasons for doing so. For example, Walseth and Fasting (2003) found that Egyptian women's participation in sport and physical activity was largely shaped by their Islamic beliefs. The women in their study believed that Islam called for people to be physically active for various reasons, including to care for their overall health and to be ready in case of war. Because Islam says that women may participate in sport so long as the sport movements are not "exciting" for men who might watch them, the extent to which the women participated in

---

alternative
P E R S P E C T I V E S

Some Sports Are Tolerated. Some authors suggest that the Puritans were adamantly opposed to all sport and recreation (Eitzen & Sage, 2003). Rader (1999), however, feels differently. True, the Puritans prohibited sport or recreational activities held on the Sabbath or that resulted in undesirable outcomes such as drunkenness. Under other circumstances, however, sport was seen as beneficial and rejuvenating. To be "acceptable," a sport should refresh people so they could better execute their worldly and spiritual callings. Rader notes, "believing that all time was sacred (and therefore one's use of it was accountable to God), conscientious Puritans approached all forms of play with excruciating caution" (p. 7). These rigid rules did not apply to children, as they played with toys and were allowed to swim and skate so long as they were orderly while doing so. Evidently, the rules also did not apply to military training. All men age 16 to 60 met regularly for required military training, engaging in jumping, foot races, horse racing, and shooting at marks (Rader, 1999). These exceptions suggest that the Puritans are often mislabeled as "anti-sport."

sport and physical activity depended on whether they adopted a more modern or more traditional view of Islam. Women who adopted a more modern view of Islam considered most activities (except gymnastics, dancing, or aerobics) appropriate and likely not to excite men. Women with a more traditional view felt that all sport forms were inappropriate unless the sport was conducted in sex-segregated venues. Because such venues were limited in Egypt, so was their sport participation.

Athletes' Use of Religion

Many athletes use religious beliefs, prayers, and rituals while participating in sport. Though research in this area is generally scarce, Coakley (2004) suggests that there are six reasons why athletes use religion (see Exhibit 7.2).

Reduce anxiety. Athletes use religion as a way of coping with the anxiety-producing uncertainty that is a fact of life with many sports, whether the uncertainty pertains to the risk of bodily harm, pressure to perform well, or not knowing what will come next. Some athletes use prayer, scriptures, meditation, or other religious rituals to reduce this anxiety. For example, DeBerg (2002) examined the way athletes used their religion in their sport performance. One athlete noted, "it gives me security, especially from injuries. It means a higher power is looking out for you" (p. 11). Another athlete explained, "sometimes you get so nervous out there. I say a little prayer" (p. 11).

Avoid trouble. Athletes may also use religion as a way of keeping out of trouble (Coakley, 2004). As previously discussed, persons who hold strong religious

---

Exhibit 7.2	**Using religion during sport participation.**

Athletes use religion to

- reduce anxiety.
- avoid trouble.
- give meaning to sport participation.
- gain perspective.
- increase team unity.
- achieve personal success.

Adapted from Coakley (2004).

beliefs may behave differently than those who do not. Their beliefs also give them a focus for their lives. This is certainly true for University of Southern California defensive end Jeff Schweiger. Commenting on the challenges he often faces in the "un-Christian" football environment, Schweiger said, "There's been points where I'm like, 'screw this, I can't do this, it's too hard right now.' But I always come back" (Malcolmson, 2005). The athletes' faith serves as a guide for their behavior, even in difficult times.

Give meaning to sport participation. Coakley (2004) notes that athletes also use religion to give personal meaning to their sport participation. Athletes spend countless hours training and practicing. Even in team sports, the focus is primarily on the self and improving individual performance. How do people rationalize spending so much time focusing on the self or, from another perspective, so much time focusing on sport in general? Athletes of faith often consider sport participation an act of worship, thereby bringing glory to God. An athlete in DeBerg's (2002) study illustrated this point: "The Lord has been in my life before football, and he will be in it afterwards. Jesus gave his all for me so how can I give less?" (p. 10).

Gain perspective. Some athletes use religion to keep their sport participation in perspective (Coakley, 2004). If an athlete perceives that her participation is part of God's calling, then facing life's challenges becomes easier. The athlete does not become "swallowed up by sports or become overwhelmed by the drama, challenges, and regular failures that occur in sports" (p. 551). The Egyptian women interviewed by Walseth and Fasting (2003) provided evidence of this phenomenon. One participant commented on why she participated in sport: "Islam tells us that we

DIVERSITY *in the field*

Costs of Prayer. As noted, athletes use prayer and their religious beliefs for various reasons in the sport context. The same is true for coaches—they often lead prayers prior to or after athletic events. Although this practice has occurred for some time (and continues to), some people view a coach leading a team prayer as a violation of the separation of church and state requirement for public schools. This very issue came to a head in October of 2005 at East Brunswick High School in New Jersey. Marcus Borden, who had compiled 5 conference championships and 7 playoff appearances during his 23-year career as head coach, was awarded the 2004 American Football Coaches Association Power of Influence Award for his positive influence on the lives of his players. However, when told by school officials that he would have to stop leading and taking part in team prayers, he resigned his position. Borden noted that the practice of leading team prayers was not uncommon and that coaches across the state led similar prayers prior to the sport events they coached. However, many team parents and school officials had a different view. Trish LaDuca, a spokesperson for the school district, noted "a representative of the school district cannot constitutionally initiate prayer, encourage it, or lead it." Rather, any team prayer must be initiated by the students or else the law is violated ("Coach," 2005; "Power," 2004). As this situation illustrates, one's religious beliefs and convictions can have a substantial influence on leadership behaviors and career decisions.

have got the body as a gift from God, and that we should take care of it. God tells us to do a lot of things. How much we do of these things, is what decides our place in heaven" (p. 53).

Increase team unity. Religion is often used to increase team unity (Coakley, 2004). Former NFL coach George Allen commented that religion and prayer united teammates like no other factor he witnessed as a coach. Murray, Joyner, Burke, Wilson, and Zwald (2005) conducted a study of university softball teams to examine this very relationship. For many of the players in their study, prayer and shared religious beliefs among the team members positively influenced the team's cohesiveness. One player explained, "I think team prayer is an awesome way to get people focused on the task at hand. I think it lets people know they can put their trust in God and whatever the outcome, it's okay. Faith helps you get through any obstacle and lets people bond over commonality" (p. 236).

Achieve personal success. Some athletes use religious beliefs as a means to improve performance (Coakley, 2004). Although performance is usually viewed in terms of wins and losses, Czech, Wrisberg, Fisher, Thompson, and Hayes (2004) found that prayers for performance can take several forms. Many athletes, for example, will pray that they perform to the best of their ability, and if success comes as a result, then so be it. As one wrestler commented, "I didn't really pray for victory so much as I prayed to help me give my best and to perform to the highest ability that God gave me" (p. 8). Other athletes use prayer as a way of showing their gratitude for their athletic abilities. One athlete said, "You kind of thank God for providing opportunity. You realize He did provide this opportunity" (p. 8).

Sexual Orientation

Sexual orientation is another deep-level characteristic that exerts substantial influence in the sport context. As with religious beliefs, sexual orientation is a characteristic that is often unknown to others unless one chooses to disclose the information. Various estimates suggest that between 4 and 17 percent of the U.S. population is either gay, lesbian, or bisexual (GLB), or between 11 and 48 million Americans (Lubensky, Holland, Wiethoff, & Crosby, 2004). This section discusses the categorical effects of sexual orientation.

Basic Concepts

Historically, people viewed sexual orientation as a binary construct—one was either heterosexual or homosexual (Lubensky et al., 2004). Kinsey and his colleagues challenged this assumption (Kinsey, Pomeroy, & Martin, 1948; Kinsey, Pomeroy, Martin, & Gebhard, 1953). They considered sexual orientation as existing on a continuum from completely heterosexual to completely homosexual, with various gradients in between the two ends, including bisexuality. Various authors continue to consider sexual orientation in this manner (e.g., Gill, Morrow, Collins, Lucey, & Schultz, 2006).

One's sexual orientation is complex, with dimensions beyond simply the sex of one's sexual partners. Sexual orientation consists of many elements, including self-image, fantasies, attractions, and behaviors (Lubensky et al., 2004). These elements can interact in seemingly contradictory ways. A person can, for example, be attracted to and have fantasies about both men and women, yet exhibit exclusively heterosexual behavior. Contradictions such as this make it difficult to obtain precise estimates of the number of GLB persons. The malleability of one's sexuality also makes it difficult to gauge the number of GLB persons. Some people do not recognize their GLB identity until late in their lives. Others form relationships with members of the opposite sex after years of having a same-sex partner. Lubensky et al. note that for persons who are not exclusively heterosexual or exclusively homosexual, "it may make sense to think in terms of sexual orientation as something with multiple facets that is influenced by social context" (p. 207).

Scientific thinking about sexual orientation has changed over the years, and so too have people's attitudes toward GLB individuals (Yang, 1997). For example, in 1973, 70 percent of people felt that sexual relations among members of the same sex was always wrong. This figure fell to 56 percent by 1996. Between 1982 and 1996, the proportion of people who believed that homosexuality was an acceptable lifestyle rose from 34 to 44 percent. In a similar way, people's attitudes toward GLB individuals have also improved. In 1984, 35 percent of people polled indicated that they had unfavorable attitudes toward homosexuals, a percentage that decreased to 20 percent by 1996. In light of the improved attitudes toward homosexuality and GLB persons, it is not surprising that people also generally hold more favorable opinions of GLB individuals' civil rights. For example, a plurality of people polled in 1996 believed that GLB persons should be able to teach in the public schools—the first time such a plurality was obtained. Furthermore, 60 percent of people polled in 1996 favored employment legislation barring discrimination based on sexual orientation. Finally, 61 percent of people surveyed in 1973 favored free speech for GLB individuals—this proportion increased 20 percent by 1996 (see Yang, 1997). These figures suggest that attitudes toward homosexuality, GLB persons, and GLB persons' rights improved over time.

Sexual Prejudice

Though attitudes related to homosexuality have improved, GLB persons still experience considerable sexual prejudice—"negative attitudes toward an individual because of his or her sexual orientation" (Herek, 2000, p. 19). These negative attitudes are directed toward homosexual behavior, GLB persons, and

GLB communities. Note that, consistent with the discussion of prejudice and discrimination in Chapter 3, manifestations of sexual prejudice can be overt or subtle. Overt prejudice comes in many forms, such as the physical abuse GLB persons sometimes experience (e.g., Matthew Shepard). Herek notes that over 1,000 hate crimes based on sexual orientation were reported in 1997 alone. Not all manifestations are that blatant, however. Hebl, Foster, Mannix, and Dovidio (2002) conducted an experiment designed to examine the discrimination faced by GLB job applicants. Although store managers did not overtly discriminate against GLB applicants, there was evidence of subtle discrimination, as employers were verbally negative and spent less time interacting with the GLB applicants than the other applicants.

Not all GLB people experience the same level of sexual prejudice. For example, attitudes toward gay men are usually more negative than attitudes toward lesbians (Gill et al., 2006; Whitley & Kite, 1995). One possible explanation for this effect is that gay men are viewed as violating "appropriate" gender roles more so than lesbians. Furthermore, the rater's sex influences the degree of sexual prejudice—men exhibit more prejudice than women (Whitley & Kite, 1995).

The discussion now turns to the prevalence of sexual prejudice, the motivation for such negative behaviors and attitudes, and the outcomes associated with sexual prejudice.

Prevalence of Sexual Prejudice

Though attitudes have improved toward GLB individuals, some negativity still persists. Herek (2000) notes that generally the public is reluctant to view homosexuality on par with heterosexuality, and the evidence, as outlined by Meyer (2003), seems to support this contention. GLB persons are twice as likely as their heterosexual counterparts to experience some form of prejudice in their lifetime. Furthermore, these persons are likely to be victims of degrading remarks, torture, assault, or murder. These abuses appear to be especially prevalent for GLB youth. Most (90 percent) GLB youth have heard sexually prejudiced remarks at their schools, with many of these remarks (37 percent) coming from teachers or administrators. As might be expected, these effects are also evident in the workplace. Various reports indicate that GLB employees earn considerably less (11–27 percent) than their heterosexual counterparts. They also face other forms of treatment discrimination and have limited access to certain organizations or jobs (Meyer, 2003).

This same pattern of prejudice exists in the sport and physical activity realm—a context in which sexual prejudice is considered rampant. Anderson (2002) notes that sexual prejudice is especially prevalent among athletes on men's teams. For example, as an openly gay cross-country coach, Anderson witnessed one of his runners being beaten by a football player who assumed the runner was gay (he was not). The football player fractured four of the runner's facial bones and tried to gouge out his eyes.

Sexual prejudice also occurs in the coaching ranks. Krane and Barber (2005) interviewed 13 lesbian college coaches. The sexual orientation of only one of the coaches was known to all members of the athletic department for which she worked. The other coaches withheld this information because of the repercussions they thought would ensue if such information was made public. In fact, some of the coaches asked if the interview records could be traced back to them or if the tapes could be subpoenaed. The coaches in the study discussed many types of sexual prejudice. As one coach noted, "the coaching world is not always a kind world. . . . It's a really strange issue within coaching. . . . There are so many lesbians in coaching, and yet it's not somewhere that people can be comfortable with that being openly known about them" (p. 71). The sexual prejudice directed toward the lesbian coaches does not come just from others in the athletic department. Other coaches against whom they compete will use sexual orientation as a "chip" in the athlete recruiting process. The openly gay coach commented, "I'm the only coach that's gay, that is open, so I'm sure it's been used as a recruiting tool. . . . I'm sure kids don't come here because of that" (p. 72). Some coaches capitalize on the prejudice toward GLB persons by generating negative attitudes among parents and athletes toward a specific coach or team.

Motivations for Negative Behaviors and Attitudes

It is important to understand the underlying motivations for the negative behaviors and attitudes directed toward GLB persons. Herek (2000) outlines four primary motivations, all of which may interact with one another. First, sexual prejudice may originate from an unpleasant interaction with a GLB individual. For example, if an athlete has a negative experience with a gay coach (e.g., incongruence in leadership style), then the athlete might hold negative attitudes toward all other gay coaches—and even gay athletes. This generalization to others is more likely to occur when the gay coach is perceived as typical or representative of other gay men in general.

A second underlying motivation is fear of homosexuality itself (Herek, 2000). This fear may develop in people who are uncomfortable with their own sexual impulses or their gender conformity. Likewise, this fear may arise from the perception that homosexuality challenges traditional heterosexual social structures (Lubensky et al., 2004).

Third, others may express sexual prejudice when group norms mandate hostility toward homosexual or bisexual persons. There are many contexts, such as the military or sport, where such group norms are prevalent. Messner (1992) notes that "boys (in sports) learn early that to be gay, to be suspected of being gay, or even to be unable to prove one's heterosexual status is unacceptable" (p. 34). Messner states that sport is a place where heterosexuality is the norm and homosexuals are seen as "others." When someone holds this "other" distinction, they are likely to face negative attitudes, be trusted less, and be sub-

DIVERSITY *in the field*

Sexual Prejudice Toward Coaches. Bloomburg is a small town in northeast Texas with a population of 374. The high school is too small to field a football team, so like many towns this size, basketball reigns supreme and is the source of town pride. For many years, however, the girl's team performed at subpar levels—that is, until Coach Merry Stephens arrived in 1999. Her team excelled at high levels, making the playoffs three times and reaching the state semifinals in 2004. These successes resulted in Stephens being named teacher of the year by the local Wal-Mart and coach of the year by the district in which the team competed. However, only nine months after guiding her team to the state semifinals, Stephens was fired.

Many aspects about Stephens made her unique. Not only was she the first female coach in Bloomburg history, but she was also a lesbian. Her partner (who also worked at the school) was formerly married, had two children, and was a school board member's niece. When their relationship became public, the school board members, along with the school superintendent, set out to make both women's lives miserable by assigning them difficult tasks and holding them to a different standard. Her partner was fired by the school's superintendent, and the school board voted to begin proceedings to terminate Stephens' contract. When Michael Shirk, a Texas State Teachers Association attorney, began to take depositions for the termination hearings, he found that the school board had no basis to fire Stephens. Unlike her partner who was

an at-will employee and could be fired without cause, Stephens was also a teacher, and in Texas teachers cannot be fired without just cause. Shirk commented, "what doomed these administrators from the start was their hubris and obvious bigotry" (Colloff, 2005, p. 60). Ultimately, a settlement was reached that required the school board to pay Stephens' salary for the 18 months remaining on her contract in exchange for her resignation.

The actions taken by the school board and superintendent left the town divided. Some believed that Stephens and her partner were treated unfairly; one such person was the pastor of the First Baptist Church, Tim Reed. Though he preaches that homosexuality is a sin, Reed was appalled at what occurred: "unless we are going to remove every abomination from the school district, I don't see why we should focus on one at the exclusion of all others." He continued, "Maybe we should have a crusade against gossipers too. Let's cut their tongues out and run them out of town! There might be three of us left" (p. 60). Others believed that the school board was justified and supported their decision.

The competing views came to a head in 2005 when the school board elections were held. Jimmy Lightfoot, the school board member who spearheaded the move to release Stephens, was challenged by Suzanne Bishop who was critical of the way Lightfoot handled the terminations. Bishop easily won the election. Of the five persons running for the seat, Lightfoot came in a distant last (Colloff, 2005).

jected to disapproving behaviors. To the extent that these beliefs are maintained, the prejudice will continue.

Finally, some people are prejudiced toward GLB persons because homosexuality is contrary to their personal belief systems (Herek, 2000). This is especially true for those who hold conservative or traditional religious beliefs (Lubensky et al., 2004). Sexual prejudice is justified by the religious beliefs. Research shows that such beliefs exist across a variety of religions including Christianity, Judaism, Islam, and Buddhism (Lubensky et al., 2004).

Outcomes Associated with Sexual Prejudice

Most of the outcomes associated with experiencing sexual prejudice relate to one's health and well-being, which may then be associated with other outcomes such as those related to work. A meta-analysis performed by Meyer (2003) indicated that GLB individuals are about 2.3 times more likely than heterosexuals to experience a mental disorder (e.g., mood disorder, increased anxiety, substance abuse) during their lifetime. GLB persons are also more likely to attempt or commit suicide than their heterosexual counterparts. These differences are particularly apparent among youth. These mental disorders are thought to result, at least in part, from the social stressors associated with being the target of sexual prejudice (Cochran, 2001).

It is not surprising that sexual prejudice has a deleterious effect on people in the workplace. As previously noted, GLB persons encounter access discrimination (Hebl et al., 2002), are paid less than their heterosexual counterparts (Meyer, 2003), and may face hostile work environments, especially in the sport context (Krane & Barber, 2005). A study by Ragins and Cornwell (2001) supports this general trend. They found that perceived workplace discrimination was negatively related to organizational commitment, career commitment, self-esteem, job satisfaction, opportunities for promotion, and the overall promotion rate. Furthermore, those persons subjected to discrimination had strong turnover intentions. These findings suggest that sexual prejudice is detrimental to one's overall health and well-being and also negatively impacts one's well-being in the workplace (see the Diversity in the Field box for other examples).

Sexual Orientation Disclosure

As might be expected, the decision by GLB persons to reveal their sexual orientation, especially within the sport context, can be a life-altering choice. After all, if GLB individuals are treated differently, have limited access to positions, are paid less than what they deserve, and face difficult work environments, then disclosing such information may not be readily embraced. However, there are advantages to disclosing this information, and sometimes the benefits outweigh the costs. The next section discusses how people decide whether to disclose their sexual orientation, the antecedents of this decision, and the decision's outcomes.

Passing and Revealing

Clair, Beatty, and MacLean (2005) outline various strategies people use to decide whether to pass or to reveal their sexual orientation. Exhibit 7.3 summarizes these concepts.

Passing. *Passing* refers to a "cultural performance whereby one member of a defined social group masquerades as another in order to enjoy the privileges afforded to the dominant group" (Leary, 1999, p. 82). In the context of sexual orientation, this refers to GLB persons passing as heterosexuals. Passing can be intentional such as deliberately providing false information, or unintentional such as a when a coworker mistakenly assumes that a lesbian is heterosexual. Passing involves people leading a "double life" such that they adopt one persona in the workplace and another in their personal life.

GLB people use three strategies to pass: fabrication, concealment, and discretion (Clair et al., 2005). *Fabrication* occurs when someone deliberately provides incorrect or false information about the self. For example, a gay coach might deny that he is gay or more subtly, bring a woman companion, rather than a man, to an athletic department event. *Concealment* occurs when people

Exhibit 7.3	**Passing and revealing.**

Passing: the practice of withholding or failing to reveal a personal identity that is invisible to or unrecognizable by others. Passing strategies include:

- *Fabrication:* someone deliberately provides incorrect or false information about the self.
- *Concealment:* people actively withhold information or prevent others from acquiring information that would reveal their sexual orientation.
- *Discretion:* people avoid questions related to their sexual orientation.

Revealing: the practice of disclosing a personal identity that would otherwise be indistinguishable to others. Revealing methods include:

- *Signaling:* people disclose their sexual orientation by sending messages, providing subtle hints, or giving certain clues.
- *Normalizing:* people reveal their sexual orientation to others and then attempt to make their difference from the others seem commonplace or ordinary.
- *Differentiating:* people disclose their sexual orientation and highlight how it makes them different from others who do not share such preferences.

Adapted from Clair et al. (2005).

actively withhold information or prevent others from acquiring information that would reveal their sexual orientation. An example might be a gay administrator who does not display a picture of his partner on his desk, thereby concealing he has a same-sex partner. Finally, *discretion* occurs when people avoid questions related to their sexual orientation. Though related, discretion and concealment differ. People who choose discretion do not hide information about their sexual orientation (as they do with concealment)—they simply sidestep the issue altogether. People who use discretion avoid conversations where their sexual orientation might become a topic or simply change the topic.

Revealing. Clair et al. (2005) refer to *revealing* as the choice to "disclose an identity that would otherwise be invisible or unrecognizable to others" (p. 82). Revealing is a general term that is used with a myriad of identities such as religious affiliation, social class, and so forth. "Coming out" is the term most often used when referring to revealing one's sexual orientation.

GLB people use three different methods to reveal their sexual orientation: signaling, normalizing, and differentiating (Clair et al., 2005). People who choose the *signaling* method disclose their sexual orientation by sending messages, providing subtle hints, or giving certain clues. Sometimes, people use signals that are meaningful to insiders but are innocuous to others, thereby making their preferences known only to those they choose. For example, a lesbian athlete might put a rainbow sticker on her car's back window.

Normalizing occurs when people reveal their sexual orientation to others and then attempt to make their difference from the others seem commonplace or ordinary (Clair et al., 2005). People who adopt the normalizing method seek to assimilate into the dominant culture and downplay the significance of the difference. For example, a lesbian coach might share the everyday difficulties she and her partner have, such as mowing the grass or paying the bills, that underscore how common their experiences are with a heterosexual couple's experiences.

Finally, *differentiating* occurs when people disclose their sexual orientation and highlight how it makes them different from others who do not share such preferences. Clair et al. (2005) note that people who differentiate "seek to present an identity as equally valid (rather than stigmatized) and many engage in an effort to change the perceptions and behavior of the groups, organizations, and institutions that may stigmatize them" (p. 83). By doing so, people claim a certain identity at work (e.g., gay coach) and redefine the way their identity is understood and viewed by others in the workplace. For example, a gay athlete might speak up when his teammates use derogatory terms (e.g., "that is so gay").

Antecedents to Passing and Revealing

As the preceding discussion illustrates, the decision to disclose personal information related to sexual orientation is complex. Clair et al. (2005) outline several factors that influence the decision to pass or reveal.

Contextual conditions. Clair et al. (2005) identify three contextual conditions that are thought to influence the decision to pass or reveal: organizational diversity climate, industry and professional norms, and legal protections. These authors suggest that people view these conditions as indicators of whether they will receive support for or be stigmatized because of their sexual orientation.

With respect to the *diversity climate,* organizations that have formal antidiscrimination policies and procedures are transparent in their decision-making processes and have several "out" individuals currently employed. These organizations are more convivial for GLB persons. Anderson (2002) found evidence of this in his study of gay athletes. For those athletes who had a supportive team environment and backing from their teammates, "coming out" was met with little or no resistance and was perceived as a generally pleasant experience. On the other hand, in organizations where support is lacking, discrimination is rampant, and no other persons are "out," then it is likely that revealing behavior will not be seen as an option (see also Griffin, 1998).

Industry and professional norms set the standard by which people can "fit in" (Clair et al., 2005). For instance, the Clinton administration implemented a "don't ask, don't tell" policy in the U.S. military, implying that GLB soldiers and other personnel should pass. Many argue that the same is true in sports (e.g., Griffin, 1998). Even if one works in a supportive organization, and thus reveals his sexual orientation, others in the sport industry might "use" that information against them. Krane and Barber (2005) documented this occurrence, especially in recruiting battles, in their study of women coaches. Because the same is true in other aspects of sport, it explains why so few people, especially gay men, reveal their sexual orientation in the sport industry.

Finally, *legal protections* may impact the decision to pass or reveal (Clair et al., 2005). Although federal laws protect people from discrimination on the basis of their race, disability, and sex, there is no such protection for sexual orientation (Clair et al., 2005). Without protection, the decision to reveal one's sexual orientation becomes more difficult.

Individual differences. The decision whether or not to disclose one's sexual orientation will likely be influenced by several individual differences: willingness to take risks, self-monitoring tendencies, stage of adult development, and the presence of other stigmatizing characteristics (Clair et al., 2005).

People who have a higher *willingness to take risks* typically make riskier decisions than those without such propensity. Clearly, revealing one's sexual orientation can be a risky proposition in the sport context. Thus, people who are less averse to risk may be more willing to reveal their sexual orientation, even absent other enabling contextual conditions, than their counterparts with an aversion to taking risks.

Self-monitoring tendencies (Clair et al., 2005) refers to the extent to which people regulate or try to control how well they fit the social expectations of their roles within certain environments. High self-monitors are very cognizant of how others perceive them and try hard to "fit in." On the other hand, low self-monitors are less concerned with how others perceive them and are more likely to be true to themselves. High self-monitors are likely to pass or reveal depending on the situation; they will pass when the social situation calls on them to do so, and reveal when it socially benefits them. Low self-monitors will likely reveal no matter the situation, as revealing is more consistent with who they are as a person.

One's *stage of adult development* should also impact the decision to pass or reveal (Clair et al., 2005). People who have higher levels of self-esteem and are more self-assured are more likely to reveal than are those who do not. The same is likely true for people who fully embrace their identity as a GLB individual.

Finally, the degree to which one has other potentially *stigmatizing characteristics* influences decisions to pass or reveal (Clair et al., 2005). If they do possess such characteristics, they already face stress and bias at work. Further exacerbating this situation by revealing that one is homosexual is often not viewed as an appealing option. For example, women already face a gender bias in many organizational settings; hence, revealing one's lesbian identity would only amplify the bias she experiences. On the other hand, people who are not already subjected to stigmatization might be more willing to reveal their GLB orientation.

Passing and Revealing Outcomes

Several studies examined the outcomes associated with passing or revealing (Button, 2001; Day & Schoenrade, 1997; Meyer, 2003). Generally, passing might be expected to be associated with more positive outcomes. After all, people choose to pass, at least in part, because of a fear that they may be subjected to verbal or physical abuse or be stigmatized—undesirable outcomes. However, research shows that passing is actually associated with more negative outcomes. People who pass are not revealing a part of who they are, and this leads to authenticity issues (Leary, 1999). They also might be isolated from others because of certain behaviors associated with passing such as avoiding particular people or issues. Indeed, research shows that people who pass at work or in sport are generally less satisfied with their experiences in those contexts (Day & Schoenrade, 1997).

Those people who reveal at work, however they choose to do so, are often pleased with their choice. Of course, not all situations are pleasant. People can be ostracized or stigmatized because of their GLB identity (Anderson, 2002). Many times, however, the choice to reveal ultimately eliminates the stress of having to live a "double life." People who disclose their GLB orientation might also feel that they are more complete and not hiding who they are. Day and Schoenrade (1997) found that GLB persons who were "open" at work did not differ from heterosexuals on any of the following important work outcomes: affective commitment, continuance commitment, job satisfaction, job stress, support from top management, role ambiguity, role conflict, and work–home conflict. These results suggest that "open" GLB employees experience work the same as any other employee might, thereby demonstrating the benefits of revealing at work (see also Griffith & Hebl, 2002).

Sheryl Swoopes' decision to reveal her sexual orientation illustrates this point. Swoopes, a three-time MVP of the WNBA, decided to disclose the fact that she was a lesbian in October of 2005. She commented, "I'm just at a point in my life where I'm tired of having to pretend to be somebody I'm not. I'm tired of having to hide my feelings about the person I care about. About the person I love" (Granderson, 2005). As this illustrates, revealing her sexual orientation relieved some of the stress associated with passing and allowed her to be more authentic as a person.

Organizational Perspectives

The discussion thus far focused on sexual prejudice and the dynamics of the decision to disclose one's sexual orientation at work in terms of individuals. This section examines sexual orientation issues from an organizational perspective. Why do some organizations make concerted efforts to target GLB persons as employees and customers? Why have some entities formed specifically as a place for GLB to participate in sport, and how do these organizations function? These questions are addressed next.

Targeting GLB Persons

Some organizations specifically target GLB persons as employees and customers (Lubensky et al., 2004). These organizations believe that increasing the number of GLB employees serves to increase the overall workforce diversity. A diverse workforce is thought to excel in certain areas—creativity, breadth of decision making, and confronting the challenges of a changing marketplace (see Chapter 1). Thus, the presence of GLB employees is highly desired.

Organizations also believe that GLB persons are "ripe for product marketing" (Lubensky et al., 2004, p. 213). GLB persons are perceived as affluent and thus serve as a key demographic on which to focus marketing and promotional efforts. Because GLB persons have been neglected for so long, even modest attempts at marketing to the GLB community are viewed in a very positive light and result in increased sales and brand loyalty. The extant data seem to support these claims. Consider the following data from an online survey by Community Marketing, Inc. (Roth, 2006):

- GLB persons have a median household income of $87,000.
- 84 percent of GLB persons have a valid passport.
- 73 percent of GLB persons belong to a frequent flyer program.
- 53 percent of GLB persons spent at least $5,000 each on a vacation.

- 96 percent of GLB persons took at least a short vacation during the 2005 year.
- 72 percent of GLB are college graduates.

Because all of these figures are greater than the U.S. national average, GLB individuals represent a viable demographic for sport and tourism organizations.

There are several organizations specifically designed to cater to the needs and wants of GLB travelers including Rainbow Tourism (www.rainbowtourism.com). This Australia-based company was founded in 2005 and specializes in niche tourism experiences. People interested in traveling to Australia can work with Rainbow Tourism to visit locations and stay in hotels that are owned and operated by gays or lesbians or are designated as gay-friendly properties. Research from Community Marketing, Inc. (Roth, 2006) suggests that such locations are very important to GLB tourists. For instance, 98 percent of those in their survey indicated that a destination's gay-friendly reputation influenced their decision to visit that destination. Further, 59 percent indicated that gay-friendly hotels were very important to them. All of these data support the notion that targeting GLB customers may be financially beneficial for sport and tourism organizations (see also the Professional Perspectives box).

Sport Entities

Elling, De Knop, and Knoppers (2003) report that an increasing number of GLB persons are choosing to participate in gay and lesbian sport clubs or informal gay sport groups. The GLB sport teams often compete against mainstream teams in various tournaments or leagues, or alternatively, may choose to participate in competitions or tournaments specifically for GLB athletes. Elling et al. examined why GLB persons chose to participate in those clubs and what their experiences were when doing

PROFESSIONAL
P E R S P E C T I V E S

Olivia Cruises and Resorts. Amy Errett is a former college athlete who earned her finance degree at the University of Connecticut and an MBA from the Wharton School at the University of Pennsylvania. She is also the CEO of Olivia Cruises and Resorts, a company dedicated to being a lesbian's lifestyle company, with a particular focus on travel and tourism. One way Olivia promotes its products is through celebrity endorsements, including Rosie Jones of the LPGA, tennis great Martina Navratilova, and Sheryl Swoopes of the WNBA. Errett notes that, "for many people, the fear of saying you're gay would then translate into nobody wanting to endorse you . . . what a great thing to have a company [such as Olivia] that wants to endorse you because you are gay." Errett believes that Swoopes serves as a good role model, especially for African American women who might be grappling with their sexual orientation. Errett also suggests that having Swoopes as a product endorser has substantially impacted Olivia's bottom-line. In the weeks immediately after Swoopes signed with Olivia, the company experienced a huge upsurge in media mentions (21 million), as well as a considerable increase in sales. The same trend occurred when they signed Jones and Navratilova. Although some companies may shy away from having GLB athletes endorse their products, Olivia found that such spokespersons provide a meaningful benefit to the organization.

so. They learned that many club participants found the culture of mainstream sport clubs to be discriminatory toward GLB athletes, especially gay men. The most important reason, however, for joining the club was that respondents felt more at ease and believed they were better able to socialize with people like them (i.e., other GLB persons) in those clubs.

An example of a sport form that embraces persons of all sexual orientations, including heterosexuals, is the Gay Games (Waitt, 2003). Established in San Francisco in 1982 by Tom Waddell, the Gay Games are held every four years. In the initial 1982 Games, 1,350 athletes from 12 different nations competed in 14 events. In 2002, the Games were held in Sydney, Australia, and hosted 12,000 athletes from 71 countries. Over 30 events were offered. Waitt notes that the Gay Games provide a sport environment free from the elitism and sexual prejudice often seen in the Olympics and also provide a sense of community for those who participate. The Games also serve to challenge stereotypes related to homosexuality and sport participation. As one participant noted, "I think it is an important statement considering the amount of homophobia there is in sport. The linking of homosexuality to sport is quite a challenging thing for a lot of people" (p. 174).

Though many view GLB-specific clubs and the Gay Games in a positive light, such sentiments are not shared by all. One participant in the study by Elling et al. (2003) believed that forming GLB-specific sport clubs served to discriminate and further alienate GLB persons: "You separate yourself when you do that, you discriminate yourself when you totally separate yourself from normal society . . . it is very contradictory: they don't want to be discriminated and at the same time they discriminate themselves" (p. 448). As this study participant noted, separate clubs actually had negative effects and was a form of self-discrimination on the part of GLB sport participants. In a related study (Waitt, 2003), some persons took exception to various aspects of the Gay Games, not understanding why a separate event was needed for people with GLB orientations. As one study respondent noted, "there's no sense in which being gay or lesbian affects your capacity to perform in sport" (p. 176). Similar sentiments were expressed by others in the study. Although GLB sport clubs and sport events have many positive effects for those who choose to join or participate, they can be viewed in a somewhat negative light by those who do not.

Social Class

This final section focuses on the categorical effects of social class. Some may question the inclusion of social class in a chapter related to deep-level diversity because it is not always invisible. There are some situations where social class may be readily known, or at least perceived. We might expect a person driving a fancy car to be in a different social class than someone who drives a less expensive car. In many cases, however, one's social class is not known unless deliberately revealed to others. Even in the example of the cars, the two drivers might actually be in the same social class, but simply put a different emphasis on the type of car they drive; thus, any noticeable differences between the two drivers are more a function of our perception than their actual social class.

As with the other forms of deep-level diversity, social class meaningfully impacts a person's experience in sport organizations. This section begins with an overview of the basic concepts—social class and social stratification. The influence of social class career success is examined next, including how class influences the jobs people have and how class differences are perpetuated through the organizations' structure. This is followed by a discussion of classism and how prejudicial attitudes toward people in certain social classes impact various outcomes. Finally, the ways sport participation influences upward social mobility is discussed.

Basic Concepts

A central component of American ideology is the notion that anyone can succeed in the workplace no matter where they were born, how much money their parents have, or how recently they immigrated to the country (Hochschild, 1995). Indeed, the United States is largely regarded as a meritocracy—a place where rewards and training are distributed based on talent and hard work, not on unfair advantage, unjust practices, or membership in a social group (Bullock, 2004). These concepts are exuded in the workplace as well as in the sport context. As former U.S. President Ronald Reagan noted, "when men and women compete on the athletic field, socioeconomic status disappears . . . it's the same way in the stands, where corporate presidents sit next to janitors . . . which makes me wonder if social class matters at all" (as cited in Coakley, 2004, p. 324).

Unfortunately, available data do not support this notion and instead point to a system of stratification across social groups. *Stratification* refers to the classification of people into specific social groups, with members of each group having similar life chances (Scott, 1996). Sociological theories largely dismiss the notion of meritocracy and argue that established patterns of inequality and power relations determine the distribution of rewards and resources—not people's performance or abilities. Applying this perspective, people in prominent, high-status social groups are likely to be afforded a wide range of opportunities—chances that people from less desirable social groups are not. The difference between a team president earning a $1 million salary and the grounds crew employee earning an hourly wage likely resides in education and access to resources, not in effort, motivation, or drive (Bullock, 2004).

People who occupy the same relative economic rank in the stratification system are thought to be from the same *social class* (Rothman, 2002). Though there is some debate as to exactly what is considered when grouping people into

DIVERSITY *in the field*

Social Class, Sport Participation, and Sport Spectatorship.

Issues related to social class permeate all parts of society, including sport participation and sport spectatorship. Participating in sport and recreational activities takes time and money, two things the elite are likely to have more of than other members of society, especially the working class and the poor. People who participate in sport are most likely to be highly educated, from a high-income bracket, and have a high-status occupation (Gibson, 1998). This pattern is evident in several segments of the sport industry including the Olympics, health and fitness, and recreational activities (Coakley, 2004). For example, skiing, golf, and tennis all have substantial costs for club dues and equipment. Therefore, persons from the elite or professional middle class are most likely to participate in these activities than those from the poor or working classes.

Social class also influences who attends sport events. A report from the *Sports Business Journal* (Genzale, 2003) illustrates this point. This publication tracked the fan demographics of the four major professional sport leagues in the United States (MLB, NBA, NFL, and NHL) from 1995 to 2001. Across each league, the proportion of people earning $20,000–$29,000 and $30,000–$49,000 decreased over the seven-year span. During the same time frame, the proportion of fans who earned $100,000 or more increased by at least 50 percent. This trend is not necessarily surprising considering the high costs of attending a professional sport event as discussed in Chapter 1. More and more, watching live sport is becoming something available only to persons in the professional middle class or the elite. The cost of attending is simply too expensive for persons from other social classes.

different social classes, there is relative consensus on three factors: income, education, and occupation (Bullock, 2004). People who share a particular social class are thought to have similar life chances—that is, they have the same odds of achieving success and gaining economic prosperity in their lives (Coakley, 2004). This is illustrated in the Diversity in the Field box.

Bullock (2004) notes that the United States is often characterized as having five social classes: elite, professional middle class, middle class, working class, and poor. At the top of this class system is the *elite*, which also happens to be the smallest class, representing 1 to 2 percent of the population. The elite can be further divided into two groups: the capitalist elite who have wealth and status based on their ownership of land, stocks, and organizations, and the institutional elite who possess powerful positions in government and corporations. The elite class is the wealthiest in the United States, with some estimates indicating that the wealthiest 1 percent of the population control about 39 percent of the wealth (Bullock, 2004).

Members of the *professional middle class* (Bullock, 2004) rely primarily on wages or salary for their income. Members are "white collar" workers and managers below the executive level. For many people in this class, their position is based on their expert knowledge (e.g., professors, sport psychologists, or sport agents). Persons in the professional middle class usually have advanced educational degrees such as an MBA or a Ph.D.

Below the professional middle class is the *middle class* (Bullock, 2004). Members of this class usually have a baccalaureate degree and are in such occupations as school teacher, data analyst, or lower-level manager. Research shows that most people strongly identify with the middle class. Many Americans classify themselves as middle class even if they do not technically meet the criteria. Bullock suggests this tendency reflects people's idea that the United States is a country not necessarily divided by class, or that the "middle" is normative. It could also be indicative of the greater value people place on membership in the middle class relative to the lower alternative: the working or lower class.

People in the *working class* are often "blue collar" workers who engage in physical labor (Bullock, 2004). For example, the employee who shapes the wood to make a baseball bat at the Louisville Slugger plant might be considered a member of the working class. Many of the jobs working class people hold require considerable skill (e.g., automobile technician); however, because a formal education is not required to achieve those skills, they are not considered to be in the middle class.

The *poor* includes those persons at the "bottom" of the class hierarchy (Bullock, 2004). People in this group are at or below the poverty level, which according to the U. S. Census Bureau, was at $11,869 for a parent with one dependent in 2000. Households headed by women, especially women of color, are overrepresented in this group. Bullock notes that many poor men and women work either full- or part-time; however, having employment does not necessarily pull one out of this class. The jobs the poor are likely to hold, such as a concessionaire at a baseball game, pay minimum wage (or slightly above) and are unlikely to offer any benefits. These jobs have minimal prospects for advancement; thus, the employee is "stuck" in that position.

Class and Career Success

The concepts of stratification and class are also seen in the workplace. In any sport organization, employees have different educational backgrounds, life experiences, work histories, and so on. In large part, these characteristics influence the type of job one holds in the organization. For example, a person with no college education and little experience in the workplace has little chance of becoming an athletic director. On the other hand, a person with a Wharton MBA and a law degree, experience, and has a history of substantial earnings is in a much better position to become an athletic director. The sport organization's structure, the power associated with certain jobs, and the earning potential of various positions further reinforce the class differences. An examination of these reciprocal relationships allows one to see how power and privilege are maintained (Bullock, 2004).

Bullock (2004) notes that in the United States, middle-class cultural norms hold that people freely choose their occupation. For example, if you ask children what they want to be when they grow up, you will receive a myriad of responses, including the President, a firefighter, a professional athlete, and a school teacher. This freedom to explore different career options and then to choose the career one wants to pursue is encouraged by middle-class parents.

This liberty to choose one's occupation also connotes the idea that one's occupation is based on personal choice, not economic factors or class-based opportunities. This belief does not factor in the demands that limit many poor and working class youth—the necessity of working at an early age to provide for one's family or being unable to afford to attend college.

Social class influences the perceived opportunities to pursue certain lines of employment and the educational opportunities with which one is presented. Both issues are examined next.

Employment Opportunities

Weinger (2000) conducted a study of how school children viewed opportunities for career success for children from poor or middle-class backgrounds. She found that among both the middle class and the poor, persons who were poor were viewed as being least likely to obtain a job with the potential for high career success. Poor children were also believed to most likely obtain working class or blue-collar jobs, as opposed to professional or management positions. Interestingly, poor children were believed to obtain entertainment positions—such as a movie star or professional basketball player—more often than middle-class children. Finally, poor children were believed to encounter more obstacles to achieving their dreams than middle-class children. The middle-class children who participated in the study believed that their dreams would be thwarted because of a lack of effort on the part of the poor child. On the other hand, the study's poor children anticipated that a poor child's dreams would be truncated because of overt prejudice and discrimination. Overall, these findings suggest that children's views of potential career success are largely shaped by social class factors.

Education

Social class also influences the level of education one receives (Bullock, 2004). Education level can be examined from a number of perspectives. First, persons who live in poor cities or poor neighborhoods are likely to receive a different type of education than those people in more affluent cities or school districts. This is especially true when property taxes are the major source of school revenue. These money differences influence teacher compensation; access to books, supplies, and technology; and building security—all factors that can influence the quality of the education received. Second, social class influences the likelihood of completing high school. Bullock (2004) reports that school children from the poorest 20 percent of families are *six times* more likely not to finish high school than persons from the richest 20 percent. Third, social class influences who attends college, as a small proportion of all undergraduates are from low-income families (Bullock, 2004). These data suggest that even if a student performs well in high school, scores well on standardized tests, and is motivated to attend college, the lack of economic and social resources is likely to restrict her ability to attend college.

As might be expected, the level of education has a substantial influence on future career success. Management or professional occupations often requires advanced degrees such as an MBA. The same is not true for other occupations such as sales or production. This is meaningful because of the earnings difference between occupations. In the year 2000, the median income for a person in a management or professional occupation was $43,000. This is considerably more than the median income for a person in sales ($21,000) or production ($28,800). Thus, the level and quality of education one receives—something that is largely influenced by social class—has a substantial impact on subsequent occupations and career earnings.

Classism in the Workplace

Classism refers to behaviors, beliefs, and negative attitudes that serve to oppress low-income people (Bullock, 2004; Lott, 2002). This concept is comprised of three distinct, yet related, dimensions: prejudice, stereotypes, and discrimination. The existence of prejudice and stereotyping is well-documented. In one study, Beck, Whitley, and Wolk (1999) examined the attitudes toward the poor held by members of the Georgia state legislature. They found consensus among the legislators that people's actions serve to perpetuate their own poverty. The poor were considered to lack effort, talent, morals, and ambition. Consistent with these findings, Chafel's (1997) summary of two decades of research shows that both children and adults view poverty as a state that is self-inflicted and something that is the product of personal factors (e.g., lack of effort) rather than structural variables (e.g., racism). These studies suggest that people not only hold negative attitudes toward the poor and working class, but that these prejudicial attitudes are widespread.

In addition to the incidence of prejudice and negative stereotypes related to the poor, research also reveals the incidence of discrimination. Lott (2002) notes that discrimination results in distancing, avoidance, or exclusion of the poor or working class. Barriers are erected such that these people cannot enjoy full societal participation. In the workplace, this discrimination is seen in the hiring process and the placement of people into particular jobs. For example, Kennelly (1999) found that employers were sometimes reluctant to hire people who they perceived to be from a poor background because the applicants were thought to possess a poor work ethic. When they are hired, people from poor backgrounds are likely to be placed in "class appropriate" jobs such as janitorial or parking lot attendant positions (Bullock, 2004).

Class discrimination is also found in the structure of many organizations (Bullock, 2004). Upper management employees are paid, on average, 120 times what a line worker earns (Frank & Cook, 1995). In some organizations, interaction between upper management and line-level workers is minimal or nonexistent. Thus, people in the elite class are able to distance themselves from the poor or working class. In those organizations where there is interaction between people from different levels, the interactions are often rooted in hierarchical norms. These norms equate middle- and upper-class status with authority, while working-class status is associated with subordination; thus, the structure serves to reinforce, rather than challenge, class stereotypes (Bullock,

DIVERSITY *in the field*

Pay to Play. The influence of social class has also penetrated the realm of high school athletics. Funding sports is expensive, and for schools in poorer districts, administrators must choose to put money into sports or money into books and new classrooms. When such decisions have to be made, few young people from low-income families have the opportunity to participate in such expensive sports as baseball and football. Meanwhile, basketball grows in popularity among low-income boys and girls because a school can offer basketball as long as it can maintain a usable gym. It should be noted here, however, that maintaining a usable gym is a serious problem in some inner-city schools, where overcrowding has required that gyms be turned into classrooms.

Similar problems are seen in schools with middle- and upper-class students; however, in these schools, administrators are likely to institute a "pay-to-play" policy such that students pay a fee, sometimes up to several hundred dollars, for each sport they play. For example, in Fairfield, Ohio, a suburb of Cincinnati, students must pay $630 for each sport in which they participate, as well as fees to participate in other extracurricular activities, such as Spanish Club.

How prevalent are such practices? A *USA Today* study (Brady & Glier, 2004) showed that 34 of the 50 states have at least some pay-to-play programs. In Kansas, 18 percent of all schools implemented a pay-to-play program, and in Michigan, the percentage is about 23 percent. Among the states that do have pay-to-play programs, the number of schools implementing such a financing structure continues to grow.

Some may question whether pay-to-play programs have a deleterious effect on sport participation rates. The answer is yes. According to sport management professor Scott Smith of Central Michigan University, participation rates do not decline noticeably when the fees are small (e.g., $50); however, when the fees increase above the $300 range, participation rates "drop noticeably," sometimes by a third or more (Brady & Glier, 2004).

What do such policies mean to a discussion of social class and sport? The answer is clear: Such policies guarantee that opportunities to participate in varsity programs will continue for those young people born into middle- and upper-class families or who attend wealthy school districts that can afford to finance sport teams. For those students in poor school districts or whose families cannot afford the hundreds of dollars in fees, their formal sport participation opportunities are eliminated.

2004). This literature suggests that classism has a prevalent effect in the workplace. (See the Diversity in the Field box on the previous page for further information related to the effects of class on sport participation).

Sport and Social Mobility

The foregoing discussion suggests that social class plays a significant role in the education people receive, opportunities people are afforded, the types of jobs they have, and the experiences they have in the workplace. Nevertheless, some are of the opinion that sport participation can serve to negate this pattern. For example, does being a star athlete at a major university provide a person with the capital needed to be successful throughout life? Does participating in sport and athletics in high school mean that people will be more successful later in life? There are certainly isolated incidents where this is the case. Most of us can think of people who were raised in lower-income households, and as a result of their sport participation, received the college education, met the important social contacts, or gained the confidence needed to be successful in life. Unfortunately, for every athlete who has risen above his humble beginnings to be successful, there are just as many who have not. How does sport contribute to occupational success or upward social mobility, if at all?

Coakley (2004) suggests that sport participation will be positively related to upward social mobility when it does the following:

- Provides the athlete with educational opportunities as well as the chance to develop skills relevant to the workplace.
- Increases the support others give the athletes for their overall growth and development.
- Provides opportunities to make friends and social contacts with people outside sport and sport organizations.
- Provides people with the material resources necessary to create future career opportunities.
- Develops identities unrelated to sports through expanded opportunities and training.
- Minimizes the risks of injuries that would incur substantial medical costs and rehabilitation.

These predictions suggest that, under some circumstances, sport will help expand one's opportunities. This is certainly true when sport allows one to obtain education, skills, and training unrelated to sport. For example, when a volleyball player from a poor family receives a scholarship to a university, she is afforded the chance to obtain an education. To the extent that she takes advantage of this opportunity, develops her skills for the workplace, gains experiences through internships, and cultivates her social relationships, her sport participation is likely to be positively related to her upward social mobility and career success.

Chapter Summary

This chapter focused on deep-level differences. Unlike other diversity characteristics that are largely visible upon seeing somebody, deep-level differences are invisible. In most cases, people are not made aware of these differences until one chooses to divulge such information. As the Diversity Challenge illustrates, though they are invisible, deep-level differences have substantial effects on people, their actions, preferences, and beliefs. Deep-level differences also influence organizational practices, marketing efforts, and the formation of sport events. After reading the chapter, you should be able to:

1. **Define religion and spirituality, and discuss the categorical effects of religious beliefs in sport organizations.**

Religion is defined as a set of beliefs and practices related to sacred things that unites all those who adhere to them (Durkheim, 1965). The influence of religion is seen at the individual, interpersonal, institutional, and social integration levels. Spirituality is the feeling of connectedness and unity with others and the universe (Mitroff & Denton, 1999).

The categorical effects of religion are widespread. From an organizational standpoint, religious beliefs influence strategic decisions, ethical behavior, leadership style, and the level of stress encountered. Religious beliefs also influence how and why people participate in sport. Sport participants use religion to (a) reduce anxiety, (b) avoid trouble, (c) give meaning to sport participation, (d) gain perspective, (e) increase team unity, and (f) achieve personal success.

2. **Define sexual orientation and sexual prejudice, and outline the categorical effects of sexual orientation, both for the individual and for organizations.**

Though sexual orientation is often viewed as a binary construct, it is actually better viewed as a continuum from completely heterosexual to completely homosexual, with various gradients in between. One's sexual orientation has several elements including self-image, fantasies, attractions, and behaviors. Sexual prejudice refers to the negative attitudes people have toward others based on their sexual orientation.

The categorical effects of sexual orientation impact both individuals and organizations. GLB persons have to decide whether or not to reveal their sexual orientation to others. Because passing and revealing both have negative and positive outcomes, GLB persons must carefully weigh the consequences of either decision. Some organizations make efforts to attract GLB employees and customers, thinking that such efforts will have meaningful positive effects for the organization. Some sport organizations are formed specifically for GLB persons, thereby giving them a place to participate in sport without encountering some of the barriers in mainstream sport clubs.

3. **Define stratification, social class, and classism, and analyze the categorical effects of social class in sport organizations.**

Stratification refers to the classification of people into specific social groups, with members of each group having similar life chances. People who occupy the same relative economic rank in the stratification system are thought to be from the same social class. Social class membership is based on income, education, and occupation. Classism refers to behaviors, beliefs, and negative attitudes that serve to oppress low-income people. This concept is comprised of three distinct, yet related, dimensions: prejudice, stereotypes, and discrimination.

Research suggests that social class influences many aspects of sport organizations. People from low-income classes do not have the power or resources necessary to obtain certain high-level positions. Organizations are also structured in such a way to reinforce the class structure, both in terms of pay levels and the organizational hierarchy. These effects may be neutralized by sport participation, but only under certain circumstances. Sport is thought to be related to upward social mobility when it allows one to obtain a higher level of education, develop skills for the workplace, gain experiences, and cultivate social networks.

Questions for Discussion

1. Some people distinguish between religion and spirituality. Do you? If so, what are the major differences between religion and spirituality? If not, how are the two concepts similar?

2. Is the influence of religion on organizational practices stronger or weaker in sport than it is in other contexts? Why or why not?

3. In your experience, how much do athletes rely on their religious beliefs while participating in sport? What is the primary reason for this reliance?

4. Many authors suggest that sexual prejudice is prevalent in the sport context. Has this been your experience? Provide some examples.

5. Research suggests that attitudes toward gay men are more negative than attitudes toward lesbians. Why do you think this is the case?

6. What are some of the outcomes, both positive and negative, for an organization seeking to specifically target GLB customers?

7. Many argue that social class does not matter in the sport context, especially on sport teams. Do you agree or disagree with this sentiment and why?

8. Which is more likely to influence the career success one has in life: social class or personal attributes such as motivation?

Learning Activities

1. Visit the Federation of Gay Games website (www.gaygames.com/en/) and research the origin of the Games, the date and location of the next Games, and information about the participants.

2. Interview former athletes, whether they participated in interscholastic or university athletics, and ask them about the way in which their sport participation influenced their social mobility.

Resources

SUPPLEMENTARY READINGS

Griffin, P. (1998). *Strong women, deep closets: Lesbians and homophobia in sport*. Champaign, IL: Human Kinetics. (Analyzes stereotypes and prejudice directed toward lesbians in the sport context; considers the influence of religion on attitudes toward lesbians; addresses identity management for lesbian coaches and athletes.)

Putney, C. (2001). *Muscular Christianity: Manhood and sports in Protestant America, 1880–1920*. Cambridge, MA: Harvard University Press. (Provides a historical account of the relationship between the Protestant church, sports, and men in the early 20th century.)

Sage, G. H. (1998). *Power and ideology in American sport: A critical perspective* (2nd ed.). Champaign, IL: Human Kinetics. (Addresses the manner in which social, political, and economic influences shape sport in the United States today.)

WEB RESOURCES

- Fellowship of Christian Athletes (www.fca.org): an organization that challenges coaches and players to use sport to spread their Christian faith.
- National Center for Minority Health and Health Disparities (www.ncmhd.nih.gov): organization aimed at reducing and ultimately eliminating health disparities.
- Outsports (www.outsports.com): site devoted to providing the most comprehensive information related to the gay sport community.

References

Anderson, E. (2002). Openly gay athletes: Contesting hegemonic masculinity in a homophobic environment. *Gender & Society, 16,* 860–877.

Bailey, J. R. (2001). Book review of J. A. Conger and associates: Spirit at work: Discovering the spirituality in leadership. *The Leadership Quarterly, 12,* 367–368.

Beck, E. L., Whitley, D. M., & Wolk, J. L. (1999). Legislators' perceptions about poverty: Views from the Georgia General Assembly. *Journal of Sociology and Social Welfare, 26*(2), 87–104.

Bennett, G., Sagas, M., Fleming, D., & Von Roenn, S. (2005). On being a living contradiction: The struggle of an elite intercollegiate coach. *Journal of Beliefs & Values, 26,* 289–300.

Brady, E., & Glier, R. (2004, July). To play sports, many U.S. students must pay. *USA Today.* Retrieved February 19, 2006, from www.usatoday.com/sports/preps/2004-07-29-pay-to-play_x.htm

Bullock, H. E. (2004). Class diversity in the workplace. In M. S. Stockdale & F. J. Crosby (Eds.), *The psychology and management of workplace diversity* (pp. 226–242). Malden, MA: Blackwell.

Button, S. B. (2001). Organizational efforts to affirm sexual diversity: A cross-level examination. *Journal of Applied Psychology, 86,* 17–28.

Cacioppe, R. (2000). Creating spirit at work: Revisioning organization development and leadership—Part I. *Leadership and Organizational Development Journal, 21,* 48–54.

Cash, K. C., & Gray, G. R. (2000). A framework for accommodating religion and spirituality in the workplace. *Academy of Management Executive, 14*(3), 124–134.

Chafel, J. A. (1997). Societal images of poverty: Child and adult beliefs. *Youth & Society, 28,* 432–463.

Clair, J. A., Beatty, J. E., & MacLean, T. L. (2005). Out of sight but not out of mind: Managing invisible social identities in the workplace. *Academy of Management Review, 30,* 78–95.

Coach resigns after high school bans pregame prayer. (2005, October). ESPN.com. Retrieved October 12, 2005, from http://sports.espn.go.com/sports/news/story?id=2188313

Coakley, J. (2004). *Sports in society: Issues and controversies* (8th ed.). New York: McGraw-Hill.

Cochran, S. D. (2001). Emerging issues in research on lesbians' and gay men's mental health: Does sexual orientation really matter? *American Psychologist, 56,* 931–947.

Colloff, P. (2005, July). She's here. She's queer. She's fired. *Texas Monthly, 33*(7), 52–61.

Czech, D. R., Wrisberg, C. A., Fisher, L. A., Thompson, C. L., & Hayes, G. (2004). The experience of Christian prayer in sport: An existential phenomenological investigation. *Journal of Psychology and Christianity, 23,* 3–11.

Day, N. E., & Schoenrade, P. (1997). Staying in the closet versus coming out: Relationships between communication about sexual orientation and work attitudes. *Personnel Psychology, 50,* 147–163.

DeBerg, B. A. (2002). Athletes and religion on campus. *Peer Review, 4*(4), 10–12.

Dunn, R., & Stevenson, C. (1998). The paradox of the church hockey league. *International Review for the Sociology of Sport, 32,* 131–141.

Durkheim, E. (1965). *The elementary forms of religious life.* New York: Free Press.

Ehrhart, M. G. (2004). Leadership and procedural justice climate as antecedents of unit-level organizational citizenship behavior. *Personnel Psychology, 57,* 61–94.

Eitzen, D. S., & Sage, G. H. (2003). *Sociology of North American sport* (7th ed.). New York: McGraw-Hill.

Elling, A., De Knop, P., & Knoppers, A. (2003). Gay/lesbian sport clubs and events: Places of homo-social bonding and cultural resistance? *International Review for the Sociology of Sport, 38,* 441–456.

Frank, R. H., & Cook, P. J. (1995). *How more and more Americans compete for ever fewer and bigger prizes, encouraging economic waste, income inequality, and an impoverished cultural life*. New York: Martin Kessler Books/The Free Press.

Freshman, B. (1999). An exploratory analysis of definitions and applications of spirituality in the workplace. *Journal of Organizational Change Management, 12,* 318–327.

Fry, L. W. (2003). Toward a theory of spiritual leadership. *The Leadership Quarterly, 14,* 693–727.

Genzale, J. (Ed.). (2003). *Sport Business Journal by the numbers 2003*. Charlotte, NC: Street & Smith's *Sport Business Journal.*

Gibson, H. J. (1998). Active sport tourism: Who participates? *Leisure Studies, 17,* 155–170.

Gill, D. L., Morrow, R. G., Collins, K. E., Lucey, A. B., & Schultz, A. M. (2006). Attitudes and sexual prejudice in sport and physical activity. *Journal of Sport Management, 20,* 554–564.

Granderson, L. Z. (2005, October). *Three-time MVP "tired of having to hide my feelings."* ESPN.com. Retrieved October 26, 2005, from http://sports.espn.go.com/wnba/news/story?id=2203853

Greenleaf, R. K. (1977). *Servant leadership*. New York: Paulist Press.

Griffin, P. (1998). *Strong women, deep closets: Lesbians and homophobia in sport*. Champaign, IL: Human Kinetics.

Griffith, K. H., & Hebl, M. R. (2002). The disclosure dilemma for gay men and lesbians: "Coming out" at work. *Journal of Applied Psychology, 87,* 1191–1199.

Hebl, M. R., Foster, J. B., Mannix, L. M., & Dovidio, J. F. (2002). Formal and interpersonal discrimination: A field study of bias toward homosexual applicants. *Personality and Social Psychology Bulletin, 28,* 815–825.

Herek, G. M. (2000). The psychology of sexual prejudice. *Current Directions in Psychological Science, 9,* 19–22.

Hicks, D. A. (2002). Spiritual and religious diversity in the workplace: Implications for leadership. *The Leadership Quarterly, 13,* 379–396.

Hochschild, A. R. (1995). *Race, class, and the soul of a nation: Facing up to the American Dream*. New York: Viking.

Hoffman, S. (1999). The decline of civility and the rise of religion in American sport. *Quest, 51,* 69–84.

Jurkiewicz, C. L., & Giacalone, R. A. (2004). A values framework for measuring the impact of workplace spirituality on organizational performance. *Journal of Business Ethics, 49,* 129–142.

Kennelly, I. (1999). "That single-mother element": How White employers typify Black women. *Gender and Society, 13,* 168–192.

Khavari, K. A., & Harmon, T. M. (1982). The relationship between the degree of professed religious belief and use of drugs. *International Journal of Addictions, 17,* 847–857.

Kinsey, A. C., Pomeroy, W. B., & Martin, C. E. (1948). *Sexual behavior in the human male*. Philadelphia: W. B. Saunders.

Kinsey, A. C., Pomeroy, W. B., Martin, C. E., & Gebhard, P. H. (1953). *Sexual behavior in the human female*. Philadelphia: W. B. Saunders.

Krane, V., & Barber, H. (2005). Identity tensions in lesbian intercollegiate coaches. *Research Quarterly for Exercise and Sport, 76,* 67–81.

Kriger, M., & Seng, Y. (2005). Leadership with inner meaning: A contingency theory of leadership based on the worldviews of five religions. *The Leadership Quarterly, 16,* 771–806.

Leary, K. (1999). Passing, posing, and "keeping it real." *Constellations, 6,* 85–96.

Lott, B. (2002). Cognitive and behavioral distancing from the poor. *American Psychologist, 57,* 100–110.

Lubensky, M. E., Holland, S. L., Wiethoff, C., & Crosby, F. J. (2004). Diversity and sexual orientation: Including and valuing sexual minorities in the workplace. In M. S. Stockdale & F. J. Crosby (Eds.), *The psychology and management of workplace diversity* (pp. 206–223). Malden, MA: Blackwell.

Malcolmson, B. (2005, April). *Religion key for many USC athletes*. Daily Trojan Online. Retrieved February 8, 2006, from www.dailytrojan.com

Messner, M. (1992). *Power at play: Sports and the problem of masculinity*. Boston: Beacon.

Meyer, I. H. (2003). Prejudice, social stress, and mental health in lesbian, gay, and bisexual populations: Conceptual issues and research evidence. *Psychological Bulletin, 129,* 674–697.

Mitroff, I. I., & Denton, E. A. (1999). A study of spirituality in the workplace. *Sloan Management Review, 40,* 83–92.

Murray, M. A., Joyner, A. B., Burke, K. L., Wilson, M. J., & Zwald, A. D. (2005). The relationship between prayer and team cohesion in collegiate softball teams. *Journal of Psychology and Christianity, 24,* 233–239.

Power of influence award. (2004, October). American Football Coaches Association. Retrieved February 15, 2006, from www.afca.com/lev2.cfm/611

Rader, B. G. (1999). *American sports: From the age of folk games to the age of televised sport* (4th ed.). Upper Saddle River, NJ: Prentice Hall.

Ragins, B. R., & Cornwell, J. M. (2001). Pink triangles: Antecedents and consequences of perceived workplace discrimination against gay and lesbian employees. *Journal of Applied Psychology, 86,* 1244–1261.

Roth, T. E. (2006). *CMI's gay & lesbian tourism profile.* San Francisco: Community Marketing, Inc.

Rothman, R. A. (2002). *Inequality and stratification: Race, class, and gender* (4th ed.). Englewood Cliffs, NJ: Prentice Hall.

Scott, J. (1996). *Stratification and power: Structures of class, status, and command.* Cambridge, UK: Polity Press.

Shafran, A. (2002, June). *Mr. Feuerstein is a legend in the corporate world: His company is now bankrupt and he doesn't regret a thing.* Aish.com. Retrieved February 6, 2006, from www.aish.com/societyWork/work/Aaron_Feuerstein_Bankrupt_and_Wealthy.asp

Spears, L. C. (Ed.). (1998). *Insights on leadership: Service, stewardship, spirit, and servant leadership.* New York: Wiley.

Waitt, G. (2003). Gay games: Performing "community" out from the closet of the locker room. *Social & Cultural Geography, 4,* 167–183.

Walseth, K., & Fasting, K. (2003). Islam's view on physical activity and sport: Egyptian women interpreting Islam. *International Review for the Sociology of Sport, 38,* 45–60.

Weaver, G. R., & Agle, B. R. (2002). Religiosity and ethical behavior in organizations: A symbolic interactionist perspective. *Academy of Management Review, 27,* 77–97.

Weinger, S. (2000). Opportunities for career success: Views of poor and middle-class children. *Children and Youth Services Review, 22,* 13–35.

Whitley, B. E., & Kite, M. E. (1995). Sex differences in attitudes toward homosexuality: A comment on Oliver and Hyde (1993). *Psychological Bulletin, 117,* 146–154.

Whittington, J. L., Pitts, T. M., Kageler, W. V., & Goodwin, V. L. (2005). Legacy leadership: The leadership wisdom of the Apostle Paul. *The Leadership Quarterly, 16,* 749–770.

Yang, A. S. (1997). Attitudes toward homosexuality. *Public Opinion Quarterly, 61,* 477–507.

Compositional and Relational Diversity

Compositional Diversity

DIVERSITY CHALLENGE

LEARNING OBJECTIVES

After studying this chapter, you should be able to:

- Discuss the underlying principles of compositional diversity.

- Identify both the positive and negative effects of compositional diversity on group processes and outcomes.

- Analyze the effects of six compositional diversity forms on a group's social and effectiveness outcomes.

Converse, founded by Marquis M. Converse in 1908, is an athletic shoe company in the United States. The company is perhaps best known for its Chuck Taylor Converse All-Star style basketball shoes, a shoe worn by nearly all basketball players in the middle part of the 20th century. Today, Converse designs and manufactures a variety of athletic footwear options, including those worn for competitive performance and for leisure.

In 2006, Converse sought a director of Global Performance Basketball Product Marketing, whose primary purpose is to "drive the global line management of the Performance Basketball category of products." One of this position's chief responsibilities is people management, which includes leading a *"cross-functional* team of design, development, and product marketing to achieve business unit goals for the Basketball performance category" (emphasis added).

Exactly what is a cross-functional team? It is a specific type of work group composed of people from a variety of functional backgrounds (e.g., marketing, finance, operations). The use of cross-functional teams is widespread, well beyond the confines of Converse. For example, Nike, Coors Brewing Company, and Johnson and Johnson are but a few of the companies now using these teams in their business structure.

The thinking underlying the creation of cross-functional teams is that people from different backgrounds have different ideas to bring to the group. These different ideas then translate into a greater breadth of decision making and increased creativity. Leroy Zimdars, the director of supply chain management at Harley Davidson, noted, "cross-functional teams are

at the heart of every motorcycle produced at Harley Davidson Motor Company."
Other companies' cross-functional teams have been the driving force behind
many of today's product innovations.*

| DIVERSITY CHALLENGE | **R E F L E C T I O N** |

1. Cross-functional teams are often used to develop products. Where else in organizations might cross-functional teams be helpful?

2. Some benefits of cross-functional teams were outlined above. What might be some of the disadvantages of such teams?

3. In your experience, do sport organizations take advantage of cross-functional teams or are most work groups functionally homogeneous? Why?

---

*Information adapted from www.cfo.com; www.converse.com; www.nag.co.uk; Parker, G. M. (2002). *Cross-functional teams: Working with allies, enemies, and other strangers.* San Francisco: Jossey-Bass.

As the Diversity Challenge illustrates, work groups are no longer comprised of only similar people; rather, team members are likely to differ across a variety of characteristics—age, race, sex, tenure, functional background, sexual orientation, values, and so forth. Many organizations such as Nike and Converse intentionally create diverse groups, thinking that such heterogeneity will increase group effectiveness. However, sometimes diverse groups actually perform worse than their homogeneous counterparts because of infighting and member turnover. Therefore, it is important to understand the dynamics of such groups, how they function, and the expected outcomes of the various group diversity forms.

The purpose of this chapter is to examine the effects of compositional diversity. Recall from Chapter 2 that compositional diversity focuses on the group as a whole (Tsui & Gutek, 1999). Unlike Tsui and Gutek (1999) who use the term "compositional *demography*," I use the term compositional *diversity* because the focus in not just on demographic differences. The latter term allows for a broader conceptualization of group diversity. The compositional approach to the study of diversity differs from the categorical approach applied in Chapters 4 through 7, where the focus was on the individual and how membership in a particular social category (e.g., being a woman) influences subsequent attitudes and behaviors. The compositional approach has the group as a focus and examines how differences in the group influence various group outcomes. The first section discusses the theoretical approaches to the study of compositional diversity and presents an integrated model. The model is used to examine both the positive and negative effects of group diversity. The second section applies the model to six forms of diversity—race, sex, age, tenure, functional background, and values and attitudes—to show the effect of each form on a group's social and effectiveness outcomes.

Underlying Principles of Compositional Diversity

The discussion of the categorical effects of diversity in Chapters 4 through 7 primarily relied on sociological and social psychological theories to explain how membership in a particular social category influenced subsequent attitudes and behaviors. Compositional diversity explanations, however, rely more on managerial theories and, to some degree, social psychological theories. Merging these two theoretical approaches into a single, gestalt approach presents a clearer picture of complex phenomena.

At first glance, the managerial and social psychological theories appear to make contradicting predictions of the effects of diversity: managerial theories hold that diversity can be beneficial to groups through the increased debate and varying viewpoints (see Gruenfeld, Mannix, Williams, & Neale, 1996; Pelled, 1996; van Knippenberg, De Dreu, & Homan, 2004); social psychological theories indicate that diversity might be bad for the group and result in factionalism, conflict, and infighting (see Byrne, 1971; Tajfel & Turner, 1979; Turner, Hogg, Oakes, Reicher, & Wetherell, 1987). A more in-depth analysis of both theory approaches suggests that they do not necessarily contradict one another; rather, they make different sets of predictions about different forms of diversity. An integrated model is shown in Exhibit 8.1.

This model shows the compositional effects of diversity using managerial theory (top) and social psychological theory (bottom). The diversity variable (e.g., race, sex) considered is thought to influence the effects (shown by the moderating variable: type of diversity). Job-related diversity variables (e.g., tenure, functional background) are expected to result in better decision-making capabilities and greater group performance (Pelled, 1996). Non–job-related variables (e.g., race, sex, age, values, and attitudes) are expected to influence group dynamics, potentially resulting in poor social outcomes such as turnover.

Although the differences between job-related and non–job-related variables is consistent with previous theorizing (Chelladurai, 2005; Pelled, 1996), the distinctions are not as clear-cut as Exhibit 8.1 makes it appear. There are some situations where job-related variables negatively impact the work group's dynamics. For example, when two companies merger, employees often categorize themselves and others using former organizational affiliations (a job-related variable), and the dynamics of those groups formed using both employee sets might be strained (Terry & O'Brien, 2001). There are some cir-

Exhibit 8.1   **Effects of compositional diversity on group outcomes.**

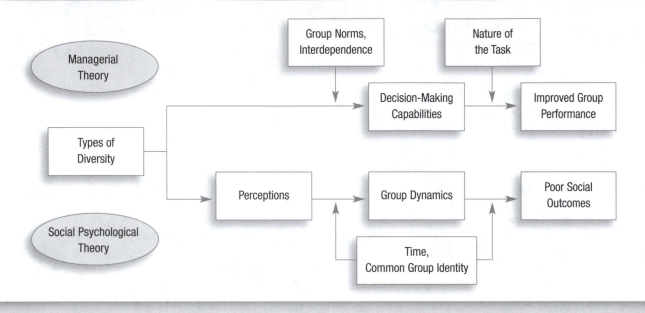

cumstances when racially diverse organizations realize better financial returns than their more homogeneous counterparts (Richard, 2000). This is thought to occur because of the competitive advantage racial diversity brings to an organization. These examples illustrate that the dichotomy presented in the integrated model—job-related diversity results in increased decision-making ability and non–job-related diversity affects group dynamics—does not always hold to form. Nevertheless, there is sufficient theoretical and empirical evidence to suggest that the patterns shown in Exhibit 8.1 will *generally* occur.

Managerial Theories

The primary assumption of managerial theories is that people from various backgrounds bring different experiences, perspectives, and knowledge to the group. These attributes are thought to ultimately result in improved group performance. The group's varied backgrounds operate to generate more topic debate, identify a wider range of alternatives, increase task conflict, and expand task-relevant information, thereby avoiding the pitfalls of groupthink (see Thompson, 2003). These group processes then relate to improved group performance (e.g., creativity, innovative decisions).

Three moderators, factors that influence the relationship between two variables, impact the group's operation: interdependence, group norms, and the nature of the task. Though there are several levels and types of interdependence (Deutsch, 1973; Van der Vegt, Emans, & Van de Vliert, 1998; Wageman, 1995), we can generally consider *interdependence* as the degree to which the group members work closely with one another. For example, a group of people developing a marketing plan work more closely with one another than a group of people on an assembly line making athletic shoes. The group diversity is likely to impact the marketing plan, whereas the individual differences among workers are unlikely to influence one's performance on an assembly line. Thus, the effects of diversity are likely to be observed in groups with high interdependence relative to those without it.

Group norms also influence the relationship between diversity and performance (e.g., van Knippenberg et al., 2004). If the group's debates are contentious, the motivation to complete the task is low, or there is little opportunity for group members to express doubt and frustration, then the influence of diversity on performance will be minimal, if not negative. On the other hand, group norms that encourage collaboration and cooperation, permit a free expression of beliefs and perspectives, and highly motivate members to complete the task all result in diversity positively influencing overall group performance.

Finally, the *nature of the task* influences the effects of diversity on a group. Complex tasks require careful contemplation, debate, and discussion among team members to arrive at a quality solution. Other more routine tasks do not. For example, developing a professional hockey team's marketing campaign for the upcoming season can be a difficult undertaking. Having varied perspectives and active debate allows the group to achieve a better solution than if such processes are not present. On the other hand, deciding when to hold a meeting is a straightforward decision that requires little thought or planning; in fact, debate and discussion could impede the process. These examples suggest that the positive effects of diversity are likely to be observed in more complex tasks (see also Doherty & Chelladurai, 1999).

Social Psychological Theories

The bottom portion of Exhibit 8.1 focuses on the social psychological effects of group diversity. Actual group diversity is expected to be positively related to perceptions of such differences, which in turn are expected to drive the subsequent processes and outcomes. That is, people's perceptions of how they are similar to or different from others in the group should then relate to the group's dynamics—how they function with others (see Cunningham, in press). The dynamics might include the levels of cohesion, communication with others, degree of factionalism, and overall liking of others. These group dynamics are then expected to influence the group's social outcomes. Social outcomes include attitudes of the group as a whole, such as satisfaction or commitment, and group behaviors, such as turnover levels.

As with the managerial theory, two moderators impact the group: time and a common group identity. As *time* passes, the effects of surface-level characteristics become less important while the impact of other diversity forms such as deep-level characteristics increases (Harrison, Price, & Bell, 1998; Harrison, Price, Gavin, & Florey, 2002). The social categorization framework suggests that people form in-groups and out-groups based on people's membership in a social group and that these categorizations are used in future interactions because of the stereotypes formed about people in various social groups. However, as people in a group spend more and more time together, they learn more about each other—their likes and dislikes, preferences, and attitudes. They come to know each other at a deep level. This is important because as deep-level characteristics become known, they become more salient in influencing the attitudes and behaviors directed at other group members. At the same time, surface-level characteristics become less important. Thus, time is thought to decrease the importance of surface-level characteristics in determining group outcomes.

A *common group identity* is also expected to moderate these relationships. When groups have a common identity, all members consider themselves as belonging to a single, common group—one group inclusive of all identities and affiliations (Gaertner & Dovidio, 2000). When such an identity is formed, the potential negative effects of diversity on group dynamics and social outcomes should be reduced (Cunningham, 2004) because group members base their social identity on group membership rather than subgroup differences. Thus, former out-group members are now afforded in-group membership. The "us vs. them" dynamics prevalent in diverse groups become less salient.

Section Summary

Exhibit 8.1 illustrates how differences at the group level might influence subsequent outcomes. From one perspective, diversity might be positively related to group processes and performance outcomes. Alternatively, diversity may negatively impact group dynamics, resulting in poor social outcomes. Though the phenomenon of group diversity is complex, the moderators provide clues as to when particular outcomes are expected to occur.

The Effects of Compositional Diversity in Sport Organizations

The previous section presented an integrated model that outlined the effects of group diversity. In this section, I apply the model to six forms of diversity to show the effect of each form on a group's social and effectiveness outcomes. An examination of available research allows for a greater understanding of the dynamics of compositional diversity in sport organizations, which factors are most salient in predicting many processes and outcomes, and how diversity can impact various group dimensions. Each diversity form is discussed separately.

Race

Racial diversity has received considerable attention in the compositional diversity literature, with the studies showing that the effects of racial diversity are seen at multiple levels.

Social Outcomes

As with categorical diversity, racial compositional diversity studies provide evidence that race does influence group functioning. From a group dynamics perspective, racial diversity negatively influences group functioning. For example, Cady and Valentine (1999) found that racial diversity was negatively related to team consideration; that is, the extent to which all team members all had input into the decision-making process and helped the team arrive at a creative decision. Thomas, Ravlin, and Wallace (1996) found that group diversity was negatively related to a myriad of poor group processes, including a lack of shared leadership and cohesiveness. Pelled, Eisenhardt, and Xin (1999) observed similar results, but also found that the effects were reduced when the task was routine. Consistent with the model predictions, research shows that these effects are likely mediated by perceptions of such differences. Cunningham (in press) studied track and field coaching staffs and found that the staff's actual racial diversity was strongly related to perceptions of such differences. These perceptions were meaningful, because they were negatively associated with the degree to which the staff members formed a common group identity.

Although racial diversity negatively influences social group processes, especially among newly formed groups, the effects are likely to decrease over time. Watson,

alternative
P E R S P E C T I V E S

Racial Diversity in Athletic Teams. Increased racial diversity is often associated with greater work group performance; however, most of the research focuses on cognitive task performance. The same relationships are not always observed for physical tasks such as those performed by athletic teams. For example, Timmerman (2000) examined the effects of racial diversity on professional basketball and baseball teams from 1950–1997. He found that on baseball teams, which have little interdependence among players, racial diversity did not influence performance. However, on basketball teams, where the interdependence among players is relatively high, diversity negatively influenced the teams' success, particularly from 1981–1997. Such effects were not seen from 1950–1980. Thus, racial diversity's negative effects on physical tasks is a more recent phenomenon, at least on some sport teams.

Kumar, and Michaelson (1993) found that homogeneous groups initially had more favorable group processes than their heterogeneous counterparts. Over time, however, these effects diminished. By the end of their study, which lasted several months, the diverse and homogeneous groups reported equally productive group processes.

Consistent with the notion that racial diversity results in poor group processes, research shows that racial diversity is negatively related to social outcomes as well. For example, Cunningham and Sagas (2004a) studied college football coaching staffs, examining the influence of staff racial diversity on attitudes and intentions toward the profession. They suspected that when people experience work poorly (or well) within their organization, they perceive these experiences to be indicative of how work is experienced within other organizations throughout the profession. The same is true for diversity. The effects of diversity on a coaching staff might be generalized as to how diversity impacts all coaching staffs, influencing their commitment to coaching or their intentions to leave coaching altogether. The study's results support this reasoning—racial diversity was negatively related to the coaches' commitment to the occupation and positively related to occupational turnover intentions. When the staff was diverse, the coaches, *as a whole,* expressed less commitment to coaching and less desire to remain a coach.

Effectiveness Outcomes

Though racial diversity can negatively influence a group's social aspects, it can also result in greater group effectiveness. Sargent and Sue-Chan (2001) found that racial diversity was positively associated with the members' belief that the group can be successful in their task. This confidence is important because it is linked to several important outcomes—task persistence and overall performance.

These findings are consistent with other research related to effectiveness outcomes. In an experimental study, McLeod, Lobel, and Cox (1996) asked different student groups to develop strategies aimed at attracting tourists to the United States. They expected that diverse groups would arrive at creative, feasible solutions because of the groups' range of perspectives. The results supported this prediction, as diverse groups produced strategies that were independently judged more feasible and more effective than those produced by homogeneous groups.

These experimental results were replicated in field research using real-life work groups. For example, Cunningham and Sagas (2004b) found that racial diversity on football coaching staffs was positively related to objective measures of team success. Drawing from the resource-based theory (Barney, 1991; see also Castanias & Helfat, 2001), they suggested that because diverse coaching staffs were valuable, rare, and imperfectly imitable, they served as a unique resource for the team and the department as a whole. Research outside the sport context (Richard, 2000) produced similar results. See the Alternative Perspectives box on page 225 for evidence of when these results do not occur.

Sex

As with race, research in the area of sex diversity is extensive, especially when compared to other diversity forms. Findings related to staff sex diversity effects are somewhat equivocal, but may be explained by incorporating moderating variables.

Social Outcomes

Pelled (1996) predicted that staff sex diversity would result in greater emotional conflict. Using her framework, we might also expect that sex diversity is associated with less team consideration and lower levels of cohesion; however, empirical research does not always support this reasoning. Cady and Valentine (1999) found that sex diversity was negatively associated with team consideration, thereby suggesting that as the team's sex diversity increases, the degree to which all members' perspectives are considered decreases. Others, however, found that sex diversity does not have an impact on task or emotional conflict (Pelled et al., 1999; Rogelberg & Rumery, 1996), or the presence of a common group identity (Cunningham, in press). The seemingly contradictory nature of these findings may be explained by the effects of time. Harrison et al. (1998) found that sex diversity negatively influenced group cohesiveness when the group first formed. Over time, however, these effects disappeared, such that the effects of deep-level characteristics became stronger predictors of cohesion. Therefore, sex diversity might be important in terms of cohesion in newly formed groups, but it is not as important as members get to know each other over time.

In a separate investigation, Knoppers, Meyer, Ewing, and Forrest (1993) examined the effects of sex diversity on the degree to which men and women communicated with similar and different others. They found that as the proportion of women in the athletic department increased, so too did the amount of interaction the women had with other women. The interaction the women had with men, as well as the interaction men had with men and women, did not change. When discussing their results, Knoppers et al. suggested that increases in sex diversity "may lead to a more rigid demarcation of gender boundaries in the sport world" (p. 266).

Effectiveness Outcomes

Research related to the effects of sex diversity on group effectiveness is also mixed. Pelled et al. (1999) found that sex diversity did not influence the amount of disagreement and debate (task conflict) related to a current task. However, Rogelberg and Rumery (1996) found that on "male-oriented" tasks (e.g., sur-

DIVERSITY *in the field*

Marketing Athletics. Each year, the National Association of Collegiate Marketing Administrators (NACMA) provides awards for excellence in the area of sport marketing. In 2005, of the 18 awards given by the NACMA, 7 went to the University of California-Davis. The university's athletic department's marketing staff created innovative programs such as the Aggie Auction, an event that draws over 1,400 people from across the United States to participate in live and silent auctions for a variety of items, including wine, travel, golf, and sports memorabilia. To date, the event has raised over $2 million, and all proceeds go to the athletic department's grant-in-aid program.

An examination of the athletic department's marketing and development staff reveals that several staff members are women. This is unique in the marketing field, especially in university athletic departments where most staffs are comprised predominantly of men. That the University of California-Davis does have several women on staff and performs quite well is consistent with the notion that sex diversity can positively influence group effectiveness.

viving a plane crash during the winter in Minnesota), the presence of women in the group hurt performance, but only somewhat. Groups with a lone female made more quality decisions than did all-male groups. The authors speculated that these findings might be attributed to the benefits that the sole woman brings to a group. All-male groups may be overly competitive and unable to coordinate the activities needed to excel. A group's woman may "calm" the males' over-competitiveness or may introduce a social variable to the group and focus on coordinating activities. When the sex distribution is more evenly matched—more than one woman—the social categorizations in the groups led to poor group functioning.

As discussed previously, Rogelberg and Rumery (1996) examined the influence of sex diversity on what they described as a task oriented toward males. Applying a different perspective, Fenwick and Neale (2001) examined the effects of sex diversity on a neutral task—a marketing simulation exercise where groups gathered competitor information and introduced new products to the market. They found that sex diversity helped with this task, as teams with two or more women outperformed the groups with fewer women. Fenwick and Neale suggest that because women may manage interpersonal relations and communications more effectively than men, the increased proportion of women on the team resulted in more coordinated efforts, a conclusion similar to that reached by Rogelberg and Rumery.

Finally, Siciliano (1996) examined the effects of a board of directors' sex diversity on subsequent performance among YMCAs (see the Diversity Challenge in Chapter 2). After accounting for the organizations' size, sex diversity was positively related to social performance, but negatively associated with the level of donations. Siciliano believes that the multiple perspectives generated by greater sex diversity may have allowed the YMCAs to fulfill their social missions, but when it came to generating donations, "women may not have access to needed economic, social, and political resources, which may have influenced their success in the fundraising area" (p. 1319).

Age

Theory suggests that the effects of age diversity should be similar to those of sex and race (Byrne, 1971; Tajfel & Turner, 1979; Turner et al., 1987) because all three characteristics are readily visible to others and are used for assessments of similarity, categorization, and stereotypes. The evidence generally supports this.

Social Outcomes

Cunningham (in press), in his study of track and field coaching staffs, found that actual group age diversity is positively associated with perceptions of such differences, but that perceived age diversity is negatively related to the presence of a common group identity. Research in other contexts supports these findings. Lichtenstein, Alexander, Jinnett, and Ullman (1997) found that age diversity is negatively associated with various indicators of team consideration including overall team functioning.

Such poor group dynamics are likely to result in undesirable social outcomes. Research consistently shows that age diversity in a group is related to greater turnover among the group members (Jackson et al., 1991; Wiersema & Bird, 1993). One exception is the Cunningham and Sagas (2004b) study, though they examined the degree to which age diversity would influence turnover in the coaching profession, not just in an organization.

Effectiveness Outcomes

Although age has some impact on a group's social outcomes, the same is not always true for effectiveness. Zenger and Lawrence (1989) found that age diversity is negatively associated with the amount of technical communication among group members. The more people differed with respect to age, the less they discussed a project's technical aspects, both with one another and with people outside the group. However, this study is the exception, as a myriad of other studies show that age diversity does not influence communications in the group (e.g., Simons, Pelled, & Smith, 1999) or the group's overall effectiveness (e.g., Wiersema & Bantel, 1992).

An exception to this generalization might be when effectiveness is contingent upon contacts outside the organization. Siciliano (1996) studied the effects of a variety of diversity variables on the ability of YMCA boards to raise funds. She found that age diversity was positively associated with the level of donations the YMCAs received. It is possible that people of varying ages also have social contacts of varying ages. A board with members all in their 50s might focus on generating donations from people who are also in their 50s, thereby limiting the number of potential donors. Conversely, a board with members whose ages range from 30 to 75 might have social contact with people in the same age range. This group's number of potential donors would be higher, as would the overall donation amount.

Tenure

Managerial theories suggest that tenure diversity should help the group's effectiveness because of the various perspectives held by the members. From this perspective, the effects on social outcomes are likely to be low, especially if people stereotype themselves and others based on other characteristics. However, research shows that tenure diversity does influence social outcomes, as well as effectiveness outcomes.

Social Outcomes

People who join an organization at the same time are likely to identify with one another (O'Reilly, Caldwell, & Barnett, 1989). This identification might relate to greater interpersonal attraction, time spent together on and off the job, and an overall satisfaction with people of a similar cohort. On the other hand, people who join an organization at times different than the self might be viewed as "others." For example, people who joined a sport organization in 1985 might be considered the "old guard," especially when compared to recently hired people. The "old guard" might share similar experiences in the organization, see things from a common point of view, and so forth. The "new guard" does not have these shared experiences and may have perspectives that differ from the "old guard." These differences can affect the group's functioning.

Empirical research supports this reasoning. Several studies show that groups with high tenure diversity are unlikely to have members who are socially integrated into the group (e.g., O'Reilly et al., 1989). These groups are also likely to be characterized by poor communication (Smith et al., 1994; Zenger & Lawrence, 1989) and high levels of emotional conflict (Pelled et al., 1999). Consistent with the integrated model in Exhibit 8.1, the effects on conflict are influenced by the level of task routineness and group longevity. The more routine the task, the smaller the effect of tenure diversity on conflict. Similarly, as the group spends more time together, the effects of tenure diversity diminish.

Given the negative effects of tenure diversity on social processes, it is not surprising that it also has a deleterious effect on social outcomes. Tenure diversity is negatively related to occupational commitment (Cunningham & Sagas, 2004a) and is positively associated with organizational turnover (McCain, O'Reilly, & Pfeffer, 1983; Wiersema & Bird, 1993) and intentions to leave the occupation (Cunningham & Sagas, 2004a).

Effectiveness Outcomes

Although tenure diversity can negatively impact a group's social processes and outcomes, such dissimilarities can improve performance under some conditions. For example, Cunningham and Sagas (2004b) found that tenure heterogeneity on football coaching staffs was positively related to objective measures of performance. Hambrick, Cho, and Chen (1996), in their study of firms in the airline industry, found that tenure diversity in the top management team positively influenced the airlines' performance. Other studies, however, demonstrate a negative effect. Smith et al. (1994) studied high-technology firms and found that occupational tenure diversity was negatively related to financial measures of success.

These seemingly contrary results can be explained by considering other variables. Industry stability and context is one such factor. Keck (1997) observed that tenure diversity in top management teams was negatively related to return on assets (a financial measure of a firm's performance) during turbulent years, but was positively related during more stable years. In turbulent years, the need for quick action is paramount because the environment is continually changing. Quick action is difficult for diverse groups because tenure diversity is likely to bring about more debate and consideration of alternatives. This increased debate extends the time it takes to make decisions (Ancona & Caldwell, 1992; Hambrick et al., 1996). This may be why the tenure diversity in the high-technology firms studied by Smith et al. (1994) negatively influenced performance—the technology industry is continually changing, and timely decision making is necessary. Only when groups have the time to debate issues and consider a broad range of possibilities will tenure diversity help performance. In support of this contention, Simons et al. (1999) found that those top management teams in the manufacturing industry that debated were more likely to arrive at comprehensive decisions, and that such decisions positively influenced performance.

How do these findings from other industries relate to sport organizations? Change takes place in all industries, including sport (Caza, 2000; Cunningham, 2002); however, many sport segments do not change as rapidly as other industries. The products offered at a fitness club, the teams supported by an athletic department, and the social activities offered at a YMCA all change less rapidly than the software needs of a computer company. Thus, in most sport contexts, tenure diversity, when accompanied by debate and lively discussions, is likely to improve performance.

Functional Background

Cross-functional groups have members from various functional areas in the organization. A kinesiology department committee with members from pedagogy, exercise science, and sport management is cross-functional. The same is true for a group at Nike with members from research and development, marketing, and operations. Many times these groups are formed for special projects (e.g., selecting a department chairperson, introducing a new product). In all cases, the diversity of perspectives is thought to result in better decisions.

PROFESSIONAL PERSPECTIVES

Creating Effective Cross-Functional Teams. Sethi is an expert in the area of cross-functional teams, especially as it involves the effects of such teams on product innovation. Sethi, Smith, and Park (2002) examined the factors that influence the outputs of cross-functional teams, and their findings are intriguing. Cross-functional teams:

- Do produce many ideas, but sometimes there are too many. It is important to sift through the ideas and identify the few on which the team should focus.

- Often face factionalism because members closely identify with others from their functional background. This is overcome by creating a strong superordinate identity in which all group members consider themselves part of a single, common group.

- Might perform poorly if members get along too well. If the social cohesion is high, group members may be unwilling to voice concerns or debate issues. It is important to have an environment where group members are free to openly express their views.

- Perform better when top managers promote group innovation. Teams that are encouraged to stretch the boundaries and think outside the box perform at higher levels than those that are instructed to seek continuous improvement.

- Benefit from having management supervision. Conventional wisdom holds that such teams perform at higher levels when managers take a "hands-off" approach; however, within limits, managerial supervision tells the team how important the project is and serves to motivate greater performance.

Social Outcomes

The effects of background diversity on social outcomes is minimal. None of the studies that examined this association directly (Jehn, Northcraft, & Neale, 1999; Pelled et al., 1999) found any significant relationship between functional background diversity and subsequent group dynamics or social outcomes.

Effectiveness Outcomes

Several studies examined the effects of functional background diversity on group effectiveness, and the findings are similar to those of tenure diversity. Cross-functional groups generally have more discussions and disagreements related to the current task (Lovelace, Shapiro, & Weingart, 2001), which can improve performance, especially when the task is not routine (Jehn et al., 1999). One of the benefits of cross-functional groups is access to outside resources (Ancona & Caldwell, 1992). Group members will talk with people from their own functional area about the task assigned to the cross-functional group. This additional information is useful because it is eventually used in the group's decision-making process.

Disagreements about task completion can make working in a cross-functional group difficult at times, but the outcomes are desirable, especially when the disagreements are handled appropriately. For example, Lovelace et al. (2001) found that when group members felt free to express their doubts and when communications were collaborative rather than contentious, task disagreements resulted in more innovative solutions. Simons et al. (1999) studied top management teams in manufacturing firms. They observed that functional diversity resulted in increased profitability when the top management teams openly debated the topics and an absence of an increase when debate did not take place. These studies suggest that the differences between the members of cross-functional groups should be appropriately leveraged; otherwise, the effects will be minimal or even detrimental. (See the Professional Perspectives box on page 232 for information on creating effective cross-functional teams.)

Values and Attitudes

Research related to other diversity forms largely concentrates on the deep-level characteristics of values and attitudes. Unlike the surface-level characteristics, those considered deep-level are thought to be revealed only after spending time with other people (Harrison et al., 1998). The effects of such differences are meaningful because groups with dissimilar deep-level characteristics generally have less desirable outcomes than their counterparts.

Social Outcomes

Harrison et al. (2002) conducted an experimental study with student groups to examine the effects of deep-level differences on subsequent outcomes. They found that actual deep-level differences are significantly associated with perceptions of such differences. Perceived deep-level diversity is negatively related to the social integration of the group members, and these effects increased as the collaboration of the group members increased. As the group members got to know each other better, they learned more about each other's values, beliefs, and attitudes. When these characteristics differed among group members, the group's social integration suffered. Research using work groups in an organizational setting supports these findings—deep-level diversity is positively associated with emotional conflict (Barsade, Ward, Turner, & Sonnenfeld, 2000; Jehn et al., 1999). It is, therefore, not surprising that deep-level

DIVERSITY *in the field*

Ramadan and Football. At Dearborn's Fordson High School, 99 percent of the football team's members are Arab. The team is among the most successful in Michigan prep football, with only 4 losing seasons in the past 38 years. Nevertheless, the team's high proportion of Arabs presents many challenges, including handling the prejudicial remarks made by other teams, especially after September 11, 2001. In addition, the players' parents often have to be convinced of the merits of playing football relative to spending time with family. Another challenge the team faces is playing football during Ramadan—a month-long Islamic holiday during which Muslims fast. When Ramadan falls during the season, the Muslim players do not eat or drink during the day, and in a show of team unity and support, the non-Muslim players also forgo water during practice and games. Unfortunately, this sometimes means that performance suffers, as the lack of hydration becomes a serious issue. In the 2005 season, the team went 3–6, the worst record in the school's history. Noted head coach Jeff Stergalas, "We didn't win one game during Ramadan. It was the most difficult season I've ever had coaching." Despite the potential challenges associated with Ramadan, the religious observance actually brings the team closer together, and this unity makes for a more successful team overall (Drehs, 2006).

diversity has a negative effect on a group's social outcomes. Members of groups with high levels of deep-level diversity are likely to be unsatisfied, uncommitted, and unlikely to remain in the organization (Jehn et al., 1999).

Effectiveness Outcomes

The effects of deep-level diversity on a group's effectiveness are intricate. Jehn et al. (1999) found that deep-level differences are associated with disagreements among team members about the nature of the task and how to complete it. Such disagreements might be helpful in arriving at an innovative solution, but only somewhat. Too many differences in values, attitudes, and beliefs hurt the group and its functioning. Indeed, Jehn et al. found that value diversity is negatively related to group performance and efficiency, and groups with high value diversity are not able to realize the benefits of functional diversity. (See the Diversity in the Field box on page 233 for an example.)

Chapter Summary

Compositional diversity has a significant influence on how a group functions, the decisions it makes, and the group's overall effectiveness. As seen in the Diversity Challenge, organizations are increasingly using diverse groups to realize greater performance gains. An in-depth analysis, such as presented in this chapter, reveals that not all diversity forms have the same effects. Therefore, it is important to carefully consider a group's diversity forms and the outcomes expected from the differences. After reading the chapter, you should be able to:

1. Discuss the underlying principles of compositional diversity.

The two theoretical approaches used to understand compositional diversity are the managerial and social psychological. Managerial theories focus on the benefits diversity brings to the group. Social psychological theories focus on how people prefer to work with similar others, and that diverse groups have more conflict and infighting, resulting in poor outcomes.

2. Identify both the positive and negative effects of compositional diversity on group processes and outcomes.

The positive effects, generally arising from managerial theories, include effective decision making and more desired group outcomes (e.g., creativity, decision quality, bold strategic moves, and improved financial performance).

The negative effects are explained using social psychological theories. People's perceptions of group diversity are thought to influence group processes (e.g., factionalism, overall liking of others) and outcomes (e.g., group attitudes and behaviors).

3. Analyze the effects of six compositional diversity forms on a group's social and effectiveness outcomes.

Research suggests that race and sex diversity are likely to influence social processes and outcomes, as well as group effectiveness. Age diversity has its strongest effects on the group's social outcomes. Job-related variables such as tenure and functional background have the strongest effects on the group's effectiveness. Finally, a group's deep-level diversity (e.g., attitudes and values) is likely to negatively influence social outcomes and have a varied effect on the group's effectiveness.

Questions for Discussion

1. Using managerial theories, how does diversity affect group outcomes? What factors might influence the outcomes?

2. Using social psychological theories, how does diversity influence group outcomes, and what factors impact the outcomes?

3. The amount of time spent together plays an important role in how well group members function. How does time influence the effects of diversity?

4. How might the integrated model in Exhibit 8.1 influence your decisions when forming work groups? Can you use the model to structure groups for desired outcomes?

5. Research suggests that surface-level characteristics influence social outcomes, but that only race and sex diversity have a meaningful impact on effectiveness. Why do race and sex influence group effectiveness but age does not?

6. Functional diversity has a stronger influence on group effectiveness than it does on the group's social outcomes. Why?

7. Deep-level characteristics generally negatively influence group functioning. How do you structure a group to capitalize on the positive effects of other diversity forms yet reduce the deep-level negative effects?

Learning Activities

1. Everyone has worked in a group at some point. How does working in a diverse group differ from working in a group where all members are similar?

2. Divide into two groups that are composed of both individuals who believe and those who do not believe that university athletes should be paid for their sport services (a form of deep-level diversity). Each group should

then develop support for paying or not paying the athletes—each group member must actively contribute to the discussion. How did the varying perspectives influence group dynamics and the group's ultimate decision-making effectiveness?

Resources

SUPPLEMENTARY READINGS

Hackman, J. R. (2002). *Leading teams: Setting the stage for great performances.* Boston, MA: Harvard Business School Press. (Draws from various examples—airline cockpit crews to symphony orchestras—to outline the conditions of effective teams; identifies various conditions that are needed to achieve high performance.)

Parker, G. M. (2002). *Cross-functional teams: Working with allies, enemies, and other strangers.* San Francisco: John Wiley & Sons. (Examines cross-functional teams in the organizational setting, including factors that influence the inner workings of such teams, their successes, and their failures.)

Poncini, G. (2004). *Discursive strategies in multicultural business meetings.* Bern, Switzerland: Peter Lang Publishers. (Focuses on the way in which language and communication can influence group processes and outcomes in multicultural business meetings.)

WEB RESOURCES

- Adventure Associates (www.adventureassoc.com): company devoted to developing effective work teams through team building exercises.

- Strategic Futures (http://strategicfutures.com/crossfun.htm): provides helpful insights into the development of cross-functional teams.

References

Ancona, D., & Caldwell, D. F. (1992). Demography and design: Predictors of new product team performance. *Organization Science, 3,* 321–341.

Barney, J. (1991). Firm resources and sustained competitive advantage. *Journal of Management, 17,* 99–120.

Barsade, S. G., Ward, A. J., Turner, J. D. F., & Sonnenfeld, J. A. (2000). To your heart's content: A model of affective diversity in top management teams. *Administrative Science Quarterly, 45,* 802–836.

Byrne, D. (1971). *The attraction paradigm.* New York: Academic Press.

Cady, S. H., & Valentine, J. (1999). Team innovation and perceptions of consideration: What difference does diversity make? *Small Group Research, 30,* 730–750.

Castanias, R. P., & Helfat, C. E. (2001). The managerial rents model: Theory and empirical analysis. *Journal of Management, 27,* 661–678.

Caza, A. (2000). Context reciprocity: Innovation in an amateur sport organization. *Journal of Sport Management, 14,* 496–515.

Chattopadhyay, P. (1999). Beyond direct and symmetrical effects: The influence of demographic dissimilarity on organizational citizenship behavior. *Academy of Management Journal, 42,* 273–287.

Chelladurai, P. (2005). *Managing organizations for sport and physical activity: A systems perspective* (2nd ed.). Scottsdale, AZ: Holcomb Hathaway.

Cunningham, G. B. (in press). Opening the black box: The influence of perceived diversity and a common in-group identity on diverse groups. *Journal of Sport Management.*

Cunningham, G. B. (2002). Removing the blinders: Toward an integrative model of organizational change in sport and physical activity. *Quest, 54,* 276–291.

Cunningham, G. B. (2004). Strategies for transforming the possible negative effects of group diversity. *Quest, 56,* 421–438.

Cunningham, G. B., & Chelladurai, P. (2004). Affective reactions to cross-functional teams: The impact of size, relative performance, and common in-group identity. *Group Dynamics: Theory, Research, and Practice, 8,* 83–97.

Cunningham, G. B., & Sagas, M. (2004a). Group diversity, occupational commitment, and occupational turnover intentions among NCAA Division IA football coaching staffs. *Journal of Sport Management, 18,* 236–254.

Cunningham, G. B., & Sagas, M. (2004b). People make the difference: The influence of human capital and diversity on team performance. *European Sport Management Quarterly, 4,* 3–22.

Deutsch, M. (1973). *The resolution conflict: Constructive and destructive processes.* New Haven, CT: Yale University Press.

Doherty, A. J., & Chelladurai, P. (1999). Managing cultural diversity in sport organizations: A theoretical perspective. *Journal of Sport Management, 13,* 280–297.

Drehs, W. (2006, February). *Middle East team in Midwest football.* ESPN.com. Retrieved March 1, 2006, from http://sports.espn.go.com/espn/black-history/news/story?id=2347173

Fenwick, G. D., & Neale, D. J. (2001). Effect of gender composition on group performance. *Gender, Work and Organization, 8,* 205–225.

Gaertner, S. L., & Dovidio, J. F. (2000). *Reducing intergroup bias: The Common Ingroup Identity Model.* Philadelphia: Psychology Press.

Gruenfeld, D. H., Mannix, E. A., Williams, K. Y., & Neale, M. A. (1996). Group composition and decision making: How member familiarity and information distribution affect process and performance. *Organizational Behavior and Human Decision Processes, 67,* 1–15.

Hambrick, D. C., Cho, T. S., & Chen, M. J. (1996). The influence of top management team heterogeneity on firm's competitive moves. *Administrative Science Quarterly, 41,* 659–684.

Harrison, D. A., Price, K. H., & Bell, M. P. (1998). Beyond relational demography: Time and the effects of surface- and deep-level diversity on work group cohesion. *Academy of Management Journal, 41,* 96–107.

Harrison, D. A., Price, K. H., Gavin, J. H., & Florey, A. T. (2002). Time, teams, and task performance: Changing effects of surface- and deep-level diversity on group functioning. *Academy of Management Journal, 45,* 1029–1045.

Jackson, S. E., Brett, J. F., Sessa, V. I., Cooper, D. M., & Peyronnin, K. (1991). Some differences make a difference: Individual dissimilarity and group heterogeneity as correlates of recruitment, promotions, and tenure. *Journal of Applied Psychology, 76,* 675–689.

Jehn, K. A., Northcraft, G. B., & Neale, M. A. (1999). Why differences make a difference: A field study of diversity, conflict, and performance in workgroups. *Administrative Science Quarterly, 44,* 741–763.

Keck, S. L. (1997). Top management team structure: Differential effects by environmental context. *Organization Science, 8,* 143–156.

Knoppers, A., Meyer, B. B., Ewing, M., & Forrest, L. (1993). Gender ratio and social interaction among college coaches. *Sociology of Sport Journal, 10,* 256–269.

Lichtenstein, R. A., Alexander, J. A., Jinnett, K., & Ullman, E. (1997). Embedded intergroup relations in interdisciplinary teams: Effects on perceptions of team integration. *Journal of Applied Behavioral Science, 33,* 413–434.

Lovelace, K., Shapiro, D. L., & Weingart, L. R. (2001). Maximizing cross-functional new product teams' innovativeness and constrain adherence: A conflict communications perspective. *Academy of Management Journal, 44,* 779–793.

McCain, B. E., O'Reilly, C., & Pfeffer, J. (1983). The effects of departmental demography on turnover: The case of a university. *Academy of Management Journal, 26,* 626–641.

McLeod, P. L., Lobel, S. A., & Cox, T. H., Jr. (1996). Ethnic diversity and creativity in small groups. *Small Group Research, 27,* 248–264.

O'Reilly, C. A., III, Caldwell, D. F., & Barnett, W. P. (1989). Work group demography, social integration, and turnover. *Administrative Science Quarterly, 34,* 21–37.

Pelled, L. H. (1996). Demographic diversity, conflict, and work group outcomes: An intervening process theory. *Organization Science, 7,* 615–631.

Pelled, L. H., Eisenhardt, K. M., & Xin, K. R. (1999). Exploring the black box: An analysis of work group diversity, conflict, and performance. *Administrative Science Quarterly, 44,* 1–28.

Richard, O. (2000). Racial diversity, business strategy, and firm performance: A resource-based view. *Academy of Management Journal, 43,* 164–177.

Riordan, C. M. (2000). Relational demography within groups: Past developments, contradictions, and new directions. In G. R. Ferris (Ed.), *Research in personnel and human resources management* (Vol. 19, pp. 131–173). Greenwich, CT: JAI Press.

Rogelberg, S. G., & Rumery, S. M. (1996). Gender diversity, team decision quality, time on task, and interpersonal cohesion. *Small Group Research, 27,* 79–90.

Sargent, L. D., & Sue-Chan, C. (2001). Does diversity affect group efficacy? The intervening role of cohesion and task interdependence. *Small Group Research, 32,* 426–451.

Sethi, R., Smith, D. C., & Park, C. W. (2002). How to kill a team's creativity. *Harvard Business Review, 80*(8), 16–17.

Siciliano, J. I. (1996). The relationship of board member diversity to organizational performance. *Journal of Business Ethics, 15,* 313–332.

Simons, T., Pelled, L. H., & Smith, K. A. (1999). Making use of difference: Diversity, debate, and decision comprehensiveness in top management teams. *Academy of Management Journal, 42,* 662–673.

Smith, K. G., Smith, K. A., Olian, J. D., Sims, H. P., Jr., O'Bannon, D. P., & Scully, J. A. (1994). Top management team demography and process: The role of social integration and communication. *Administrative Science Quarterly, 39,* 412–438.

Tajfel, H., & Turner, J. C. (1979). An integrative theory of intergroup conflict. In W. G. Austin & S. Worchel (Eds.), *The social psychology of intergroup relations* (pp. 33–47). Monterey, CA: Brooks/Cole.

Terry, D. J., & O'Brien, A. T. (2001). Status, legitimacy, and ingroup bias in the context of an organizational merger. *Group Processes and Intergroup Relations, 4,* 271–289.

Thomas, D. C., Ravlin, E. C., & Wallace, A. W. (1996). Effect of cultural diversity in work groups. In P. A. Bamberger, M. Erez, & S. B. Bacharach (Eds.), *Research in the sociology of organizations* (Vol. 14, pp. 1–33). London: JAI Press.

Thompson, L. (2003). Improving the creativity of organizational work groups. *Academy of Management Executive, 17,* 96–111.

Timmerman, T. A. (2000). Racial diversity, age diversity, interdependence, and team performance. *Small Group Research, 31,* 592–606.

Tsui, A. S., & Gutek, B. A. (1999). *Demographic differences in organizations: Current research and future directions.* New York: Lexington Books.

Tsui, A. S., Egan, T. D., & O'Reilly, C. A., III (1992). Being different: Relational demography and organizational attachment. *Administrative Science Quarterly, 37,* 549–579.

Turner, J., Hogg, M. A., Oakes, P. J., Reicher, S. D., & Wetherell, M. S. (1987). *Rediscovering the social group: A self-categorization theory.* Oxford, UK: B. Blackwell.

Van der Vegt, G. S., Emans, B., & Van de Vliert, E. (1998). Motivating effects of task and outcome interdependence in work teams. *Group & Organization Management, 23,* 124–144.

van Knippenberg, D., De Dreu, C. K. W., & Homan, A. C. (2004). Work group diversity and group performance: An integrative model and research agenda. *Journal of Applied Psychology, 89,* 1008–1022.

Wageman, R. (1995). Interdependence and group effectiveness. *Administrative Science Quarterly, 40,* 145–180.

Watson, W. E., Kumar, K., & Michaelson, L. K. (1993). Cultural diversity's impact on interaction processes and performance: Comparing homogeneous and diverse task groups. *Academy of Management Journal, 35,* 590–602.

Wiersema, M. F., & Bantel, K. (1992). Top management team demography and corporate strategic change. *Academy of Management Journal, 35,* 91–121.

Wiersema, M. F., & Bird, A. (1993). Organizational demography in Japanese firms: Group heterogeneity, individual dissimilarity, and top management team turnover. *Academy of Management Journal, 36,* 996–1025.

Zenger, T. R., & Lawrence, B. S. (1989). Organizational demography: The differential effects of age and tenure distributions on technical communication. *Academy of Management Journal, 32,* 353–376.

Relational Diversity

DIVERSITY CHALLENGE

David Perlmutter is an associate professor of mass communications at Louisiana State University at Baton Rouge. During his first year of teaching, he received an inspiring written student assignment that was articulate and witty. He did not recognize the student's name, so when he handed the assignments back, he was amazed to learn that the paper was written by what he termed "one of the 'lost girls.'" This is the nickname he had given to the women who sat in the back of his class and attended on a sporadic basis. They all were basketball players, and most were African American.

Perlmutter spoke with the student after class and throughout the semester, encouraging her to continue the impressive writing, to develop her skills, and to consider taking creative writing courses. Although she continued to be a stellar student, their meetings—either after class or when she handed in assignments—were always brief. After the course ended, he never heard from her again.

Disappointed that he could not connect with her, Perlmutter relayed the story to a friend, who was a teacher at an inner-city school. His friend noted that the student may have been apprehensive because of the racial and status differences. At first, Perlmutter dismissed this idea, but after further contemplation, he decided the notion may be valid. He investigated the issue by asking his students in subsequent classes how often they visited their professors outside class. Those students who rarely met with their professors were almost always athletes, most of whom were African American.

Perlmutter's findings led to additional conversations with athletes, professors, and athletic department personnel. He learned that athletes often hold a dual identity on campus—athlete and student—and faced pressures

LEARNING OBJECTIVES

After studying this chapter, you should be able to:

- Identify and discuss the basic tenets of relational diversity.

- Discuss the factors that influence the relationship between dissimilarity and subsequent outcomes.

- Analyze how being different in various relationships influences subsequent outcomes and behaviors.

from the growing commercialization of college sports. These pressures were amplified for minority athletes, especially when they attended predominantly White institutions, such as his. Under these circumstances, the athletes may feel isolated or dissimilar from the others around them.

According to Perlmutter, these difficulties are exacerbated by various professor behaviors, including:

- *Overlooking*—professors do not call on athletes in class because they do not believe the athletes are there to seriously pursue academic success.

- *Lowering expectations*—professors do not believe the athlete can meaningfully contribute to class conversations.

- *Cutting off*—an athlete does speak in class, but the professor cuts the comment short.

- *Intensifying scrutiny*—professors single out athletes, or athletes of color, in class or closely monitor their performance more than other students.

- *Commenting negatively*—professors make such a statement as "you people should be thankful to even be here."

This differential treatment is also felt from other students. As one athlete noted, "it's funny, but you can cheer a guy on the court and still resent him sitting next to you in class." All of these actions provide a negative college experience for the athlete. When the athlete also differs from the rest of the student body in some other respect (e.g., racial minority), such actions can result in distancing behaviors, lack of attention in class, and a lack of trust toward the professor by the athlete.*

DIVERSITY CHALLENGE **R E F L E C T I O N**

1. Have you been in situations where you differed from others? How did your differences influence your attitudes and behaviors?

2. Athletes differ from the rest of the student body in many ways. In what other areas does being different possibly affect their experiences as college students?

3. How may the many identities of athletes of color influence their college experiences?

---

*Information adapted from Perlmutter, D. D. (2003, October). Black athletes and white professors: A twilight zone of uncertainty. *The Chronicle Review*. Retrieved March 2, 2006, from http://chronicle.com.

As the Diversity Challenge illustrates, being dissimilar in a particular setting can have a meaningful impact. How people think of you as "different," their attitudes toward you, and their associated behaviors all influence your experiences with that group, athletic team, or organization. Being different might also influence your attitudes and behaviors toward other members of your social entity. The basketball player in Perlmutter's class might have reacted differently to her professor had the professor been a woman, an African American, or both. Under such circumstances, the athlete and the professor would share key attributes—their sex or race—and such similarities might result in greater interpersonal attraction.

The purpose of this chapter is to examine these issues in greater depth. The focus is on relational diversity, or the degree to which being different from others in a dyad or group influences subsequent attitudes, preferences, and behaviors (see also Tsui & Gutek, 1999). As in Chapter 8, I use the term diversity instead of demography (Tsui & Gutek, 1999) to allow for a broader conceptualization of the effects of being different. (See the Diversity in the Field box for an example of how this approach is advantageous.) The first section outlines the basic tenets of relational diversity and presents an integrated model to guide later discussions. In the second section, I discuss the four relationships people may encounter in an organization, focusing on how being different from others in these relationships might impact subsequent outcomes.

DIVERSITY *in the field*

Differences in the NBA. People differ from others in a group in many ways including demographic characteristics, cognitive abilities, and deep-level attributes. In the NBA, many of the players are similar. Most are African American, highly skilled athletes who make more money per year than many people will make in a lifetime. When dissimilarities do exist, they are usually related to deep-level characteristics. Etan Thomas and Steve Nash are two players who differ from most of their colleagues. These two are outspoken about substantive societal issues—not just those dealing with sports—such as affirmative action, oppression, and war. They make political statements, march in various protests, and Thomas even published poetry about these issues. Such activism is rarely seen among professional athletes. According to noted columnist Scoop Jackson (2006), other athletes largely remain silent on controversial issues because of the fame and fortune they have received from doing so. After all, opining about hot-button topics can polarize an individual, resulting in fewer sponsorship dollars and endorsement deals. By addressing such issues head-on, Nash and Thomas take a financial risk, but they are taking a stand on issues important to them. Thus, they, and others such as Jim Brown, Craig Hodges, and Mahmoud Abdul-Rauf, differ from their professional athlete counterparts.

Basic Tenets of Relational Diversity

n Chapter 2, I provided an overview of the two social psychological theories related to the study of diversity: the social categorization framework (Tajfel & Turner, 1979; Turner, Hogg, Oakes, Reicher, & Wetherell, 1987) and the similarity-attraction paradigm (Byrne, 1971). It is useful here to briefly outline how these theories are used to understand the influence of being different from others, and thus, understand the concept of relational diversity. An illustrative model of the discussion is presented in Exhibit 9.1.

Relational diversity focuses on the individual in relation to the group. The degree to which one differs from other group members is thought to influence subsequent attitudes, preferences, and behaviors. A woman in a group with four men might experience work differently than another woman who is in a group with four other women. Although seemingly straightforward, there are actually many other intervening and moderating factors that influence these relationships.

In general, dissimilarity is thought to result in the categorization of self and others, which then is expected to result in intergroup bias. This intergroup bias should then result in poor attitudes, preferences, and behaviors in the group context. A woman in a group with four men might perceive herself as different from the men. To the extent that she prefers to work with other women (i.e., intergroup bias), she might have negative attitudes toward working in her current group or toward the individuals in it. Indeed, past research shows that people who are different from other group members might be less satisfied, prefer to work in other groups, and put forth less effort (see Chattopadhyay, 1999; Mueller, Finley, Iverson, & Price, 1999). Three primary moderators are thought to influence these relationships: identity salience, identity threat, and nonsymmetrical effects. Each primary moderator is discussed next.

Exhibit 9.1	**Basic tenets of relational diversity.**

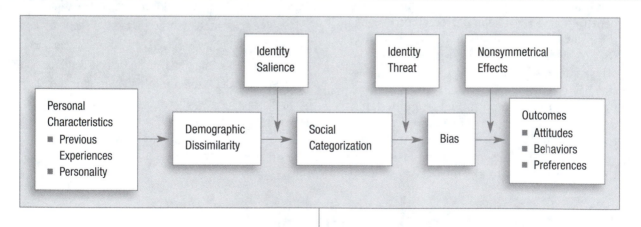

General Moderators: Time, Context, Culture

Identity Salience

People differ from other social unit members in many ways. Consider Helen, a 53-year-old White lesbian woman who works in the research and development branch of Adidas. If she belongs to a cross-functional team, several "us versus them" distinctions can be made: woman versus man, old versus young, lesbian versus heterosexual, research and development versus operations. Which characteristic does she use to categorize herself and others? One view holds that Helen would choose to categorize the self and others based on the importance of a certain social category or identity at that particular time (see Randel, 2002); that is, if being a woman is particularly relevant in a specific situation, then her sex will be most salient. Other factors such as her functional background, sexual orientation, and age, while still important to her in other areas of life, are less important *in that specific situation*. Thus, being different on a particular attribute (e.g., sex) is likely to lead to the categorization of others based on that attribute only when it is important to the categorizer. If the attribute is not important, then such categorizations are unlikely to occur (see van Knippenberg, De Dreu, & Homan, 2004, for further discussion of this issue).

Identity Threat

As noted in Chapter 2, the categorization process is not the same as intergroup bias. The former term simply refers to the perceptual grouping of members of a social entity (Turner et al., 1987). The latter term refers to the favorable perceptions of, pleasant attitudes toward, and helping behaviors directed to in-group members relative to out-group members (Brewer, 1979). Such distinctions are important because the negative effects of being different from others are thought to arise from intergroup biases, not the categorization process (van Knippenberg et al., 2004).

Identity threat is thought to provide the impetus for intergroup bias (see van Knippenberg et al., 2004). People generally want to maintain a positive image of the self, and this is also how they would like to see their group—with a positive and dis-

alternative PERSPECTIVES

The Totality of Being Different. People differ from their supervisors and group members in many respects. For example, a professional athlete such as MLB player Alex Rodriguez differs from his teammates in nationality (he has dual citizenship in the Dominican Republic and the United States), age, and salary (he is the highest paid player in MLB history). As noted in the text, he might categorize himself and others based on the importance of a particular social category. Some authors, however, suggest that the focus of relational diversity should be the totality of the differences; thus, dissimilarity between the self and others should be considered as an amalgamation (Chatman & Spataro, 2005). Applying this approach, Rodriguez will consider how different he is from his teammates, as a whole, rather than considering the social categories individually. It is this estimation of his overall difference from others that will impact subsequent attitudes, preferences, and behaviors.

tinct identity (e.g., Hogg & Abrams, 1988). Thus, people's group membership reflects how they view themselves.

When the existence of a positive identity is challenged, intergroup bias is likely to result. Challenges to the distinctiveness and positive perceptions of the group (and hence, the self) take many forms—competition for status or prestige, derogation of the group, or blatant discrimination. In the earlier example with Helen, differing from other group members based on her sex might lead to bias if women receive fewer rewards and opportunities in the organization than men. Another example relates to sports fans. The competition between teams serves to challenge the league status of the fans' teams, thereby prompting bias against the opposing team and its fans. Even people who might be friends in other contexts (e.g., the classroom) might be viewed as "enemies" or "the opposition" if they root for the opposing team. Identity threat is therefore thought to increase the positive association between categorization and bias—without a threat, bias is unlikely to exist.

Nonsymmetrical Effects

Bias is expected to result in negative attitudes toward others or toward the group; however, these effects might be stronger for some people than they are for others. Tsui, Egan, and O'Reilly (1992) found that the effects of being different on subsequent outcomes were stronger for Whites and for men than for other persons—a concept called *nonsymmetrical effects*. It is expected that some groups of people, such as Whites or men, are not accustomed to being a minority. When they are, the effects of being different from others (e.g., the effects on satisfaction or commitment) are likely to be stronger than they are for those who may be more used to holding minority status in a group (e.g., women, racial minorities). Research in this area (Cunningham & Sagas, 2004b; Tsui et al., 1992) is largely focused on sex and race, but the same findings would likely hold true for other attributes. For example, the effects of being different from other group members due to sexual orientation might be stronger for heterosexuals than for GLB persons, as the latter group may be accustomed to having a different sexual orientation. The literature suggests that nonsymmetrical effects should moderate the relationship between bias and subsequent work outcomes.

General Moderators

In addition to the three primary moderators, three general moderators are thought to influence relationships: time, context, and culture. The effects of *time* are likely to decrease the effects of being dissimilar, especially for demographic characteristics (Vecchio & Bullis, 2001). As time passes, work outcomes are based more on behaviors and performance than on stereotypes and biases. Furthermore, surface-level differences may become less salient, while deep-level differences become more prevalent (Harrison, Price, Gavin, & Florey, 2002).

Context as a moderating factor (Oakes, 2001) means that the influence of being different in one situation is not necessarily the same in another. For example, a police officer may be viewed negatively while issuing a traffic citation, but is viewed positively when apprehending a mugger. The same is true in sport organization settings. As illustrated in the Diversity Challenge, students may resent having student-athletes in their classes but will root for them during athletic contests. This suggests that the categorization process differs from one situation to another.

Culture is the third general moderator. Research in the organizational context shows that differing from others is less likely to result in negative outcomes when the organization is characterized by collectivistic rather than individualistic norms (Chatman, Polzer, Barsade, & Neale, 1998). In a similar way, the effects of being different on subsequent affective reactions to the groups are less for those people working in groups where all members consider themselves as belonging to a single, common group (Cunningham, 2005). Under these circumstances, the "us" and "them" dynamics often present in diverse groups is replaced by a more inclusive "we" (Gaertner & Dovidio, 2000).

Antecedents

One's personal characteristics may also serve as antecedents, or precursors, to these relationships. Previous experiences are one such example. People who have had pleasant experiences in the past with people who differ from the self might be less affected by being different in a group context (e.g., Allport, 1954). The same is true for those who have had considerable contact with persons who differ from the self—they may be minimally affected by being different from other group members. Personality is another personal characteristic that influences these relationships (Flynn, Chatman, & Spataro, 2001). For example, extroverted people might be more willing to share information with others and take steps to form relationships. Such steps are likely to decrease the negative effects of differing from others.

Section Summary

Although the model in Exhibit 9.1 suggests that being different from others should be associated with negative outcomes for the individual, this is not always true. The attribute by which one differs from other group members may not be salient, the identity threat may be low, or the group norms and culture may support diversity and communication. In all of these situations, the effects of being different on subsequent outcomes are likely to be low. The same is likely true for those who have spent an extended period of time in the group.

Relational Diversity in Sport Organizations

The previous section discussed the basic tenets of relational diversity. In this section, the integrated model in Exhibit 9.1 is used as a guide to highlight specific findings related to being different from others. There are four relationship types found in organizations: vertical dyads, horizontal dyads, individual–group relationships, and employee–customer interactions. A summary of these relationships is presented in Exhibit 9.2.

Vertical dyads are those relationships between a supervisor and subordinate; for example, parent and child, manager and employee, teacher and student, or coach and player. *Horizontal dyads* are relationships between two

---

Exhibit 9.2	**Relational diversity relationships.**

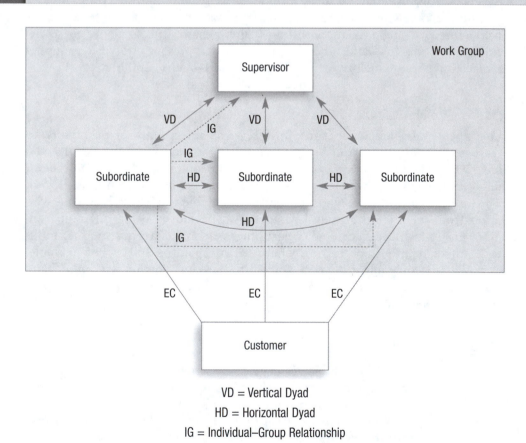

VD = Vertical Dyad

HD = Horizontal Dyad

IG = Individual–Group Relationship

EC = Employee–Customer Interactions

people at the same hierarchical level or status. Pairs of children, employees at the same organizational level, students, or athletes all represent horizontal dyads. *Individual–group* relationships move beyond the dyadic level and consider how different someone is from other group members. Examining the experiences of the lone Muslim on a basketball team is an example of this relationship type. Finally, *employee–customer interactions* are those between an organization's employee and the organization's client or customer. In each of these relationships, being different from the other dyad member or other group members can negatively influence one's experiences. The presence of differences may also influence the behaviors directed toward the others in those relationships. These effects are discussed next.

Vertical Dyads

Because the presence of differences in vertical dyads affects two people, the supervisor and the subordinate, we can examine how being different influences the supervisor's attitudes and behaviors directed toward the subordinate, or how being different from the supervisor influences the subordinate's reactions and behaviors. Although the two are strongly related, examining both sides allows us to accurately identify the link between dissimilarity and subsequent subordinate outcomes.

Supervisor Attitudes and Behaviors

In general, supervisors view those subordinates who are similar to themselves in a more positive light than they do dissimilar subordinates. For example, Judge and Ferris (1993) found that the more similar a subordinate is to the supervisor in terms of age and experience, the more the supervisor reports liking that subordinate. Tsui and O'Reilly (1989) found similar effects for sex, education, and job tenure. The concept of "liking" in these studies is consistent with the intergroup bias previously discussed. Judge and Ferris also found that liking is strongly associated with performance ratings. These findings comport with other research that focused on race—the performance of African Americans is rated higher by other African Americans than it is by Whites (Stauffer & Buckley, 2005). Drawing from this research, we can surmise that performance rating differences are likely the result, at least in part, of the more positive affect afforded to similar others.

Research also shows that supervisors and subordinates are often "matched" based on their demographic characteristics. Elliott and Smith (2001) analyzed data from a large-scale study of persons in Boston, Atlanta, and Los Angeles. Consistent with previous discussions in Chapter 4 relating to coaches and administrators, they found that Whites held most of the supervisory positions. When racial minorities did hold these positions, they were usually charged with supervising members of their own racial groups. For example, Hispanics were 11.2 times more likely to be supervised by another Hispanic than they were to be supervised by a White. Similar trends emerged for African Americans (10.8) and Asians (71.0). Such racial "matching" is important because the incidence of supervisor discrimination was less in same-race vertical dyads.

The "matching" concept also occurs in the sport context. Brown (2002) reported that African American coaches often believe that they are hired to help recruit minority athletes to the program; that is, the coach is "matched" to the prospective athlete such that a racial similarity is achieved. The same applies in women's sports, especially when the head coach is male. Efforts to recruit women might be more effective if a woman is charged with the recruiting efforts or at least is a staff member. Indeed, Sagas, Cunningham, Teed, and Waltemyer (2004) found that among women's university athletic teams, male head coaches were more likely to have staffs consisting primarily of women than they were to have all-male staffs. This may be due to the need for demographic "matching" between the coaches and the players.

Other studies focus on dissimilarity and the leader–member exchange (LMX) quality (Epitropaki & Martin, 1999; Green, Anderson, & Shivers, 1996; Sagas & Cunningham, 2004). LMX focuses on the quality of the relationship between the leader and the follower. Leaders are thought to classify employees into in-groups and out-groups and afford in-group members greater trust, give them more challenging assignments, and so forth. In return, in-group followers are thought to be loyal to the supervisor and perform better. Research shows that leaders are *unlikely* to form their in-groups and out-groups based on demographic similarity or a lack thereof. One reason for this occurrence could be that LMX focuses on the employee's performance and how that performance benefits the supervisor (Schriescheim, Neider, Scandura, & Tepper, 1992). Thus, it is possible that high follower performance negates the effects of vertical dyad dissimilarity.

Subordinate Reactions

Because the research related to subordinate reactions to being different from the supervisor was conducted in a variety of contexts, it is useful to divide the discussion into employee reactions and athlete reactions.

Employee reactions. Those employees who differ from their supervisors generally have poorer work experiences than do those who are similar. Generally, persons in diverse vertical dyads, relative to other persons, express:

- greater role conflict and role ambiguity (Tsui & O'Reilly, 1989)
- less procedural justice (Jeanquart-Barone, 1996; Wesolowski & Mossholder, 1997)
- less job satisfaction (Wesolowski & Mossholder, 1997)

■ a greater frequency of absences from work (Perry, Kulik, & Zhou, 1999)

■ less loyalty (Iverson & Buttigieg, 1997)

Several factors influence these relationships including time spent with the supervisor (Vecchio & Bullis, 2001), status incongruence (e.g., older employee with younger supervisor; Perry et al., 1999), and the supervisor's attitudes toward diversity (Vecchio & Bullis, 2001).

Recent studies examined these issues in sport organizations. Fink and her colleagues (Fink & Cunningham, 2005; Fink, Pastore, & Riemer, 2001) examined the influence of supervisor–subordinate dissimilarity in the context of university athletic departments. Their results show that people in mixed-sex and mixed-race dyads have less pleasant work experiences (i.e., they are less satisfied, feel they are less able to be creative) than their counterparts in homogeneous dyads (Fink & Cunningham, 2005). Fink et al. (2001) found that differences in race and parental status (i.e., whether or not the person has children) between the supervisor and subordinate also influenced perceptions of the diversity management strategy used in that athletic department. Relative to others, people who differ from their supervisor believe that the department employs a less effective strategy for managing diversity.

These same patterns, however, are not observed between assistant coaches and the head coaches. Cunningham and Sagas (2005) studied 237 assistant coaches of men's and women's basketball teams. They found that although the demographics of the assistant coach and the demographics of the head coach had independent effects on future coaching aspirations and job satisfaction, there were no interactive effects. The demographic diversity of the vertical dyad did not influence the assistant's job satisfaction or intentions to seek a head coaching position. Sagas, Paetzold, and Cunningham (2006) may have identified the reason why those results seem contradictory. They studied 415 assistant coaches of a variety of women's teams, including basketball, softball, soccer, and volleyball, and although no direct effects were found in this study (as with the Cunningham and Sagas study), they did report a significant dissimilarity-by-tenure interaction. Consistent with the model in Exhibit 9.1, the time spent with the head coach influenced the effects of being different, such that, in general, the otherwise negative effects of being different decreased with time.

Athlete reactions. Past research shows that diversity in the head coach–athlete dyad influences the athlete's experiences. For example, Anshel (1990) interviewed African Americans about their experiences while participating in college football. Anshel found that these players had different relationships with their White coaches relative to their African American coaches. The athletes viewed the White coaches as only being interested in them for their athletic abilities. They also expressed a lack of trust in the White coaches and believed that discrimination and a lack of sensitivity to racial differences existed. In general, these attitudes were not held about the African American coaches.

Taking another approach, Everhart and Chelladurai (1998) examined how sex diversity in the head coach–player relationship influenced athletes' subsequent attitudes toward the coaching profession. They collected data from 197 athletes who participated in Big Ten Conference athletics. Female athletes with a female head coach believed that coaching was a more attractive career option than did those women who were coached by men. A similar trend occurred with respect to perceived discrimination in coaching: women coached by men anticipated more barriers in the coaching profession than did the women coached by women.

Horizontal Dyads

Research of horizontal dyads is scarce. Conceptually, we might expect trends observed with vertical dyads to occur with horizontal pairs. People who are similar to a particular colleague, classmate, or teammate are also likely to have positive attitudes toward that person. It is possible that people seek relationships with others who are similar to the self, or who are at least perceived to be. In one of the few studies to examine this issue, Antonioni and Park (2001) examined the influences of differences and similarities on peer performance evaluations. People rated peers with deep-level similarities (e.g., conscientiousness) higher than those peers who were dissimilar. Thus, consistent with the model presented in Exhibit 9.1, a similarity between peers manifests in more positive attitudes.

Individual–Group Relationships

Much of the relational diversity research focuses on people who differ from others in a group setting. Consistent with the effects seen in vertical and horizontal dyads, as well as the model depicted in Exhibit 9.1, people generally like working with coworkers similar to the self. When employees are dissimilar, they experience work poorly. Consider the following:

- In general, people who are demographically different are less likely to communicate with colleagues. This effect, however, is influenced by the organization's culture. In collectivistic cultures, dissimilarity is related to a higher frequency of contact with colleagues. In individualistic cultures, those people who are demographically similar are more likely to communicate (Chatman et al., 1998).

- The greater the number of other women working at a particular woman's job level, the less likely she is to voluntarily leave the organization. Furthermore, for those women in mid-level or upper-level management positions, the presence of women hierarchically above them is inversely related to organizational turnover (Elvira & Cohen, 2001).

- People with dissimilar deep-level characteristics (e.g., values), are likely to have greater conflict with their colleagues (Hobman, Bordia, & Gallois,

2003), be less involved in the work group (Hobman et al., 2003), and experience less job satisfaction (Cunningham & Sagas, 2004a).

- Differing from others in a cross-functional group can negatively influence performance. When group members are in the minority and they closely identify with their original functional background, their performance suffers (Randel & Jaussi, 2003).

- Demographically different people who readily share information with others, especially information that is appropriate for specific situations (i.e., high self-monitors), are perceived more positively than those without such a disposition (Flynn et al., 2001).

These studies are just a sample of those that show that differing from others can have a substantial influence on subsequent work outcomes, behaviors, and attitudes.

As previously discussed, these effects are not always as straightforward as they seem. People vary in their reactions to being different. According to the nonsymmetrical hypothesis, those who are unaccustomed to being a minority in a group are affected more negatively than are their counterparts (Tsui & Gutek, 1999). In most sport organizations, these people are White, Protestant, able-bodied, heterosexual males.

For those unaccustomed to holding minority status, being dissimilar can influence citizenship behaviors (Chattopadhyay, 1999), attachment to the organization (Tsui et al., 1992), and job satisfaction (Mueller et al., 1999). For example, Mueller et al. (1999) collected data from over 1,400 public school teachers in the United States. They found that White teachers in schools with mostly White teachers and White students had more positive attitudes toward their work than their White counterparts in schools with other demographic profiles. African American teachers were not impacted by the racial composition of the students or teachers at the school. In another study, Cunningham and Sagas (2004b) examined the influence of being different among coaches on basketball coaching staffs. White coaches on staffs composed of primarily minority coaches had lower organizational commitment than White coaches on other staffs. Also, their commitment was lower than African American coaches on mostly White staffs.

The effects of being different can be mitigated by the organization's culture and norms (Chatman et al., 1998; Cunningham, 2005; Hobman et al., 2003). For example, Hobman et al. (2003) found that people with high perceived value dissimilarity were more likely to socially integrate into the group when members were open to diversity—that is, when they valued differences among people. In the coaching context, Cunningham (2005) found that the negative effects of racial dissimilarity on coworker satisfaction were reduced when the coaching staff had a common group identity. When such an identity was not present, however, people who differed racially from other staff members experienced low levels of satisfaction with their coworkers.

DIVERSITY *in the field*

When Differences Do Not Matter. Differing from others, whether the differences are based on demographics, values, attitudes, or preferences, is often difficult. Under some circumstances, however, the group's norms and culture are such that dissimilarity does not have a substantial impact. This occurs because membership in the group is the *central* identity for the group members. Andrew Goldstein found this to be true with his Dartmouth College lacrosse team. Goldstein, who was the team's All-American goalie, also happened to be gay. Goldstein was initially apprehensive about revealing his sexual orientation to others because nobody else on the team, or in the conference, was openly gay. How would being different from his teammates influence his standing on the team, the team's cohesiveness, or the behaviors directed toward him by opponents? To his surprise, revealing that he was gay *did not* hurt his relationships with the other players or the overall group dynamics— something he attributes to his teammates' support. Describing the support he felt from one teammate in particular, Goldstein noted, "He wasn't literally patting me on the back, but I felt like there was, there was a hand on my back, pushing me forward and supporting me. There's really no feeling like that." Not only did his teammates support him as a player, but they also joined him in advocating rights for GLB persons on campus (Garber, 2005). Being part of the team and having a strong identity as teammates muted the effects of being different in terms of sexual orientation.

Similar effects occur among athletic team members, as shown in the Diversity in the Field box.

Finally, past research shows that both demographic and deep-level dissimilarity negatively influences one's experiences in a group; however, these effects are not mutually exclusive. People's demographic dissimilarity is often indicative of more deep-level differences. Cunningham (2006) examined these issues in the context of college physical activity classes. He found that students who were demographically different from others in the class also perceived such differences. Also, perceived demographic dissimilarity had a significant, positive association with perceived deep-level dissimilarity. Finally, deep-level differences were negatively associated with affective reactions (e.g., student involvement and pleasure) to the class. As this study shows, the various diversity forms are closely related, not distinct concepts.

Employee–Customer Interactions

The three relationship types discussed earlier involved people who work in the same organization. With employee–customer interactions, the focus is on the potential differences between a service provider and an organization's customer. These dissimilarities are important because they can influence the customer's satisfaction with the service experience, products purchased, and future purchase intentions and behaviors (see Tsui & Gutek, 1999). Because most of the sport industry's products are services (Chelladurai, 1992), it is important to understand the factors that lead to successful service interactions. For an example, see the Professional Perspectives box on the following page.

There are two types of service interactions: encounters and relationships (Tsui & Gutek, 1999). Service *encounters* are brief and the customer generally does not expect to have subsequent interactions with the service provider—a close relationship between the employee and the customer is not expected to develop. The interaction between a ticket clerk and a fan at a professional baseball game is an example of a service encounter.

Service *relationships* have extended interactions between the employee and the customer. The services may be provided over a long period or many occasions. Employees and customers in these relationships may get to know one another on a personal level. The interactions one has with a doctor, physical therapist, golf instructor, or personal trainer are all service relationships.

The effects of employee–customer dissimilarity in service interactions is likely to vary based on the type of interaction. For service relationships, people may prefer someone who is similar to the self because these interactions usually require some level of trust, and people are more likely to trust someone who is similar than someone who is different. If people who are dissimilar do enter into a service relationship, the effects of the differences are likely to diminish over time as the people learn more about each other on a personal level. Time operates to diminish any stereotypes or bias.

An opposite trend might occur with service encounters, however. If one is simply purchasing tickets for a game, it usually does not matter whether the tickets are purchased from someone who is different from or someone who is similar to the self. This is true for other encounters such as purchasing licensed team merchandise or food services (e.g., Kochan et al., 2003). However, as the time spent in the encounter increases, social categorizations and subsequent stereotyping are likely to occur. Under these circumstances, time is thought to increase the potential negative effects of employee–customer dissimilarity.

A study by Cunningham and Sagas (2006) of fans who attended a professional tennis tournament supports these predictions related to service encounters. They asked customers about their encounters with tournament employees, including their perceived dissimilarity from the service provider, the time spent in the interaction, and their satisfaction with the service. In general, people who perceived that they were different from the service provider expressed less customer service satisfaction as compared to their counterparts. These effects were augmented over time—as the length of the encounter increased, so too did the level of dissatisfaction.

PROFESSIONAL PERSPECTIVES

The Need to Focus on Diversity. Customer service satisfaction is often high if similarity exists between the service provider and the customer. In some situations, however, diversity may be emphasized, as is the case with Australian tourism—a context in which customer service is the driving force. Marketing expert Daniel Rogers (2002) suggests that Australian tourism agencies focus on the nation's diversity and modernity. He notes that "Australia is a multi-cultural society full of new thoughts, new ideas, and infectious optimism. It should capture the imagination of people who want to see what a society in the future could be like." People traveling to Australia can enjoy the diversity of the people and the culture and "get inspired about modern life."

Chapter Summary

As seen in the Diversity Challenge, being different from others—in that case, a student who is different from her professor—can negatively influence the interaction's experiences. Although the types of interactions vary, the effects of being different are generally the same—they are negative. The impact of being different is fairly robust, as effects have been observed for both surface- and deep-level characteristics (see Chatman & Spataro, 2005, and Cunningham, 2006, for examples of each). After reading this chapter, you should be able to:

1. **Identify and discuss the basic tenets of relational diversity.**

The integrated model in Exhibit 9.1 draws from both the social categorization framework and the similarity-attraction paradigm. According to the social categorization framework, people use various characteristics to classify the self and others into social groups. This categorization process likely results in intergroup bias, whereby people positively evaluate those similar to the self (i.e., in-group members) as opposed to people different from the self (i.e., out-group members). The similarity-attraction paradigm suggests that people are attracted to those who are perceived to be similar to the self. This attraction results in greater interpersonal contact and communications. In both cases, similarity to others is preferred. When people differ from their supervisor or coworkers, their experiences in the group are likely to be negative.

2. **Discuss the factors that influence the relationship between dissimilarity and subsequent outcomes.**

Though dissimilarity from others is thought to negatively influence subsequent outcomes, several moderators influence these relationships. These moderators include the identity salience, identity threat, nonsymmetrical effects, time, context, and the group's culture. Furthermore, the effects of being different are stronger for those people not accustomed to holding the minority role; that is, men and Whites.

3. **Analyze how being different in various relationships influences subsequent outcomes and behaviors.**

Four types of relationships were discussed: vertical dyads, horizontal dyads, individual–group relationships, and employee–customer interactions. Generally speaking, individual outcomes are more positive when similarities, as opposed to differences, are present. Supervisors express positive attitudes and behaviors toward those subordinates similar to the self, and subordinates have better experiences when working for a supervisor with similar characteristics to the self. Employees have better work experiences when they are similar to their colleagues. Finally, customer satisfaction is higher when similarities exist between the self and the service provider. Although various factors influence these relationships, these basic trends exist for both surface- and deep-level characteristics.

Questions for Discussion

1. Some characteristics are more likely than others to engender perceptions of dissimilarity. In your experience, what are those factors? Why are these factors important?

2. Context is a moderator that influences the relationship between dissimilarity and subsequent outcomes. Describe a time when you felt different from a certain group of people in one situation, but felt similar to those same people in another situation.

3. Four relationship types were discussed. On which relationship type is relational diversity likely to have its strongest effects? On which relationship type is it likely to have its weakest effects? Why?

4. On sport teams, diversity in the player–coach relationship is rather commonplace. However, in many cases, a player who is different from his or her coach has a close bond with that coach. How are the player and coach able to overcome the potential negative effects of diversity to form this bond?

5. Sport teams are often diverse, meaning that diversity is observed in both the horizontal dyads and the individual–group relationships. In a team setting, how does being different influence individual players?

6. Diversity in employee–customer interactions may have negative effects in some situations, but not others. Why?

Learning Activities

1. In most any social situation, you will differ from others on some attribute. There are some situations, however, when you feel different and others when you do not. Divide into student groups and identify those factors common to the group that impact when you feel different in various situations.

2. Suppose you are charged with staffing the volunteers at a professional tennis tournament. Draft a staffing plan. Given what you know about relational diversity and its influence on employee–customer interactions, what role, if any, will demographics play in your staffing decisions?

Resources

SUPPLEMENTARY READINGS

Jackson, S., & Ruderman, M. (Eds.). (1996). *Diversity in work teams: Research paradigms for a changing workplace.* (Edited text that contains a well-written chapter focusing on relational demography.)

Li, J. T., Tsui, A. S., & Weldon, E. (Eds.). (2000). *Management and organizations in the Chinese context.* London: Macmillan. (Edited text focusing on management in the Chinese culture; contains an excellent chapter concerning Guanxi, which is a unique relational diversity-type relationship.)

Riordan, C. M. (2000). Relational demography within groups: Past developments, contradictions, and new directions. In G. R. Ferris (Ed.), *Research in personnel and human resources management* (Vol. 19, pp. 131–173). Greenwich, CT: JAI Press. (Selection from the annual review; provides comprehensive overview of relational diversity and issues concerning the topic.)

WEB RESOURCES

Footballers Against Racism in Europe (FARE; www.farenet.org): contains information about how being dissimilar, with respect to race, can influence sport participation.

Understanding Prejudice (www.understandingprejudice.org): site for students, teachers, and researchers seeking to understand prejudice and the effects of dissimilarity.

References

Allport, G. W. (1954). *The nature of prejudice.* Cambridge, MA: Addison-Wesley.

Anshel, M. H. (1990). Perceptions of Black intercollegiate football players: Implications for the sport psychology consultant. *The Sport Psychologist, 4,* 235–248.

Antonioni, D., & Park, H. (2001). The effects of personality similarity on peer ratings of contextual work behaviors. *Personnel Psychology, 54,* 331–360.

Brewer, M. B. (1979). In-group bias in the minimal intergroup situation: A cognitive–motivational analysis. *Psychological Bulletin, 86,* 307–324.

Brown, G. T. (2002). Diversity grid lock. *The NCAA News.* Retrieved February 15, 2003, from www.ncaa.org/news/2002/20021028/active/3922 n01.html

Byrne, D. (1971). *The attraction paradigm.* New York: Academic Press.

Chatman, J. A., Polzer, J. T., Barsade, S. G., & Neale, M. A. (1998). Being different yet feeling similar: The influence of demographic composition and organizational culture on work processes and outcomes. *Administrative Science Quarterly, 43,* 749–780.

Chatman, J. A., & Spataro, S. E. (2005). Using self-categorization theory to understand relational demography-based variations in people's responsiveness to organizational culture. *Academy of Management Journal, 48,* 321–331.

Chattopadhyay, P. (1999). Beyond direct and symmetrical effects: The influence of demographic dissimilarity on organizational citizenship behavior. *Academy of Management Journal, 42,* 273–287.

Chelladurai, P. (1992). A classification of sport and physical activity services: Implications for sport managers. *Journal of Sport Management, 6,* 38–51.

Cunningham, G. B. (2005). The importance of a common in-group identity in ethnically diverse groups. *Group Dynamics: Theory, Research, and Practice, 9,* 251–260.

Cunningham, G. B. (2006). The influence of demographic dissimilarity on affective reactions to physical activity classes. *Journal of Sport and Exercise Psychology, 28,* 127–142.

Cunningham, G. B., & Sagas, M. (2004a). Examining the main and interactive effects of deep- and surface-level diversity on job satisfaction and organizational intentions. *Organizational Analysis, 12,* 319–332.

Cunningham, G. B., & Sagas, M. (2004b). The effect of group diversity on organizational commitment. *International Sports Journal, 8*(1), 124–131.

Cunningham, G. B., & Sagas, M. (2005). Diversified dyads in the coaching profession. *International Journal of Sport Management, 6,* 305–323.

Cunningham, G. B., & Sagas, M. (2006). The role of perceived demographic dissimilarity and interaction in customer service satisfaction. *Journal of Applied Social Psychology, 36,* 1654–1673.

Elliott, J. R., & Smith, R. A. (2001). Ethnic matching of supervisors to subordinate work groups: Findings on "bottom-up" ascription and social closure. *Social Problems, 48,* 125–276.

Elvira, M. M., & Cohen, L. E. (2001). Location matters: A cross-level analysis of the effects of organizational sex composition on turnover. *Academy of Management Journal, 44,* 591–605.

Epitropaki, O., & Martin, R. (1999). The impact of relational demography on the quality of leader–member exchanges and employees' work attitudes and well-being. *Journal of Occupational and Organizational Psychology, 72,* 237–240.

Everhart, C. B., & Chelladurai, P. (1998). Gender differences in preferences for coaching as an occupation: The role of self-efficacy, valence, and perceived barriers. *Research Quarterly for Exercise and Sport, 69,* 188–200.

Fink, J. S., & Cunningham, G. B. (2005). The effects of racial and gender dyad diversity on work experiences of university athletics personnel. *International Journal of Sport Management, 6,* 199–213.

Fink, J. S., Pastore, D. L., & Riemer, H. A. (2001). Do differences make a difference? Managing diversity in Division IA intercollegiate athletics. *Journal of Sport Management, 15,* 10–50.

Flynn, F. J., Chatman, J. A., & Spataro, S. E. (2001). Getting to know you: The influence of personality on impressions and performance of demographically different people in organizations. *Administrative Science Quarterly, 46,* 414–442.

Gaertner, S. L., & Dovidio, J. F. (2000). *Reducing intergroup bias: The common ingroup identity model.* Philadelphia: Psychology Press.

Garber, G. (2005, May). *Now I get to be like everybody else.* ESPN.com. Retrieved March 16, 2006, from http://sports.espn.go.com/espn/print?id=2069239&type=story

Green, S. G., Anderson, S. E., & Shivers, S. L. (1996). Demographic and organizational influences on leader–member exchange and related work attitudes. *Organizational Behavior and Human Decision Processes, 66,* 203–214.

Harrison, D. A., Price, K. H., Gavin, J. H., & Florey, A. T. (2002). Time, teams, and task performance: Changing effects of surface- and deep-level diversity on group functioning. *Academy of Management Journal, 45,* 1029–1045.

Hobman, E. V., Bordia, P., & Gallois, C. (2003). Consequences of feeling dissimilar from others in a work team. *Journal of Business and Psychology, 17,* 301–324.

Hogg, M. A., & Abrams, D. (1988). *Social identifications: A social psychology of intergroup relations and group processes.* London: Routledge.

Iverson, R. D., & Buttigieg, D. M. (1997). Antecedents of union commitment: The impact of union membership differences in vertical dyads and work group relationships. *Human Relations, 50,* 1485–1510.

Jackson, S. (2006, February). *Etan Thomas' voice is one worth listening to.* ESPN.com. Retrieved March 1, 2006, from http://sports.espn.go.com/espn/blackhistory/news/story?id=2343032

Jeanquart-Barone, S. (1996). Implications of racial diversity in the supervisor–subordinate relationship. *Journal of Applied Social Psychology, 26,* 935–944.

Judge, T. A., & Ferris, G. R. (1993). Social context of performance evaluation decisions. *Academy of Management Journal, 36,* 80–105.

Kochan, T., Bezrukova, K., Ely, R., Jackson, S., Joshi, A., Jehn, K., et al. (2003). The effects of diversity on business performance: Report of the diversity research network. *Human Resource Management, 42,* 3–21.

Mueller, C. W., Finley, A., Iverson, R. D., & Price, J. L. (1999). The effects of group racial composition on job satisfaction, organizational commitment, and career commitment. *Work and Occupations, 26,* 187–219.

Oakes, P. (2001). The root of all evil in intergroup relations? Unearthing the categorization process. In R. Brown & S. L. Gaertner (Eds.), *Blackwell handbook of social psychology: Intergroup processes* (pp. 3–21). Malden, MA: Blackwell.

Perry, E. L., Kulik, C. T., & Zhou, J. (1999). A closer look at the effects of subordinate–supervisor age differences. *Journal of Organizational Behavior, 20,* 341–357.

Randel, A. E. (2002). Identity salience: A moderator in the relationship between group gender composition and work group conflict. *Journal of Organizational Behavior, 23,* 749–766.

Randel, A. E., & Jaussi, K. S. (2003). Functional background identity, diversity, and individual performance in cross-functional teams. *Academy of Management Journal, 46,* 763–774.

Rogers, D. (2002, August 29). Can the Aussies bring in upmarket tourists? *Marketing,* p. 11.

Sagas, M., & Cunningham, G. B. (2004). Treatment discrimination in college coaching: Its prevalence and impact on the career success of assistant basketball coaches. *International Sports Journal, 8*(1), 76–88.

Sagas, M., Cunningham, G. B., Teed, K. C., & Waltemyer, D. S. (2004, November). *Examining homologous reproduction in the representation of assistant coaches.* Paper presented at the annual conference for the North American Society for the Sociology of Sport, Tucson, AZ.

Sagas, M., Paetzold, R., & Cunningham, G. B. (2006). Effects of supervisor–subordinate demographic diversity on the job satisfaction experienced by assistant coaches. *International Journal of Sport Management, 7,* 141–159.

Schriescheim, C. A., Neider, L. L., Scandura, T. A., & Tepper, B. J. (1992). Development and preliminary validation of a new scale (LMX-6) to measure leader–member exchange in organizations. *Educational and Psychological Measurement, 52,* 135–147.

Stauffer, J. M., & Buckley, M. R. (2005). The existence and nature of bias in supervisory ratings. *Journal of Applied Psychology, 90,* 586–591.

Tajfel, H., & Turner, J. C. (1979). An integrative theory of intergroup conflict. In W. G. Austin & S. Worchel (Eds.), *The social psychology of intergroup relations* (pp. 33–47). Monterey, CA: Brooks/Cole.

Tsui, A. S., Egan, T. D., & O'Reilly, C. A., III. (1992). Being different: Relational demography and organizational attachment. *Administrative Science Quarterly, 37,* 549–579.

Tsui, A. S., & Gutek, B. A. (1999). *Demographic differences in organizations: Current research and future directions.* New York: Lexington Books.

Tsui, A. S., & O'Reilly, C. A., III. (1989). Beyond simple demographic effects: The importance of relational demography in supervisor–subordinate dyads. *Academy of Management Journal, 32,* 402–423.

Turner, J., Hogg, M. A., Oakes, P. J., Reicher, S. D., & Wetherell, M. S. (1987). *Rediscovering the social group: A self-categorization theory.* Oxford, UK: B. Blackwell.

van Knippenberg, D., De Dreu, C. K. W., & Homan, A. C. (2004). Work group diversity and group performance: An integrative model and research agenda. *Journal of Applied Psychology, 89,* 1008–1022.

Vecchio, R. P., & Bullis, R. C. (2001). Moderators of the influence of supervisor–subordinate similarity on subordinate outcomes. *Journal of Applied Psychology, 86,* 884–896.

Wesolowski, M. A., & Mossholder, K. W. (1997). Relational demography in supervisor–subordinate dyads: Impact on subordinate job satisfaction, burnout, and perceived procedural justice. *Journal of Organizational Behavior, 18,* 351–362.

Managing Workplace Diversity

PART IV

Legal Aspects of Diversity

Justin Tatum attended Christian Brothers College High School in St. Louis, Missouri. During his senior season on the boys' basketball team, he averaged 16.9 points, 8.6 rebounds, and 2.9 assists per game. He helped lead his team to the Class 4A State Championship in 1997. Because of his success, many top college programs recruited Tatum, including Minnesota, Oklahoma State, and Cincinnati.

Tatum scored poorly the first time he took his college entrance exam, the ACT. His guidance counselor recommended that he be evaluated for a learning disorder. A doctoral candidate examined him, found that he did not have a learning disorder, and suggested that he study harder for the exam. A month later, Tatum was examined by a licensed psychologist and was diagnosed with generalized anxiety disorder. The ACT administrators accepted this diagnosis and allowed Tatum to take a modified version of the exam—it was not timed, allowed breaks, and the questions were read to him. After three attempts using this modified testing format, Tatum scored high enough to "qualify" for athletic competition.

Under NCAA guidelines, students who take modified entrance exams must have their credentials reviewed by their learning specialist. Tatum's specialist concluded that although he did have test-taking problems, he did not have a learning disability. Based on this determination, the NCAA refused to accept Tatum's modified test score and denied him "qualifier status." Tatum sued the NCAA, challenging its ruling, but the court found in favor of the NCAA.

Tatum's suit against the NCAA is not an isolated incident—other athletes with learning disabilities, many of whom were diagnosed with a learning disability early in their academic life (e.g., second grade), have sued the organization. In most cases, the courts have ruled in favor of the NCAA.

After studying this chapter, you should be able to:

- Discuss the major equal employment opportunity laws and their influence on workplace diversity.

- Describe the steps people can take if they face discrimination in the workplace and the defenses employers have against such charges.

- Discuss the basic tenets of Title IX and the law's impact on sport and physical activity.

In response to these suits, the U. S. Department of Justice determined that the NCAA discriminated against athletes with disabilities. After negotiations, the two parties entered into a Consent Decree, an agreement that required the NCAA to change its operations. The purpose of the Consent Decree was to reduce the incidence of discrimination, but it has had little practical effect. Of the students with disabilities who seek eligibility certification from the NCAA, only 66 percent receive it, substantially less than the over 85 percent of persons without disabilities who receive such certification. These numbers suggest that athletes with disabilities face discrimination when trying to play college sports.*

DIVERSITY CHALLENGE   R E F L E C T I O N

1. Based on this information, do you believe that athletes with disabilities are discriminated against by the NCAA?

2. The Consent Decree between the NCAA and the U. S. Department of Justice expired on May 1, 2003. In your opinion, should another agreement be established?

3. Purported violations of the Americans with Disabilities Act (ADA) is but one of many legal issues affecting the NCAA and its member institutions. What other legal issues might be raised in the college sports context?

---

*Information adapted from Denbo, S. M. (2003). Disability issues in higher education: Accommodating learning-disabled students and student-athletes under the Rehabilitation Act and the Americans with Disabilities Act. *American Business Law Journal, 41,* 145–203; McCallum, J., & O'Brien, R. (1998, February 16). The disability issue. *Sports Illustrated, 88*(6); http://slubillikens.collegesports.com/.

As the Diversity Challenge illustrates, sport managers and administrators may be confronted with various legal issues. Local, state, and federal laws impact organizations' employment and human resource decisions. The way employees are treated, the compensation they receive, and how employees are hired and fired are governed by various legal mandates. Within U. S. athletic departments, the sports that are offered, the scholarships that are allocated, and the distribution of resources must comply with federal mandates concerning gender equity. The degree to which an organization complies with these laws can have a meaningful impact on its overall effectiveness (Wright, Ferris, Hiller, & Kroll, 1995).

This chapter provides an overview of several legal issues related to diversity in sport organizations. After discussing the evolution of employment discrimination law, I then outline how the equal employment opportunity laws influence hiring and other personnel decisions. Employment discrimination claims are addressed in the third section. In the last section, I provide an overview of Title IX—a law that substantially influences virtually all aspects of American sport today.

Evolution of Employment Discrimination Law

Though many might believe that diversity-related legislation is a recent phenomenon, it is not. For example, the 5th Amendment to the U. S. Constitution (ratified in 1791) gave *all* persons the right to due process. The 13th Amendment, which was ratified in 1865, outlawed slavery, and the courts have ruled that it prohibits racial discrimination. The 14th Amendment (ratified in 1868) prohibits states from making or enforcing laws that abridge the privileges and immunities of any U. S. citizen. This amendment prevents states from denying citizens due process and equal protection. Thus, as Dessler (2003) notes, there are over 200 years of legislation outlawing various forms of discrimination.

In this section, I discuss the evolution of employment discrimination law in the courts. In doing so, I draw from Dessler (2003), who outlined how various court cases have influenced the way equal employment laws are applied.

Early Court Decisions

The earliest landmark case was *Griggs v. Duke Power Co.*, 401 U.S. 424 (1971). Duke Power Company required all employees to have a high school diploma. Lawyers for Willie Griggs argued that this policy was discriminatory because (a) possessing such a degree was not necessary to perform the required duties at the power plant and (b) the requirement's effect discriminated against African Americans as they were more often denied employment than Whites. Writing the decision for a unanimous Supreme Court, Chief Justice Warren Burger provided three guidelines affecting equal employment opportunities:

1. **Discrimination need not be intentional.** The power plant was not accused of intentionally discriminating against African Americans; rather, the policies unintentionally discriminated. Thus, employees need only show that discrimination occurred—not that it was deliberate.

2. **Employment practices must be job-related.** When certain employment practices have an adverse effect on members of a protected class, then the employer must show that the policy is directly related to how well people can perform the job. In *Griggs*, having a high school diploma did not influence how well people worked at the power plant.

3. **The burden of proof is on the employer.** It is up to the employer to show that a certain policy or test is job-related.

Another case that had a meaningful impact on equal employment laws is *Albemarle Paper Co. v. Moody*, 422 U.S. 405 (1975). In its ruling, the Court specified the steps employers should take to use screening tools. A company must carefully analyze and document the specific job duties and responsibilities. The performance standards used to evaluate people currently on the job should be clear and unambiguous so the employer can identify who is the most qualified.

Burden of Proof Changes

For over three decades, the courts supported protected persons in employment cases; however, in 1989 two Supreme Court decisions changed this practice (Dessler, 2003). In *Price Waterhouse v. Hopkins*, 490 U.S. 228 (1989), the plaintiff (a woman) sued her employer for being passed over for promotion. She showed that her sex was a contributing factor in the decision, while the firm demonstrated that her "abrasiveness" was a factor as well. The Court, in finding for the employer, ruled that although sex was a factor, she would not have been promoted anyway because of her abrasiveness.

The second influential decision came in *Wards Cove Packing Co. v. Atonio*, 490 U.S. 642 (1989). In this case, the company was sued because racial minorities were overrepresented in lower-level positions, while Whites were overrepresented in upper-management positions and received better housing. Ever since the *Griggs* decision, the employee only had to statistically demonstrate evidence of discrimination, and then the burden of proof shifted to the company. The *Wards Cove* court ruled that the employee had to demonstrate statistical evidence of discrimination *and* prove that the underrepresentation was the result of a policy or practice by the employer. This ruling substantially shifted who had the burden of proof in employment discrimination cases, and placed the expense and onus of proving the case on the employee.

Employment Discrimination Law Since 1991

The *Wards Cove* and *Price Waterhouse* rulings limited the protection minority group members had under Title VII and prompted Congress to pass new legislation: the Civil Rights Act of 1991 (Dessler, 2003). This Act had the following major provisions:

- **Burden of proof.** The Act shifted the burden of proof back to the employer—a company must show that a test or policy is a business necessity.
- **Money damages.** The Act allows those persons who have been intentionally discriminated against to sue for both compensatory and punitive damages. To recover punitive damages, the employee must show that the employer acted with malice or reckless disregard to the rights of the aggrieved employee.

- **Mixed motives.** Recall in the *Price Waterhouse* case, the Court ruled that although sex discrimination was a contributing factor, the plaintiff would have been passed over for promotion in any event because of her abrasive behavior. The Civil Rights Act of 1991 overturned this ruling by making it unlawful for discrimination to have any bearing on employment decisions. That is, the employee's sex cannot impact any part of the decision.

- **Normed tests.** The Act also forbids adjusting test scores to equalize groups, a practice known as within-group norming (Ployhart, Schneider, & Schmitt, 2006). Prior to the Act, some employers hired a minority at one test score (e.g., 80) and a White applicant at another test score (e.g., 90), thereby holding persons from different racial groups to different standards. The Civil Rights Act of 1991 makes this practice unlawful.

The Civil Rights Act of 1991 returned employment discrimination laws to where they were prior to *Wards Cove,* at least with respect to the protections employees have.

Equal Employment Opportunity Legislation

Unfortunately, people still face discrimination today. As discussed in previous chapters, there are substantial differences among various social groups in (a) hiring decisions, (b) compensation, (c) opportunities for training and advancement, and (d) the overall incidence of discrimination in the workplace. Although such differences exist, they are still illegal under most circumstances. In the following sections, I discuss the major equal employment laws as they relate to the various diversity forms. Unless otherwise indicated, the information was gathered from the Equal Employment Opportunity Commission (EEOC) website, www.eeoc.gov.

Title VII of the 1964 Civil Rights Act is the primary law prohibiting employment discrimination on the basis of race or color, national origin, sex, and religion. This law applies to (a) all organizations with at least 15 employees, including state and local governments, (b) labor unions, (c) employment agencies, and (d) the federal government.

Race

Title VII protects people from discrimination based on their race or skin color in hiring and firing decisions, promotions, compensation, and training opportunities. This law also prohibits people from making employment decisions based on the stereotypes associated with people from a particular race—assumptions about people's work ethic, personal traits, or their overall abilities. The law also forbids employers from making employment decisions based on a spouse's race, membership in or affiliation with race- or ethnic-based organizations (e.g., the

Black Coaches Association), or attendance at schools or places of worship that might be associated with a particular racial group (e.g., having attended a Historically Black College or University, such as Grambling State University).

Title VII prohibitions also include the following:

■ **Race-related characteristics and conditions.** Discrimination based on a characteristic often associated with a particular race (e.g., specific hair texture, skin color) is unlawful. Organizations cannot make employment decisions based on conditions that predominantly affect members of one race more than they do members of other races unless it can be conclusively demonstrated that such practices are job-related and are a business necessity. For example, a fitness club that has a policy of not hiring people with sickle cell anemia discriminates against African Americans because that condition is predominantly found among members of that race.

■ **Harassment.** Harassment takes many forms, including racial slurs, racial jokes, comments that could be deemed offensive, and other verbal or physical contact that is based on one's race.

■ **Segregation or classification of employees.** An organization may not physically isolate members of a racial minority group from other employees or from customers. This prohibition also relates to the assignments people receive. It is unlawful, for example, to assign Hispanics to a mostly-Hispanic establishment or geographic region. Finally, it is also illegal to group people from a protected class into certain positions. Suppose an athletic department always assigns African American employees to life skills coordinator or academic advisor positions, as opposed to positions dealing with development or finances, based on the assumption that people in those positions have the most contact with the athletes, many of whom are also African American. Classifying employees in this manner is unlawful. Based on NCAA data (DeHass, 2004), this actually does occur frequently.

■ **Preemployment inquiries.** With a few exceptions, it is always unlawful to ask job applicants what their race is. Employers that use affirmative action in the hiring process or track applicant flow may ask for information on race. Under these circumstances, it is best to use a separate form to keep the information away from the application. This ensures that the information is not used in the remainder of the selection process.

According to the EEOC, there were over 27,000 complaints of racial discrimination reported in 2004. In that same year, the Commission recovered $61.1 million in damages for the charging parties and other aggrieved persons. This figure does not include the additional monies obtained through litigation. In addition to race discrimination, color discrimination charges are prevalent. From 1994 to 2004, the number of charges increased 125 percent (413 and 932, respectively). For information related to national origin discrimination, see Exhibit 10.1.

A topic related to racial discrimination is national origin discrimination. Persons of different ancestries have historically added value to the United States. As EEOC Chairperson Carli M. Dominguez notes, "Immigrants have long been an asset to the American workforce. This is more true than ever in today's increasingly global economy." As with racial discrimination, Title VII prohibits discrimination on the basis of national origin. Treating people differently because they come from a different country or region, have a different accent, or because they are believed to have a different ethnic background is forbidden. The law prohibits hiring, firing, or promoting people on the basis of their national origin. Ethnic slurs and jokes about a person's homeland are prohibited because they can create a hostile work environment. Employers are also barred from making employment decisions based on one's accent or English proficiency unless they substantially influence the manner in which people perform in their job. Incidents of national origin discrimination are widespread. In 2004, the EEOC fielded 8,361 complaints, and the people who brought these claims recovered over $22 million.

Information gathered from EEOC website (www.eeoc.gov).

Sex

Title VII prohibits discrimination based on one's sex. It is unlawful to make employment decisions related to hiring, firing, compensation, the availability or type of training, or any other term, condition, or privilege of employment based on an employee's sex. Employment decisions that are based on stereotypes concerning the traits, abilities, or performance of one sex compared to the other are also forbidden. This law prohibits employers from intentionally or unintentionally creating policies that disproportionately exclude people on the basis of sex and that are not related to the job.

Title VII prohibitions also include the following:

■ **Sexual harassment.** The term *sexual harassment* covers a variety of behaviors including requesting sexual favors and creating a hostile work environment. A hostile work environment exists "when an employee is subjected to repeated unwelcome behaviors that do not constitute sexual bribery but are sufficiently severe and pervasive that they create a work environment so hostile that it substantially interferes with the harassed employee's ability to perform his or her job" (Sharp, Moorman, & Claussen, 2007, p. 240). People of either sex can be sexually harassed. This prohibition also covers same-sex harassment. This concept is discussed in greater detail in Exhibit 10.2.

| *Exhibit 10.2* | **Sexual harassment in the workplace.** |

According to the EEOC, sexual harassment is a form of sex discrimination that violates Title VII. This type of discrimination can take several forms: unwanted sexual advances, solicitation of sexual favors, and other forms of sexual conduct, verbal and physical, that implicitly or explicitly influence one's continued employment, negatively influence performance, or create a hostile, intimidating workplace environment. The harassers can be either men or women, and they do not have to harass members of the opposite sex. In 2004, for example, over 15% of all charges of sexual harassment were made by males. The harassment may be inflicted by peers, subordinates, customers, or other nonemployees. Sexual harassment victims are not always the particular person who is being harassed; a victim may be someone who is otherwise negatively affected by the direct harassment of others.

Fitzgerald and her colleagues developed an instrument designed to measure the incidence of sexual harassment in the workplace (Gelfand, Fitzgerald, & Drasgow, 1995; Fitzgerald et al., 1988). They identified three behavioral dimensions: (a) gender harassment, which consists of those behaviors that connote a negative or hostile view toward women but are not necessarily aimed at seeking sexual cooperation; (b) unwanted sexual attention, which is conduct that is explicitly sexual in nature such as requesting dates or discussing one's sex life; and (c) sexual coercion, which consists of demands for sexual favors backed by either a threat or a promise of future rewards.

The effects of being harassed can be detrimental to one's career. Research shows that women who are harassed report decreased morale on the job, are absent more frequently, and generally have negative experiences in the workplace. Women may leave their job after experiencing harassment—they resign, are transferred to another work environment, or are even fired. There are also psychological costs associated with harassment. Clinical studies show that women who have been harassed have greater levels of fear, anxiety, and depression than those who have not been harassed (see Marshall, 2005, for a review).

Sexual harassment is seen in all work contexts, including sport. United States Olympics coach Tim Nardiello was suspended from his skeleton team coaching position because of sexual harassment charges ("Accused," 2006). Jean Brooks, who was the women's basketball coach and a part-time instructor at the Southern University at New Orleans, recovered over $275,000 in damages for the years of sexual harassment to which she was subjected (Matisik, 2005).

Because of the frequency of sexual harassment in sport, many professional organizations adopted official statements and positions against that form of discrimination. For example, the National Association for Sport and Physical Education issued a statement in 2000 titled "Sexual harassment in athletic settings," outlining the issues related to sexual harassment, examples of the discrimination, and the steps that coaches, players, and administrators can take to confront it. Other entities such as WomenSport International developed similar statements.

Information gathered from indicated sources.

■ **Pregnancy-based discrimination.** Title VII was amended by the Pregnancy Discrimination Act. Pregnancy-related protections include hiring, pregnancy and maternity leave, health insurance, and fringe benefits. Exhibit 10.3 provides an overview of these protections.

Another issue related to sex discrimination is differences in compensation between men and women. The Equal Pay Act of 1963 requires that men and women in the same organization receive equal pay for equal work. The jobs do not have to be identical; rather, the jobs only have to be substantially equal. For example, if a kinesiology department hires two professors, a man and a woman, who have the same rank, roughly the same experience, and perform the same duties, both professors must be paid the same salary.

Five factors are applied to determine whether the Equal Pay Act was violated:

1. **Skill.** As between men and women, the pay may differ if the two people have dissimilar job-related skills. For example, a coach with 500 career wins has more skill than a coach with only 42 career wins because the number of games won is a job-related skill. Two ticket clerk jobs at a professional sport franchise are considered equal even if one of the clerks has a master's degree because the advanced degree is not required for the job.

2. **Effort.** Compensation can vary if there are differences in the physical or mental efforts needed to complete a certain task or hold a particular job. For example, an employee at a fitness club who is charged with moving the weight machines around the facility exerts considerably more physical effort than the employee who checks the membership status of patrons when they enter the facility. Thus, the former employee may be paid more than the latter, regardless of the employee's sex.

3. **Responsibility.** People who hold more meaningful responsibilities may be paid more than their counterparts. A regional salesperson who also coordinates the efforts and responsibilities of other salespeople earns a greater salary because of the extra responsibilities. It should be noted, however, that the increased responsibilities must be meaningful.

4. **Working conditions.** Two factors are considered with respect to working conditions: the physical surroundings and hazards. People with more challenging or difficult work conditions may be paid more than others.

5. **Establishment (place of employment).** The Equal Pay Act only applies to differences in compensation among employees of the same organization.

Based on the number of complaints filed with the EEOC (25,000 in 2004), it appears that incidents of sex discrimination are rather common. Companies that discriminate based on sex receive severe financial punish-

Exhibit 10.3	**Pregnancy-based discrimination.**

The Pregnancy Discrimination Act, an amendment to Title VII, applies to all organizations with at least 15 employees, including state and local governments, employment agencies, labor unions, and the federal government. In general terms, this Act requires that women who are pregnant or who are affected by related conditions be treated the same as their colleagues who have comparable abilities or limitations. Pregnancy-related protections include:

- **Hiring.** Organizations cannot refuse to hire a woman because she is pregnant, has a pregnancy-related condition, or because of any prejudices that her coworkers, clients, or customers might have. For example, a pregnant woman who applies for a position with an athletic shoe company may not be denied employment merely because the manager believes that the company's clients will not respond well to a pregnant salesperson.

- **Pregnancy and maternity leave.** If a woman is unable to perform her job because of her pregnancy, the employer must treat that condition as any other temporary disability. For example, if employees with temporary disabilities are able to modify the way they accomplish their tasks, the pregnant woman must be permitted to modify her tasks. In addition, employers must hold open a job for a woman who is absent because of her pregnancy the same length of time the employer would for a person who is sick or on disability leave.

- **Health insurance.** If an employer provides medical insurance, then pregnancy must be covered. The charges for pregnancy-related expenses must be at the same rate as other illnesses. Employers must provide the same health benefits for spouses of male employees as they do for spouses of female employees.

- **Fringe benefits.** The same pregnancy-related benefits provided to married women must be available to single women. If an employer provides benefits for people who are on leave, the benefits must also be given to women on leave for pregnancy-related conditions. Finally, women on pregnancy leave must be treated the same as people on other types of leave when it comes to issues such as seniority, vacation calculation, pay increases, and temporary disability benefits.

In 2004, the EEOC received 4,512 complaints of pregnancy-based discrimination. In that same year, the Commission recovered $11.3 million for the people who brought the claims (this figure does not include money recovered through litigation).

Information gathered from EEOC (www.eeoc.gov).

ments. In 2004 alone, over $100 million in damages were collected for persons who made complaints (this figure does not include damages recovered through litigation).

Religion

Discrimination on the basis of religion is also prohibited by Title VII. Under Title VII:

- Employers cannot treat people more or less favorably because of their religious affiliation.

- Employees cannot be forced to participate in religious ceremonies or prayers as a condition of employment. As discussed in Chapter 7, this issue often arises in the context of team prayers.

- Employers must accommodate their employees' sincerely held religious beliefs unless doing so would cause undue hardship to the employer. Reasonable accommodations include flexible work hours and the ability to change working assignments with other employees. Unreasonable accommodations are those that impose hardships on other employees, jeopardize workplace safety, or decrease efficiency.

- Employers cannot restrict an employee's religious expression any more than other forms of expression that might have a comparable effect. For example, an employer may not restrict personal, silent prayers when they do not negatively impact performance.

- Employers must take all reasonable steps to prevent religious harassment in the workplace.

Charges of religious discrimination are not as prevalent as other forms. In 2004, the EEOC received 2,466 complaints. This is only a fraction of the racial (9 percent), sex (10 percent), age (14 percent), or disability (16 percent) claims. In 2004, the EEOC recovered $6 million in damages for those claiming religious discrimination.

Age

People over age 40 are protected from discrimination by the Age Discrimination in Employment Act of 1967 (ADEA). This law protects both current employees and job applicants. Employers cannot discriminate against people because of their age with respect to any aspect of employment, including hiring, firing, promotion, compensation, benefits, and the quality of job assignments. It also protects people from retaliation if they do file a complaint. The ADEA applies to all organizations with at least 20 employees, including state and local governments, employment agencies, labor unions, and the federal government. Protections under the law also include the following:

■ **Apprenticeship programs.** Under most circumstances, it is unlawful for apprenticeship programs to set age limits.

■ **Job notices and advertisements.** When advertising for a position, it is unlawful to include age preferences or limitations. The only exception to this policy is when age is a bona fide occupational qualification.

■ **Preemployment inquiries.** Although it is *not* unlawful to ask prospective employees for their age or date of birth, the EEOC has indicated that the requests will be closely scrutinized to ensure that they are made for lawful purposes.

■ **Benefits.** Some older employees may need more medical care than their younger counterparts. Because this costs money, it may serve as a disincentive to hire older employees or provide them with benefits—both of which are unlawful. The Older Workers Benefit Protection Act of 1990 amended the ADEA to guarantee these rights.

■ **Waivers of ADEA rights.** Some organizations offer special early retirement packages to their older employees for a variety of cost-saving and human resource reasons. The ADEA and the Older Workers Benefit Protection Act of 1990 allow for early retirement if the employee willingly chooses to waive his rights. A valid waiver must (a) be written and understandable by all parties; (b) explicitly refer to ADEA rights and claims; (c) not surrender future rights or claims; (d) be in exchange for something that is valuable (e.g., a retirement package worth more than a standard retirement); (e) recommend that the employee seek legal advice before signing; and (f) provide the employee with at least three weeks to consider the agreement and one week to revoke the agreement, even after the document is signed.

Though not as commonplace as sex or racial discrimination, age discrimination is still prevalent in the workplace. In 2004, the EEOC received approximately 18,000 claims of age discrimination. Not including other money awards from litigation, the EEOC recovered $60 million from organizations that were found to discriminate on the basis of one's age.

Disability

The Americans with Disabilities Act of 1990 (ADA) prohibits private organizations, local, state, and federal government entities, employment agencies, and labor unions from discriminating against persons with disabilities (either mental or physical). As outlined in Chapter 6, people are considered to have a disability when they possess an impairment (whether physical or mental) that significantly restricts one or more major life activities. A major life activity, as defined in the ADA, is an activity that is fundamental to human life—"caring for oneself, performing manual tasks, walking, seeing, hearing, speaking, breathing, learning, and working" (ADA, 1985).

Within the sport context, a qualified person with a disability is one who can perform the basic elements of the job with reasonable accommodations. Reasonable accommodations are those that the employer can make without undue hardship, and may include restructuring the nature of the job (e.g., modifying the work schedule), making existing facilities readily accessible by persons with a disability, or modifying equipment.

Employers are not required to lower the job standards. If a person with a disability cannot perform the basic job functions with reasonable accommodations, then the person need not be hired. The employer is also not required to provide employees with items such as glasses or hearing aids.

The ADA covers medical examinations and inquiries, as well as drug and alcohol abuse. Employers cannot ask job applicants if they have preexisting medical conditions, but they can ask if the applicants are able to perform the basic duties related to the job. Medical examinations are permissible when they are required of *all* job applicants. The examinations must be job-related and consistent with the employer's overall business needs. With respect to drugs and alcohol, the ADA does not apply to people who take illegal drugs. Mandatory drug testing is legal, and employers can hold substance abusers to the same performance standards as other employees.

In 2004, the EEOC received 15,376 claims of disability discrimination, recovering over $47 million in damages. For a sport industry example, see the Diversity in the Field boxes.

DIVERSITY *in the field*

ADA Compliance in Fitness Organizations. A 2003 report in the periodical *Club Industry* (Cardinal, 2003) suggested that fitness clubs are not doing all they should to comply with ADA guidelines. Investigations of 84 facilities in two demographic regions (Kansas City, Missouri, and Western Oregon) found that *not a single facility* was ADA compliant! The areas with the poorest compliance were accessibility to and around the exercise equipment, access to the customer service desk, and in restrooms and locker rooms. Facility and telephone access received the highest marks. According to Marc D. Spaziani, many of the problems are easily addressed such as reducing the thickness of the rubber mats so they can be accessed by persons in wheelchairs. Other problems, though, are more perplexing. "Many of the problems related more to a lack of space," Spaziani noted. "A club will add new equipment or cardio machines and cram them into existing space—and suddenly there's no room to maneuver anymore." Despite these issues, there are some fitness clubs that are very "disability friendly." Crosstrainers Fitness Forum, which is located in Clinton Township, MI, boasts full access for persons with disabilities. These efforts have not gone unrecognized, as 10 percent of all members are persons with disabilities. Thus, it is possible for the fitness industry to excel in the area of ADA compliance.

Obesity

As of 2006, there are no laws in place that specifically address the issue of obesity discrimination. This does not mean, however, that people have not successfully sued on the basis of such differential treatment. These suits are usu-

DIVERSITY *in the field*

Casey Martin and the PGA. Casey Martin is a person with a severe circulatory disorder in his legs, prohibiting him from walking long distances at one time. He is also a golfer who is good enough to compete at the highest levels. Because of his condition, he needs to ride in a golf cart during play. This became an issue when Martin tried to qualify for the Professional Golf Association (PGA) Tour, as Tour rules prohibit participants from riding in carts. Martin sued the PGA Tour under the ADA. In 2001, the Supreme Court ruled in favor of Martin (*PGA Tour, Inc. v. Martin,* 532 U.S. 661), saying that allowing Martin to ride a cart during an event would not fundamentally alter the nature of the game (Sharp, Moorman, & Claussen, 2007).

ally brought under the Rehabilitation Act of 1973, which prohibits discrimination on the basis of disability alone (Bell, McLaughlin, & Sequeira, 2004). In *Cook v. Rhode Island,* 10 F.3d 17 (1st Cir. 1993), Cook was denied employment at a state facility because it was believed her obesity would limit her job performance even though Cook had performed at high levels in her previous job. The employer also believed that Cook would miss more time from work and that the state would face more compensation claims because of her condition. The court, in finding in Cook's favor, ruled that obesity was a disability because it (obesity) resulted in a metabolic dysfunction.

Because most suits similar to Cook's are not successful, various groups advocate the adoption of laws and ordinances prohibiting weight discrimination (Bell et al., 2004). Local ordinances in San Francisco and Santa Cruz, California, and the District of Columbia prohibit discrimination on the basis of weight. As noted in the Diversity Challenge in Chapter 6, these laws and ordinances have helped people such as Jennifer Portnick fight discrimination and overcome the barriers they encounter because of their weight.

Sexual Orientation

As of 2006, no federal laws prohibited sexual orientation discrimination. According to the U. S. Office of Personnel Management (www.opm.gov), Executive Order 13087, issued by President Clinton on May 28, 1998, explicitly forbids sexual orientation discrimination in Executive Branch civilian employment.

As of 2001, only 24 percent of states provided protection against sexual orientation discrimination (Hayes-Thomas, 2004). Some major cities such as Atlanta have local ordinances barring such discrimination. Many of the larger U.S. firms also have such policies, including IBM and the Marriott Corporation (Hayes-Thomas, 2004).

Section Summary

For most forms of diversity, federal laws protect people against discrimination. In general, employers cannot use demographic characteristics, ethnic background, or religious preferences in employment decisions. The two notable exceptions are weight and sexual orientation.

Employment Discrimination Claims

 n this section, I highlight the steps involved when charges of discrimination do arise. This issue is addressed from both the employee and employer perspectives.

Employee Perspective

Discrimination in the employment context can take two forms: disparate treatment and disparate impact. *Disparate treatment* occurs when an employer intentionally discriminates against persons from various groups (e.g., women, racial minorities). As noted in the *Griggs* case, however, not all forms of discrimination are intentional. *Disparate impact* occurs when some neutral company policy results in discrimination. For example, some employment policies or tests negatively impact one group relative to another even though that is not the employer's intent.

Employees must establish a prima facie case of discrimination by demonstrating that a certain policy had an adverse impact on members of a protected group. For example, if 80 percent of men pass an employment test, but only 10 percent of women pass the same test, then this test has an adverse impact on women, who are a protected group. After the prima facie case is established, the burden of proof then shifts to the employer to demonstrate the legality and validity of its actions.

What steps, then, can employees take to show disparate impact? Although a variety of methods are available (see Bobko & Roth, 2004), the EEOC applies the "four-fifths rule." As Mathis and Jackson (2006) explain, "if the selection rate for a protected group is less than 80 percent (four-fifths) of the selection rate for the majority group or less than 80 percent of the majority group's representation in the relevant labor market, discrimination exists" (p. 116). For example, suppose an athletic sporting goods company has 1,000 job applicants, 800 of whom are White and 200 of whom are African American. If 450 Whites and 80 African Americans are hired from that pool, the "four-fifths rule" is violated.

$$80/200 = .40$$
$$450/800 = .56$$
$$.40 \, / \, .56 = .71$$
$$.71 < .80$$

The burden then shifts to the employer to show that the selection rate differences are legally justified (discussed next). (See Exhibit 10.4 for the steps for filing a discrimination complaint with the EEOC.)

Exhibit 10.4	**Filing a complaint with the EEOC.**

According to the EEOC, *any* person who believes his employment rights have been violated can file a charge of discrimination either by mail or in person at the nearest EEOC Office (see www.eeoc.gov/offices.html for a list of offices nationwide). The following information must be provided in the complaint: (a) the name, address, and telephone number of the complainant; (b) the name, address, and telephone number of the entity charged with discriminating; and (c) a brief description of the alleged discrimination including when it occurred. All Title VII complaints must be filed within 180 days of the discriminating event.

Employer Perspective

If a prima facie case is established, the burden then shifts to the employer to show that there was no discrimination. There are several defenses available to an employer (Dessler, 2003).

Business Necessity

One defense to an allegation of discrimination is to demonstrate that there was an overriding business purpose or necessity for a policy or test, thereby warranting its use. Dessler (2003) notes that proving a business necessity is often difficult. The courts have dismissed the notions that inconvenience, annoyance, or expense to the employer qualify as a business necessity. Those jobs that require minimal training preemployment standards are usually closely scrutinized by the courts.

Bona Fide Occupational Qualification

Another defense available to employers is that a particular employment practice is a bona fide occupational qualification (BFOQ) for performing the job. Dessler (2003) notes that the BFOQ defense is most often used in cases of intentional discrimination, not in cases of disparate impact.

One's age, sex, religion, and national origin may all be considered BFOQs under certain circumstances. For example, age is often a BFOQ for persons involved in transportation (e.g., bus drivers, pilots) or acting. Sex can be a BFOQ for some jobs such as acting, modeling, or locker room attendants. One's religious beliefs might be a BFOQ when it involves jobs with religious-based societies or organizations—the position's tasks must be related to the particular religion. For example, a physical educator's religious preferences might be a determining factor in whether or not she receives a position at a private, religious-based high school because a physical educator at this school is expected to incorporate religious principles in his or her classes. Finally, there are some cases where one's national origin might be considered a BFOQ. For example, an employer who is running a Korean Sport Forum might prefer persons of Korean heritage as employees. Title VII prohibits the use of other characteristics (e.g., race) as a BFOQ.

Title IX

The previous sections outlined equal employment opportunity laws and how they influence employment decisions. These laws have a substantial impact on the way *all* business in the United States is conducted today. A law that has a significant influence on sport is Title IX, which states that:

> No person in the United States shall, on the basis of sex, be excluded from participation in, be denied the benefits of, or be subjected to discrimination under any educational program or activity receiving Federal financial assistance. (Title IX of the Education Amendments of 1972, P.L. 92-318, 20 U.S.C.S § 1681)

Note that the words "sport," "athletics," "physical education," and "recreation" are not included in the law. Nevertheless, this legislation impacts sport perhaps more than any other. In essence, it requires that equal opportunities be provided to men and women participating in federally funded activities. Because almost every high school and institution of higher education in the United States receives some federal financial assistance, either directly or indirectly, the law influences almost all aspects of amateur athletics. In the following sections, I give a brief historical overview of Title IX and then discuss the law's influence on sport today. Unless otherwise noted, the information was gleaned from Carpenter and Acosta's (2005) comprehensive and authoritative text, *Title IX*.

History of Title IX

Title IX was passed in 1972 as part of the Education Amendments. The law provided little direction to administrators on how to provide equal opportunities for men and women in educational settings. Thus, the Office of Civil Rights (OCR) developed regulations that "would breathe an enforceable life into Title IX" (Carpenter & Acosta, 2005, p. 6). Congress approved these regulations in 1975, giving them the force of law. The regulations are used by organizations and the courts to interpret, measure, and enforce Title IX.

Of particular application to athletics are the following regulations:

- **Section 106.37:** When athletic scholarships are offered, they must be offered to both men and women in proportion to the number of men and women participating in athletics overall.

- **Section 106.41(a):** No person shall, on the basis of sex, be excluded from, denied the benefits of, or be discriminated against in any form of athletics (e.g., interscholastic, intercollegiate, club, or intramural).

- **Section 106.41(b):** Separate athletic teams can be formed for men and women. If a school supports a men's team but does not offer a similar sport for women, then women must be allowed to try out for the men's team. The exception to this is contact sports such as rugby, ice hockey, football, and basketball.

- **Section 106.41(c):** Schools that support athletic teams should provide equal opportunities to both men and women. To do so, the athletic director should consider 10 factors: (a) whether the teams are congruent with the interests and abilities of members of both sexes; (b) the provision of equipment and supplies; (c) the manner in which games and practices are scheduled; (d) travel and per diem; (e) coaching and academic counseling; (f) compensation of the coaches and academic tutors; (g) the provision and quality of locker rooms and facilities (both practice and game); (h) the provision of medical and training staff and their facilities; (i) the provision of housing, dining facilities, and dining services; and (j) overall publicity.

Later policy interpretations identified two additional factors: recruitment and support services. Thus, the financial aid regulations identified in Section 106.37, the 10 regulations in Section 106.42(c), and the two factors identified in the policy interpretations established 13 areas to consider when enforcing Title IX.

Institutions had until 1978 to comply with the law, but few met the deadline (Carpenter & Acosta, 2005). In 1984, a meaningful blow was dealt to Title IX by the Court's decision in *Grove City College v. Bell,* 465 U.S. 555. The U.S. Supreme Court addressed two issues:

1. Does the word "program" refer to the institution as a whole or to individual programs within that entity?

2. Does an institution have to receive direct federal funding in order for it to be subject to Title IX guidelines?

With respect to the first issue, the Court found that only those units receiving federal monies were included in the term "program." Therefore, if an athletic department did not receive federal funds, it was not bound by Title IX regulations. However, with respect to the second issue, the Court ruled that an institution did not have to receive direct federal funds to be subject to the Title IX regulations.

The effects of the *Grove City* decision were severe. Because many (if not most) university athletic departments did not receive federal monies, they were now not subject to Title IX. As a result, many schools immediately cut women's scholarships, women's teams were slated to be cut at the end of the academic year, all complaints that had been filed with the OCR were closed, and Title IX lawsuits were dismissed.

According to Carpenter and Acosta (2005), Congress considered the Supreme Court's interpretation of "program" to be incorrect. To remedy this situation, the Civil Rights Restoration Act of 1987 was passed over President Reagan's veto in 1988. This Act clarified issues surrounding the word "program." According to the Civil Rights Restoration Act, the term "program" refers to the entire institution, not just individual programs within that entity. Most physical education departments and athletic departments do not receive federal funds; however, the universities in which they are housed *do* receive such funds. Thus, every entity within a university now fell under Title IX guidelines.

Two other cases of particular relevance to the history of Title IX are *Franklin v. Gwinnett County Public Schools*, 503 U.S. 60 (1992) and *Jackson v. Birmingham Board of Education*, 544 U.S. 167 (2005). The key issue in *Franklin* was whether or not monetary damages could be awarded to persons who successfully sued under Title IX. In this case, a student who had been sexually harassed filed a Title IX lawsuit, but neither the statute nor the regulations contained any language related to monetary damages. The Supreme Court unanimously ruled that monetary damages could be awarded under Title IX. As a result of this ruling, Title IX enforcement changed dramatically. It was now in the best financial interest of institutions to comply with Title IX mandates. Failing to do so meant losing potentially large sums of money—money the institutions could ill afford to relinquish. The *Jackson* case is also relevant. Roderick Jackson, a male coach of a girls' high school basketball team, alleged that the girls on the team were discriminated against. He complained to the board about this discrimination and was subsequently fired. He sued the Board of Education claiming that his termination was in retaliation for complaining about the discrimination. The Supreme Court ruled that Title IX whistle-blowers who were subjected to retaliation for filing a Title IX claim could recover damages.

Much of the Title IX discussion thus far focused on the athletics context; however, the law impacts all educational activities. For information related to the influence of Title IX on physical education and recreation, see Exhibits 10.5 and 10.6, respectively.

Title IX Compliance

The 1979 policy interpretations together with a 2003 letter of clarification established a three-prong test for evaluating Title IX compliance by universities and colleges (Carpenter & Acosta, 2005). According to this framework, often referred to as the three-prong test, a school must select one of the following in order to be compliant with the law:

1. Provide participation opportunities for male and female athletes that are in proportion to their respective enrollments at the university (referred to as substantial proportionality).

   [Note that the numbers need not be equal; they need only be in proportion. Consider the following examples using data obtained from the

| *Exhibit 10.5* | **The influence of Title IX on physical education.** |

Within the sport context, Title IX is most often discussed in relation to athletics; however, the law also impacts physical education (Carpenter & Acosta, 2005). According to Title IX, schools may not:

- Treat males and females differently when determining whether they satisfy necessary requirements or conditions prior to receiving physical education services. For example, a teacher may not require girls to pass a skills test if such screening is not also required of boys.

- Provide differing physical education benefits or services to boys and girls. For example, it may be improper to group students in a class by sex, or to hire experienced teachers for boys' classes and novices for the girls' classes.

- Deny students of one sex access to the benefits or services associated with physical education. Weight rooms, for example, were traditionally reserved for boys. This practice is unlawful because it denies girls access to the facilities.

- Subject students to a different set of rules based on their sex. Behavioral issues might fall under this category. It is not uncommon for teachers to punish girls for misbehaving in class but attribute similar behaviors on the part of boys to the notion that "boys will be boys."

- Apply different rules concerning the residence of a student or an applicant. It is a violation of Title IX to enroll an out-of-district male student because he might be an asset to the basketball team and then deny a similar request by a female student.

- Aid or assist discrimination by providing help to an entity that discriminates on the basis of sex. A school may not allow an all-male tennis league to use its facilities because the league discriminates on the basis of sex by not allowing girls to participate.

- Otherwise limit the students' enjoyment of their rights and privileges as they relate to physical education. For example, if boys are allowed to use a gym after school for "free play" basketball, girls must be given the same opportunity.

Information gathered from Carpenter and Acosta (2005).

Equity in Athletics website (http://ope.ed.gov/athletics/index.asp). In 2004, women represented 45 percent of the athletes at both the University of Alabama at Birmingham and the University at Buffalo. During that same year, women constituted 60 percent of the undergraduates at the University of Alabama at Birmingham and 45 percent of the athletes at the University at Buffalo. Using these data, we can conclude that the University of Alabama at Birmingham was *not* in compliance with Title

Recreation programs and Title IX.   *Exhibit 10.6*

Title IX impacts those recreational activities that meet the three requirements for Title IX jurisdiction:

1. sex discrimination occurs,

2. the activity is educational in nature, and

3. the entity sponsoring the activity receives federal financial assistance.

The first two of these conditions are usually easily demonstrated because recreation and sport activities are generally considered educational. If the discrimination occurs on a college campus, the third condition is met, as most universities receive federal funding of some form. Outside school context, however, demonstrating the third condition may be more difficult.

Carpenter and Acosta (2005) discuss several scenarios that, as of 2005, had not been decided by the courts, but may provide evidence of federal financial assistance. First, if an entity does not receive federal monies directly, but its member organizations do, is Title IX triggered? Suppose a governing body (e.g., National Intramural-Recreational Sport Association, NIRSA) is a private organization, but some of its institutional members receive federal funding. These institutions pay dues to the governing body; thus, some argue that federal monies are, in an indirect fashion, being received by the governing organization. If this is true, then the organization is subject to the Title IX requirements. Second, what if an organization is tax-exempt? Is the federal government supporting the organization by not collecting taxes, thereby activating Title IX? These issues do raise the possibility of bringing Title IX claims against sport organizations that might not otherwise fall under the jurisdiction of the law.

Information gathered from Carpenter and Acosta (2005).

IX, while the University at Buffalo was. The two schools had different compliance outcomes even though they provided the same opportunities for female athletes.]

2. Demonstrate a history and continued practice of program expansion for athletes of the underrepresented sex.

    [Under this condition, the school need not be compliant at the time of its evaluation; rather, it only has to demonstrate that it has continually strived to be more equitable and provide opportunities for persons of the underrepresented sex to develop their skills and compete in athletic events.]

3. Effectively demonstrate that the programs and opportunities offered are congruent with the interests and abilities of the underrepresented sex (referred to as the accommodation of interest and ability test).

[Critics from both sides have weighed in on this. If women are the underrepresented sex and do not have an interest in playing varsity sports, why should the athletic department spend the time and money to field a team? On the other hand, interest in sports may wane if opportunities are not provided. How can an athletic department claim in good faith that women are not interested in participating in sports if few women's sports are offered? If sports are offered, perhaps they would attract women to the campus who might not otherwise have come.]

In its 2003 letter of clarification, the OCR notes that, traditionally, schools have viewed substantial proportionality (i.e., the first prong) as a "safe harbor" for Title IX compliance. That is, they primarily sought to satisfy this requirement to the neglect of the other prongs. This is unnecessary. According to the OCR, each of the three tests is a viable option for Title IX compliance, and no single test is preferred over the others.

Title IX Outcomes

The final section examines three relevant Title IX outcomes: increased participation by girls and women in sport, increased prestige of women's sport, and the effects on women coaches and administrators. For additional information, see the Professional Perspectives box on the following page.

Participation

One of the primary purposes of Title IX is to create equal opportunities for males and females to participate in educational activities, including sport and recreation. By all measures, the law has achieved this goal. Carpenter and Acosta (2005) note, "The often heard phrase 'if you build it, they will come' is true of females and sport opportunities. Indeed, they have come. Each year the participation of females in sport breaks new records" (p. 168).

This growth of female participation in sport is seen in several areas. Carpenter and Acosta (2005) indicate that one of the largest increases has been in the high school context. In 1972, girls represented just 5 percent of all high school athletes. This proportion increased to 32 percent by 1978 (the first year of mandatory compliance) and to 41 percent by 2002. During this time, the number of girls participating in high school sports increased by over 900 percent (from 294,015 to 2,856,358).

Similar increases have been seen at the university level (Carpenter & Acosta, 2005). Results from their longitudinal work show many advances, including the following:

- When Title IX was passed in 1972, the average number of women's teams offered per university was 2.50. By 2004, this figure increased to 8.32.
- From 1998–2004, 1,155 new teams for females were added.

■ In 1977, less than 3 percent of all schools offered women's soccer. By 2004, this figure increased over 4,000 percent to 88.6 percent of all schools.

These data indicate that more girls and women are participating in sport today than ever before. These trends have also spilled over to other types of sport and recreation. Many female professional sport leagues such as the WNBA exist today—something that many thought impossible prior to Title IX. Girls and women are also regular participants in such recreational activities as running and weight training. The sport opportunities made available because of Title IX are a primary reason for these increases.

Increased Prestige

Title IX requires schools to provide equal opportunities for men and women in sports; this means sponsoring teams, hiring coaches and support staff, paying for scholarships, building facilities, and publicizing the teams—all of which take time, effort, and money. With the monetary resources now directed at female athletes and their teams, the prestige of women's sport also increased. As noted in Chapter 5, coaches for and players on women's teams are still paid less than men; however, the salaries they do receive are substantially higher than the salaries prior to Title IX. Furthermore, recruiting budgets, scholarship allocations, and monies spent on facilities are all greater than they would be had Title IX never been enacted.

Leadership Effects

The increased prestige and attention to female athletes and their teams has, in many respects, been positive, but there have also been problems. One drawback of the increased prestige is the decline of women

PROFESSIONAL
P E R S P E C T I V E S

Title IX. Lori Miller is a Professor of Sport Administration and an Associate Dean in the College of Education at Wichita State University and has written numerous articles and coauthored a book about legal issues in the sports world. Miller suggests that Title IX has "had a tremendous impact" on all aspects of education. In the sport context, Title IX created additional opportunities for girls and women to participate in sport. Similar effects are seen in other contexts. According to Miller, prior to Title IX, only 9 percent of all law degrees were awarded to women. The equal opportunities for men and women resulting from Title IX changed these figures substantially.

Though strides have been made in terms of gender equity as a result of Title IX, Miller contends that there is "still a lot of territory to cover." For example, she notes that only 2 percent of all claims with the EEOC are Title IX–related, meaning that either the agency does not take the claims seriously, or people are not filing charges under this law. When charges are made, most schools use the accommodation of interests and abilities defense under the three-prong test. Miller notes, however, that this defense is inherently flawed because it does not address the history of inequality between men and women. "What really needs to be addressed is accommodation at lower levels," Miller argues. This means bringing suits against high schools and elementary schools for not providing equal opportunities for girls and women in the sport context. If lawsuits are initiated, they might increase the interest in sport and physical activity among younger girls. As Miller explains, "there needs to be litigation at the lower levels so we can start addressing the needs of the young girls."

in leadership positions (Carpenter & Acosta, 2005). Although enacting Title IX meant more women's teams were formed, the coaching vacancies for these teams are usually filled by men. For example, in 1972, about 90 percent of all coaches of women's teams were women. This figure dramatically declined in the first years after Title IX (58 percent in 1978) and has continued to do so over time. In 2006, only 42.4 percent of all coaches of women's teams were women (Acosta & Carpenter, 2006).

A similar trend has occurred with administrators, with more drastic effects (Acosta & Carpenter, 2006). In 1972, 90 percent of the administrators of women's programs were women, a figure that dropped to 20 percent by 1980 and was at 18.6 percent as of 2006. Just as with coaching, there are more men serving as the administrator of women's sports than women.

Recall that the reasons for these declines were discussed in Chapter 5. First, the increased prestige of women's sport made coaching females and their teams a viable option for men; thus, they became more apt to seek positions coaching women's teams than in the past. Second, women are likely to leave coaching at an earlier age than men. This results in fewer women in the field and, consequently, a supply-side shortage (Hasbrook, 1988). Finally, among assistant coaches, men have a greater interest and desire to become a head coach (Cunningham & Sagas, 2002; Cunningham, Sagas, & Ashley, 2003). When positions do become available, men are more likely to apply for the openings than their female counterparts.

The second and third reasons for the underrepresentation of women in leadership positions seem to place the blame on the women. As noted in Chapter 5, this is not true. There are structural forces in place (e.g., access and treatment discrimination) that exert influence on the female coaches. There are also gender roles and norms that influence ideas about what women "can" and "should" do with their careers, families, and friends. All of these factors interact to influence who seeks leadership positions, who is selected for these roles, and how long they remain in them.

Chapter Summary

This chapter focused on diversity laws as they affect sport organizations. As noted in the Diversity Challenge, these laws have a substantial influence not only on the organization and its practices, but also on its employees and customers. Who is hired or fired, who receives training, and the level of compensation they receive are all influenced by employment discrimination laws. Within the sport, recreation, and physical education context, laws govern the opportunities provided to people, as well as the monies and facilities devoted to them. The laws impact virtually every aspect of organizational life. After reading the chapter, you should be able to:

1. **Discuss the major equal employment opportunity laws and their influence on workplace diversity.**

Employment laws protect against discrimination on the basis of race (Title VII of the Civil Rights Act of 1964), color (Title VII), national origin (Title VII), sex (Title VII, Title IX of the Education Amendments, Equal Pay Act of 1963), age (Age Discrimination in Employment Act of 1967, Older Workers Benefit Protection Act of 1990), disability (American with Disabilities Act of 1963), and religion (Title VII). There are no federal laws barring discrimination based on weight or sexual orientation.

2. **Describe the steps people can take if they face discrimination in the workplace and the defenses employers have against such charges.**

A person must file a charge with the EEOC prior to instituting any legal action in the courts. Once a lawsuit is initiated, the employee must establish a prima facie case by demonstrating that organizational policies or behaviors had an adverse impact on members of a protected group. The onus is then on the organization to prove that the adverse impact was based on legitimate reasons. They can do so by proving that the policies or behaviors relate to a business necessity or a bona fide occupational qualification.

3. **Discuss the basic tenets of Title IX and the law's impact on sport and physical activity.**

Title IX requires that educational programs receiving federal funds provide equal opportunities for males and females. Athletic departments must abide by one of three standards to comply with the law. The standards are aimed at providing athletic opportunities and funding for members of the underrepresented sex, which is most often women. The effects have been substantial: The number of females participating in sport has increased, as has the funding for these activities. On the negative side, however, the proportion of women in leadership positions has decreased, as more men assumed these roles.

Questions for Discussion

1. The ADA is the primary legislation protecting persons with disabilities. Think about a health and fitness organization with which you are familiar. In what ways is that organization not ADA compliant? Are there steps the managers can take to become compliant?

2. What are the primary defenses against discrimination available to an organization? In your estimation, is one defense better than the other? Why?

3. What are the basic tenets of Title IX, and what are the steps an athletic department can take to comply with the law?

4. What are the various outcomes of Title IX, both good and bad?

Learning Activities

1. Interview a manager of a sport organization. Ask her about the collective impact of equal employment legislation on her staffing and employment decisions. Based on the interview, do you think that this legislation will be needed in the future? Why or why not?

2. Though federal mandates outlawing weight and sexual orientation discrimination do not exist, various cities and municipalities have adopted their own ordinances. Use the Web to identify some of these cities and municipalities. Compare the ordinances. Which do you think will prove most effective and why?

Resources

SUPPLEMENTARY READINGS

Carpenter, L. J., & Acosta, R. V. (2005). *Title IX*. Champaign, IL: Human Kinetics. (Most comprehensive text related to Title IX available; examines the law as applied to numerous areas; considers the influence of the law on subsequent outcomes, such as participation and coaching.)

Landry, F. J. (Ed.). (2005). *Employment discrimination litigation: Behavioral, quantitative, and legal perspectives*. San Francisco: Jossey-Bass. (Edited text that provides scenarios from the perspective of both the plaintiff and the defendant; includes questions related to race, sex, disability, and age.)

Sharp, L. A., Moorman, A. M., & Claussen, C. L. (2007). *Sport law: A managerial approach*. Scottsdale, AZ: Holcomb Hathaway. (Approaches legal issues in sport from a managerial perspective; sections on Title IX, sexual harassment, and disabilities.)

WEB RESOURCES

- Department of Justice (www.usdoj.gov/crt/emp/faq.html): answers frequently asked questions related to employment discrimination.

- National Women's Law Center (www.titleix.info/): site devoted to Title IX issues.

- U. S. Equal Employment Opportunity Commission (www.eeoc.gov/): contains guidelines, facts, and figures.

- WomenSport International (www.sportsbiz.bz/womensportinternational/taskforces/wsi_position_statement.htm): position statement on sexual harassment and abuse of girls and women in sport.

References

Accused skeleton coach's suspension upheld. (2006, January 10). MSNBC.com. Retrieved March 22, 2006, from www.msnbc.com/id/10658008/print/1/displaymode/1098/

Acosta, R. V., & Carpenter, L. J. (2006). *Women in intercollegiate sport: A longitudinal study—twenty-nine year update—1977–2006.* Unpublished manuscript, Brooklyn College, Brooklyn, NY.

Americans with Disabilities Act, 45 C.F.R. 843(j)(2)(i) (1985).

Bell, M. P., McLaughlin, M. E., & Sequeira, J. M. (2004). Age, disability, and obesity: Similarities, differences, and common threads. In M. S. Stockdale & F. J. Crosby (Eds.), *The psychology and management of workplace diversity* (pp. 191–205). Malden, MA: Blackwell.

Bobko, P., & Roth, P. L. (2004). The four-fifths rule for assessing adverse impact: An arithmetic, intuitive, and logical analysis of the rule and implications for future research and practice. In J. Martocchio (Ed.), *Research in personnel and human resource management* (Vol. 23, pp. 177–198). Oxford, UK: Elsevier.

Cardinal, B. J. (2003). Fitness for all: Is your club ADA compliant? *Club Industry, 19*(5), 31–34.

Carpenter, L. J., & Acosta, R. V. (2005). *Title IX.* Champaign, IL: Human Kinetics.

Cunningham, G. B., & Sagas, M. (2002). The differential effects of human capital for male and female Division I basketball coaches. *Research Quarterly for Exercise and Sport, 73,* 489–495.

Cunningham, G. B., Sagas, M., & Ashley, F. B. (2003). Coaching self-efficacy, desire to head coach, and occupational turnover intent: Gender differences between NCAA assistant coaches of women's teams. *International Journal of Sport Psychology, 34,* 125–137.

DeHass, D. (2004). *2003–04 race and gender demographics of NCAA member institutions' athletic personnel.* Indianapolis, IN: The National Collegiate Athletic Association.

Dessler, G. (2003). *Human resource management* (9th ed.). Upper Saddle River, NJ: Prentice Hall.

Fitzgerald, L. F., Shullman, S. L., Bailey, N., Richards, M., Swecker, J., Gold, Y., et al. (1988). The incidence of dimensions of sexual harassment in academia and the workplace. *Journal of Vocational Behavior, 32,* 152–175.

Gelfand, M. J., Fitzgerald, L. F., & Drasgow, F. (1995). The structure of sexual harassment: A confirmatory analysis across cultures and settings. *Journal of Vocational Behavior, 47,* 164–177.

Hasbrook, C. A. (1988). Female coaches: Why the declining numbers and percentages? *Journal of Physical Education, Recreation, and Dance, 59*(6), 59–63.

Hayes-Thomas, R. (2004). Why now? The contemporary focus on managing diversity. In M. S. Stockdale & F. J. Crosby (Eds.), *The psychology and management of workplace diversity* (pp. 3–30). Malden, MA: Blackwell.

Marshall, A. M. (2005). *Confronting sexual harassment: The law and politics of everyday life.* Burlington, VT: Ashgate.

Mathis, R. L., & Jackson, J. H. (2006). *Human resource management* (11th ed.). Mason, OH: Southwestern.

Matisik, E. N. (2005, January 21). Men's basketball coach sexually harassed women's basketball coach. *College Hoopsnet.* Retrieved March 22, 2006, from www.collegehoopsnet.com/specials/050121.htm

NASPE (2000, Fall). Sexual harassment in athletic settings. Naspe@aahperd.org. Retrieved November 7, 2006 from www.aahperd.org/naspe/pdf_files/pos_papers/sex-harr.pdf

Ployhart, R. E., Schneider, B., & Schmitt, N. (2006). *Staffing organizations: Contemporary practice and theory* (3rd ed.). Mahwah, NJ: Lawrence Erlbaum.

Sharp, L. A., Moorman, A. M., & Claussen, C. L. (2007). *Sport law: A managerial approach.* Scottsdale, AZ: Holcomb Hathaway.

Wright, P., Ferris, S. P., Hiller, J. S., & Kroll, M. (1995). Competitiveness through management of diversity: Effects on stock price valuation. *Academy of Management Journal, 38,* 272–287.

Managing Diverse Organizations

Aboriginal, or First Nations, people in Canada are disadvantaged in many ways. Consider the following statistics: the poverty rate is comparable to that in developing nations, 25 percent of all adults are unemployed, the suicide rate among youth is 500 percent greater than non-Aboriginals, and the incidence of alcohol and drug abuse is high. Aboriginal persons have several barriers to sport and physical activity participation including:

■ a general lack of awareness,

■ economic difficulties,

■ insensitivity to Aboriginal culture and traditions,

■ a lack of Aboriginal coaches and/or coaches who are cognizant of the Aboriginal culture,

■ the substantial distance of many villages from sport venues,

■ lack of governmental financial support,

■ racism, and

■ an inadequate sport infrastructure.

Because of these issues, the Canadian federal government took several steps to improve the quality of life among Aboriginals. Together with economic and social policies, the government is using sport as a way to achieve this goal. Sport is viewed as a tool for economic development and as a mechanism that engages citizens, overcomes social constraints, and contributes to cohesion among people in a community. Sport Canada, the sport governing body in Canada, is on record as being "committed to contributing, through sport, to the health, wellness, cultural identity, and quality of life of Aboriginal Peoples."

Sport Canada actively works with governmental agencies, Aboriginal communities and leaders, and other entities to achieve the following goals:

LEARNING OBJECTIVES

After studying this chapter, you should be able to:

■ Discuss the four models for managing diversity in sport organizations.

■ Outline the methods managers can use to implement diversity management strategies.

■ Provide an overview of the leadership competencies necessary in diverse organizations.

- *Enhanced participation.* Sport Canada is increasing the participation of Aboriginal peoples in sport at all levels by providing equitable access, developing programs that meet their unique needs, involving Aboriginal persons in the planning and development of sport, and targeting youth participation.

- *Enhanced excellence.* Sport Canada creates an environment that welcomes Aboriginal peoples to national teams and encourages high performance levels by increasing the number of qualified Aboriginal athletes, coaches, and officials by providing access to and support for quality facilities, training, and development.

- *Enhanced capacity.* Sport Canada seeks to improve the capacity of individuals, groups, and communities in support of Aboriginal sport in Canada by identifying the needs of Aboriginal people, providing facilities, promoting Aboriginal leaders, and maintaining cultural sensitivity.

- *Enhanced interaction.* Sport Canada increases the levels of communication and interaction among Aboriginal peoples and other sport and governmental entities at the federal, provincial, and local levels.

The Canadian government recognizes that for Canadian sport to be successful, all people must have access to it and provided an opportunity to achieve excellence. Sport Canada's policies are aimed at driving "the actions necessary to create and maintain an inclusive Canadian sport system that supports Aboriginal participation in sport from playground to podium."*

DIVERSITY CHALLENGE   R E F L E C T I O N

1. In your opinion, how viable is sport as a vehicle for creating social change? Explain.

2. How effective are the goals outlined by Sports Canada? Are there any you feel might be especially effective? Less effective?

3. What are other sport-related strategies that could be implemented to decrease the disparities Aboriginal peoples face?

4. Are you aware of other instances where sport has been used as a vehicle for promoting change among members of a social group?

---

*Information adapted from *Sport Canada's Policy on Aboriginal Peoples' Participation in Sport.* Retrieved March 28, 2006, from www.canadianheritage.gc.ca/progs/sc/pol/aboriginal/2005/1_e.cfm.

A s the Diversity Challenge illustrates, organizations or government entities will often implement strategic initiatives aimed at diversity issues. Here, Sport Canada's strategies sought to (a) decrease the negative effects of diversity in a particular context by improving the quality of life of a certain group of people and (b) capitalize on the unique cultural attributes that Aboriginal peoples and their sports could bring to the overall fabric of Canadian sport. These strategies are referred to as diversity management. Recall from Chapter 1 that diversity management is a proactive, strategic action aimed at capitalizing on the benefits diversity brings to organizations. In its ideal form, diversity management is strategic and proactive, and emphasizes the manner in which managers realize the advantages of diversity while minimizing its potential disadvantages.

The purpose of this chapter is to provide an overview of strategies that can be used to manage diversity in sport organizations. The focus here is largely macro, as we will consider the organization as a whole, as well as the top leaders within the organization. Chapter 12 deals with more micro issues related to diversity management at the group level. The first section discusses four primary models for managing diversity in sport organizations. The next two sections consider how organizations implement diversity strategies and how managers can ensure the success of their diversity management efforts. The final section discusses the influence of leadership in diverse organizations.

Implicit in the arguments presented in this chapter is the notion that diversity management techniques are desired, especially by persons from diverse backgrounds. However, this might not always be true. It is possible that such strategies may be perceived as providing remedial training for racial minorities, women, and so on. For example, a special program designed to provide racial minorities with leadership opportunities may create the perception they are deficient from Whites in

PROFESSIONAL
P E R S P E C T I V E S

Potential Unintended Effects of Diversity Management Programs. Fitzgerald Hill is the President of Arkansas Baptist College, located in Little Rock. He earned a Ph.D. in Higher Education Leadership from the University of Arkansas in 1997, served as the assistant head football coach at the University of Arkansas from 1998 to 2000, and was the head football coach at San Jose State University from 2000 to 2004.

Hill participated in many conferences and programs while coaching in the NFL (prior to college coaching) and NCAA. Reflecting on those experiences, he suggested that the diversity management programs in place in these sport organizations, as well as others like them, may have unintended effects. These entities often have special programs to provide extra training for minority coaches. According to Hill, these programs, in essence, suggest to African American coaches that they are not qualified, so they need extra training. The same message, however, is not conveyed to White coaches, as no special programs exist for them. "They are saying we are not qualified or that we are inept," Hill explained. "This can be dehumanizing in nature."

As Hill's comments suggest, the diversity programs in the NFL and NCAA may have negative effects on those they are intended to benefit. It is important to remain cognizant of these potential effects when implementing such initiatives.

that area and thus need additional training. Fitzgerald Hill articulates this point in the Professional Perspectives box on the previous page. This is not the intention of the diversity management initiatives described in this chapter. Rather, all of the initiatives are aimed at capitalizing on the positive effects of diversity while minimizing its potential disadvantages. Capitalizing on the positive effects of diversity entails providing an equitable workplace for all people, irrespective of their surface- or deep-level differences.

Diversity Management Strategies

Many examples are presented throughout this book of insensitivity toward others or a general lack of understanding of cultural differences that resulted in negative outcomes for organizations. Yet another example is found in the Diversity in the Field box on the following page. Often these problems can be avoided by using appropriate diversity management strategies. Although many diversity management models exist, both in the general business and psychology literature (e.g., Cox, 1991; Thomas, 1996), this section focuses on four models that are specific to the sport context.

DeSensi's Model

DeSensi (1995) developed one of the earliest models for managing diversity in the educational and sport context. Her model was built on the notion that managing diversity "involves increasing the consciousness and appreciation of differences associated with heritage, characteristics, and values of different groups" (p. 35). She adopted the term *cultural diversity* to refer to both the surface- and deep-level differences discussed in earlier chapters. DeSensi suspected that effective diversity management strategies would provide many benefits to organizations, such as an increased understanding of different people and cultures and a reduction or elimination of prejudice and discrimination.

Drawing from various sources (e.g., Chesler & Crowfoot, 1990; Cox, 1991), DeSensi (1995) proposes that diversity revolves around five organizational dimensions: mission, culture, power, informal relations, and major change strategies. Examining these dimensions reveals at which of three stages of multiculturalism an organization exists.

■ **Monocultural:** Diversity and diverse people are either ignored or deliberately excluded. The organization's culture revolves around the norms and mores of those people who traditionally have been in charge—that is, White men. These organizations are likely to be hierarchical in nature, with power residing at the top with White men. Communication patterns are likely to be segregated, such that people are more likely to communicate with others who are similar to the self. Diversity initiatives in these organizations usually only result from litigation, demands placed on the organization by external constituents, or in rare cases, elite people within the organization.

- **Transitional:** There is a stated desire to increase organizational diversity. Though gains are made, some of the remnants of the monocultural organization remain: (a) aspects of discrimination are still present, albeit in lesser forms; (b) the norms of White men dictate the organizational culture, though they may be challenged; (c) the power is still primarily in the hands of White men, though a few women and minorities might rise to the top; (d) informal communications may cross social group boundaries, but discussions of very important issues are only held with like others; and (e) some diversity initiatives are present (e.g., administrative mandates, affirmative action programs, "awareness" training).

- **Multicultural:** Diversity is valued and viewed as contributing to the organization's overall effectiveness. The organizational culture values diverse perspectives, and prejudice and discrimination are largely nonexistent as a result of stiff sanctions imposed for such actions and beliefs. A multicultural team holds the power. The organization has a sense of community, and communication lines cross racial, gender, and other cultural boundaries. These organizations actively combat external social oppression and have performance appraisal systems in place that reward people for multicultural work.

DIVERSITY *in the field*

A Little Diversity Management Would Have Helped. The NFL's San Francisco 49ers created a video that was shown to the players as part of a diversity training seminar. The video was supposed to illustrate how the players should handle the media in a town as diverse as San Francisco. Although the film was intended for diversity purposes, its "over the top" content had the opposite effect—it was offensive to many who viewed it. The film included racial slurs, a spoof of an Asian man trying to translate the sports section of a newspaper, a lesbian wedding followed by the two women engaging in heavy petting, considerable profanity, and ended with a man and three topless women engaging in a four-way hug. The video, intended only for the players, was secretly released to the media. As a result, many in the 49er organization spoke out against it, arguing that it was "absolutely contradictory to the ideals and values" of the sports franchise. The person who made the video, Kirk Reynolds, subsequently left the franchise (Matier & Ross, 2005). As this situation illustrates, even people who are charged with developing diversity initiatives may need diversity training themselves.

DeSensi's (1995) work is significant for several reasons. First, it was the earliest theory-based conceptualization of diversity management in the sport context. Although others have since followed suit, DeSensi's work provided the groundwork. Second, she specifically identified many organizational factors that she perceived as contributing to workplace diversity. Such specification allows managers to focus on key areas in the organization to implement their diversity strategies. For these reasons, DeSensi's model is valued.

Doherty and Chelladurai's Model

Doherty and Chelladurai (1999) define cultural diversity as "the unique sets of values, beliefs, attitudes, and expectations, as well as language, symbols, customs, and behaviors, that individuals possess by virtue of sharing some common characteristic(s) with each other" (p. 281). They began with the premise that aligning diversity with organizational objectives creates synergy for the organization, thereby improving the overall effectiveness. They also suggest that it is the *management* of diversity—not just diversity itself—that results in positive outcomes for the organization.

Doherty and Chelladurai (1999) believe that organizations can be characterized as either those with a culture of similarity or those with a culture of diversity. Organizations with a *culture of similarity* are generally rigid, avoid risks, are intolerant of uncertainty, are task-oriented, and view differences as deficits. As a result, these organizations are likely to have closed communication lines, a process-based performance appraisal system, one-sided decision making, and closed group membership. Organizations with a *culture of diversity* have very different values, assumptions, and outcomes—they are characterized by a respect for differences, a tolerance of risk and ambiguity, are people- and future-oriented, and acknowledge that there are often many ways to accomplish tasks. The organization's communication lines are likely to be open, and they are likely to have outcome-based reward systems, multilevel decision-making systems, and open group membership.

Drawing from this dichotomy, Doherty and Chelladurai (1999) identify cultural diversity outcomes that result from each type of organizational culture—similarity or diversity. See Exhibit 11.1. Their two-by-two framework is as follows:

- **Low cultural diversity, organizational culture of similarity:** The organization is unlikely to realize any benefits of diversity.

- **High cultural diversity, organizational culture of similarity:** The organization is unlikely to realize any benefits of diversity; negative outcomes may result.

- **Low cultural diversity, organizational culture of diversity:** The organization *may* realize some benefits of diversity, but not many because of the low cultural diversity.

- **High cultural diversity, organizational culture of diversity:** The positive effects of cultural diversity are likely to be strongest, and the organization is most responsive to its environment.

Doherty and Chelladurai's (1999) work is significant for several reasons. First, it has a strong theoretical foundation. As discussed in Chapter 2, models with such a grounding are likely to be the most useful for sport organization managers. Second, Doherty and Chelladurai explicated on both the values and assumptions underlying a particular culture and manifestations of that culture,

Graphic representation of the Doherty and Chelladurai model.   *Exhibit 11.1*

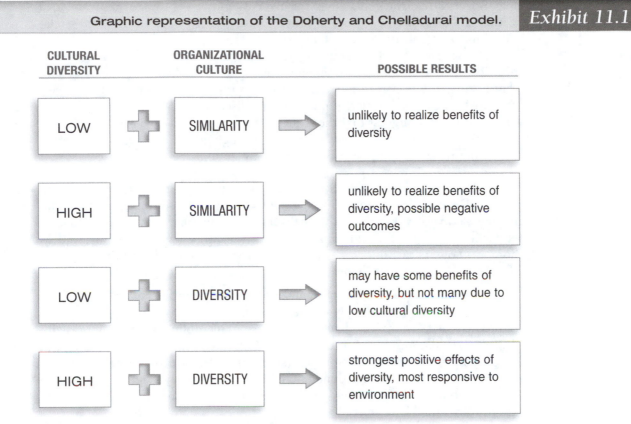

CULTURAL DIVERSITY		ORGANIZATIONAL CULTURE		POSSIBLE RESULTS
LOW	+	SIMILARITY	→	unlikely to realize benefits of diversity
HIGH	+	SIMILARITY	→	unlikely to realize benefits of diversity, possible negative outcomes
LOW	+	DIVERSITY	→	may have some benefits of diversity, but not many due to low cultural diversity
HIGH	+	DIVERSITY	→	strongest positive effects of diversity, most responsive to environment

allowing us to decouple the intricate effects of culture on subsequent outcomes. Third, their model specifically considers context. Cultural diversity is not expected to result in positive effects in all situations. Rather, there must be a fit, or a match, between the diversity level and the organization's culture for the positive effects to be realized.

Fink and Pastore's Model

Fink and Pastore (1999) drew extensively from the business literature to develop their model of diversity management. They support the social need for diversity in organizations and the moral obligation to provide an equitable workplace for *all* people. They recognize, however, that not all organizations will embrace the social aspects of diversity; rather, a business reason provides a stronger rationale. They note, "while it would be wonderful for all of those in positions of power to recognize the moral and social advantages of diversity, it may not be a realistic goal. Thus, for diversity initiatives to be truly embedded within the organization, those in power must be convinced of diversity's relationship to organizational effectiveness" (p. 315).

Using these ideas, Fink and Pastore (1999) propose four categories of organizations: noncompliance, compliance, reactive, and proactive. They realize that an organization may not fall neatly into one category or another; nevertheless, it is useful, for clarity purposes, to discuss them in isolation. Further, Fink and Pastore suggest that the strategies can be viewed on a continuum such that an organization is likely to move through a compliance stage before becoming reactive. The specific categories are as follows:

- **Noncompliance:** Noncompliant organizations are monocultural in nature (DeSensi, 1995) and do very little to follow state and federal guidelines related to diversity. Employees view diversity as a liability or a deficit (Doherty & Chelladurai, 1999), and those in power seek to keep the organization as homogeneous as possible. Lines of communication are rigid, and there are few prospects for voluntary change.

- **Compliance:** Compliant organizations still view diversity as a liability, but efforts are made to comply with equal employment opportunity laws—likely because of a feeling of "having to" do so. This obligation to comply with diversity regulations may breed resentment among Whites and among men in the organization toward persons unlike them or toward diversity in general. Persons from diverse backgrounds may be employed, but little is done to help them succeed in the "majority" culture. Lines of communication are rigid, and the power is held by a select few.

- **Reactive:** Reactive organizations are viewed as a "big leap" (Fink & Pastore, 1999, p. 323) from compliance organizations because diversity is deemed an asset, not a liability. Top decision makers acknowledge that diversity, and its effective management, can result in greater organizational success. Therefore, efforts are made to create a diverse work environment, one that gleans the positive effects of employee differences. Because of their reactive nature, however, many attempts at effective diversity management are "one shot" (e.g., once-a-year diversity seminar). If these attempts fail, then other efforts may be thwarted. Furthermore, as with compliance organizations, diversity initiatives are sometimes met with resistance, and a backlash is felt from those who traditionally have held the power.

- **Proactive:** Only proactive organizations realize the full benefits of diversity. These entities take a broad view of diversity and value diversity to its fullest extent. Company policies, procedures, and practices are all focused on developing a diverse workforce and effectively managing differences. Because all employees benefit from the positive outcomes associated with diversity, the backlash against such initiatives seen in other organizations is not present. These organizations generally have a different structure than their counterparts—one that is flexible, with open lines of communication, and where the power is shared by diverse persons.

Although there are many similarities between Fink and Pastore's (1999) model and the models proposed by DeSensi (1995) and Doherty and Chelladurai (1999), only Fink and Pastore's model was empirically tested, allowing us to determine whether their propositions materialize in real-life settings.

Both studies were conducted in the athletic setting. The first study, by Fink, Pastore, and Riemer (2001), involved collecting data from persons in NCAA Division I athletic departments. Their results revealed that most athletic departments employed compliance strategies, followed by proactive strategies, and finally reactive strategies. They also examined the strategies' outcomes. Both the compliance and proactive strategies significantly contributed to desired organizational outcomes such as attracting and retaining talented workers, employee satisfaction, employee involvement in decision making, the presence of a creative workplace, and overall workplace diversity. These findings largely support their proposed model.

In a subsequent study, Fink, Pastore, and Riemer (2003) focused on the diversity management strategies in NCAA Division III athletic departments because of the major differences between Division I and Division III departments. Because the former have more employees, larger budgets, and are generally more diverse than the latter, they serve as an interesting contrast. The study's results identified interesting similarities to and differences from their previous work. As in their Division I study, Fink et al. found that compliance strategies were more characteristic of Division III programs, followed by proactive strategies and reactive strategies. However, the effects of using proactive strategies were stronger in the Division III context than in the Division I setting. Among Division III universities, only the proactive strategies held a significant association with the recruitment of talented workers, the existence of a diverse fan base, the presence of a creative workplace, and overall workplace diversity. These results suggest that because Division III universities are generally not known for their diversity, those departments that do employ proactive strategies are better able to realize the strategies' benefits.

Chelladurai's Model

The final model was developed by Chelladurai in 2005. In addition to being the most contemporary, it is perhaps the most comprehensive macro-level model developed for the sport context. Chelladurai's model primarily differs from the three models discussed previously in its explicit emphasis on competence, a point also emphasized by others (Lawson & Shen, 1998; Thomas, 1996). From his perspective, employers will be able to attract a diverse workforce if the primary focus of all hiring decisions is the applicants' competency. As Lawson and Shen argue, "no one group of members has a monopoly on competence; rather, dif-

alternative
P E R S P E C T I V E S

The False Hope of Competency. Chelladurai (2005) and others (Lawson & Shen, 1998; Thomas, 1996) emphasize the need to focus on competency when making employment or other similar decisions. On the surface, this idea has considerable merit, as it potentially diminishes the influence of biases and other factors not directly pertinent to the job. In some situations, however, this practice can have an adverse impact on members of particular social groups. For example, consider a university that uses only academic competence to select its students. This is a sound selection technique because universities typically try to select the brightest students for their programs. By using such an admission standard, we might expect that those students who attend prestigious high schools, who take college preparatory courses, or who receive private tutoring have the best chance for admission. Of course, these options cost money and require resources—something only available to certain people. This selection technique, therefore, has a disparate impact on racial minorities, persons from lower socioeconomic circumstances, and persons in rural settings. It is not that these other people cannot learn or lack motivation; rather, they simply were given different opportunities in their lives. In most cases, when these students attend universities, they excel in the classroom. This example illustrates the problem with focusing solely on competency—it ignores situational and historical factors that influence one's outcomes. Although competence should be a cornerstone, other factors must be considered, such as one's ability to learn or be trained, motivation, personality, and overall fit with the organization.

ferent persons have different competencies" (p. 80). Employers who focus on competency first should attract a wide variety of people, all of whom, though they may have a similar level of competency, may differ in other respects. See the Alternative Perspectives box for a discussion about focusing *solely* on competency.

Chelladurai (2005) adopts a different approach to classifying the various diversity forms (recall the discussion of surface- and deep-level characteristics in Chapter 1) by identifying four categories:

- *Appearance or visible features* refer to such characteristics as sex, race, age, or skin color—surface-level attributes.
- *Behavioral preferences* refer to penchants for things such as certain foods or clothing.
- *Values and attitudes* are forms of deep-level differences that can only be ascertained through interaction with a person.
- *Cognitive orientations* are forms of how people differ at a deep level and relate to one's technical, human, and conceptual skills.

Chelladurai suggests that the four categories are expressed in one of two ways: symbolically or substantively. *Symbolic expressions* are identified by symbols such as Muslims' clothing preferences or Catholics' food preferences during Lent. *Substantive expressions* are related to the values, attitudes, preferences, and orientations that people have.

Chelladurai (2005) suggests that all management efforts begin with valuing diversity—that is, an awareness of the personal differences among employees, an acknowledgment of such differences, and an understanding that they can add value to the workplace.

Managers who value diversity use one of two management strategies—accommodation or activation. *Accommodation* occurs when managers permit symbolic expressions of diversity so long as the expressions do not interfere with task performance. For example, it is reasonable to allow a woman from India to wear a sari or a Christian to wear a cross necklace because neither expression impedes the work process. Setting aside a room for the Muslim employees to use for their daily prayers is another accommodation strategy.

Activation strategies are concerned with more substantive expressions, and involve intentionally bringing employees with divergent values or perspectives together to work in groups on projects because such heterogeneous perspectives produce better decision making and more creative solutions—a position consistent with the managerial theories discussed in Chapter 2 (Gruenfeld, Mannix, Williams, & Neale, 1996; Pelled, 1996).

It is hard to envisage a time when accommodation strategies should not be permitted; however, activation strategies might work better in some situations than in others. Chelladurai (2005) recognized this and identified two key moderating variables: task complexity and task interdependence. For simple tasks, activation strategies are not necessary and may even impede the process. When activities are simple and straightforward, employees can rely on past experiences or organizational procedures to guide their actions (Jehn, Northcraft, & Neale, 1999). With more complex tasks, however, it is desirable to have many perspectives in the group. Complex tasks are not routine and a good outcome is likely to be a function of the various group ideas and preferences.

Task interdependence, or the degree to which employees work closely with one another, is also thought to influence the usefulness of activation strategies. When employees do not work closely with one another, the effects of diversity are likely to be neutralized. When employees work closely and rely on one another to complete their tasks, the effects of diversity are likely to be realized (see also Doherty & Chelladurai, 1999).

Chelladurai's (2005) model draws from previous works in the sport context to provide a comprehensive integrated model. This is a user-friendly model because it considers the four diversity forms, acknowledges that the ways in which people differ are not the same, and uses moderators to determine whether and when particular strategies should be implemented.

Sport Industry Support for Diversity Management

Several sport industry reports and awards related to diversity indicate how well the various sport entities manage it. Although rarely published in academic journals, these contributions are noteworthy because of the attention they receive among industry professionals and in the popular press. A brief overview of two are presented next.

Racial and Gender Report Card

Richard Lapchick, often referred to as the "racial conscience of sport," is the founder of the Institute for Diversity and Ethics in Sport, an organization that regularly publishes reports focusing on racial equality issues and/or student-athlete education. Perhaps the most influential of these publications is the semi-annual *Racial and Gender Report Card*. This comprehensive report outlines the racial and sex distribution of administrators, employees, and athletes in virtually every segment of American sports including all of the professional sport leagues, university athletic departments, and the NCAA. Scores are assigned based on the proportion of persons from various social groups relative to their representation in the general U. S. population. The *Report Card* also outlines the major diversity initiatives each sport entity has initiated (for an overview, see Exhibit 11.2). Without doubt, Lapchick's publications are regarded as the most authoritative works related to diversity in the sport context.

Exhibit 11.2	Diversity initiatives among the major sport entities in the United States.

Diversity management strategies used by major sport entities.

- **Major League Baseball (mlb.com):** This league seeks diversity not only in its employees, but also in a wide range of product and service offerings. The league has initiatives in place to ensure diversity in the following areas: suppliers, player development, community relations, education, and philanthropic awards.

- **Major League Soccer (mlsnet.com):** MLS was the first league to require diversity training for all employees *and* players in 1998. The league adopted a Diversity Initiative that guarantees a focus on diversity throughout league operations. There is also a Diversity Committee that consists of administrators from each team who share best practices in diversity management. MLS Futbolito (MLSFutbolito.com), which targets Hispanic youth, is the largest grassroots diversity strategy among any of the professional sport leagues.

- **National Basketball Association (nba.com):** The first professional sport league to require diversity training for its employees, the league's office has mandatory training each year for its employees and encourages member teams to do so as well. The NBA maintains diverse applicant pools for its jobs and makes concerted efforts to ensure employee diversity, such as actively recruiting at Historically Black Colleges and Universities. The league also offers a Jr. NBA program that focuses on overall life skills people can maintain through their athletic careers and once those careers are over (nba.com/jmba/).

(continued)

- **National Football League (jointheteam.com):** Much of the attention on diversity in the NFL focuses on race issues. In 2002, the Rooney Rule was implemented, requiring clubs to interview at least one racial minority for head coach openings. In 2003, the Fritz Pollard Alliance, named after the first African American head coach in the league, was formed to work with the NFL to create better opportunities for racial minorities including developing a Minority Coaching Fellowship program. Such efforts have been successful, as the number of African American head coaches increased substantially from 2002 to 2005. Teams that do not follow these guidelines are fined heavily (e.g., Matt Millen, general manager of the Detroit Lions, was fined $200,000 for not interviewing a minority applicant for a then-vacant head coach position).

- **National Hockey League (nhl.com):** The NHL has many policies in place aimed at improving the diversity within the league. NHL Diversity was founded in 1995 and serves as the league's group that focuses on diversity (nhl.com/nhlhq/diversity). The annual Willie O'Ree All-State Game, named after the NHL's first African American hockey player, puts 14–16-year-old inner-city hockey players together to participate in an East versus West hockey game. The league also sponsors a "Hockey Is for Everyone Month," where the teams provide tickets to those inner-city youth who want to attend games. Finally, there are scholarship and equipment programs, both of which are aimed at inner-city youth.

- **Women's National Basketball Association (wnba.com/community/):** Much of the WNBA's diversity initiatives derive from the NBA's efforts because of the link between the leagues. However, the WNBA has other programs, most of which are aimed at girls and women. The WNBA—Be Smart—Be Fit—Be Yourself program encourages girls and women to learn more about their bodies and the importance of physical activity. The program's focus is on nutrition, self-esteem, and overall health. The league also has a Breast Health Awareness campaign aimed at increasing awareness about breast illnesses such as cancer. As of 2006, the league had earned over $2,000,000 for breast cancer research. The league also offers a Jr. WNBA program that focuses on overall life skills that people can maintain through their athletic careers and once those careers are over (nba.com/jrnba/).

- **Professional Golf Association (pga.com/home/):** In an effort to increase diversity within the golf industry, the PGA established the Diversity Internship Program in 1992. The program is available to racial minority students of African American, Hispanic, Asian, Pacific Islander, and Native American descent, providing the participants with internships in marketing, communications, information systems, and event management, among others. The PGA partnered with industry leaders (e.g., Nike Golf, Titleist) to help them diversify their workforces.

(continued)

| Exhibit 11.2 | **Continued.** |

■ **United States Tennis Association (usta.com):** The USTA views diversity as essential to achieving its overall goal of promoting and developing the growth of tennis. To this end, the organization created a Multicultural Participation Committee—its goals include (a) identifying multicultural barriers to participation; (b) developing programs to increase multicultural participation in the USTA; (c) ensuring that tennis has the appropriate links to multicultural communities; and (d) monitoring and evaluating multicultural participation in USTA programs. In addition, the USTA also promotes an adaptive tennis program (usta.com/news/fullstory.sps?iType=946&inewsid=33099).

■ **NASCAR (nascar.com):** NASCAR's Executive Steering Committee for Diversity has implemented both on- and off-track initiatives to diversify the sport. For example, the Drive for Diversity program seeks to develop drivers and crew members from diverse backgrounds. NASCAR also has diversity internship programs, an urban youth racing school, and scholarship programs at Historically Black Colleges and Universities.

■ **National Collegiate Athletic Association (ncaa.org/wps/portal):** Steps taken by the NCAA to improve the diversity and its related outcomes in college athletics include providing postgraduate scholarships for racial minorities and women, developing internship programs aimed at racial minorities and women who want to work in university athletics administration, providing matching funds to Division II and III universities that hire full-time administrators to increase the department's sex and racial diversity, giving matching grants for minority women coaches, creating a leadership institute for racial minority males, and requiring diversity education.

Adapted from *2004 Gender and Racial Report Card,* www.nhl.com, www.usta.com, www.pgatour.com, and www.workplacefairness.com.

Diversity in Athletics Award

The Laboratory for Diversity in Sport presents the Diversity in Athletics Award on an annual basis. The award's purpose is to recognize those NCAA Division I-A athletic departments that excel in seven diversity-related categories: diversity strategy, sex diversity of department employees, racial diversity of department employees, graduation of African American male student-athletes, graduation of African American female student-athletes, Title IX compliance, and overall excellence in diversity. A list of the 2005 award recipients for each category is found in Exhibit 11.3.

| Recipients of the 2005 Diversity in Athletics Award. | *Exhibit 11.3* |

OVERALL EXCELLENCE IN DIVERSITY

- Arizona State University
- Temple University
- University of Arizona
- University at Buffalo
- University of Louisiana, Monroe
- University of Nevada
- University of Tulsa
- University of Washington
- University of Wisconsin, Madison
- Washington State University

DIVERSITY STRATEGY

- Arizona State University
- Bowling Green State University
- Kent State University
- University of California, Los Angeles
- University of Iowa
- University of Washington
- University of Wisconsin, Madison

AFRICAN AMERICAN GRADUATION: MALE STUDENT-ATHLETES

- Ball State University
- California State University, Fresno
- Indiana University
- Kansas State University

- Marshall University
- Mississippi State University
- San Diego State University
- University of Akron
- University of Cincinnati
- University of Louisiana, Monroe
- University of Southern Mississippi
- University of Toledo
- Western Michigan University

AFRICAN AMERICAN GRADUATION: FEMALE STUDENT-ATHLETES

- Marshall University
- University of Akron
- University of Arizona
- University of Cincinnati
- University of Loulsville
- University of Missouri, Columbia
- University of Toledo
- University of Wisconsin, Madison

TITLE IX COMPLIANCE

- Boston College
- Clemson University
- North Carolina State University
- The Ohio State University
- Oregon State University

- San Diego State University
- Tulane University
- University at Buffalo
- University of Michigan
- Washington State University
- West Virginia University

EMPLOYEE DIVERSITY: SEX

- Arizona State University
- Auburn University
- Michigan State University
- The Ohio State University
- Syracuse University
- University at Buffalo
- University of Nevada
- University of Tennessee
- University of Tulsa
- University of Wisconsin, Madison

EMPLOYEE DIVERSITY: RACE

- Arizona State University
- Temple University
- University of Arizona
- University of California, Berkeley
- University of Hawaii, Manoa
- University of New Mexico
- University of Southern California
- University of Tulsa
- University of Washington

Source: Laboratory for Diversity in Sport, http://lds.tamu.edu

The Diversity in Athletics Award differs from Lapchick's *Report Card* in several respects. First, it examines the diversity within each department rather than college sports overall. Second, although the award does consider the proportion of racial minorities and women in the individual departments (as does the *Report Card*), it also includes other variables thought to impact the department diversity, including Title IX compliance, graduation of minority athletes, and the overall diversity strategy implemented. Even though the award focuses on a much narrower sector of the sport industry, university athletics, it provides a more in-depth analysis of the entities.

Diversity Management Processes

As you may have noticed, the theoretical models and the reports and awards by and large focus on the desired end state. They describe what an organization using, for example, a proactive strategy looks like and some of the strategy's expected outcomes. What is missing from the earlier discussions is the process of achieving that end state. Even in the Chelladurai (2005) model, which indicates when to use certain diversity management strategies, the process organizational leaders may use to achieve a diverse workforce is not explicitly described. This critique applies to most diversity management strategies in all of the management literature (Agars & Kottke, 2004), not just those in the sport context. It is important to understand, therefore, the process organizations use to successfully implement a desired diversity management strategy. To explain this process, the discussion draws from a related literature—organizational change and development.

Moving from a current diversity state (e.g., a compliance organization) to another (a proactive organization) requires change efforts. But how can managers overcome resistance to change, people's uncertainty, or the propensity for change efforts to fail? Organizational change literature identifies several possibilities—forming change teams, providing education, implementing reward systems related to diversity, and supporting top management. All of these strategies should engender employee commitment to the change efforts, which should, in turn, be related to positive outcomes (e.g., positive coping behaviors, championing behavior, remaining in the organization). A schematic representation of the relationships is presented in Exhibit 11.4.

Overcome Resistance to Change

Research shows that people resist change for a variety of reasons. Robbins (2003) notes that resistance to change can occur at both the individual (e.g., habit, security) and organizational (e.g., threat to power relationships, organizational inertia) levels (see Exhibit 11.5). For example, one of the most common reasons for resisting change is fear of the unknown. It is not that peo-

Conceptual model implementing diversity-related change. | *Exhibit 11.4*

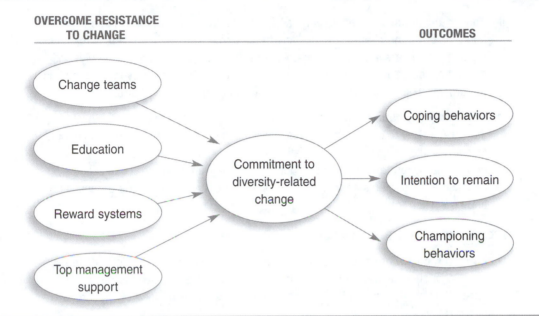

Exhibit 11.5

Forms of resistance to diversity-related change.

INDIVIDUAL RESISTANCE

- **Prejudice:** People may prefer a homogeneous workplace. This preference may come from a strong liking of in-group members or disliking out-group members.

- **Habit:** People use habits to reduce uncertainty in their lives and to increase efficiencies. The same is true for organizational policies and procedures. When diversity-related strategies are implemented, they might represent a departure from a habit, and therefore be met with resistance.

- **Security:** People with a high need for security may resist any and all change efforts because the changes might impact the power they have, the roles they assume, and so forth, all of which decrease the security people have at work.

- **Economic factors:** Some people resist change that they perceive will negatively affect them monetarily. For example, if a diversity strategy meant (or was perceived to mean) that some people would receive reduced pay increases, then they would likely resist the initiative.

(continued)

| Exhibit 11.5 | Continued. |

■ **Fear of the unknown:** People generally prefer to have an understanding of what the future holds for them, and change alters those perceptions. When diversity management strategies are implemented, people may be unsure of how the strategies will affect their jobs, the relationships they have with others, and their overall standing in the organization. If this is true, they will likely resist any change efforts.

■ **Selective information processing:** Once people form perceptions of their world, they are unlikely to change them. This unwillingness to change may result in people selectively interpreting some information, while ignoring other input. For example, people may ignore arguments as to how diversity will improve the organization because the arguments are counter to their current perceptions of the organization and how it functions.

ORGANIZATIONAL RESISTANCE

■ **Limited focus of change:** Because organizations are comprised of interrelated systems, changing one part requires changing another if the change is to have a lasting effect. Diversity initiatives often have a narrow focus that is nullified by the larger organizational system.

■ **Inertia:** Organizational inertia is the propensity for organizations to resist change and remain in their current state. Even if certain people want the change, the organizational norms and culture may act as constraints.

■ **Threat to expertise:** Changes that threaten the expertise of particular groups cause resistance. For example, hiring a diversity officer to oversee the organization's diversity efforts might be resisted by the human resource staff because that threatens their expertise in the area of hiring and employee relations.

■ **Threat to established power relationships:** In proactive organizations, the power is held by a multicultural group of people. In other organization types, the power rests primarily with White males. To the extent that diversity is viewed as disrupting established power relationships, it may face resistance.

■ **Threat to established resource allocations:** Those groups that control sizeable resources may view change efforts as a threat. For example, in university athletics, men's teams traditionally have received the lion's share of the budget. Thus, moves to increase the gender equity might be met with resistance by these players or coaches if they believe it means they will receive fewer resources.

Adapted from Robbins (2003).

ple are opposed to diversity in the workplace, they are just unsure of how it will affect them, the organization, and the relationships they have with others. This uncertainty makes people hesitant to "jump on board" with change initiatives. Therefore, it is important for managers to devise strategies to overcome this resistance.

Change Teams

Organizations are so complex and complicated that any efforts from only one person to spearhead change may be futile (Hirschhorn, 2002; Kotter, 1995). Thus, there is a need for coalitions or teams to garner support for change. This is seen in the political realm, where politicians create coalitions to gain voter support. The same principle applies to change teams in the organizational context. A change team can serve to inform others in the organization about the positive aspects of the proposed strategy, how the change will benefit them and the organization, and why they should support it. The use of teams can go a long way toward overcoming resistance.

The team's composition is important. Top managers should select those employees who hold substantial power and influence and are representative of all employees. Change teams that represent only one department or division will have difficulty gaining support from *all* employees. Finally, change team members should have a vested interest in the change itself. Championing a particular initiative is impossible if there is not a strong belief in the cause.

Education

As seen in Exhibit 11.5, much of the resistance to change might simply be due to not understanding (or being misinformed) how the change will affect people on an individual level. For example, how does an organizational focus on diversity influence the way people complete their work, the power they maintain, and the organization's outcomes? How will working with people different from the self impact such work outcomes as satisfaction, identification, or commitment? All organizational efforts to educate people about the proposed change serve to allay these fears of the unknown (Robbins, 2003). Managers should use memorandums, leader speeches, change teams, and seminars to educate employees. Regardless of the method used, it is imperative that people are apprised of *what* the change means for them and *why* it is taking place.

Reward Systems

Rewards play a powerful role in organizational life. The actions people take, the work they complete, and the quality they bring to their work are all influenced by the rewards they expect as a result of that behavior. Therefore, creative managers devise strategies to reward employees for their support of the diversity-related change efforts (Powell & Graves, 2003; Robbins, 2003). These rewards can range from a pat on the back to a bonus. For example, managers might offer a reward to those who attend diversity training workshops. When linked to rewards, participation is likely to be high, as is the perceived importance of the training.

Top Management Support

There is perhaps no more reliable reinforcement of a strategic initiative than strong, steady support from top management. When a program or procedure is perceived to lack the support of top managers, the likelihood that it will succeed is low. This is certainly true when diversity management is involved (Gilbert & Ivancevich, 2000). If diversity is made a part of the organization's overall mission, values, and goals, the managers can demonstrate their support by behaving consistently with that mission. By making diversity a central part of the organization, it factors into all strategic decisions, from who is hired to the products and services offered to the mechanisms used to market the organization's products. Strong managerial support for diversity is likely to reduce resistance to the initiative.

Commitment to Diversity-Related Change

Using change teams, educational materials, reward systems, and top management support positively influences attitudes toward diversity-related change and increase the commitment employees are likely to have toward the change.

Meyer and Herscovitch (2001) describe commitment to change as "a force (mind-set) that binds an individual to a course of action deemed necessary for the successful implementation of a change initiative" (p. 475). Though some may view commitment as a one-dimensional construct, Herscovitch and Meyer believe that commitment can take three forms: affective, normative, and continuance. People with an *affective commitment* to change support the initiative based on the belief that it will benefit the organization, while those with a *normative commitment* have a sense of obligation to support the change. Finally, those who express a *continuance commitment* to change support the initiative because they recognize the costs associated with failing to do so.

Managers are most likely to desire an affective commitment to diversity-related changes, because this type of commitment is likely to result in the most positive outcomes for the individual and the organization. Normative commitment is also desired, though the subsequent outcomes are not likely to be as strong or as positive as with affective commitment. Finally, though it might be desired in some situations, a continuance commitment to change is the least desired form (Herscovitch & Meyer, 2002).

Available research indicates that the managerial strategies to overcome resistance described earlier all have positive associations with affective and normative commitment. Herscovitch and Meyer (2002) posited that affective commitment increases when employees become involved in and recognize the significance of the change effort. All of the managerial strategies are aimed at influencing this process (e.g., Gilbert & Ivancevich, 2000; Hirschhorn, 2002; Kanter, 2004). If efforts to enlighten employees about the benefits of the change are strong enough, employees may feel obligated or a normative commitment to support the change, as failing to do so might result in the organization not achieving optimal performance. Thus, employee commitment to diversity is likely to increase when specific actions are taken to enlighten them as to the benefits of the change.

Outcomes of Commitment to Diversity-Related Change

If organizations are able to engender an affective or normative commitment to diversity-related change among the employees, then subsequent outcomes are likely to be positive. Research shows, for example, that people with affective commitment to change are also likely to effectively cope with the change (Cunningham, 2006), an important part of the change process. Cunningham et al. (2002) demonstrated that employees' confidence in their ability to cope with organizational change held a positive association with their readiness for change, participation in the change process, and perceived contribution to the change. Judge, Thoresen, Pucik, and Welbourne (1999) found that coping behavior was associated with several career outcomes—organizational commitment, satisfaction, and job performance. These are clearly desired outcomes in the context of diversity-related change.

Those employees with an affective or normative commitment to change are also unlikely to leave the organization because of the change (Cunningham, 2006)—one of the risks associated with implementing any kind of change effort. Some might argue that such turnover may be desirable because it reduces the friction created by those people who do not support the change. However, turnover is expensive. The costs of replacing an employee can range from several thousand dollars to a quarter of a million (Robinson & Dechant, 1997), and these costs do not include the potential process losses that occur when people leave their workgroups. Thus, the effects of employee turnover can be severe for an organization.

Finally, people with affective or normative commitments to change are likely to demonstrate behaviors that support the change efforts (Herscovitch & Meyer, 2002). Within the context of organizational change, championing represents the highest form of discretionary behavior. Championing requires considerable sacrifice and entails promoting the value of the change to persons within and outside the organization (Herscovitch & Meyer, 2002). As Simon, Elango, Houghton, and Savelli (2002) note, champions fight for an initiative's success, even in the face of opposition or resistance. Clearly, when implementing diversity management strategies, it is important to have people fighting for the changes because they will then take the necessary steps to ensure that the change is a success.

Diversity and Leadership

A separate but related issue to that of diversity management is leadership in diverse organizations. After all, it is the leaders in these organizations who are ultimately responsible for selecting a diverse workforce and implementing diversity strategies. Thus, it is important to consider the leadership skills and behaviors necessary for diverse workplaces. Considering this issue, Chrobot-Mason and Ruderman (2004) suggest that leaders of diverse organizations must develop a multicultural competence, which they defined as "a proficiency in diagnosing diversity issues and resolving diversity-related conflicts and organizational problems by reaching a mutually satisfying solution for all parties involved" (p. 114). They argue that developing such competence means increasing one's knowledge of cultural differences, increasing self-awareness, and developing multicultural skills, each of which is discussed next.

Knowledge of Cultural Differences

Effective leaders have an awareness of the differences in values, beliefs, and norms across various cultures (Chrobot-Mason & Ruderman, 2004). Having such knowledge allows for an organizational culture that respects differences among people. Without an awareness and understanding of the dissimilarities, it is likely that some behaviors may be offensive to others. For example, when the former San Jose MLS team moved to Houston, Texas, officials originally renamed the team Houston 1836. This was the year that Texas won its independence. What team officials failed to consider, however, is that the name might be offensive to the area's large Hispanic population, as it was from Mexico that Texas won its independence (Trecker, 2006). Because Hispanics represent a large portion of MLS fans, the team changed the name to the Dynamos. A greater knowledge of cultural differences by the Houston team officials would have enabled them to avoid this public relations problem.

Increased Self-Awareness

Chrobot-Mason and Ruderman (2004) suggest that, in addition to a knowledge of cultural differences, leaders of diverse organizations also must increase their self-awareness. Effective leaders interact with their followers on an interpersonal level. To have meaningful interactions, leaders must be aware of their own biases, prejudices, and attitudes toward those who differ from the self. This understanding helps leaders to reduce or rid themselves of such biases, thereby improving their interactions with others.

Multicultural Skills

Effective leaders develop such important multicultural skills as conflict management, interpersonal communication, feedback seeking, and role modeling (Chrobot-Mason & Ruderman, 2004).

Conflict Management

Many conflicts arise because of multicultural differences between people, and it is often incumbent upon the leader to resolve the conflicts. Haslam (2000) believes that conflicts are best resolved when the values and preferences of both sides are considered. Therefore, managers must not only understand these issues, but also develop techniques to reduce destructive forms of conflict between employees (Chrobot-Mason & Ruderman, 2004).

Interpersonal Communication

Effective leaders often interact with people on an interpersonal level (Chrobot-Mason & Ruderman, 2004). For these interactions to be useful, leaders must develop effective communication skills, and encourage trust, honesty, and openness with their followers. This is challenging in diverse organizations, where differences in power, demographic characteristics, or deep-level attributes make meaningful interactions with some followers difficult. There may be times when leaders have not had the same life experiences as their diverse followers; this is especially true when the leader is a White male. Despite these potential hurdles, effective leaders find ways to develop a closeness with their followers. As Chrobot-Mason and Ruderman note, "although it is easier to understand and empathize with people who are similar, multiculturally competent leaders will listen to dissimilar others with an open mind and attempt to understand the issues that minority members face in the workplace, even if they have never shared or witnessed this experience" (p. 119).

Feedback Seeking

Effective leaders constantly seek feedback from sources internal and external to the organization in order to evaluate their own leadership as well as the organization's policies and procedures (Chrobot-Mason & Ruderman, 2004). It is often necessary to explicitly seek feedback from diverse constituents, as they might provide unique perspectives concerning diversity issues. This feedback is acquired through interviews, questionnaires, focus groups, or informal conversations with others. For example, a manager at a city recreational center might ask local diversity leaders, the NAACP, or other entities for feedback on how well the organization is performing in such areas as staffing, the provision of recreational opportunities, and community outreach. The insights received are then used to shape future decisions.

Role Modeling

Effective leaders show a commitment to diversity. This is perhaps best accomplished through role modeling behaviors (Chrobot-Mason & Ruderman, 2004). For example, leaders should be actively involved in recruiting and hiring diverse employees, developing congruent missions and goals that emphasize diversity, and initiating and developing relationships with people from diverse backgrounds. Leaders should expand their comfort zone by placing themselves in situations where they might be the minority, thereby increasing their understanding of the experiences of dissimilar others.

 *Chapter Summary*

This chapter provided an overview of macro-level diversity management strategies, those aimed at the organization as a whole as opposed to specific groups or individuals. As illustrated in the Diversity Challenge, there is often a need to employ specific strategies to provide equal opportunities to all parties. Without such strategies, dissimilar others may have negative work experiences. Effective diversity management strategies generate positive outcomes for the organization as a whole. After reading the chapter, you should be able to:

1. Discuss the four models for managing diversity in sport organizations.

Four primary diversity management strategies are used in the sport context. DeSensi (1995) described three stages of organizational multiculturalism: monocultural, transitional, and multicultural. Organizations were classified based on five organizational dimensions: mission, culture, power, informal relations, and major change strategies. Doherty and Chelladurai (1999) proposed a model that characterized organizations as having either a culture of diversity or a culture of similarity. They expected that an organization's diversity-related outcomes would be a function of the level of its employee diversity and the specific culture. Fink and Pastore (1999) categorize organizations as noncompliant, compliant, reactive, or proactive, with the latter category being the most desirable. Finally, the Chelladurai (2005) model is based on the manifestations of diversity (i.e., symbolic or substantive) and the specific strategies a manager could employ (i.e., accommodation or activation). The choice of strategy is dependent upon the manifestation of diversity, the task complexity, and group interdependence.

2. Outline the methods managers can use to implement diversity management strategies.

Implementing any change initiatives is difficult because of people's resistance. To overcome this resistance, managers should use change teams, educate the workforce about the change and what it means for them, link change efforts to reward systems, and show strong support.

3. Provide an overview of the leadership competencies necessary in diverse organizations.

Leaders of diverse organizations must develop a knowledge of culture differences, increased self-awareness, and multicultural skills, including skills in conflict management, interpersonal communication, feedback seeking, and role modeling.

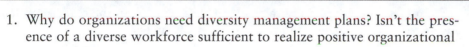

Questions for Discussion

1. Why do organizations need diversity management plans? Isn't the presence of a diverse workforce sufficient to realize positive organizational outcomes?

2. Four diversity management models were discussed in the chapter. What are the models' similarities? What are the major differences?

3. Refer to the forms of resistance listed in Exhibit 11.5. Which one might be the most prevalent in sport organizations? Which one is the most difficult to overcome?

4. Are there any methods not discussed in the chapter that managers could use to decrease resistance to diversity management programs?

5. Of the competencies that leaders of diverse organizations must have, which is likely to be most important and why?

Learning Activities

1. Suppose you are hired to manage a recreational sport facility. Which diversity management strategies would you implement? Or, would a combination of two or more strategies be the best fit? Develop a written plan for the strategy you select, and include the rationale for your decision.

2. Suppose you are trying to implement a particular diversity management strategy in your organization. Develop a written action plan outlining the steps would you take to ensure the success of the program. Address the steps necessary to present the desirability of the program to your employees and to overcome any opposition to it.

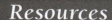

Resources

SUPPLEMENTARY READING

Mor Barak, M. (2005). *Managing diversity: Toward a globally inclusive workplace.* Thousand Oaks, CA: Sage. (Provides an overview for establishing inclusive diversity management perspectives; adopts a global perspective of diversity.)

Thomas, K. M. (2004). *Diversity dynamics in the workplace.* San Francisco: Wadsworth. (Describes the impact of diversity on a variety of organizational process and outcomes, including recruitment, socialization, and leadership.)

Thomas, R. R., Thomas, D. A., Schrank, R., Ely, R. J., & Fletcher, J. K. (2001). *Harvard Business Review on Managing Diversity.* Boston: Harvard Business School Publishing. (Leaders in the field use firsthand accounts, case studies, and practical guidance to inform the reader about ways to create inclusive, equitable work environments.)

WEB RESOURCES

- Bernard Hodes Group (www.hodes.com): consulting agency whose purpose is to develop and institute diversity management plans.

- Catalyst (www.catalyst.org): leading research and advisory organization whose aim is to help organizations build inclusive, diverse work environments.

- Diversity, Inc. (www.diversityinc.com): provides a "best practices" page for diversity management.

References

Agars, M. D., & Kottke, J. L. (2004). Models and practice of diversity management: A historical review and presentation of new integrated theory. In M. S. Stockdale & F. J. Crosby (Eds.), *The psychology and management of workplace diversity* (pp. 55–77). Malden, MA: Blackwell.

Chelladurai, P. (2005). *Managing organizations for sport and physical activity: A systems perspective* (2nd ed.). Scottsdale, AZ: Holcomb Hathaway.

Chesler, M., & Crowfoot, J. (1990). Racism on campus. In W. May (Ed.), *Ethics and higher education* (pp. 195–230). New York: Macmillan.

Chrobot-Mason, D., & Ruderman, M. N. (2004). Leadership in a diverse workplace. In M. S. Stock-

dale & F. J. Faye (Eds.), *The psychology and management of workplace diversity* (pp. 101–121). Malden, MA: Blackwell.

Cox, T. (1991). The multicultural organization. *Academy of Management Executive, 5*(2), 34–47.

Cunningham, C. E., Woodward, C. A., Shannon, H. S., MacIntosh, J., Lendrum, B., Rosenbloom, D., et al. (2002). Readiness for organizational change: A longitudinal study of workplace, psychological and behavioral correlates. *Journal of Occupational and Organizational Psychology, 75,* 377–392.

Cunningham, G. B. (2006). The relationship among commitment to change, coping with change, and turnover intentions. *European Journal of Work and Organizational Psychology, 15,* 29–45.

DeSensi, J. T. (1995). Understanding multiculturalism and valuing diversity: A theoretical perspective. *Quest, 47,* 34–43.

Doherty, A. J., & Chelladurai, P. (1999). Managing cultural diversity in sport organizations: A theoretical perspective. *Journal of Sport Management, 13,* 280–297.

Fink, J. S., & Pastore, D. L. (1999). Diversity in sport? Utilizing the business literature to devise a comprehensive framework of diversity initiatives. *Quest, 51,* 310–327.

Fink, J. S., Pastore, D. L., & Riemer, H. A. (2001). Do differences make a difference? Managing diversity in Division IA intercollegiate athletics. *Journal of Sport Management, 15,* 10–50.

Fink, J. S., Pastore, D. L., & Riemer, H. A. (2003). Managing employee diversity: Perceived practices and organizational outcomes in NCAA Division III athletic departments. *Sport Management Review, 6,* 147–168.

Gilbert, J. A., & Ivancevich, J. M. (2000). Valuing diversity: A tale of two organizations. *Academy of Management Executive, 14*(1), 93–105.

Gruenfeld, D. H., Mannix, E. A., Williams, K. Y., & Neale, M. A. (1996). Group composition and decision making: How member familiarity and information distribution affect process and performance. *Organizational Behavior and Human Decision Processes, 67,* 1–15.

Haslam, S. A. (2000). *Psychology in organizations: The social identity approach.* Thousand Oaks, CA: Sage.

Herscovitch, L., & Meyer, J. P. (2002). Commitment to organizational change: Extension of a three-component model. *Journal of Applied Psychology, 87,* 474–487.

Hirschhorn, L. (2002). Campaigning for change. *Harvard Business Review, 80*(7), 98–104.

Jehn, K. A., Northcraft, G. B., & Neale, M. A. (1999). Why differences make a difference: A field study of diversity, conflict, and performance in workgroups. *Administrative Science Quarterly, 44,* 741–763.

Judge, T. A., Thoresen, C. J., Pucik, V., & Welbourne, T. M. (1999). Managerial coping with organizational change: A dispositional perspective. *Journal of Applied Psychology, 84,* 107–122.

Kanter, R. M. (2004). The middle manager as an innovator. *Harvard Business Review, 82*(7/8), 150–161.

Kotter, J. P. (1995). Leading change: Why transformation efforts fail. *Harvard Business Review, 73*(2), 59–67.

Lawson, R. B., & Shen, Z. (1998). *Organizational psychology: Foundations and applications.* New York: Oxford University Press.

Matier, P., & Ross, A. (2005, June). 49ers' personal foul: Team's in-house training video includes lesbian porn, racial slurs, and barbs at Newsom. *SFGate.com.* Retrieved April 13, 2006, from www.sfgate.com/cgi-bin/article.cgi?f=/c/a/2005/06/01/MNGHQD1IOT1.DTL

Meyer, J. P., & Herscovitch, L. (2001). Commitment to the workplace: Toward a general model. *Human Resource Management Review, 11,* 299–326.

Pelled, L. H. (1996). Demographic diversity, conflict, and work group outcomes: An intervening process theory. *Organization Science, 7,* 615–631.

Powell, G. N., & Graves, L. M. (2003). *Women and men in management* (3rd ed.). Thousand Oaks, CA: Sage.

Robbins, S. P. (2003). *Essentials of organizational behavior* (7th ed.). Upper Saddle River, NJ: Prentice Hall.

Robinson, G., & Dechant, K. (1997). Building a business case for diversity. *Academy of Management Executive, 11*(3), 21–31.

Simon, M., Elango, B., Houghton, S. M., & Savelli, S. (2002). The successful product pioneers: Maintaining commitment while adapting to change. *Journal of Small Business Management, 40,* 187–203.

Thomas, R. R., Jr. (1996). *Redefining diversity.* New York: AMACOM.

Trecker, J. (2006, February). Report: *Houston 1836 close to name change.* Foxsports.com. Retrieved April 13, 2006, from http://msn.foxsports.com/soccer/story/5331940

12

Managing Diverse Groups*

DIVERSITY CHALLENGE

Melaleuca Elementary School is less than 10 miles from Palm Beach, Florida, where multimillion dollar mansions line the beachfront. Most of its students, however, do not come from high-income families or live in luxurious homes; rather, most students come from working-class families and 70 percent are racial minorities. Two out of three students receive free or reduced lunches.

Despite the class-related dissimilarities, these students have at least one thing in common with students from the more affluent neighborhoods: lacrosse. It is the working together toward a common goal—winning—that brings the students together. Claire Lawson, a midfielder on the team, explains, "when we're on the team, we're not focused on color or ethnic background. We're just focused on playing as team." Though the potential for race- or social class–related friction certainly exists, sport brings this diverse collection of athletes together.

In a similar fashion, in Seattle, Washington, efforts are underway to make rowing more accessible to everyone. Those students who participate learn several life lessons such as the importance of working together. Steve Gerritson, who serves as the Executive Director of the George Pocock Rowing Foundation, notes: "It teaches values that are important no matter what you are doing. . . . If you can't cooperate, you don't stay dry." It is lessons such as these that demonstrate to people the importance of team-work and overlooking potential differences in the interest of the team.**

*Portions of this chapter are adapted from Cunningham (2004).

**Information adapted from Sharp, D. (2003, June). *High-brown sports seek diversity.* USAToday.com. Retrieved April 15, 2006, from www.usatoday.com/news/nation/2003-06-15-croquet-usat_x.htm.

LEARNING OBJECTIVES

After studying this chapter, you should be able to:

- Discuss the conditions of contact under which prejudice should be reduced.

- Discuss how categorization-based strategies are used to manage diverse groups.

- Explain the integrated model of managing diverse groups.

1. In your experience, does sport serve to bring people together such that any differences are ignored? If so, explain why this occurs.

2. Have you had experiences where team member dissimilarities remained the primary focus instead of team cooperation? If so, why did this happen?

3. Does sport serve to unify other people, not just the athletes? If so, what are some examples?

As the Diversity Challenge illustrates, some groups' dynamics ameliorate any potential negative effects of member differences. This is often seen in the sport context because demographics usually do not matter on the playing field. This is not true of all athletic teams, however—we all can think of situations where the differences among team members were too great to overcome. The likelihood of individual differences subverting an otherwise positive group dynamic occurs even more often when we move away from the athletic context and consider work groups in the organizational setting, thereby suggesting that strategies must be used at the group level to reduce the potentially negative effects of diversity.

I begin this chapter with an overview of the early perspectives upon which more contemporary theories were built. The focus then turns to the social categorization perspective, with the suggestion that the key to reducing the negative effects of diversity in the group setting is to target the categorization process. This can be done in one of three ways: breaking down the categories, differentiating between the groups, or building up a superordinate identity. This chapter concludes with a discussion of an integrated model that combines the three categorization-based strategies.

The Contact Hypothesis

Allport's (1954) contact hypothesis is among the earliest and most influential theories related to reducing prejudice. Most of the contemporary theories on bias reduction are grounded in his work (Brewer & Gaertner, 2001), and many scholars and practitioners still incorporate his original piece in their efforts to reduce prejudice. The basic premise underlying Allport's *contact hypothesis* states that prejudice is sustained against others because of unfamiliarity and separation; thus, the key to reducing prejudice is to enable members of various social groups to have contact with one another under the right conditions (see also Exhibit 12.1).

| Contact under the right conditions reduces prejudice. | *Exhibit 12.1* |

PROCESSES

- Contact allows people to learn about out-group members, resulting in stereotype disconfirmation.
- Intergroup contact acts as a form of behavioral change.
- Continued positive contact will likely reduce any anxieties and may generate empathy toward out-group members.
- Contact causes a reappraisal of the in-group.

CONDITIONS

- Social and institutional support is available.
- The possibility of intimate contact exists.
- Members of the various groups have equal status.
- Cooperative interaction is required.

Adapted from Allport (1954) and Pettigrew (1998).

Pettigrew (1998) suggests that contact with dissimilar others reduces prejudice and bias because of the operation of four processes (see also Allport, 1954):

1. Contact allows people to learn about out-group members, and this increased knowledge should result in stereotype disconfirmation.
2. Intergroup contact acts as a form of behavioral change. People normally do not have extensive interactions with others who differ from the self; thus, when in-group and out-group members do interact, it is a behavior that is outside the norm, and this behavioral modification is a first step toward attitudinal change.
3. Continued positive contact will likely reduce any anxieties one feels toward out-group members and may generate empathy toward them, resulting in more positive affective ties between both groups.
4. Intergroup contact causes a reappraisal of the in-group. People learn that the in-group's norms, preferences, and values are not the only way of viewing the world. This recognition reshapes the way people view themselves and similar others.

As suggested earlier, Allport's contact hypothesis recognized that contact under *any* circumstances may not reduce prejudice, and, in fact, in some situations it might exacerbate it. Thus, Allport suggests that contact between dissimilar people improves intergroup relations under the four conditions presented in Exhibit 12.1 and discussed below.

Social and Institutional Support Is Available

Institutional support, such as from top administrators, should lead to social norms that favor intergroup interaction, tolerance, and acceptance (Allport, 1954). Early research focusing on people in housing projects demonstrated this effect (Deutsch & Collins, 1951; Wilner, Walkley, & Cook, 1955). Prejudice was higher among Whites in segregated housing projects than it was for Whites in integrated projects. For the latter group, bias was especially low when the Whites believed that interactions with racial minorities were expected.

This idea is certainly applicable to the organizational context. Group leaders often set the norms for the group, thereby prescribing acceptable modes of behavior. If the leader endorses interaction among members from different social groups (e.g., Hispanics and Whites), then that becomes the accepted way of doing things in that group. This available support, coupled with the other conditions, reduces bias among group members.

The Possibility of Intimate Contact Exists

Allport (1954) suggests that close, intimate contact is more effective in reducing bias than brief, impersonal encounters for two reasons. First, developing friendships is usually rewarding and provides a pleasurable affective experience. Second, if people interact with one another on a close, intimate level, then it is likely that this contact will result in stereotype disconfirmation. Recall from Chapter 2 that stereotypes are largely based on faulty information; thus, closely interacting with someone will expose the faulty information as such. The housing project research mentioned earlier supports Allport's contention. Those White families who lived close to African American families reported more interaction and significantly more favorable attitudes toward them, relative to the other White families (Wilner et al., 1955).

This principle is applicable to the sport organization context. Consider, for example, groups working on a project in a physical education or kinesiology class. Many times projects require students to work closely with one another over an extended period of time, allowing them to get to know one another on a more personal level. During this process, friendships may be formed or, at the very least, preconceptions and stereotypes about one another may be discredited.

Members of the Various Groups Have Equal Status

Prejudice is more likely to be reduced when the various social groups have equal status (Allport, 1954). If some members are in a subordinate role, then it is likely that stereotypes will be reinforced and strengthened (Cohen, 1984); however, if everyone is on a "common ground," then the interaction will likely result in bias reduction.

Applying this principle to sport organizations, interaction with dissimilar colleagues on the same hierarchical level is more likely to reduce bias than when the interaction is between a supervisor and a subordinate. For example, bias held by a White assistant athletic director toward Asians is reduced more when his interactions are with Asian assistant athletic directors as opposed to an Asian student worker. The interaction with the Asian assistant director involves two people who have the same power and organizational rank; hence, the equal status might result in reduced bias and prejudice. With the Asian student worker, power differences are still present between the two, so stereotypes may remain.

Cooperative Interaction Is Required

Prejudice is thought to be reduced when the situation requires cooperative interdependence among group members (Allport, 1954). Prejudice directed toward out-group members is likely to be reduced when members of separate groups have to work with one another in order to accomplish the task. Without the others' contributions, the task cannot be completed.

Brewer and Gaertner (2001) suggest that it is this principle that has received the greatest attention and support since the 1950s. This awareness was spurred in large part by Sherif's (Sherif, Harvey, White, Hood, & Sherif, 1961) Robbers Cave study, which involved 22 boys who signed up for three weeks of summer camp. They were randomly assigned to groups of 11 and subsequently named themselves the Eagles and the Rattlers. During the camp's first week, the boys participated in activities with members of their own group, not knowing that the other group even existed. During the second week, the two groups competed against one another in a series of activities such as touch football, resulting in intergroup competition and bias. However, unlike laboratory settings where in-group favoritism is common, the boys actually displayed out-group derogation—they harbored negative feelings toward the out-group—to the extent that there were hostile relations between the two groups (Gaertner et al., 2000). During the third week, the campers were brought together under noncompetitive conditions, but the hostility remained. It was not until the two groups worked together under cooperative conditions (e.g., working together to fix a truck) that the bias between the two groups began to subside. The results of this study, and the studies that support its results (e.g., Johnson, Johnson, & Maruyama, 1984), suggest that cooperative interdependence among group members can decrease levels of intergroup bias.

The efficacy of cooperative interdependence is routinely seen in sport organizations. Recall that in the Diversity Challenge, one of the players commented that her teammates' demographics did not matter while they were playing because all members focused on the team. In a highly interdependent sport such as lacrosse, teammates must cooperate in order for the team to be successful. Therefore, it is understandable that the team, not the individual differences among the members, becomes the focus of attention, thereby reducing intergroup bias.

Contact Hypothesis Limitations

Although Allport's (1954) contact hypothesis has been used extensively through-out the years, it does have three primary limitations (Brewer & Gaertner, 2001). First, most of the research was conducted in laboratory settings where contact conditions are controlled. It is possible that the expected contact outcomes may not occur when there is a history of hostility between the groups. For example, would the contact conditions reduce the biases between Palestinians and Jews? In the context of sport organizations, biases might not be as strong as those in the Middle East, but strong prejudicial attitudes exist nonetheless.

Second, bias reduction in one context might not translate to a correspond-ing reduction in another—it might not generalize to other contexts. For example, suppose players on a boys' basketball team experience a reduction in racial bias because the contact conditions are met. Does this mean that bias is reduced toward *all* racially different people in *all* subsequent situations? Probably not. That a White player's bias toward racial minority teammates is reduced in that situation does not mean that bias toward racial minority students in the class-room context will also be reduced. Thus, the effects might be context-specific. See Exhibit 12.2 for additional information related to generalization.

Third, Brewer and Gaertner (2001; see also Pettigrew, 1998) suggest that subsequent studies related to the contact hypothesis placed many boundary conditions on the general theory, resulting in the attachment of an inordinate number of qualifiers. As noted in Chapter 2, boundary conditions can be use-ful because they provide answers as to when and where certain effects are thought to occur. However, when too many conditions are placed on a theory, it is essentially rendered useless. Commenting on these conditions, Pettigrew believes that it is important to distinguish between those factors essential to bias reduction and those that facilitate the operation of the processes. For our purposes, the four conditions described previously are considered essential fac-tors, while any remaining boundary conditions (see Brewer & Gaertner, 2001) are facilitators.

Social Categorization Approaches to Reducing Bias

The limitations of the contact hypothesis meant that more sophisticated conceptualizations were needed. As Brewer and Gaertner (2001) note, "contact researchers needed a more elaborate theory of what the under-lying processes are and how they mediate the effects of intergroup contact under different conditions" (p. 456). The social categorization framework (Tajfel & Turner, 1979; Turner, Hogg, Oakes, Reicher, & Wetherell, 1987) pro-vides one such perspective. Although this approach is discussed at length in Chapter 2, it is instructive to recall the following two points:

1. In an attempt to organize their social world, people will categorize the self and others into social groups, and this process minimizes differences *within* groups while heightening differences *between* groups; and

2. People who are similar to the self are considered in-group members and are afforded more positive affect and trust than are those who differ from the self—out-group members. The end result is intergroup bias—in-group members are viewed in a more positive light than out-group members.

This theory suggests, therefore, that the potential negative effects of diversity are a function, at least in part, of the intergroup bias that exists between

---

Generalizing the effects of contact.   *Exhibit 12.2*

When bias is reduced, it can either result only for that specific situation or be transferred to other situations. The latter circumstance is termed *generalizability* and is more desired because it means bias is reduced in more than a single situation. Pettigrew (1998) identified three forms of generalization: across situations, from the individual to the entire out-group, and from the immediate out-group to other out-groups.

1. *Generalization across situations.* This form refers to the reduction in bias toward an out-group member in multiple contexts. If diversity strategies are applied in only one context (e.g., workplace training center), then bias toward specific out-group members will likely be reduced in that specific setting, but not others. When the bias reduction is generalized across settings, this means that the strategies were effective in that specific setting (e.g., workplace training center) as well as other settings (e.g., a place outside work).

2. *Generalization from an individual to the entire out-group.* Bias reduction might also be transferred from an individual to all other members of an out-group. Suppose that, as a result of a diversity training seminar, a White male coach expresses less bias toward the two African Americans in his work group—a good result. A better result is if the training results in the White coach expressing less bias toward all African Americans in all situations.

3. *Generalization from the immediate out-group to other out-groups.* To extend the previous example further, the best result is when the White coach not only expresses less bias toward individual African American coaches and African Americans in general, but also toward *all* racial minorities. This is what is meant by generalizing from the immediate out-group to all out-groups. Though seldom observed, this form of generalization has occurred in some studies (Pettigrew, 1997). As might be expected, those diversity strategies and training endeavors that have this effect are the most desirable.

Information gathered from Pettigrew, 1998.

groups. Tsui, Egan, and O'Reilly (1992) argue that the social categorization process is "fundamental to the formation of in-groups and the widely documented tendency of individuals to prefer homogeneous groups of similar others" (p. 522). Williams and O'Reilly (1998) arrived at similar conclusions after reviewing over 40 years of diversity research. They note that "it is clear that there are potentially negative consequences from social categorization processes operating in groups" (p. 118).

This literature suggests that the key to reducing the potentially negative effects of diversity in the group setting is to target the categorization process. Indeed, researchers drew from the contact hypothesis and social categorization's basic tenets to develop three strategies—decategorization, recategorization, and mutual group differentiation—thought to overcome categorization boundaries (see Exhibit 12.3). For yet another approach, see the Alternative Perspectives box.

Decategorization

Decategorization seeks to reduce intergroup bias by breaking down the categorization boundaries between interacting groups (Brewer & Miller, 1984). This strategy holds that repeated, individualized interactions among members of different groups will ultimately reduce bias. This is accomplished in two ways. First, recall that, through the categorization process, all members of a specific social group are perceived as largely homogeneous (e.g., "all women act *that* way"), and distinctions are not made between members of the group. Decategorization allows one to make distinctions between out-group members, a process called *differentiation*. Second, when people interact on a personal level with others, they compare that person to the self. This results in a process called *personalization,* where out-group members are viewed "in terms of their uniqueness and in relation to the self" (Hewstone, Rubin, & Willis, 2002, p. 589). Both processes allow one to see the self and the person

Exhibit 12.3	**Categorization-based strategies for managing diverse groups.**

- **Decategorization.** Reduces bias by breaking down categorization boundaries through repeated individualized interactions with out-group members.

- **Recategorization.** Reduces bias by building up a superordinate group identity that is inclusive of all groups.

- **Mutual group differentiation.** Reduces bias by emphasizing both the categorization boundaries and the unique contributions of each subgroup to the overall group.

with whom the interaction is occurring as *individuals,* not members of homogeneous in-groups or out-groups. To the extent that these interactions are repeated over time, this breaking down of categorization boundaries might also be applied in new situations or to hitherto unfamiliar out-group members (Gaertner et al., 2000).

alternative PERSPECTIVES

Cross-Categorization Approaches to Managing Diverse Groups. It is possible for people to maintain several identities, but each identity may simply be salient at different times and in different contexts. For example, a person might hold the identity of coach in the workplace, husband at home or during time spent with his family, Christian at church or when religious questions arise, and son when in the presence of his parents. Clearly, not all of these identities hold equal weight across all situations. Within a particular situation, each may serve as the source of categorization. At work, the person might consider other coaches as in-group members and therefore hold those coaches in higher regard than other persons in the organization. This is consistent with the categorization process outlined throughout this book.

We have been working with the assumption that people's identities are orthogonal, such that when one is important in a certain context, others are not. What would happen, however, if one could blur the distinctions of the categorization boundaries? What if a person could concurrently trigger multiple identities in a specific social context, such that, for example, the categorizations of being a coach and being a male were both salient in the work context? The answer is that the prejudice and bias that can result from a particular category distinction may be reduced. This is the essence of the *cross-categorization* argument. As

Brewer and Gaertner (2001) note, "there are reasons to expect that simultaneous activation of multiple ingroup identities both is possible and has potential for reducing prejudice and discrimination based on any one category distinction" (p. 463).

There are several reasons why this might be true. First, when multiple identities are activated in a specific context, the significance of in-group and out-group distinctions become blurred. Second, the bias toward out-group members in one category is thought to be lessened when that person is an in-group member in another category. Finally, cross cutting categorization boundaries allows for increased interactions with former out-group members—something that should ultimately reduce the level of bias toward that person (Brewer, 1999).

To illustrate, suppose the coach in the earlier example attends the same church as an opposing coach. In this situation, two categories are crossed—that of a Christian and that of a coach. In this context, the distinction of the opposing coach as an out-group member may be blurred because the coach attends the same church and is thus an in-group member in that regard. Because of the cross-categorization, the coaches are likely to spend more time with one another than they otherwise would, and biases might be reduced. Thus, the cross-categorization decreased the intergroup bias.

Considerable laboratory research supports this rationale (Bettencourt, Brewer, Croak, & Miller, 1992; Gaertner, Mann, Murrell, & Dovidio, 1989; Marcus-Newhall, Miller, Holtz, & Brewer, 1993). For example, Bettencourt et al. (1992) found that personalized interactions with out-group members reduced bias toward those out-group members who were physically present as well as toward those who were viewed on a video. Gaertner et al. (1989) found a reduction in bias when members of separate groups came to conceive of themselves as separate individuals as opposed to members of differing social groups. They also identified the manner by which the bias was reduced—decategorization resulted in less attraction toward former in-group members, or reduced in-group favoritism (see also Brewer, 1999).

Application

Although it may not be referred to as decategorization, this approach is often used in organizational and team settings. For example, many organizations use rope courses or other adventure escapes, such as those offered by Adventure Associates (www.adventureassoc.com) as methods to build a team. These programs allow people to become acquainted outside the office, build communication skills among team members, and strengthen interpersonal relationships. It is expected that boundaries among team members will be reduced, thereby increasing the team's effectiveness.

As another example, the Dallas Cup, a competitive weeklong soccer tournament held in Dallas, Texas, is designed to host youth teams from around the world. To attract these teams to the tournament, housing must be provided. This is accomplished by having those area athlete participants host several international players for the week. According to tournament organizers, the local players initially are apprehensive about hosting players so different from the self. However, by week's end, the players have become so close that tears often accompany the goodbyes. Tournament organizers attribute this closeness to the fact that the players get to know one another on a very personal level during that week and grow quite fond of one another (personal communication, Gordon Jago, November 15, 2005).

Potential Limitations

Despite the support of decategorization by various studies and its use in professional settings, the approach does have limitations. First, it is unclear how well decategorization is maintained over time or across situations (Brewer & Gaertner, 2001). For example, a common criticism of ropes courses and other adventure activities is that they might reduce bias in that specific context, but the effects may not transfer back to the workplace or athletic team. Just because two people learn information about one another and come to like each other in a particular setting does not mean that those same feelings will be expressed outside the adventure course context. On the contrary, it might be more likely that once they're back in the workplace—a setting to which the parties are accustomed—the usual routines, behaviors, preferences, and biases will recur. Even if the bias reduction is sustained for a short time, it is unclear whether the effects will last.

Second, even if bias is reduced toward specific individuals, it is unclear whether this effect can be transferred to similar persons (Brewer & Gaertner, 2001). For example, suppose that a Jew and a Muslim share personal information about one another over a period of time, lessening the categorization boundaries. Because this occurred with these two people, does that mean that the categorization boundaries that might exist between the Jew and other Muslims in other contexts will also be reduced? Although that is possible, it is more likely that the bias reduction was directed toward a specific person; consequently, the same process would have to occur with other targets.

Despite these limitations, decategorization is an effective approach to reduce bias in the group setting.

Recategorization

According to Gaertner and Dovidio (2000), who developed the Common Ingroup Identity Model, the purpose of *recategorization* is to encourage "members of both groups to regard themselves as belonging to a common superordinate group—*one group* that is inclusive of both memberships" (p. 33, emphasis in original). If members of different groups consider themselves members of a single, common group, then former membership boundaries become unimportant—now, all people are members of the same in-group. It serves to replace the "us" and "them" dynamics with a more inclusive "we." Suppose members of a racially diverse sport marketing team considered themselves as *all* belonging to a common in-group—for example, the organization's "sport marketers." If this is the primary identity source in that organization, then the group members would consider themselves "sport marketers" first, and perceive other attribute differences (e.g., race) second.

Note the differences between this approach and decategorization. In the latter, the focus is on breaking down categorization boundaries. The goal is to recognize that not all out-group members are the same, and in fact, some out-group members have characteristics similar to the self (Brewer & Miller, 1984). With recategorization, the focus is on creating a new, more inclusive category that encompasses *both* in-group *and* out-group members. Although bias is reduced through decategorization by devaluing former in-group members (Gaertner et al., 1989), bias is reduced through recategorization by bringing former out-group members closer to the self through a process known as pro-in-group bias (Gaertner & Dovidio, 2000; Gaertner et al., 2000). Former out-group members are now afforded in-group status, and because in-group members are generally viewed in a positive light, the former out-group members are now viewed that way as well.

Several studies lend support to this model, both in the laboratory and the field context. One of the earliest laboratory studies was conducted by Gaertner et al. (1989). They designed an experiment whereby they could manipulate the conditions under which groups worked with one another. They found that when two groups came together and considered themselves members of a single, common group, then intergroup bias was reduced. In line with their theoretical predictions, the bias was reduced because attitudes toward former out-group members became more positive. This supports the notion that bias in recategorized groups is reduced through the pro–in-group bias process. Subsequent laboratory research shows that recategorization is associated with more helping behaviors directed to out-group members (Dovidio et al., 1997), a satisfaction with the group (Cunningham & Chelladurai, 2004), and a preference to work with the group in the future (Cunningham & Chelladurai, 2004).

Terry and O'Brien (2001) conducted a field study involving people who had recently experienced an organizational merger. They found that these people who perceived a common identity with the employees with whom they recently merged also expressed higher levels of satisfaction. Nier, Gaertner, Dovidio, Banker, and Ward (2001, Study 2) conducted a field study related to helping behaviors directed toward African Americans by Whites. They found that Whites were more likely to help African Americans when the African Americans rooted for the same team as the Whites did, as opposed to when they did not. Finally, Cunningham (2005) conducted a field study of NCAA Division I track and field coaches. He found that coworker satisfaction among people who differ racially from their colleagues was higher when they were on staffs characterized by a common in-group identity, relative to when they were not.

All of these studies suggest that developing a common in-group identity among group members helps to reduce the potential negative effects of diversity.

Application

Gaertner and Dovidio (2000) propose several methods a group leader can use to form a common in-group identity, including

- spatial arrangement,
- common threat,
- common fate, and
- common goals.

Gaertner and Dovidio (1986) found that the *spatial arrangement* of group members could influence perceptions of a common in-group identity—members from various groups sit with one another rather than with members of their own group. Sitting only with in-group members reinforces categorization boundaries; however, sitting with people from other groups, while still in the context of a work group, team, or classroom, reinforces the perception that all of the people are members of a common group, not separate groups. See the Professional Perspectives box on the following page for another example.

Establishing a *common threat* is another method to engender a common in-group identity (Rothgerber, 1997). This is perhaps best illustrated by the September 11 terrorist attacks on the United States. After the attack, people from all backgrounds, irrespective of race, religion, sex, or other characteristics, joined together to form a united front against those who attacked the United States. The same principle applies in work groups. When there is a common enemy or common threat, people in the group will unite together to combat that threat. From a managerial standpoint, it is important to explicitly identify the threat and the danger it poses to the group or organization. For example, employees at Adidas might view other sporting goods companies such as Nike as a threat to the company's economic well-being. To the extent that the Adidas employees all perceive the threat, they are likely to be united in confronting the competitor in the marketplace.

Groups that share a common fate are also likely to form a common in-group identity (Gaertner & Dovidio, 2000). *Common fate* means that if the group does well, then all group members are rewarded. Similarly, if the group performs poorly, then all members suffer. This is often seen in highly interdependent athletic teams where irrespective of individual performances, if the team loses, then all team members suffer the effects. A common fate has a way of bringing the team together and forming solidarity among the members. It is interesting that this same principle is often ignored in the organizational context (DeNisi, 2000). For example, people who work on a team and are collectively responsible for a particular product are often erroneously compensated and evaluated on an individual basis. A work group whose members are dependent upon one another to complete their tasks are collectively responsible for the group's outputs (e.g., the products or services produced); thus, it is reasonable to reward all group members the same for the group's outputs (see Cunningham & Dixon, 2003). Managers or group leaders who adopt this approach are likely to not only incorporate effective performance appraisal systems, but are also likely to create a common identity among the group members.

The presence of common goals is also likely to create an in-group identity (Gaertner & Dovidio, 2000). *Common goals* have a way of unifying efforts among the group members toward a singular objective. When this occurs, the members are likely to work together for the sake of the team, thereby overlooking individual differences in the interest of the team. This phenomenon is seen on athletic teams where the primary objective, winning, brings the players together such that a common identity is formed. Not only is the common iden-

PROFESSIONAL
P E R S P E C T I V E S

Recategorization on a Soccer Team. Stoney Pryor, the head coach of the A&M Consolidated High School varsity girls' soccer team, observed that the team is diverse in many ways. First, the players differ in ability, so one of his primary tasks is "to get these girls of varying abilities to work together." Second, the levels of motivation differ across the team—some players participate in the hope of playing at the college level, some play to win, and others play for the mere enjoyment of doing so; thus, the girls' work ethic may not be uniform. Third, the players have varying personal styles (e.g., aggressive, offensive-minded, defensive-minded, etc.). Fourth, socioeconomic differences among the girls influence the team dynamics. Finally, the attitudes on the team can (and frequently do) vary, thereby opening the possibility of cliques.

In light of these differences, it is imperative that Pryor develop strategies that help the girls work together as a team. He accomplishes this team building by emphasizing the common group identity and conducting team building activities throughout the year. For example, team goals (e.g., district championship) are established prior to the season to ensure that the players "are working on the same goals as a team." In addition, the team members participate in considerable group work during practice to reinforce the team concept. This concept of a team is also carried outside the playing field—players regularly have team dinners (usually organized by the seniors) that encourage additional bonding and team building.

All of these activities focus on reducing the potential negative effects of differences and working together as a team. As Pryor explains, "Some differences are good. We need different positions and different personalities. But, in order for a team to work effectively, we must embrace our particular role, perform it well, and enable those around us to perform their roles. Then, we can begin to achieve the goals set forth as a team. Individual goals are fine, but in team sports, success is generally measured in how the team achieves its goals."

tity likely to reduce bias, but it is also likely to create more positive outcomes for the group (Murrell & Gaertner, 1992).

Potential Limitations

As with decategorization, there are limitations to the recategorization approach. Perhaps the most substantial question is whether a common identity is possible when the opposing groups have a history of strong animosity toward each other (Hewstone et al., 2002; Pettigrew, 1998). For example, would the formation of a common in-group identity be possible between Serbians and Croatians? Most would suspect not. Of course, not all intergroup bias is as pronounced as that example. Even in sport organizations, however, there may be a history of ill will between groups. If the bias is strong enough, if there are substantial differences in group size, or if variations exist in the status, power, or resources allocated to the groups, then efforts to recategorize might be thwarted (Brewer & Gaertner, 2001).

Just because members conceive of themselves as belonging to a single common in-group does not necessarily mean that bias will be reduced. Cunningham (2006) conducted an experiment in which demographically diverse students were randomly assigned to three-person groups. All groups worked on projects independently and then came together to form six-person groups. The six-person groups then worked on projects with the interaction, common goals, and common fate conditioning present. Subsequent checks indicated that the group members believed that the six-person group represented a single, common group, inclusive of both three-person groups. Though all groups recategorized, not all groups experienced the same level of bias reduction. Homogeneous three-person groups that merged with other homogeneous three-person groups experienced substantial bias reduction, as did diverse groups that merged with other diverse groups. However, the bias reduction was not as great when a homogeneous group merged with a diverse group. Cunningham's study showed that even when recategorization occurs, the bias reduction might be dependent upon the diversity of the groups merging together.

Finally, some critics argue that creating a single, common group forces people to give up their other identities (Swann, Polzer, Seyle, & Ko, 2004). For example, if people's strongest identification is with their organization, work group, or athletic team, this implicitly means that their other identities (e.g., race or sex) must be secondary or nonexistent. Such a group structure is akin to the cultures of similarity (Doherty & Chelladurai, 1999) or monocultural organizations (DeSensi, 1995) discussed in Chapter 11 and are not desired. Gaertner and Dovidio (2000) counter that the formation of a common in-group identity does *not* require one to give up their other identities; rather, it is possible for people to have multiple identities, all of which are important to them. In the context of academics, for example, it is possible for people to strongly identify with their functional background (e.g., sport management, biomechanics) *and* their academic department. A coach might identify as a Hispanic, a male, and a coach—three salient identities.

The limitations associated with recategorization do not necessarily negate the approach's effectiveness. Many groups successfully recategorize and reduce the level of intergroup bias and poor group dynamics.

Mutual Group Differentiation

The two previous strategies sought to reduce bias by altering the categorization boundaries, either by breaking them down (decategorization) or by creating a superordinate identity (recategorization). A third approach to reducing bias is to actually emphasize the categorization boundaries but in a way that shows the value of the differences, as is reflected in Hewstone and Brown's (1986) *mutual group differentiation* model (see also Hewstone, 1996). Specifically, bias is thought to be reduced when group members work with one another in the context of cooperative interdependence and the labor is divided so that each group's distinct capabilities are maximized. People then come to see and appreciate the unique contributions of the various groups. As a result, positive stereotypes might be formed about those group members, thereby decreasing the prevalence of bias.

Perhaps the best illustration of how these dynamics work is found in Brown and Wade's (1987) study where two separate groups came together to complete a two-page magazine article under three distinct scenarios. In the first scenario, the groups worked separately on the task, with one group completing the writing portion and the other working on the article layout. In the second scenario, the groups continued to work separately, but each completed both parts of the project; that is, they each completed some of the writing and some of the layout. In the final scenario, members of both groups worked together on the task without designating specific roles to either of the subgroups. As might be expected, intergroup attitudes were most positive when all members worked on the task, each uniquely contributing to its success; the groups came to appreciate the other's contributions, and positive attitudes resulted.

Application

The mutual group differentiation model can certainly be applied to diverse groups, especially those with functional diversity. Past research shows that bias is best reduced when members focus on their specific areas of expertise (Deschamps & Brown, 1983) and when the contributions are mutually valued (Dovidio, Gaertner & Validzic, 1998). Along these lines, Gaertner and Dovidio (2000) argue that cooperation among interacting groups "can lead to more positive intergroup attitudes when the division of labor maximizes the likelihood of achieving the groups' mutual goals" (p. 41). Within the context of cross-functional groups then, it is important for each group to contribute to the task in accordance with their area of expertise, and the group leader or manager to emphasize that the contributions of *all* participating groups led to the overall success.

Many sport organization executive boards consist of people from such functional areas as sport, banking, and marketing (see Siciliano, 1996, for an example). As noted in Chapter 8, cross-functional teams sometimes encounter process losses because of divisions along functional lines. A manager wishing to reduce the bias among the group members might assign group tasks to members from each functional area. For example, sport-related tasks (e.g., scheduling games, hiring coaches) are assigned to people with a sport background; tasks related to fund-raising and development are assigned to people with a banking or financial background; and executive board members with a marketing background are asked to obtain sponsorships for the organization. All of these are important and all contribute to the ultimate effectiveness of the sport organization. Further, because the activities are divided according to the functional groups' areas of expertise, all members can appreciate everyone's contribution (c.f. Gaertner & Dovidio, 2000).

Potential Limitations

As with the other approaches, there are shortcomings associated with the mutual group differentiation model. Refer back to the example using a cross-functional team to illustrate how people from different groups might use their unique capabilities to contribute to the overall success of the group. It is not exactly clear how the same approach might be used in groups where other forms of diversity are prevalent, for example, sexual orientation diversity. Do heterosexual employees possess specific skills or attributes that GLB employees do not? Probably not. Thus, the mutual group differentiation approach might not be appropriate in all settings.

Another limitation is that emphasizing categorization boundaries might actually have a *negative* effect. Recall that this approach holds that emphasizing group boundaries might be beneficial if both (or all) groups see the value that the out-group brings to the entity. However, there may be situations where one group might not bring value to the larger group, or the contributions might not be perceived to be as important as the other group's contributions. As Brewer and Gaertner (2001) note, "by reinforcing perceptions of group differences, the differentiation model risks reinforcing negative beliefs about the outgroup" (p. 462). Under these circumstances, emphasizing the differences among the groups actually does more harm than good.

The limitations associated with the mutual group differentiation model do not negate its effectiveness; rather, they simply inform managers and group leaders when the strategy is best used and when it should be avoided.

Integrated Model

At first glance, the three approaches for reducing intergroup bias may seem to conflict with one another. One approach calls for reducing categorization boundaries, another calls for creating a common identity, and the third calls for emphasizing the differences among the groups. Which is correct? How can they be reconciled? Pettigrew (1998) and Cunningham (2004) answer these questions. An integrated model is presented in Exhibit 12.4 and is discussed next.

Exhibit 12.4   Integrated model of categorization-based diversity management strategies.

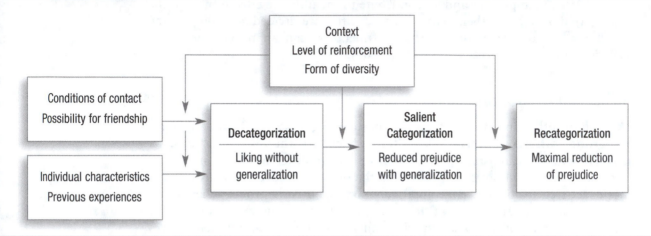

General Principles

Pettigrew (1998) suggests that Allport's (1954) conditions of contact, the potential for friendships to be formed, one's personal characteristics, and one's previous experiences all influence the initial contact between in-group and out-group members. This contact should then initially result in *decategorization,* increasing the level of liking and positive affect directed toward out-group members. This is then followed by established contact between former in-group and out-group members. Pettigrew calls this the *salient categorization* stage, which is similar to Hewstone and Brown's (1986) mutual group differentiation model. This contact between in-group and out-group members leads to a reduction in prejudice with some degree of generalization to others. The reduction of bias toward out-group members is thought to be generalized to all other members of the out-group. In the final stage, members of the various groups are *recategorized* such that a common in-group is formed. Pettigrew believes that it is in this stage that a maximal reduction in bias and prejudice is observed. Ellers and Abrams (2003) provide general support for this model, particularly with respect to the importance of friendships in reducing bias.

Moderators

Cunningham (2004) added to this model by emphasizing the importance of context as a moderator. Other potential moderators are the level of reinforcement and form of diversity.

Context. Context plays an important role in discussions of bias and prejudice because one's identity is often context specific. As Oakes (2001) notes, "we know that meaning varies with context—tears at a wedding are not the same as tears at a funeral" (p. 9). For example, an in-group member at the office might be an out-group member in another context. The same is true for diversity and categorization-based strategies in groups. Efforts to recategorize members of an athletic team, for example, may reduce racial bias among members of that specific team, but not in other situations such as when the athletes interact with members of other teams or students at the school.

It is important for managers and group leaders, therefore, to realize that categorization-based diversity strategies may only be effective in specific contexts. Usually, this is not an issue because the purpose of implementing the strategy is to reduce intergroup bias *in that context*. However, when the purpose is to generalize the reduction of bias to other contexts, strategies may have to be reinforced in those specific contexts.

Level of reinforcement. As with the diversity strategies described in Chapter 11, the categorization-based strategies require continual reinforcement to be effective (Tsui & Gutek, 1999). This is especially true if the effects are to be long-lasting. Consistent with the discussion in Chapter 11, managers and group leaders must continually monitor the diversity climate in the group and reinforce the categorization-based strategies that were implemented. Without doing so, the short-term reduction in intergroup bias is not likely to last.

Form of diversity. As previously discussed, the efficacy of categorization-based strategies may vary depending on the form of diversity. Consider the following:

■ The importance of various forms of diversity might change over time. For example, Harrison, Price, Gavin, and Florey (2002) found that demographic differences were important at the beginning of a group's formation, but deep-level diversity became more prominent as the group members remained together.

■ Some diversity forms may have historically been a source of categorization and conflict within particular organizations or work groups. For example, one's race is highly salient because of its visibility, and race issues have historically been at the forefront in society (Feagin, 2006).

■ Still other forms of diversity might be so central to one's identity that efforts to alter the categorization process associated with that form of diversity might be met with strong resistance or even hostility. For example, one's sexual orientation is usually central to who that person is, and as such, efforts to downplay or diminish that identity might be met with considerable resistance.

Chapter Summary

This chapter outlined several diversity management strategies that are used at the group level to reduce bias. As demonstrated in the Diversity Challenge, it is possible for members of diverse groups to work effectively with one another. To facilitate the groups' ability to work together, it is incumbent upon managers and team leaders to create team dynamics that alter the otherwise negative effects of social categorization. After reading the chapter, you should be able to:

1. **Discuss the conditions of contact under which prejudice should be reduced.**

According to Allport's (1954) contact hypothesis, prejudice will be reduced when the following conditions of contact exist: social and institutional support is available, the possibility of intimate contact exists, members of the various groups have equal status, and cooperative interaction is required.

2. **Discuss how categorization-based strategies are used to manage diverse groups.**

There are three primary categorization-based strategies for reducing the potential negative effects of diversity in the group context. Decategorization focuses on reducing bias by breaking down categorization boundaries through repeated individualized interactions with out-group members. Recategorization focuses on reducing bias by building up a superordinate group identity that is inclusive of in-group and out-group members. Mutual group differentiation focuses on reducing bias by emphasizing categorization boundaries and the unique contributions of each subgroup to the overall group.

3. **Explain the integrated model of managing diverse groups.**

Pettigrew (1998) suggests that the three categorization-based strategies could be integrated into a single model. Allport's (1954) conditions of contact, the potential for friendships to be formed, one's personal characteristics, and one's previous experiences all influence the initial contact between in-group and out-group members. This contact should then initially result in decategorization, which is expected to influence salient categorization (i.e., mutual group differentiation), and then recategorization. Three moderators were explicated: context, the level of reinforcement, and the form of diversity.

Questions for Discussion

1. Are there situations where asking in-group and out-group members to interact, even under the conditions of contact, might result in negative outcomes? If so, why would this happen?

2. If the conditions for contact reduce bias in one situation, will that transfer to bias reductions in other situations? Why or why not?

3. Three categorization-based strategies for reducing bias in diverse groups were discussed. Which of the three do you believe is the most effective? Why?

4. How does decategorization reduce bias between in-group and out-group members? What are the limitations of this approach?

5. How does recategorization reduce bias between in-group and out-group members? What are the limitations of this approach?

6. How does mutual group differentiation reduce bias between in-group and out-group members? What are the limitations of this approach?

Learning Activities

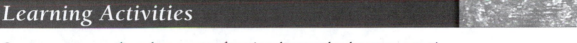

1. Suppose you are selected as a cross-functional group leader at an sporting goods company. While working in student groups, decide which of the categorization-based strategies is the best to implement to manage the diversity within the group. Be sure to identify the advantages and disadvantages of the selected strategy.

2. Interview a coach at your university or a local high school about the strategies he uses to manage the differences present on his team. How do his strategies compare with those outlined in the chapter?

Resources

SUPPLEMENTARY READING

Allport, G. W. (1954). *The nature of prejudice.* Cambridge, MA: Addison-Wesley. (The classical work on which much of the theories and perspectives espoused in this chapter are based.)

Gaertner, S. L., & Dovidio, J. F. (2000). *Reducing intergroup bias: The common ingroup identity model.* Philadelphia: Psychology Press. (Provides an excellent overview of the recategorization process, including research and practical examples.)

Turner, J., Hogg, M. A., Oakes, P. J., Reicher, S. D., & Wetherell, M. S. (1987). *Rediscovering the social group: A self-categorization theory.* Oxford, UK: B. Blackwell. (Presents the foundations of self-categorization theory and its application in various contexts.)

WEB RESOURCES

- Diversity Australia (www.diversityaustralia.gov.au/index.htm): Australian agency that promotes the benefits of diversity to various entities.

- Program of Intergroup Relations (www.umich.edu/~igrc/): program at the University of Michigan aimed at promoting an understanding of intergroup relations.

- Society for Human Resource Management (www.shrm.org/diversity/): site related to various human resource issues, including the management of diversity in work groups.

References

Allport, G. W. (1954). *The nature of prejudice*. Cambridge, MA: Addison-Wesley.

Bettencourt, B. A., Brewer, M. B., Croak, M. R., & Miller, N. (1992). Cooperation and the reduction of intergroup bias: The role of reward structure and social orientation. *Journal of Experimental Social Psychology, 28,* 301–319.

Brewer, M. B. (1999). The nature of prejudice: Ingroup love or outgroup hate? *Journal of Social Issues, 55,* 429–444.

Brewer, M. B., & Gaertner, S. L. (2001). Toward reduction of prejudice: Intergroup contact and social categorization. In R. Brown & S. L. Gaertner (Eds.), *Blackwell handbook of social psychology: Intergroup processes* (pp. 451–472). Malden, MA: Blackwell.

Brewer, M. B., & Miller, N. (1984). Beyond the contact hypothesis: Theoretical perspectives on desegregation. In N. Miller & M. B. Brewer (Eds.), *Groups in contact: The psychology of desegregation* (pp. 281–302). New York: Academic Press.

Brown, R. J., & Wade, G. (1987). Superordinate goals and group behavior: The effect of role ambiguity and status on intergroup attitudes and task performance. *European Journal of Social Psychology, 17,* 131–142.

Cohen, E. G. (1984). The desegregated school: Problems in status power and interethnic conflict. In N. Miller & M. B. Brewer (Eds.), *Groups in contact: The psychology of desegregation* (pp. 77–96). New York: Academic Press.

Cunningham, G. B. (2006). The influence of group diversity on intergroup bias following recategorization. *The Journal of Social Psychology, 146,* 533–547.

Cunningham, G. B. (2004). Strategies for transforming the possible negative effects of group diversity. *Quest, 56,* 421–438.

Cunningham, G. B. (2005). The importance of a common in-group identity in ethnically diverse groups. *Group Dynamics: Theory, Research, and Practice, 9,* 251–260.

Cunningham, G. B., & Chelladurai, P. (2004). Affective reactions to cross-functional teams: The impact of size, relative performance, and common in-group identity. *Group Dynamics: Theory, Research, and Practice, 8,* 83–97.

Cunningham, G. B., & Dixon, M. A. (2003). New perspectives concerning performance appraisals of intercollegiate coaches. *Quest, 55,* 177–192.

DeNisi, A. S. (2000). Performance appraisal and performance management: A multilevel analysis. In K. J. Klein & S. W. Kozlowski (Eds.), *Multilevel theory, research, and methods in organizations: Foundations, extensions, and new directions* (pp. 121–156). San Francisco: Jossey-Bass.

Deschamps, J. C., & Brown, R. J. (1983). Superordinate goals and intergroup conflict. *British Journal of Social Psychology, 22,* 189–195.

DeSensi, J. T. (1995). Understanding multiculturalism and valuing diversity: A theoretical perspective. *Quest, 47,* 34–43.

Deutsch, M., & Collins, M. E. (1951). *Interracial housing: A psychological evaluation of a social experiment.* Minneapolis: University of Minnesota Press.

Doherty, A. J., & Chelladurai, P. (1999). Managing cultural diversity in sport organizations: A theoretical perspective. *Journal of Sport Management, 13,* 280–297.

Dovidio, J. F., Gaertner, S. L., & Validzic, A. (1998). Intergroup bias: Status, differentiation, and a common in-group identity. *Journal of Personality and Social Psychology, 75,* 109–120.

Dovidio, J. F., Gaertner, S. L., Validzic, A., Matoka, K., Johnson, B., & Frazier, S. (1997). Extending the benefits of recategorization: Evaluations, self-disclosure, and helping. *Journal of Experimental Social Psychology, 33,* 401–420.

Ellers, A., & Abrams, D. (2003). "Gringos" in Mexico: Cross-sectional and longitudinal effects of language school-promoted contact on intergroup bias. *Group Processes & Intergroup Relations, 6,* 55–75.

Feagin, J. R. (2006). *Systematic racism: A theory of oppression.* New York: Routledge.

Gaertner, S. L., & Dovidio, J. F. (1986). Prejudice, discrimination, and racism: Problems, progress, and promise. In J. F. Dovidio & S. L. Gaertner (Eds.), *Prejudice, discrimination, and racism* (pp. 315–332). Orlando, FL: Academic Press.

Gaertner, S. L., & Dovidio, J. F. (2000). *Reducing intergroup bias: The common ingroup identity model.* Philadelphia: Psychology Press.

Gaertner, S. L., Dovidio, J. F., Banker, B. S., Houlette, M., Johnson, K. M., & McGlynn, E. A. (2000). Reducing intergroup conflict: From superordinate goals to decategorization, recategorization, and mutual differentiation. *Group Dynamics: Theory, Research, and Practice, 4,* 98–114.

Gaertner, S. L., Mann, J., Murrell, A., & Dovidio, J. F. (1989). Reducing intergroup bias: The benefits of recategorization. *Journal of Personality and Social Psychology, 57,* 239–249.

Harrison, D. A., Price, K. H., Gavin, J. H., & Florey, A. T. (2002). Time, teams, and task performance: Changing effects of surface- and deep-level diversity on group functioning. *Academy of Management Journal, 45,* 1029–1045.

Hewstone, M. (1996). Contact and categorization: Social psychological interventions to change intergroup relations. In C. N. Macrae, C. Stangor, & M. Hewstone (Eds.), *Stereotypes and stereotyping* (pp. 323–368). New York: Guilford.

Hewstone, M., & Brown, R. (1986). Contact is not enough: An intergroup perspective on the "contact hypothesis." In M. Hewstone & R. Brown (Eds.), *Contact and conflict in intergroup encounters* (pp. 1–44). Oxford, England: Basil Blackwell.

Hewstone, M., Rubin, M., & Willis, H. (2002). Intergroup bias. *Annual Review of Psychology, 53,* 575–604.

Johnson, D. W., Johnson, R. T., & Maruyama, G. (1984). Goal interdependence and interpersonal attraction in heterogeneous classrooms: A meta-analysis. In N. Miller & M. B. Brewer (Eds.), *Groups in contact: The psychology of desegregation* (pp. 187–212). New York: Academic Press.

Marcus-Newhall, A., Miller, N., Holtz, R., & Brewer M. B. (1993). Cross-cutting category membership with role assignment: A means of reducing intergroup bias. *British Journal of Social Psychology, 32,* 125–146.

Murrell, A. J., & Gaertner, S. L. (1992). Cohesion and sport team effectiveness: The benefit of a common group identity. *Journal of Sport and Social Issues, 16,* 1–14.

Nier, J. A., Gaertner, S. L., Dovidio, J. F., Banker, B. S., & Ward, C. M. (2001). Changing interracial evaluations and behavior: The effects of a common ingroup identity. *Group Processes and Intergroup Relations, 4,* 299–316.

Oakes, P. (2001). The root of all evil in intergroup relations? Unearthing the categorization process. In R. Brown & S. L. Gaertner (Eds.), *Blackwell handbook of social psychology: Intergroup processes* (pp. 3–21). Malden, MA: Blackwell.

Pettigrew, T. F. (1997). Generalized intergroup contact effects on prejudice. *Personality and Social Psychology Bulletin, 23,* 173–185.

Pettigrew, T. F. (1998). Intergroup contact theory. *Annual Review of Psychology, 49,* 65–85.

Rothgerber, H. (1997). External intergroup threat as an antecedent to perceptions of in-group and out-group homogeneity. *Journal of Personality and Social Psychology, 73,* 1206–1212.

Sherif, M., Harvey, O. J., White, B. J., Hood, W. R., & Sherif, C. (1961). *Intergroup conflict and cooperation: The Robbers Cave experiment.* Norman: University of Oklahoma Book Exchange.

Siciliano, J. I. (1996). The relationship of board member diversity to organizational performance. *Journal of Business Ethics, 15,* 313–332.

Swann, W. B., Polzer, J. T., Seyle, D. C., & Ko, S. J. (2004). Finding value in diversity: Verification of personal and social self-views in diverse groups. *Academy of Management Review, 29,* 9–27.

Tajfel, H., & Turner, J. C. (1979). An integrative theory of intergroup conflict. In W. G. Austin & S. Worchel (Eds.), *The social psychology of intergroup relations* (pp. 33–47). Monterey, CA: Brooks/Cole.

Terry, D. J., & O'Brien, A. T. (2001). Status, legitimacy, and ingroup bias in the context of an organizational merger. *Group Processes and Intergroup Relations, 4,* 271–289.

Tsui, A. S., Egan, T. D., & O'Reilly, C. A., III. (1992). Being different: Relational demography and organizational attachment. *Administrative Science Quarterly, 37,* 549–579.

Tsui, A. S., & Gutek, B. A. (1999). *Demographic differences in organizations: Current research and future directions.* New York: Lexington Books.

Turner, J., Hogg, M. A., Oakes, P. J., Reicher, S. D., & Wetherell, M. S. (1987). *Rediscovering the social group: A self-categorization theory.* Oxford, UK: B. Blackwell.

Williams, K. Y., & O'Reilly, C. A., III. (1998). Demography and diversity in organizations: A review of 40 years of research. In B. M. Staw & L. L. Cummings (Eds.), *Research in organizational behavior* (Vol. 20, pp. 77–140). Greenwich, CT: JAI Press.

Wilner, D. M., Walkley, R. P., & Cook, S. W. (1955). *Human relations in interracial housing.* Minneapolis: University of Minnesota Press.

13

Diversity Training

DIVERSITY CHALLENGE

Diversity is a significant issue in sport organizations today, and college sports is no exception. In fact, the major governing body of college sports in the United States—the NCAA—mandates diversity training for its member institutions. Noncomplying colleges and universities cannot be certified to participate in athletic competition. Such educational endeavors are aimed at providing "a positive learning environment that teaches the values of diversity and maximizes team effectiveness."

The training sessions, however, are met with mixed reviews. In one situation, all members of the 41 varsity teams at Harvard University were required to attend a training session entitled "Community Building and Diversity for Athletes." The session featured Elaine Penn, who is a motivational speaker as well as a former athlete. Penn discussed various issues related to tolerance, gender stereotypes, and racism. Although well-intentioned, the training session was viewed in a negative light. Some athletes believed that the speaker "overestimated the level of prejudice" among the athletes, while others questioned why they were required to attend the session at all. "In general sports break down stereotypes," opined one athlete. "We're exposed to a very diverse mix of people. The meeting would've been better geared toward the rest of the student body, who are exposed to much less diversity than we are." Many of the athletes left the training session feeling frustrated, claiming that the meeting was not necessary and, at times, even insulting.

Although the diversity training at Harvard had a negative effect, others hail the positive effects of these educational programs. Critical Measures,

LEARNING OBJECTIVES

After studying this chapter, you should be able to:

- Discuss the positive and negative effects of diversity training.

- Discuss the essential elements of effective diversity training programs.

LLC is an organization that specializes in cultural diversity, with the mission of "offering the finest and most authoritative diversity-related expertise in the U.S." According to this company, there are a myriad of benefits to providing diversity training in the university athletics setting, including:

- the ability to recruit and retain top athletes, coaches, and administrators from a variety of backgrounds,
- better team chemistry and performance,
- the creation of a market for women's sports, thereby potentially increasing ticket sales, and
- the reduction of both public relations and legal quandaries.

Critical Measures, LLC suggests that diversity training can positively influence an athletic department's staff, players, and overall effectiveness.*

DIVERSITY CHALLENGE **R E F L E C T I O N**

1. Have you attended a diversity training program? If so, what were your impressions of it?

2. The Diversity Challenge suggests that diversity can have both positive and negative effects. Which are more likely and why?

3. What are some of the reasons that people such as the athletes at Harvard University would oppose the diversity training? How would you address the concerns?

---

*Information adapted from www.criticalmeasures.net, www.ncaa.org, and www.thecrimson.com.

Diversity training is the educational process whereby people acquire skills, knowledge, attitudes, and abilities about diversity-related issues. The training is used to glean various benefits, both for the organization and the individuals in it. However, training generally does not always have its intended benefits, and this is certainly true with diversity training. Some people question why it is necessary, others feel they are being targeted, while still others believe that it does more harm than good. What, then, are the actual effects? Further, how do organizations that are required to conduct such training (e.g., NCAA member institutions) provide programs that generate the intended benefits? Are there steps managers can take to institute effective diversity management sessions?

The purpose of this chapter is to address these issues. The first section notes the prevalence of diversity training among organizations today. The potential positive and negative effects of such programs are then discussed. The third section discusses the four steps involved in designing effective diversity training programs: conducting a need analysis, evaluating antecedent training conditions, selecting the training methods, and ensuring effective post-training conditions. The final section addresses general program considerations. This chapter is designed to provide managers of sport organizations with the tools needed to conduct effective diversity training.

Prevalence of Diversity Training

Organizations routinely implement training programs to educate and develop their employees. Industry estimates suggest that companies spend between $55.3 billion and $200 billion annually to provide training for their employees (see Salas & Cannon-Bowers, 2001). Mathis and Jackson (2006) report that the typical organization spends about 1.5 to 2 percent of payroll costs on training its employees. This means that the average organization spends over $600 per employee on training and development activities. For some organizations—those that believe training is integral to their competitive advantage—the costs rise to $1,665 per eligible employee!

These figures are related to all forms of training—new employee orientation, technology training, and so forth. The figures for diversity training are considerably lower, though they are growing. A 1988 study of medium and large firms showed that diversity was not included among the 40 most common topics covered in training sessions (Gordon, 1988). By 2001, the Society for Human Resource Management reported that 66 percent of companies surveyed indicated that they either had a diversity training program in place or were implementing one in the near future. Large companies are more likely to implement diversity training than smaller ones, as these firms are more likely to employ a diversity manager (Rynes & Rosen, 1995). These figures represent data available for all organizations, not just those related to sport and physical activity. Data pertaining to the prevalence of diversity training in the latter organizations do not exist.

Effects of Diversity Training

At first glance, instituting a diversity training program would seem very beneficial. Providing people with necessary knowledge, skills, attitudes, and abilities about diversity would seem to be the first step toward a workplace where the positive effects of diversity are realized. However, there are some instances where these educational programs are met with resistance and actually do more harm than good, as illustrated in the Diversity Challenge. This section outlines both the positive and negative effects of diversity training in the organizational context.

Positive Effects

A review of the literature (Bendick, Egan, & Lofhjelm, 2001; Holladay, Knight, Paige, & Quinones, 2003; Mathis & Jackson, 2006; Plummer, 1998; Rynes & Rosen, 1995; Wentling & Palma-Rivas, 1999) suggests that diversity training can have many positive effects (see Exhibit 13.1).

- **Attract and retain a diverse set of employees:** Organizations that have diversity training programs show a commitment to diversity and the inclusion of all people irrespective of their individual differences. This commitment is a source of organizational attraction for potential job applicants from diverse backgrounds. Diverse job holders who react positively to such efforts strengthen their attachment to the organization and their stay intentions.

- **Maintain high worker morale:** Diversity training programs can reduce friction among in-group and out-group members. If this occurs, then the overall morale may increase.

- **Foster understanding among groups:** Diversity training sessions are usually designed to identify the fallacies of stereotypes. At the same time, they give people from various groups an appreciation of how out-group members experience work and interact with others. These factors should result in a greater understanding and harmony among members of various groups.

- **Curb lawsuits:** Diversity training can reduce the number of lawsuits brought against the organization. When employees have a greater understanding and knowledge of equal employment, discrimination, and harassment laws, it is likely that the incidence of diversity-related lawsuits will decline.

- **Contribute to organizational success:** The purpose of all training programs is to ultimately contribute to the organization's success by generating greater financial returns, reducing turnover, and so forth.

This review suggests that diversity training brings real benefits to an organization. The positive outcomes are seen in human resource issues, legal issues, and overall firm effectiveness.

Negative Effects

Although diversity training can positively benefit the organization, there are times when the programs are actually detrimental. A review of the diversity training literature (Arai, Wanca-Thibault, & Shockley-Zalabak, 2001; Bendick et al., 2001; Hemphill & Haines, 1997; Holladay et al., 2003; Jackson, 1999; Karp & Sammour, 2000; Lindsay, 1994; Plummer, 1998; Tallarigo, 1998; Thomas, 1996) identifies several potential drawbacks (see Exhibit 13.1).

- **Discusses sensitive issues:** Oppression, lack of opportunity, prejudice, discrimination, sexual harassment, and other related issues are sometimes viewed as "hot button" issues. Those issues, along with politics and religion, are generally considered to be outside the realm of polite conversation. Lindsay (1994) equated diversity training to discussing the "undiscussable" (p. 19). Training session conversations can create a tense environment, one in which people do not feel open to freely convey their thoughts. Such contexts are generally not enjoyed.

- **Code for affirmative action:** Occasionally diversity training initiatives are viewed as efforts by the organization to implement affirmative action strategies. For White men, such actions are often viewed in a negative light and ultimately reduce their support for the programs.

- **White men feel they are being "blamed":** Some White men who participate in diversity training may feel that they are the targets of the training

| Positive and negative effects of diversity training programs. | *Exhibit 13.1* |

POSITIVE EFFECTS

- Attract and retain a diverse set of employees
- Maintain high worker morale
- Foster understanding among groups
- Curb lawsuits
- Contribute to organizational success

NEGATIVE EFFECTS

- Discusses sensitive issues
- Code for affirmative action
- White men feel they are being "blamed"
- Reinforce stereotypes and categorization boundaries
- Sensitize trainees to existing problems
- Lack of positive organizational effects

or that they are being blamed for any negative effects of diversity. This is especially true when the training focuses on topics such as prejudice and discrimination. When White men have these perceptions, they are unlikely to support the training.

- **Reinforce stereotypes and categorization boundaries:** Many diversity training sessions focus on relevant stereotypes intending to expose employees' faulty perceptions of out-group members. Unfortunately, it is possible that the training has the opposite effect—rather than breaking down categorization boundaries between in-group and out-group members, the boundaries are likely to be reinforced.

- **Sensitize trainees to existing problems:** Diversity training programs make people more aware of diversity-related issues, the prejudice present in organizations and society at large, and the inequitable distribution of resources and opportunities. Trainees become more attuned to such issues and take special note of their work experiences, intent upon discovering whether discrimination is taking place. If this occurs, the incidence of diversity-related lawsuits and grievances may actually increase rather than subside, thereby having the opposite effect of what was intended.

- **Lack of positive organizational effects:** When poorly designed, diversity training has a null or negative effect on the organization's overall effectiveness.

These findings suggest that not only might such training create friction and discomfort among the trainees, but it might also actually *increase* the number of diversity-related grievances and negatively influence organizational processes and outcomes.

Making Sense of the Effects

The literature reviews provide conflicting information. On the one hand, diversity training has positive effects on the trainees, decreases legal issues, and provides value to the organization. On the other hand, this training may be viewed negatively by certain employees, sensitize people to existing issues, or negatively influence the organization's outputs. How, then, do people make sense of these varying effects? The answer lies in the design, implementation, and transfer of the diversity training. When the training sessions are ill-conceived, held simply for the sake of satisfying external constituents, or do not have the support from important organizational decision makers, they are unlikely to be successful. When the training is designed for the organization's specific needs, is a central part to the organization's mission, and has top management support, it is likely to benefit the trainees and the organization as a whole. Therefore, it is important to learn how to design and deliver effective diversity training programs. This is discussed in the next section.

Designing and Delivering Effective Diversity Training Programs

When developing a diversity training program be aware that *there is no one model that is best for all organizations* (Plummer, 1998; Sussman, 1997). Many consulting organizations offer the same "cookie cutter" diversity training program to every organization with which they consult. Some administrative bodies require that certain elements be covered in the training held by its institutions. Many university systems offer the same training (usually in an electronic format that takes several *minutes* to complete) on all of its campuses. There are several reasons why such standardization occurs, including issues related to consistency, reliability, and cost effectiveness. Nevertheless, most, if not all, of these programs are likely missing out on the true positive effects that diversity training offers.

To truly realize the benefits, it is imperative that the training be tailored to the needs of the specific organization. For some organizations, issues related to sexual orientation or religious differences may be most salient. For others, harassment of and discrimination against women may be the source of stress and friction. For still other organizations, diversity issues may not be a source of consternation; the organization simply seeks to reinforce principles and values. Because the list of potential diversity issues present in a specific organization is virtually endless, it is foolish and irresponsible to offer the same training to all organizations. Instead, the training must be personalized for each organization. Designing and delivering an effective diversity training program requires managers to conduct a needs analysis, examine the antecedent training conditions, decide on the specific training topics and methods, and consider various post-training factors (e.g., training evaluation, transfer of training). Each of these issues is discussed in turn (Mathis & Jackson, 2006; Salas & Cannon-Bowers, 2001). An illustrative summary is presented in Exhibit 13.2.

Designing effective diversity training programs.   *Exhibit 13.2*

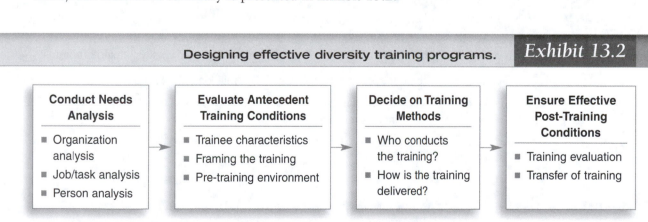

Conduct Needs Analysis	Evaluate Antecedent Training Conditions	Decide on Training Methods	Ensure Effective Post-Training Conditions
■ Organization analysis ■ Job/task analysis ■ Person analysis	■ Trainee characteristics ■ Framing the training ■ Pre-training environment	■ Who conducts the training? ■ How is the training delivered?	■ Training evaluation ■ Transfer of training

Needs Analysis

Salas and Cannon-Bowers (2001) note that "it is well acknowledged that one of *the most* important steps in training development is conducting a training needs analysis" (p. 475, emphasis added; see also the Diversity in the Field box for related information). Unfortunately, there is some evidence that preliminary analyses are not conducted (Arthur, Bennett, Edens, & Bell, 2003). This is disappointing because a *needs analysis* is instrumental to understanding *where* training is needed, *who* needs the training, and *what* material should be included in the training (Goldstein, 1993). A needs analysis covers three areas: the organization, the jobs tasks, and the people. See Exhibit 13.3 for the four primary motivations organizations have for conducting diversity training.

When conducting a needs analysis, remember that not all deficiencies are training-related problems. For example, poor customer relations may be due to a lack of cultural awareness on the part of the service provider. It could also be, however, that the method for providing the services is flawed, that the service provider simply lacks the motivation to provide high-quality services, or that the support needed to provide the service is lacking. Obviously, these latter issues pertain more to structural or managerial factors than they do diversity issues; thus, once a problem is identified, managers must critically analyze the source of the problem and take appropriate action.

Organizational Analysis

The organizational analysis requires managers to examine all of the elements of an organization that may affect the training's effectiveness (Salas & Cannon-Bowers, 2001). This includes the congruence of the training with the

---

Exhibit 13.3	Motivations for diversity training.

A recent study identified four primary motivations for initiating diversity training programs:

- To increase productivity and improve customer relations (82.1%)
- To comply with federal, state, and local mandates related to equal employment opportunity and prevent related lawsuits (37.4%)
- To enable an organization to effectively operate in the international business arena (27.2%)
- To fulfill requirements associated with a diversity-related lawsuit (4.8%)

Adapted from Bendick et al. (2001). Respondents could choose more than one response.

organization's overall mission and strategy, the monies available to deliver the training, and the level of support from top management. This is a critical first step in the overall needs analysis process because it will identify any constraints or barriers to delivering an effective training program. Salas and Cannon-Bowers note that too many organizations neglect this step; consequently, the training is not as successful for them as it is for those organizations that do the analysis.

Research suggests that the organizational climate and support from top management are particularly important to the training process (Rouiller & Goldstein, 1993; Wentling & Palma-Rivas, 1999). Organizations with a culture of diversity (Doherty & Chelladurai, 1999) are likely to have more supports in place to allow the trainees to apply the information they learn in the training session to the workplace. Because diversity and individual differences are valued in these organizations, the importance attached to the training is likely to be amplified. Top management support is also key. Without management backing, employees might question how important diversity and the related training really is, potentially undermining the training's overall effectiveness.

Job/Task Analysis

A job/task analysis entails collecting information related to the specific duties of each job, the conditions under which employees complete the job, and the specific knowledge, skills, and abilities necessary to complete the tasks (Salas & Cannon-Bowers, 2001). The job and task requirements are then compared to the existing performance level, and if a discrepancy exists, training might be needed

DIVERSITY *in the field*

How a Needs Analysis Shows the Need for Diversity Training. Kemp Elementary School is a public school located in Bryan, Texas. The students are largely economically disadvantaged (97 percent receive free or reduced lunches), and the racial composition of the school is very diverse, with 45 percent African American, 50 percent Hispanic, and 5 percent White. The staff recently conducted an organizational needs analysis to assess how well the school was serving the students' needs. According to school principal Kellie Deegear, several of the findings pointed to the need for diversity training. First, the staff is comprised predominantly of White females and thus does not match the demographic composition of the students. Second, African American students are overrepresented in special education, alternative education, and in-school suspension, while being underrepresented in the gifted and talented programs and on the honor roll. Third, the top 12 most challenging students from a discipline standpoint are all African American males. Fourth, there are large gaps between African American test scores on standardized tests and the scores of students of other races. Deegear notes, "as a staff, we believe we need to change so we can meet the needs of all students." She also notes that the following quote from Lisa Delpit, director of the Center for Urban Educational Excellence and the Benjamin E. Mays Professor of Urban Educational Leadership at Georgia State University, serves to guide their diversity efforts: "The key here is not the kind of instruction but the attitude underlying it. When teachers do not understand the potential of the students they teach, they will underteach them no matter what methodology."

(Mathis & Jackson, 2006). This analysis is useful because it identifies areas where the employee training can be made more effective.

A job/task analysis is certainly necessary to accurately forecast what skills will be needed for future jobs (Arvey, Salas, & Gialluca, 1992), but it is also useful for developing diversity training for existing employees. For example, the level of interaction with others likely varies from job to job within most sport organizations. Employees in customer service, public relations, and marketing have the most interaction with a sport organization's customers and clients. Thus, it is more useful to tailor their diversity training to meet the needs of the customers rather than other organization employees. Although this example is somewhat simplistic, it does show how conducting a job/task analysis is beneficial to developing the training program.

Person Analysis

The third prong of the needs analysis involves the organization's people (Salas & Cannon-Bowers, 2001). Analyzing the people can be accomplished by examining employees' performance appraisals and focusing on those portions that highlight deficiencies (Mathis & Jackson, 2006). Although some organizations include diversity-related criteria on their performance appraisals (Gilbert & Ivancevich, 2000), most do not. Thus, managers must develop alternative methods to identify the employees' specific needs. One option is to distribute an organization-wide questionnaire that assesses employee attitudes (and potentially behaviors) toward diversity issues. A sample item might be, "All employees within the organization, irrespective of their differences, are treated fairly" (agree or disagree). Another option is to purposefully observe employees and their interactions with others and with clients.

However the information is collected, it is imperative that managers understand the training needs of each employee. As is discussed through this book, each person brings different diversity-related experiences, attitudes, preferences, and behavioral tendencies to the workplace. These differences influence the employees' attitudes toward work, the manner in which they interact with their colleagues, and the way they serve the customers. Where deficiencies exist, training is needed to achieve the desired behaviors and attitudes.

Antecedent Training Conditions

Before designing and implementing the training program, it is important to ensure that optimal training conditions are in place. Salas and Cannon-Bowers (2001) argue that "events that occur before training can be as important as (and in some cases more important than) those that occur during and after training" (p. 447). Managers should be particularly mindful of three antecedent training conditions: the trainees' characteristics, the framing of the training, and the pre-training environment.

Trainee Characteristics

Four characteristics influence the trainees' readiness to learn the material: (a) ability to learn, (b) self-efficacy, (c) motivation to learn (Mathis & Jackson, 2006; Salas & Cannon-Bowers, 2001), and (d) learning style.

Ability to learn. All employees do not have the same ability to learn the training material. For some, a lack of overall cognitive ability may impede their capacity to learn new material. Many studies show that one's general cognitive ability is a reliable predictor of training effectiveness and knowledge acquisition (see Colquitt, LePine, & Noe, 2000; Kaemar, Wright, & McMahan, 1997). For other trainees, there may be language differences that inhibit the learning process. Still other trainees might simply lack the reading and writing capabilities necessary to learn the material. To correct these deficiencies, Mathis and Jackson (2006) suggest three options:

- Offer remedial training to current employees who lack those skills.
- Knowingly hire people who are deficient in those skills and provide specific training in the workplace.
- Work with local schools and agencies to better educate future employees.

These recommendations are global, and for some companies (e.g., smaller sport organizations), might represent unrealistic demands. The key is to ensure the employees have the ability to learn. For example, if the majority of the workforce is Spanish speaking, then perhaps the training should also be presented in Spanish, or at least the option should be available. If the workforce is not computer-savvy, then develop the training in both an electronic and a paper-and-pencil format. The point is to guarantee that employees are at least capable of learning the material.

Self-efficacy. Bandura (1986) defines self-efficacy as "people's judgments of their capabilities to organize and execute courses of action required to attain specific types of performances" (p. 391). Self-efficacy is related to a variety of behavioral outcomes such as the choice of activities and the effort expended in those activities. Within the training context, self-efficacy refers to an individual's belief that she *can* learn the material presented. Research in this area shows that the self-efficacy people possess prior to the training session is reliably related to their performance (i.e., knowledge acquisition) in the training and their ability to apply the concepts to the work context (Colquitt et al., 2000).

What steps can managers take to increase trainees' self-efficacy? The extant literature (Colquitt et al., 2000; Gist & Mitchell, 1992) points to several possibilities, including:

- Showing that people with characteristics similar to the trainee successfully completed the training session. For example, a manager of a group of elderly volunteers could provide data that illustrates the high number of people of a similar age who successfully completed the training.

- Explaining why the training is needed and how it will benefit them. A manager of an inner-city recreational facility might demonstrate how multicultural training will help reach, communicate with, and positively affect the organization's clientele.

- Persuading trainees that they have the skills and capabilities necessary for knowledge acquisition. Trainers might make the initial training sessions easy to ensure early success among the participants. This success is then used to show the trainees that they have the required skill set.

Motivation. Noe and Schmitt (1986) define training motivation as the "specific desire on the part of the trainee to learn the content of the training program" (p. 501). Trainees must not only have the capacity to learn, but they must also have the desire to learn. Without the latter, even the best-developed program will be for naught (Tannenbaum & Yulk, 1992). Indeed, research shows that training motivation is positively associated with a variety of important training outcomes, including learning outcomes (Mathieu, Tannenbaum, & Salas, 1992; Tracey, Hinkin, Tannenbaum, & Mathieu, 2001), affective reactions (Quinones, 1995; Tracey et al., 2001), post-training self-efficacy (Cunningham & Mahoney, 2004), and perceived training transfer (Facteau, Dobbins, Russell, Ladd, & Kudish, 1995). Furthermore, Colquitt et al. (2000) found that training motivation predicted important training outcomes even beyond the effects of one's general mental ability.

Research identifies various factors that influence training motivation. One factor is personality, as people who are conscientious are more likely to have confidence in their capacity to learn the material (Martocchio & Judge, 1997) and are likely to possess a strong desire to do so (Colquitt & Simmering, 1998). Others found that organizational attachment positively relates to training motivation (Cunningham & Mahoney, 2004)—those people who are vested in the organization and strongly identify with it will want to learn the training material in order to better the entity. Furthermore, people are likely to be more motivated to learn when they see the value in the learning (Colquitt et al., 2000; Cunningham & Mahoney, 2004). Managers should demonstrate how diversity training not only benefits the individual trainees, but also the organization as a whole. Finally, people's general attitudes toward diversity influence their attitudes toward diversity training. For example, Wiethoff (2004) argues that people who have experienced discrimination in the past might be more likely to express a motivation to learn in diversity training sessions. We might expect similar trends with people who strongly value fairness or who believe that diversity is beneficial to the organization and its employees.

Learning style. Because people learn in different ways, it is important for managers to understand the differences before designing and implementing a

training session. Mathis and Jackson (2006) suggest that there are three primary learning styles: auditory, tactile, and visual. *Auditory* learners retain the most
information when they can hear the instructions or material. *Tactile* learners
prefer to touch and feel things; thus, they should be given material they can
touch. Finally, *visual* learners retain more when they can watch or see the material. Although it may be difficult to individualize the material for each trainee,
all three learning styles should be incorporated into the material. Part of the
training may be presented using a lecture format, another portion delivered
electronically, and a final portion through hands-on activities such as role-play-
ing. This approach allows for the most effective training by diversifying the
training techniques to account for different learning styles.

Framing the Training

Managers must consider how they frame or depict the training. Research across
a variety of disciplines shows that the manner in which an event or behavior is
framed substantially influences people's behaviors and attitudes. Framing is
particularly important when it involves "hot button" issues (Holladay et al.,
2003). For example, people's view toward affirmative action often depends on
how those policies are framed (Crosby, Iyer, & Sincharoen, 2006). People are
more likely to favor affirmative action when it is viewed as a way organizations
reach out to traditionally disadvantaged groups as opposed to when it is perceived as a quota system. The way that a policy is framed or contextualized
influences subsequent reactions to it.

In the context of diversity training, considerable research suggests that
pre-training attitudes and beliefs influence subsequent motivation and performance (Hanover & Cellar, 1998; Holladay et al., 2003). Holladay et al.
explicitly considered two aspects of framing on trainees' subsequent attitudes:
the title of the training ("Diversity Training" versus "Building Human
Relations") and the scope of the training (a focus only on racial issues versus
a broad focus on race, sex, personality, and lifestyle differences). They found
that these two factors interacted to predict backlash to the training and likelihood of training transfer. Training that had a direct title (e.g., "Diversity
Training") and a broad focus received less backlash than the other training
formats. The same was true for the likelihood of transfer—trainees in a program that had a direct title and broad focus were the most likely to use the
information in their work. Thus, the manner in which managers frame the
training is likely to substantially influence the way people view the training
and the likelihood that they will use the information in the future.

Pre-Training Environment

The last antecedent of which managers must be mindful is the pre-training
environment. Several factors contribute to the pre-training environment: sup-

port for the training from both managers and coworkers, the training's (in)voluntary nature, and the link between the material and subsequent job-related behaviors.

Support. As previously noted, support is one of the most important factors contributing to the training's success (Wentling & Palma-Rivas, 1999; Wiethoff, 2004). This support comes from supervisors and coworkers. Wiethoff argues that, although support can positively influence people's training motivation, this effect is likely to be moderated by the extent to which employees are motivated to comply with their supervisors and coworkers. Trainees who believe there is support for the training and who are highly motivated to act in accordance with their coworkers and supervisors are more likely to reap the benefits of diversity training than their counterparts.

(In)voluntary nature of training. There is some debate as to whether diversity training should be mandatory or voluntary. As you recall from the Diversity Challenge, the athletes at Harvard resented being required to attend the diversity training. Wiethoff (2004) suggests that mandatory training might be counterproductive because it may result in less positive attitudes among the trainees. On the other hand, others argue that mandatory training conveys the message that the training is important to upper management (Cunningham & Mahoney, 2004). This is especially true when the top management team members attend the training session.

Link between the training and other outcomes. Trainees are likely to be motivated to learn and apply the information when doing so is linked to subsequent job performance and evaluations (Bendick et al., 2001; Wiethoff, 2004). If people believe that they can use the information in their jobs, that their performance evaluations will be tied to doing so, and that their pay raises are linked to applying the information to their everyday work, then the training is likely to be successful. If employees do not make such causal links, then the motivation to learn and transfer the information is likely to be low, thereby limiting the training's effectiveness. After presenting information related to multicultural competence, a manager might have the trainees role-play situations where they can use the recently learned knowledge in a scenario they will likely encounter in their everyday work settings.

Training Methods

The next steps in designing a diversity training program are to consider who will conduct the training and how the material will be delivered. Exhibit 13.4 provides information about the topics that are routinely covered in diversity training sessions.

| Topics typically covered in diversity training programs. | *Exhibit 13.4* |

- Issues of discrimination, prejudice, and stereotypes in the workplace

- Ways in which diverse groups can work well with one another

- Explanation of how a diversity training program contributes to organizational effectiveness

- Explanation of the client organization's policies related to diversity issues

- Fair and nondiscriminatory processes for recruitment, hiring, performance appraisals, and promotion

- Backlash from White males

- Cultures of various demographic groups (e.g., employees, customers/clients, community)

- Using the training on the job

Adapted from Bendick et al., 2001.

Conducting the Training

Although many people can conduct the training program, it is necessary to determine whether the training is done by someone within the organization or by an outside consultant. The advantages and disadvantages of each alternative are presented next.

Internal training. It is usually advantageous for the diversity training to be conducted by a person within the organization. Some sport organizations may have human resource personnel on staff who are specifically trained in this area. When there is no staff person available, persons with an expertise in diversity issues or who have had diversity training could lead the sessions. Using in-house personnel reduces the costs associated with the training. Because an in-house trainer likely has a working knowledge and understanding of the specific diversity issues facing the organization, the training can be made more individualized.

Despite these advantages, there are disadvantages to an internal approach. First, the scope of diversity issues is broad, and the trainer's expertise might be limited in some areas. Second, many sport organizations do not have a full-time human resource professional on staff, and others who might conduct the training may have had limited training. Thus, the training's effectiveness may be reduced. Third, trainees might be reluctant to discuss issues or disclose certain information to trainers with whom they work—another factor that can limit the program's overall success.

Outside training. There are many advantages to hiring an individual or firm to conduct the training session. There are many organizations that offer these services such as Critical Measures, LLC (www.criticalmeasures.net), highlighted in the Diversity Challenge. These firms specialize in diversity training and have the knowledge and expertise necessary to conduct high-quality programs. Outside trainers are detached from the organization and therefore from the emotional baggage that might accompany some of the diversity issues. They can, therefore, provide a more objective assessment of the diversity issues and effectively train the employees from a third-party perspective. Employees may be more inclined to discuss sensitive diversity issues with people outside the organization.

Using outside personnel, however, also has its disadvantages. The costs may be substantial, consuming a substantial portion of a small organization's training and human resource budget. In addition, some outside agencies standardize their training, presenting the same information to every organization with which they consult. Although efficient, this practice is not likely to benefit the sport organization, as it has specific diversity-related needs that must be addressed.

Training Delivery

If an in-house trainer will be used, the next decision is to consider how the training will be delivered. (If the training is conducted by an external agent, that person or organization will design the delivery.) Mathis and Jackson (2006) identify four delivery methods: cooperative training, instructor-led classroom, distance training, and simulations.

Cooperative training. This approach blends classroom training with on-the-job experience, and usually involves a school-to-work transition, internships, or apprenticeship training. It is most often used with new employees, combining the classroom learning with the real-life experience on the job.

Among the many advantages to this approach, perhaps the greatest is the opportunity for the trainee to combine the theories and principles learned in the classroom with the work context, gaining practical firsthand experience. This form's primary disadvantage is that it is more useful in some situations, such as with new employees, than others.

Instructor-led classroom. The most widely used form of training involves a trainer presenting the material primarily using a lecture format, discussions, case studies, and videos. Using many methods to deliver the information accommodates the trainees' various learning styles.

This method has several advantages. First, the information can be conveyed to a relatively large group of people. Second, this approach lends itself to the presentation of diversity issues aimed at providing factual information or, in some instances, to programs aimed at changing attitudes. A disadvantage is that trainees may be adverse to listening to a straight lecture, especially if it lasts for an extended period of time. Also, trainees get little hands-on experience with this method.

Distance training. Distance training is one of the newest and fastest growing forms of training delivery. This training can be delivered using correspondence packets, video conferencing, Internet classes, and voice-over PowerPoint presentations. Software such as WebCT (www.webct.com), Blackboard (www.blackboard.com), Camtasia (www.techsmith.com), and Impatica (www.impatica.com) offer many options that sport organizations and universities can use for distance training and education.

As with the other training designs, this approach also has its advantages and disadvantages. Distance training allows an expert speaker in one location to reach thousands of people around the world. This is especially useful for multinational corporations like Nike and Adidas. Technological advances allow for more innovative, high-tech forms of delivering information. For other benefits, see the Diversity in the Field box. Unfortunately, the lack of interaction that typically accompanies distance courses limits their effectiveness. Not every organization can afford the initial start-up costs, even though the future cost savings may compensate for the large upfront costs. In addition, not all trainees will be sufficiently technologically savvy to effectively use the materials.

Simulations. Many organizations use simulations for various training needs, with the military and aviation sectors using them most often (Salas & Cannon-Bowers, 2001). This training form uses computer-

DIVERSITY *in the field*

Diversity Through Distance Education. Distance training is one of the fastest growing education forms used by organizations, and this is certainly true for educational institutions. Students can earn undergraduate and graduate degrees online. For example, the Department of Health and Kinesiology at Texas A&M University began offering a limited number of distance education courses in the fall of 2004. Among the classes offered are four related to diversity issues—Race, Ethnicity, and Health; Women's Health; Diversity in Sport Organizations; and International Sport Business. These courses, delivered over the Internet using either voice-over PowerPoint presentations or electronic videos of lectures, are extremely popular with students—over 1,000 enroll in the online sections per semester. The courses are attractive to students for various reasons: (a) they offer flexibility as to when the students listen to the lectures; (b) they allow students to complete the course at their own pace; and (c) they allow students who might not otherwise be on campus to continue to take classes. Though the classes are also offered in the classroom setting, the online versions have much higher enrollments, by about a 5 to 1 ratio. Providing the classes online allows the department to offer them to a broader range of students. In fact, many of the enrolled students are from majors outside Health and Kinesiology.

supported games and scenarios that reflect many of the psychological and behavioral requirements of the general work environment. In the context of diversity training, trainees might work through a computer-based game related to hiring and recruiting a diverse workforce. CBT Planet (www.cbtplanet.com) offers a training session that lasts two to four hours. Trainees work through five simulations that teach them about (a) the general principles related to diversity, (b) cultural differences, (c) overcoming barriers to diversity, (d) communicating with a diverse workforce, and (e) managing workplace diversity. The advantages and disadvantages of this method are generally the same as with distance education.

The specific delivery method choice should be driven by the specific training needs, the trainees' learning styles and preferences, and the organization's budgetary constraints (see also Arthur et al., 2003). See Exhibit 13.5 for other training design considerations.

Post-Training Conditions

The final part of designing an effective diversity training program pertains to the two post-training factors that impact the program's long-term effectiveness: training evaluation and ensuring the transfer of training (Mathis & Jackson, 2006; Salas & Cannon-Bowers, 2001).

Exhibit 13.5	Effective diversity training design principles.

Research suggests that the most effective training programs are centered around four basic principles:

1. *Present pertinent information and material about the training.* Trainees should know what they are expected to learn and how they will do so.

2. *Demonstrate the knowledge, skills, and abilities the trainees are expected to learn.* Trainers must demonstrate to the participants what is to be learned. Simply telling them is often insufficient, especially when physical or behavioral skills are involved.

3. *Create environments for people to practice the skills.* Provide trainees many opportunities to actually practice each skill themselves.

4. *Provide feedback during and after the training.* Trainees must have corrective feedback so they can practice the skills properly. Not only is feedback important during the actual training, but it is also important after the training when the trainees are expected to apply the material they learned to their everyday jobs.

Adapted from Salas and Cannon-Bowers, 2001.

Training Evaluation

When evaluating the training's effectiveness, managers must consider what should be evaluated and the method for doing so.

Evaluation content. Kirkpatrick (1976) developed a framework for assessing training effectiveness. He argues that training outcomes can be grouped into one of four categories (see also the Alternative Perspectives box on page 365 for another method of evaluating training effectiveness):

1. **Reactions.** Sport organizations can evaluate trainees' reactions to the session by interviewing them or asking them to complete post-training questionnaires. The questions might relate to trainees' perceptions as to the overall value of the training, how well they liked the instruction style or the trainers, or how useful they believe the training will be in their work. Most often, trainee reactions are gathered immediately after the training; however, data can also be gathered weeks or months after the training takes place to assess how useful the information has been in their everyday job duties.

2. **Learning.** Sport organizations can assess how well the trainees learned the material by asking the trainees to complete a simple test on the material covered in the session. This method is particularly useful when the subject matter is primarily factual (e.g., legal issues related to Title IX, sexual harassment, or equal employment opportunity laws).

3. **Behavior.** A third outcome to be evaluated is actual behavior. Suppose a sport organization is subjected to claims of discrimination in the hiring and promotion process arising from differential evaluations of racial minorities and Whites. Teaching the evaluators how to construct and implement objective evaluations should reduce or eliminate this problem. The trainers can assess the training's effectiveness by tracking the behavior prior to the training and again at several points after the training.

4. **Results.** A final outcome is realizing organizational objectives, or results. Some results of interest are the retention of employees, decreased absenteeism, increased customer satisfaction, increased employee affect, and increased financial gains. Managers should compare the level prior to training with the level after training to determine whether the training was effective.

Which outcome should be assessed? The answer is largely driven by the training content. In general, it is easy to assess the reactions and difficult to assess the results. What is interesting, however, is that the results data are likely the most important to the organization and reaction data are generally considered to be least significant (Mathis & Jackson, 2006). Thus, managers must make tradeoffs and consider the training content and the outcomes the organization wishes to achieve.

Evaluation designs. There are many designs managers can use to assess the training's effectiveness. In an increasing order of the design's effectiveness, they include a post-training only design, pre- and post-training design, pre- and post-training design with a control group, and a post-training only design with a control group (see Exhibit 13.6 for an illustration).

With a *post-training only* design, data is collected from the trainees after the training. Trainees can take a test or complete a questionnaire. This approach is easy to design and administer; however, there are no data to which the results can be compared. It is impossible to determine whether the trainees improved over the course of the training or how they compare to people who have no training.

The *pre- and post-training* design evaluates the trainees prior to and after the training. If an increase in, for example, knowledge related to diversity laws is observed, then it might indicate that the training was effective. Because there is no control group, it is impossible to determine whether the increase would be greater than that observed of people who had not received the training.

Exhibit 13.6	**Evaluation of diversity training.**

POST-TRAINING

Training Group   T   E

PRE- AND POST-TRAINING

Training Group   E   T   E

PRE- AND POST-TRAINING WITH A CONTROL GROUP

Training Group   E   T   E

Control Group   E   E

POST-TRAINING ONLY WITH A CONTROL GROUP

Training Group   T   E

Control Group   E

T = Training   E = Evaluation

The third evaluation design—*pre- and post-training with a control group*—addresses the issue of comparing the results to people who have not received the training. Managers randomly assign people to one of two groups—the training group or the control group, whose members do not receive the diversity training. Members of both groups are then evaluated both prior to and after the training. Because the members are randomly assigned to the training or control group, differences between the groups are not expected for the pre-training scores. After the training, however, we would expect those people who went through the training to score higher (or have more positive reactions or more desired behaviors) than people who did not complete the training. This design is desired because it addresses the issues of (a) improvement after the training and (b) improvement relative to a control group. A design drawback is that it can be cumbersome and time-consuming to collect data prior to and after the training.

The final design—*post-training only with a control group*—is the most desired. Here, managers randomly assign people to one of two groups: training or control group. An evaluation is made after the training, and any differences between the groups would suggest that the training was effective. The pre-training evaluation is not needed because, theoretically, the randomly assigned group members should not differ in their scores prior to training. Of course, this assumption rests on the complete random assignment of employees to the two groups. If this cannot be achieved, then a pre-test is required.

In two of the designs, the control group did not receive diversity training, but would we not want those persons to ultimately do so? One way to address this issue is to evaluate the training's effectiveness with small pilot test groups before administering it to the entire organization. If the training is effective, then require *all* employees to complete it.

alternative PERSPECTIVES

Evaluating Diversity Training Effectiveness.
Kirkpatrick's (1976) model is the most popular method for evaluating training effectiveness. Salas and Cannon-Bowers (2001) note that although the method is useful and provides a firm foundation, newer and more elegant models are needed. Kraiger, Ford, and Salas (1993) developed a three-component model of training effectiveness. The first component, *cognitive outcomes,* includes such outcomes as the development of verbal knowledge, organization of knowledge, and cognitive strategies. Understanding laws that impact diversity in the workplace is an example of a cognitive outcome. *Skill-based outcomes,* the second component, pertain to skill compilation—the continued practice of a skill beyond initial success—and skill automaticity—practicing a skill in a fluid, accomplished, and individualized manner. For example, managers who can develop and administer fair performance appraisals have learned skill-based outcomes. Finally, *attitudinal outcomes* encompass two elements—affective outcomes (e.g., group norms) and motivational outcomes (e.g., motivational disposition, post-training self-efficacy, and goal setting). If trainees reduce their level of bias toward out-group members as a result of the training process, this is an attitudinal outcome. Although there are similarities to Kirkpatrick's model, Kraiger et al.'s framework is a possible alternative.

Ensuring a Transfer of Training

Lim and Morris (2006) note that one of the most important goals of training should be the application of the knowledge, skills, and abilities to the workplace setting—a process known as transfer of training. Research, however, suggests that this transfer often does not occur—the material learned in the training session is not used in the work setting (Kupritz, 2002). Why provide diversity training if the trainees do not use the information in their work lives? Fortunately, recent research points to several factors that can improve the transfer of training (Colquitt et al., 2000; Lim & Morris, 2006; Salas & Cannon-Bowers, 2001).

Organizational climate. The organizational climate can have a substantial influence on whether people apply the information from the training to their work. As Salas and Cannon-Bowers (2001) note, the organizational climate can shape "motivations, expectations, and attitudes for transfer" (p. 489). Transfer of training is likely to take place in sport organizations that (a) encourage employees to try new things, (b) promote continuous learning by employees, (c) do not punish people when they are not immediately successful in implementing the information they learned, and (d) reward people for the transfer of training.

Applicability. Trainees are most likely to actually use the information they learn when they believe it is applicable to their work. If they cannot see the connection between what was presented in the training and their job performance, then the information, no matter how valuable it is perceived by the organization, is unlikely to be used. Thus, trainers must not only present the information so it can be understood, but they must also explicitly outline how the information benefits the trainees in their everyday job.

Support. One of the most influential factors affecting the transfer of training is the support trainees receive from their peers and supervisors to actually do so. Research shows that the influence of peers is especially important in the transfer process (Colquitt et al., 2000). Much of what people do is influenced by those people who are important to them. If one's peers and supervisors show support for the training, think it is important, try to transfer the information to their own work, and are supportive of others doing the same, then transfer of training is likely to be high.

General Principles

In this final section, general principles that should be considered when delivering a diversity training program are discussed. Wentling and Palma-Rivas (1999) interviewed a panel of diversity experts from across the United States, all of whom had published extensively in the diversity literature and had consulted with public and private entities about diversity and diversity training.

Wentling and Palma-Rivas asked the experts what they considered to be the primary components of an effective diversity training program. After analyzing the experts' responses, the following themes emerged (see Exhibit 13.7).

■ **Ensure commitment and support from top management.** Effective diversity training programs must have support from top management. Top management should be actively involved in the training process and convey to employees how important the training is to them and the organization as a whole.

■ **Include diversity training as part of the overall strategic plan.** The training must be linked to the overall goals, needs, and objectives of the sport organization. Effectiveness is likely to be highest when the training is linked to the overall business strategy.

■ **Ensure training meets the sport organizations' specific needs.** The most successful training programs are those that are based on the results of a needs analysis. Without such an assessment, "training may focus on issues that are not real problems in the organization, which may result in a waste of resources without achieving desired results" (Wentling & Palma-Rivas, 1999, p. 222).

■ **Use qualified trainers.** Qualified trainers are essential. The best trainers are those who have a good mix of professional and academic skills, coupled with

Effective diversity training program components.	*Exhibit 13.7*

- ■ Commitment and support from top management.
- ■ Diversity training as part of the overall strategic plan.
- ■ Training that meets the sport organization's specific needs.
- ■ Qualified trainers.
- ■ Combining the training with other diversity programs.
- ■ Mandatory attendance.
- ■ Inclusive programs.
- ■ Ensuring trust and confidentiality.
- ■ Accountability.
- ■ Evaluation of the training.

Adapted from Wentling & Palma-Rivas (1999).

PROFESSIONAL
P E R S P E C T I V E S

Diversity Behind the Face. Cheryl Kravitz is a diversity training consultant who uses an interesting technique to create empathy and understanding in the programs she delivers. She calls the technique The Person Behind the Face. In this exercise, participants receive a piece of paper with balloons drawn all over it. They then use as many balloons as they deem necessary to define their personal identities. As the exercise facilitator, Kravitz goes first. She describes herself as "a young mom and an old mom" because she had a child at age 16 and adopted her second child at age 40. She also reveals other bits of information about herself: that she is Jewish, her mother has Alzheimer's, she was once in a coma, and she almost died at the hands of her abusive ex-husband. Revealing such personal information is beneficial, Kravitz notes, because people will then share information about themselves. Revealing such information has a way of creating empathy among the trainees and sometimes results in bonds being forged among otherwise different people. For example, another woman in the group might reveal that she too was a battered wife, or another group member might identify with having an ill parent. Thus, people come to realize that although they differ physically, they might share common deep-level characteristics. The exercise "can help unfreeze people's preconceptions of others and help melt prejudice and stereotypes" (Koonce, 2001, p. 30).

a dynamic personality. Because diversity training often touches on sensitive issues, trainers should not only be well-versed in the subject matter, but should also be skilled at diffusing disruptive forms of conflict.

■ **Combine the training with other diversity programs.** Diversity training works best when it is just one of several diversity-related initiatives (e.g., the organization also has an overall strategy aimed at diversifying the workforce and clientele). If conducted in isolation—absent of other diversity initiatives—the training will likely have a minimal impact, if any. In addition, "linking diversity training to existing training programs such as leadership training, team building, total quality management, and employee empowerment and participation will increase its effectiveness" (Wentling & Palma-Rivas, 1999, p. 222).

■ **Make attendance mandatory.** Diversity training is most successful when attendance is mandatory. Mandatory attendance shows support and commitment to the program. Mandatory attendance should apply to *all* people—including top management. Requiring top managers to attend the training may result in them modeling the desired behaviors to their employees.

■ **Create inclusive programs.** The best diversity training programs are those that are inclusive of all people because they avoid the "us" versus "them" dynamics. Also, White males are more likely to support the diversity initiatives if they believe it is inclusive of all people and does not single them out for "blame."

■ **Ensure trust and confidentiality.** Establishing trust and confidentiality ensures a safe training environment and minimizes risks to the employees and the organization. Setting guidelines early in the training process, such as "respect other people's opinions" and "keep the conversations here confidential," help to establish these norms. See the Professional Perspectives box for other examples.

■ **Require accountability.** Holding people accountable provides a means for the trainees to actively advance diversity in the workplace. Accountability practices include establishing a link between what is learned in the session and work performance, including diversity in performance appraisals and merit raises, and associating diversity performance with the organization's overall objectives.

■ **Evaluate the training.** "Evaluation is one of the most important ways of providing accountability and support for continuing with diversity programs" (Wentling & Palma-Rivas, 1999, p. 223). Indeed, evaluating the program demonstrates its success, provides information about trainees' reactions to the training, and informs the design and implementation of subsequent training sessions.

Managers should use these principles as a guide when designing and implementing diversity training programs to ensure greater success with the initiative.

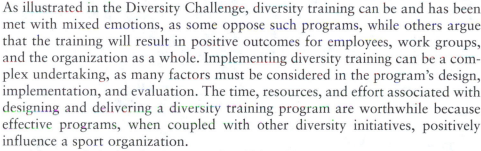

Chapter Summary

As illustrated in the Diversity Challenge, diversity training can be and has been met with mixed emotions, as some oppose such programs, while others argue that the training will result in positive outcomes for employees, work groups, and the organization as a whole. Implementing diversity training can be a complex undertaking, as many factors must be considered in the program's design, implementation, and evaluation. The time, resources, and effort associated with designing and delivering a diversity training program are worthwhile because effective programs, when coupled with other diversity initiatives, positively influence a sport organization.

After reading the chapter, you should be able to:

1. Discuss the positive and negative effects of diversity training.

The positive outcomes include attracting and retaining a diverse set of employees, maintaining worker morale, fostering understanding among groups, curbing lawsuits, and contributing to the organizations' overall effectiveness. Negative effects include the uneasiness associated with discussing sensitive issues, the belief that diversity training is "code" for affirmative action, the incidence of White men feeling "blamed," the reinforcement of stereotypes and categorization boundaries, the sensitization of trainees to diversity issues, and a potential lack of organizational effects.

2. Discuss the essential elements of effective diversity training programs.

There are several factors that must be considered when delivering diversity training. Organizations must first conduct a needs analysis, which includes an organizational analysis, a job/task analysis, and a person analysis. The antecedent training conditions must be examined, including trainee characteristics, the manner in which the training is framed, and the pre-training environment. Next, the training methods, such as who should deliver the training and what delivery method should be used must be addressed. Finally, post-training conditions—training evaluation and ensuring the transfer of training—must be completed.

Questions for Discussion

1. The incidence of diversity training has increased in Fortune 500 companies over the past decade such that more companies conduct this training than those that do not. Do you believe that there has been a corresponding increase in the number of sport organizations that provide diversity training? Why or why not?

2. Companies that view diversity training as a central part of their strategic plan spend almost three times per employee on training compared to other organizations. Why is there such an increase in spending, and do you think the organizations receive the benefits of the spending?

3. How does one conduct a needs analysis, and why is it important to do so?

4. Several trainee characteristics influence training effectiveness. Of those listed in the chapter, which do you think is the most influential and why? What can managers do to improve these characteristics?

5. Several training delivery options were discussed. What are the advantages and disadvantages associated with each approach? Which is your preferred approach and why?

6. Trainees bring differing needs, attitudes, preferences, and learning styles to the diversity training session. What steps can trainers take to ensure that *all* people learn the material?

7. Several factors were identified that could help with the transfer of training. Which of these factors is likely to be most influential and why?

Learning Activities

1. Using the Web, identify companies that specialize in diversity training. Which of these companies do you believe would provide the best training and why?

2. Working in small groups, consult the Lambert and Myers book (listed in the Supplementary Readings) and try one of the diversity training activities. Present the activity to the class and evaluate its effectiveness. Which were the most successful and why?

Resources

SUPPLEMENTARY READING

Clements, P., & Jones, J. (2002). *The diversity training handbook: A practical guide to understanding and changing attitudes* (2nd ed.). London, UK: Kogan Page, Ltd. (Offers practical advice for implementing diversity training programs, with many evaluation models and learning points.)

Katz, J. H. (2003). *White awareness: Handbook for anti-racism training* (2nd ed.). Norman: University of Oklahoma Press. (Provides a detailed analysis for designing training aimed at reducing racism and creating change in the White community.)

Lambert, J., & Myers, S. (2005). *Trainers' diversity source book: 50 ready-to-use activities, from ice breaker through wrap ups.* Alexandria, VA: Society for Human Resource Management. (Provides trainers with a variety of exercises to use during a training session to actively engage the participants.)

WEB RESOURCES

- Diversity Builder (www.diversitybuilder.com/diversity_training.php): provides diversity training in a variety of areas; provides specialized programs for each client.

- Diversity Training Group (www.diversitydtg.com/): specializes in providing diversity training workshops for organizations.

- Scottsdale National Gender Institute (http://gendertraining.com/): helps organizations to provide diversity training, with an emphasis on gender issues.

References

Arai, M., Wanca-Thibault, M., & Shockley-Zalabak, P. (2001). Communication theory and training approaches for multiculturally diverse organizations: Have academics and practitioners missed the connection? *Public Personnel Management, 30,* 445–455.

Arthur, W., Jr., Bennett, W., Jr., Edens, P. S., & Bell, S. T. (2003). Effectiveness of training in organizations: A meta-analysis of design and evaluation features. *Journal of Applied Psychology, 88,* 234–245.

Arvey, R. D., Salas, E., & Gialluca, K. A. (1992). Using task inventories to forecast skills and abilities. *Human Performance, 5,* 171–190.

Bandura, A. (1986). *Social foundations of thought and action: A social cognitive theory.* Englewood Cliffs, NJ: Prentice Hall.

Bendick, M., Jr., Egan, M. L., & Lofhjelm, S. M. (2001). Workforce diversity training: From anti-discrimination compliance to organizational development. *Human Resource Planning, 24*(2), 10–25.

Colquitt, J. A., LePine, J. A., & Noe, R. A. (2000). Toward an integrative theory of training motivation: A meta-analytic path analysis of 20 years of research. *Journal of Applied Psychology, 85,* 678–707.

Colquitt, J. A., & Simmering, M. J. (1998). Conscientiousness, goal orientation, and motivation to learn during the training process: A longitudinal study. *Journal of Applied Psychology, 83,* 654–665.

Crosby, F. J., Iyer, A., & Sincharoen, S. (2006). Understanding affirmative action. *Annual Review of Psychology, 57,* 585–611.

Cunningham, G. B., & Mahoney, K. L. (2004). Self-efficacy of part-time employees in university athletics: The influence of organizational commitment, valence of training, and training motivation. *Journal of Sport Management, 18,* 59–73.

Doherty, A. J., & Chelladurai, P. (1999). Managing cultural diversity in sport organizations: A theoretical perspective. *Journal of Sport Management, 13,* 280–297.

Facteau, J. D., Dobbins, G. H., Russell, J. E. A., Ladd, R. T., & Kudish, J. D. (1995). The influence of general perceptions of the training environment on pretraining motivation and perceived training transfer. *Journal of Management, 21,* 1–25.

Gilbert, J. A., & Ivancevich, J. M. (2000). Valuing diversity: A tale of two organizations. *Academy of Management Executive, 14*(1), 93–105.

Gist, M. E., & Mitchell, T. R. (1992). Self-efficacy: A theoretical analysis of its determinants and malleability. *Academy of Management Review, 17,* 183–211.

Goldstein, I. L. (1993). *Training in organizations: Needs assessment, development and evaluation* (3rd ed.). Monterey, CA: Brooks/Cole.

Gordon, J. (1988). Who is being trained to do what? *Training, 25*(10), 51–60.

Hanover, J. M., & Cellar, D. F. (1998). Environmental factors and the effectiveness of workplace diversity training. *Human Resource Development Quarterly, 9,* 105–124.

Hemphill, H., & Haines, R. (1997). *Discrimination, harassment, and the failure of diversity training: What to do now.* Westport, CT: Quorum Books.

Holladay, C. L., Knight, J. L., Paige, D. L., & Quinones, M. A. (2003). The influence of framing on attitudes toward diversity training. *Human Resource Development Quarterly, 14,* 245–263.

Jackson, L. C. (1999). Ethnocultural resistance to multicultural training: Students and faculty. *Cultural Diversity and Ethnic Minority Psychology, 5,* 27–36.

Kaemar, K. M., Wright, P. M., & McMahan, G. C. (1997). The effects of individual differences on technology training. *Journal of Managerial Issues, 9,* 104–120.

Karp, H. B., & Sammour, H. Y. (2000). Workforce diversity: Choices in diversity training programs and dealing with resistance to diversity. *College Student Journal, 34,* 451–458.

Kirkpatrick, D. L. (1976). Evaluation of training. In R. L. Craig (Ed.), *Training and development handbook* (2nd ed., pp. 301–319). New York: McGraw-Hill.

Koonce, R. (2001). Redefining diversity. *Training & Development, 55*(12), 22–33.

Kraiger, K., Ford, J. K., & Salas, E. (1993). Application of cognitive, skill-based, and affective theories of learning outcomes to new methods of training evaluation. *Journal of Applied Psychology, 78,* 311–328.

Kupritz, V. W. (2002). The relative impact of workplace design on training transfer. *Human Resource Development Quarterly, 13,* 427–447.

Lim, D. H., & Morris, M. L. (2006). Influence of trainee characteristics, instructional satisfaction, and organizational climate on perceived learning and training transfer. *Human Resource Development Quarterly, 17,* 85–115.

Lindsay, C. (1994). Things that go wrong in diversity training: Conceptualization and change with ethnic identity models. *Journal of Organizational Change Management, 7*(6), 18–33.

Martocchio, J. J., & Judge, T. A. (1997). Relationship between conscientiousness and learning in employee training: Mediating influences of self-deception and self-efficacy. *Journal of Applied Psychology, 82,* 764–773.

Mathieu, J. E., Tannenbaum, S. I., & Salas, E. (1992). Influences of individual and situational characteristics on measures of training effectiveness. *Academy of Management Journal, 35,* 828–847.

Mathis, R. L., & Jackson, J. H. (2006). *Human resource management* (11th ed.). Mason, OH: Southwestern.

Noe, R. A., & Schmitt, N. (1986). The influence of trainee attitudes on training effectiveness: Test of a model. *Personnel Psychology, 39,* 497–523.

Plummer, D. L. (1998). Approaching diversity training in the year 2000. *Consulting Psychology Journal: Practice and Research, 50,* 181–189.

Quinones, M. A. (1995). Pretraining context effects: Training assignment as feedback. *Journal of Applied Psychology, 80,* 226–238.

Rouiller, J. Z., & Goldstein, I. L. (1993). The relationship between organizational transfer climate and positive transfer of training. *Human Resource Development Quarterly, 4,* 377–390.

Rynes, S., & Rosen, B. (1995). A field survey of factors affecting the adoption and perceived success of diversity training. *Personnel Psychology, 48,* 247–270.

Salas, E., & Cannon-Bowers, J. A. (2001). The science of training: A decade of progress. *Annual Review of Psychology, 52,* 471–499.

Society for Human Resource Management. (2001, June 11). Keeping your edge: Managing a diverse corporate culture. *Fortune,* S1–S17.

Sussman, L. (1997). Prejudice and behavioral archetypes: A new model for cultural-diversity training. *Business Communication Quarterly, 60,* 7–18.

Tallarigo, R. (1998). Book review of *Discrimination, harassment, and the failure of diversity training: What to do now. Personnel Psychology, 51,* 749–752.

Tannenbaum, S. I., & Yulk, G. (1992). Training and development in work organizations. *Annual Review of Psychology, 43,* 399–441.

Thomas, R. R. (1996). *Redefining diversity.* New York: AMACOM.

Tracey, J. B., Hinkin, T. R., Tannenbaum, S., & Mathieu, J. E. (2001). The influence of individual characteristics and the work environment on varying levels of training outcomes. *Human Resource Development Quarterly, 12,* 5–23.

Wentling, R. M., & Palma-Rivas, N. (1999). Components of effective diversity training programmes. *International Journal of Training and Development, 3,* 215–226.

Wiethoff, C. (2004). Motivation to learn and diversity training: Application of the theory of planned behavior. *Human Resource Development Quarterly, 15,* 263–278.

Author Index

Subject Index

379